Six-Shooters and Shifting Sands

"The Coffee and the Colt," 24" X 36" oil on canvas by Donald M. Yena, used by permission.

Six-Shooters and Shifting Sands

The Wild West Life of Texas Ranger Captain Frank Jones

Bob Alexander

Foreword by Chief Kirby W. Dendy, Texas Rangers

Number 15 in the Francis B. Vick Series

UNT PRESS
University of North Texas Press
Denton, Texas

Printed in the United States of America.

10 9 8 7 6 5 4 3 2 1

Permissions:
University of North Texas Press
1155 Union Circle #311336
Denton, TX 76203-5017

The paper used in this book meets the minimum requirements of the American National Standard for Permanence of Paper for Printed Library Materials, z39.48.1984. Binding materials have been chosen for durability.

Library of Congress Cataloging-in-Publication Data

Alexander, Bob, 1947– author.
Six-shooters and shifting sands : the Wild West life of Texas Ranger Captain Frank Jones / Bob Alexander ; foreword by Chief Kirby W. Dendy, Texas Rangers.—Edition: First.
pages cm—(Number 15 in the Francis B. Vick series)
Incudes bibliographical references and index.
ISBN 978-1-57441-592-6 (cloth : alk. paper)—ISBN 978-1-57441-601-5 (ebook)
1. Jones, Frank, 1856–1893. 2. Texas Rangers. Frontier Battalion. Company D—Biography. 3. Frontier and pioneer life—Texas. I. Title. II. Series: Frances B. Vick series ; no. 15.
F391.A28 2015
363.2092—dc23
[B]

2014044076

Six-Shooters and Shifting Sands: The Wild West Life of Texas Ranger Captain Frank Jones is Number 15 in the Frances B. Vick Series

The electronic edition of this book was made possible by the support of the Vick Family Foundation.

Contents

Foreword

WHEN BOB ALEXANDER ASKED IF I WOULD consider writing a foreword for his biography of Texas Ranger Captain Frank Jones, I was extremely honored. While having some mediocre knowledge of Ranger history, I am an absolute neophyte in comparison to Bob. Like many others, my knowledge of Captain Jones was primarily limited to a basic understanding of the circumstances surrounding his death and the subsequent recovery of his body. My immediate concern and question regarding writing the foreword was what approach to take, how to do justice to a fellow Texas Ranger of years past. The uncertainty was quickly put to rest when Bob graciously, upon my request, provided me with several general topics relating to Captain Jones' life and potential comparisons to the duties and responsibilities of those commanding modern day Texas Ranger companies. My immediate thought was to highlight the vast differences the passage of years, changes in society's values, and technological advances have made on the position and its law enforcing functions in general. I will touch on that aspect, but while reviewing the working manuscript for *Six-Shooters & Shifting Sands* it became even more apparent that while there have obviously been huge changes, there are far more similarities still present than I would have previously surmised. While evolution of the job from that time to now is certainly noteworthy, the parallels and areas which have remained constant deserve appropriate mention as well.

Even for those not familiar with Texas history or the progressions of the law enforcement profession, it is an obvious and reasonable assumption that a great deal has changed regarding the practices and operations of modern day Texas Rangers from the time of Captain Frank Jones' service on the frontier. The basic equipment required to be a Texas Ranger in his time consisted primarily of a good pony, usually the best repeating rifle (primarily Winchesters), at least one Colt's revolver, suitable clothing and tack. As with those of today, the individuals recruited to become Rangers were expected to be of sound moral character and impeccable integrity. Unlike today, any formal education was spotty at best. Previous law enforcement experience was appreciated but by no means required. Training was informal and received on the job from tenured Rangers and the command staff.

Now, Texas Rangers must meet the significant and rigid basic entry requirements set for the Texas Department of Public Safety, successfully complete the twenty-six week recruit training school and have a miniminum of eight years law enforcement experience just to be eligible to compete for Ranger positions. The majority of present-day Texas Rangers have bachelor's degrees and some have master's degrees. Many have prior military service.

Today's Ranger receives extensive training in basic and advanced criminal investigation and related subjects, crime scene search techniques, evidence collection and processing. Many are trained in the use of computer generated replication of crime scenes. During Captain Jones' time, criminal investigation was still in its infancy. The value of recovering, analyzing, and maintaining evidence for future court prosecutions had only recently been realized. Certainly the widespread application of scientific examination and analysis to determine evidentiary value was still years away. Although the criminal justice system was gradually migrating toward the requirement and use of substantive, creditable evidence, most arrests and convictions were based on witness testimony and circumstantial evidence relating to motive and/or opportunity and often, not much more. The modern day level of actual investigation, evidence collection and preservation, examination, analysis and utilization of all resources to obtain criminal convictions is at an opposite end of the spectrum in comparison with practices of the late 19th Century.

Upon successful completion of basic training the Rangers receive a multitude of tools and assorted equipment for processing crime scenes, including Nikon digital cameras. They are also assigned either late model pick-up trucks or SUVs for transportation. Each new Ranger is issued a variety of weaponry, including a .308 caliber LaRue Tactical OBR (Optimized Battle Rifle), a .223 caliber Bushmaster M-4, a Sig Sauer .357 pistol, and a Remington or Mossberg 12 gauge shotgun. Soft body armor and heavier level IV armor are also provided. Adopting the latest equipment and adapting as situations demand is as relevant now as it was back then, when Captain Frank Jones was in command of Company D.

During the early 1880s with the arrival of the railroad El Paso began the transition from a dusty little adobe burg of a few hundred people into a boomtown with a population just over 10,000 by 1890. As was the case in many other frontier towns the railroad brought increased population, construction, and wealth, along with all of the attendant crime and associated vices, such as prostitution and gambling. When combined with the ubiquitous presence of saloons, the environment was ripe for exploitation by the criminal element. Even without some individuals' predisposition for criminal activity, intoxication when combined with highly elevated emotions often resulted in gunplay and assaults. For most populated areas of the period, this lawless element would be considered "normal," an expected and accepted consequence of rapid growth and progress.

What made El Paso and, in fact, the entire Texas/Mexico border unique from a crime perspective was the age old occupation of smuggling anything and everything that could put money in one's pocket. People from both banks of the Rio Grande for generations had engaged in smuggling. It was a means of providing for their families and they thought absolutely nothing wrong with the practice. With little, if any, law enforcement interference in early years, border society turned a blind eye toward transnational movement of contraband. With the influx of people, more law enforcement activity (especially on the federal side in the early 20th Century) and changing personal values toward a more "civilized" society, public perception in regards to smuggling changed, just as attitudes about gambling and prostitution had at the local level. Prior to the turn of the century, El Paso enacted laws prohibiting these type endeavors, businesses which just a few years previously had been overtly operated, widely accepted by the public while generating enormous incomes. To the more sophisticated and progressive citizenry the bawdy and gambling houses were no longer acceptable. It was an enlightened populace. The reality was that those businesses were simply forced to operate underground on a covert level. Regardless, Captain Frank Jones and his company of Rangers dealt with the crimes and the lawless element perpetrating them just as do the 21st Century Texas Rangers. Cross border smuggling, whether it be controlled substances or people remains a hot topic of current media attention and a focus of law enforcement awareness. Criminal cartels located in Mexico have organized smuggling to a level their counterparts in the 19th Century could not have imagined.

Unfortunately, they have also elevated the level of violence to a previously unthinkable plane while accomplishing their illegal goals. Local, state, and national politics on each side of the river are still formidable factors, playing a large part and adding to the complexities of borderland law enforcement. Texas Ranger Majors now commanding Company E at El Paso and Company D at Weslaco make investigative assignments based on actionable intelligence relating to smuggling of people and drugs, thefts, and in response to the associated violence, such as murders, kidnappings, home invasions, as well as investigating instances of public corruption. Today's Texas Rangers are tasked with filing criminal cases and making arrests just as Captain Jones and his Rangers were more than a century ago.

While reading the *Six-Guns and Shifting Sands* manuscript it was quite apparent that in spite of the passage of time and tremendous advances in technology, many of the duties of a Texas Ranger Company Commander remain amazingly similar, especially in regard to supervising personnel. On further contemplation, however, it really wasn't so surprising. Certain aspects of supervision will probably always be constant as long as human nature is what it is. Close interaction between Type A personalities, especially under less than desirable environmental conditions, has a tendency to lead to conflict, something Captain Frank Jones experienced firsthand. A Ranger Captain (Company Commanders today have the rank of Major) must possess the patience and wisdom to successfully deal with conflict in such a way that the least amount of damage to relationships results, while maintaining order, effectiveness, and respect for the chain of command as the problem is being corrected. This is not always easy. As evidenced in this book, there have been times when persons were hired as Rangers and at some point after the fact it became evident the individual was not as suitable as originally believed. Then, as now, quality control in the form of supervisory action had to be taken to correct the mistake. This is never a pleasant experience. Even some of the best employees are potentially subject to episodes of poor judgment which need to be addressed and which sometimes result in disciplinary action or even termination. Throughout history of the Rangers, more than one good man has been lost because of a temporary loss of discipline relating to overindulgence in intoxicating beverages. Maintaining the integrity and honor of the Texas Rangers overrides all such indiscretions and must be upheld. Modern Ranger history contains several unfortunate examples of indiscretion, poor judgment, or substandard performance that supervisory personnel have dealt with, just as Captain Jones did over one hundred years ago.

Another area that has seen little if any change is the necessity of field commanders to keep their chain of command in Austin fully apprised of all activities undertaken by their personnel. This often involves the submission of a seemingly unending number of reports documenting activities, expenditures, and a myriad of other paperwork necessary for statistical analysis, property inventories, planning, and other, more nebulous purposes. A reader can almost sense Captain Jones' frustration dealing with the administrative side of running Company D. It was clear he would have much preferred to be in the field with his Rangers pursuing bandits, murderers, and fugitives. The time span between preparation of monotonous reports, mundane office work and deadly conflict can sometimes be measured in minutes today, as it was in 1893. Captain Frank Jones' murder illustrates another constant that has not changed: Regardless rank, all law enforcement personnel face life threatening situations and must make decisions which may very well result in their death, that of a co-worker, or a criminal violator.

Upon further review of historical data and reflection upon current duties, the list of similarities' between Ranger duties separated by the past one hundred plus years could probably be continued *ad nauseam*. Suffice to say that there are far more than this writer would have ever imagined, especially in the area of supervisory responsibilities. Difficult decisions must still be made on a frequent basis, regardless of rank.

As noted, occasionally those real decisions have life or death consequences. A Ranger's job is yet dangerous. Evidence indicates there is an innate, timeless desire on the part of Texas Rangers to be armed with the absolute best weaponry available, whether it was that Winchester Model 73 chambered for .44-40 in 1877 or the aforementioned .308 caliber Larue Tactical OBRs for work in 2014. Texas Rangers must still be relied upon to display courage and place themselves in life threatening situations. They are also charged with maintaining the highest level of personal integrity and honor in their on duty as well as their off duty lives. Failure to do so today, as then, determines whether or not the term "former" is applied to one's Texas Ranger status. Although cliché, the real surprise in comparing Captain Frank Jones' career and that of a modern Ranger commander is that the more things change, the more they stay the same. . . . computers, DNA, laser scanners, and cell phones aside.

I will readily admit up front that I am biased in my opinion of this book, which is based at least in part to my long friendship and working relationship with Bob Alexander. During the 1980s we both worked many of the same Central Texas counties; he as a Special Agent with the U.S. Treasury Department's ATF (now in the Justice Department) and I as an Agent for the Texas Department of Public Safety's Narcotics Division. Our relationship continued after my promotion to Texas Ranger and his retirement from federal law enforcement. However, another aspect of that partiality for this book is based upon my esteem and sincere appreciation for his literary efforts during the last several years. While reading many of the books he has authored prior to *Six-Shooters & Shifting Sands* it was apparent that Bob was not presenting a personal agenda or making predisposed statements by shading his canvas in tones most aligned with individual preferences, unless one would consider truth and objectivity as the focus of that work. Because, that's exactly what I've seen in every book I've read that Bob Alexander has written: An unbiased and factual treatment based on incredibly detailed references. In those books relating to Texas Rangers, there have actually been a few instances where I wished he could have been a little less vigorous in describing and detailing warts and all. Unfortunately, some authors do have their own agendas to advance, and they seldom allow truth or literary objectivity to interfere with portraying their subject matter in a less than flattering light. At an opposite end of the spectrum, some books have been written that would make sales consultants jealous; their works canonize individuals who in reality were operating at a much lower performance level than depicted. Some are historical revionists who have a tendency to judge acts committed a century ago by today's standards. To make such judgments is terribly flawed when not accounting for, much less personally experiencing, decision shaping events of the day and changing societal values over that subsequent extensive passage of time. Bob Alexander has consistently avoided these pitfalls and has provided work which paints a clear, accurate picture. His writing approach reminds me fondly of my days as a young boy sitting in my grandfather's barber shop, listening with fascination to the tales of hunting, war, and everyday life told by his colorful clientele. Like the pages of Bob's books, I couldn't wait for the next customer to arrive. The difference between then and now, being that Bob Alexander's book about Captain Frank Jones is credible and of significant historical value, unlike most of those barber shop tales from my boyhood.

Kirby W. Dendy
Chief, Texas Rangers
Austin, Texas

August 2014

Preface and Acknowledgments

TEXAS RANGER CAPTAIN FRANK JONES MERITS a standalone biography. Many well-read students, historians, and loyal aficionados of Texas Ranger lore know the name, but not the man. If not all, most sweeping Texas Ranger histories, those within the parameters of a nineteenth-century timeframe, make mention of Frank Jones in the context of a blistering gunplay and typically leave it at that. True it's a rousing story, a subchapter in the life of a lawman, one affording a sketchy overview about harsh realities of wearing a badge while working the Southwest's borderlands. On the other hand, taking the measure of any man demands a broader tactic than focusing on a singular episode, somewhat ignoring the wider framework of place and time, achievements and failures. Frank Jones' biographical narrative is remarkably rich: Exciting and enlightening, factual and fascinating. Background and perspective does matter.

Although it might stand theoretical challenge today, early on it was proffered that there were four great Ranger captains: William Jesse McDonald, John Harris Rogers, James Abijah Brooks, and John Reynolds Hughes. Thankfully the Texas Ranger service of all four has now been preserved in thoroughly researched modern-era biographies. There was a historical chain linking them together, however. These noteworthy Ranger captains began their careers horseback in the Frontier Battalion, then transcending the timeline moved into the twentieth century. For awhile they sat tall in the saddle; then sat tall behind the steering-wheels of sputtering Fords. The call endorsing this quartet as the Texas Rangers' greatest captains of the twentieth century, before the clock had even struck midnight closing that gate, may have been somewhat premature. In this particular situation the span of one hundred years rightly leaves room for inclusion of others, especially since these stalwarts' Ranger careers had already ended with three-quarters of a century remaining on the calendar. Knowledgeable academics and grass-root historians—with benefit of much more hard data and hindsight—might now supplement the list, naming other impressive Texas Ranger captains. Today's working Rangers and/or those currently kicking back and enjoying retirement years—though the opinions would no doubt be varied—might have their own ideas about who of the twentieth-century captains they worked for or with should be measured for greatness. Certainly such an award is subjective.

Myriad are the reasons even an up and coming Texas Ranger—a good Ranger—might not climb the stairway to a captaincy. One, Sergeant Austin Ira Aten, comes to mind. In the annals of Texas Ranger history Ira Aten was, well, not a megastar, but distinctly and favorably known throughout wild and woolly frontier Texas. Scrutinizing quantifiable tallies of selected so-called gunfighters can prove disappointing, if evidence is meaningful. Some guys were huffing and puffing during twilight years, hawking Hollywood movie moguls with overblown tripe—selling it as truth, or trying to. Texas Ranger Ira Aten was legit—not a single counterfeit vertebra in his spine—a backbone of steel. Unlike fakers and fabricators, when push came to shove Ira Aten could and did stand his ground, sometimes all alone. Or as spitting and whittling old timers were prone to say: "Ira could stay hitched."

Fidelity, in the historic sense, also reveals that it was Ira Aten who recruited John R. Hughes into the Frontier Battalion. History also bears explicit witness, in the chain-of-command structure it was Private John Hughes who was officially answering to Sergeant Aten—never vice versa. The same may be said of Sergeant Aten and Captain Frank Jones; Ira was always subordinate in the Texas Ranger staffing models. There was not an iota of dislike in the relationship between supervisor and subordinate. Captain Frank Jones and the Aten brothers maintained affable and deferential working relationships. In the case of Ira Aten and John Reynolds Hughes, they became lifelong friends with an unbreakable bond. Their admiration for each other was limitless—provably. Why did Hughes eventually become a fêted Texas Ranger captain—one of those four great captains—and Captain Frank Jones and Ira Aten did not? The answer is not elusive, not even a little. In the case of Ranger and two-time Texas sheriff Aten that topic is addressed in his biography, *Rawhide Ranger, Ira Aten: Enforcing Law on the Texas Frontier* and will be touched on lightly herein. Regarding Frank Jones that question and many others will be tackled in *Six-Shooters and Shifting Sands*, the womb to tomb story of his life.

Objectively there is still an interest—at least a niche marketplace—for thrilling nonfiction tales of the Old West, the setting for *Six-Shooters and Shifting Sands*. Those absorbing narratives, thanks to insatiable appetites of the ravenous public and hungry publishers, are yet alive and kicking in the New West. Having nineteenth-century Texas as the backdrop for a storyline is splendid. It's near a guarantee that the menu of what follows will necessarily be peppered with high drama and lowdown deaths: Titillating and tantalizing true stuff.

While the subtitle plainly divulges Frank Jones' stirring life's story is a Western in every sense of the word, it is a good deal more. At an early age Frank Jones, a native Texan, would become a Frontier Battalion-era Ranger. Tracking the footprints of his chosen career from rookie through ascendency to captain is informative, not only about Frank the man, but the Rangers as a law enforcing entity as well. Frank Jones' timing was fortuitous. His enlistment with the Rangers was juxtaposed during the exhilarating period that they were—as an institution—transitioning from Indian fighters to lawmen. He and they had a lot to learn. And, too, so did everyday citizens—the general public—now that they had another group of horseback gendarmes with statewide legal authority. The transitions would not be minus a hiccup—or two.

Allowing Frank Jones to take center stage affords readers opportunity to explore those ever-evolving methods for interdicting and solving crimes, as well as the impact advancing technological development contributed to those efforts. It's more than a little interesting to witness that upgrading: the expansion of familiarity with forensics and incorporating new proactive policing procedures.

Those speeding changes drastically enhanced the capability of Texas Rangers to wrap up criminal cases creditable for prosecution. As Jones' story unfolds, so, too, do the disclosures regarding the U.S. Constitution's Bill of Rights and its bearing vis-à-vis the enforcement activity of Texas Rangers and their aptitude at building sustainable criminal cases worthy of withstanding appellate court review. Aside from the specifics of utilizing informants—snitches—reconstructing crime scenes, handling evidence, and employing tested strategies for clearing cases—jugging felons and misdemeanants—peeking in on Frank's life as a Ranger also illustrates the impressive upshot of an expanding infrastructure. Extension of railway lines, improvements in communications, and the invention and mad-dash distribution of barbed-wire, was not an intentional crime-fighting line of attack. Those dynamics, however, revolutionized the application of criminal justice. The sociological influence was dramatic. Frank's biography is a mirror reflecting that drama.

So, while capitalizing on Frank Jones' daring chases and arrests and shoot-outs pushes his biographical profile forward with the theme of a first-rate Western production, other relevant but less apparent aspects play into the story. Circumspectly analyzing the wealth of preserved Texas Ranger correspondence files and official Monthly Returns is revealing, not only about the law enforcing outfit as a whole, but the headaches, heartburn, and heartbreaks germinating from administrative chores and handling touchy personnel issues. There's near a universal adage about law enforcement supervisors shared by on-the-ground folks—men and women—earning their paychecks policing: "Not all good cops are good bosses, but all good bosses were good cops." Was Captain Frank Jones a run-of-the-mill political hack or a conscientious Texas Ranger and good boss? With a nonpartisan methodology *Six-Shooters and Shifting Sands* will endeavor to answer that question sans malarkey or mythos.

The cast of unforgettable characters in Captain Jones' remarkable narrative is mindboggling. While serving in the Frontier Battalion officer's corps of Company D, although seldom—if ever—mentioned is a fact. As senior commander during an extended deployment Frank Jones supervised three of those four popularly professed "great" captains: J. A. Brooks, J. H. Rogers, and J. R. Hughes. As well, besides Austin Ira Aten and his younger brothers Calvin Grant Aten and Edwin Dunlap Aten, Captain Jones also managed law enforcement activities of not just a few other noteworthy Rangers, such as Philip Cuney "P. C." Baird, Benjamin Dennis Lindsey, Bazzell Lamar "Baz" Outlaw, J. Walter Durbin, Jim King, Frank Schmid, Charley Fusselman, John Woodard "Wood" Saunders, Ed Bryant, Carl Kirchner, and a Texas Ranger undercover operative extraordinaire, Ernest "Diamond Dick" St. Leon—and the list goes on. It's more than just a little germane to keep in mind, these fellows, and the others subordinate to Captain Frank Jones, were daring and independently-minded gun-carrying guys. And some of them, according to a plucky noncommissioned officer, "could be a little fussy and dangerous—when drinking." Not all Rangers were real nice guys, twenty-four and seven. Managerial skills can be tested in a heartbeat when involved with settling interpersonal disputes between iron-willed employees or issuing explicit orders to a steely-eyed workforce all heavily armed with a razor-sharp sheath knife, a lever-action Winchester, and one or two Colt's .45 six-shooters. Dealing with hot tempers and hair-triggers can be dicey. Prudently, diplomacy is the watchword.

Doggedness is the byword on another front—catching crooks. Frank Jones' law enforcing life was anything but boring. His biography is jam-packed with the hunts for dangerous desperadoes. Not only would Frank Jones find himself dodging bullets and returning fire, but those Rangers under his supervision—many times—would also find gunplay for their résumés. In fact, for the nineteenth-century it would be Company D contributing the highest number of on-duty deaths within Texas Ranger ranks. Therefore, even if Captain Frank Jones was not a participant in the exchange of gunfire, he was forced—administratively—to investigate: Was the Ranger wrong or was the Ranger right? Perhaps surprising to some folks is a down-to-earth reality. When they killed or wounded or whipped someone Texas Rangers were not automatically given a free pass. The ravenous demands of an impartial criminal justice system needed—required—satisfaction, or an overt facade of satisfaction. Legal headaches accompanying a Texas Ranger's resort to deadly and/or physical force could and did become nightmarish problems for the outfit's leadership staff. Personal commentary—drawn from Jones' correspondence—regarding several of these shooting incidents is illuminating.

Frank Jones' written remarks and dealings are windows into his soul, of sorts. Those words and actions reveal passion and prejudice, honor and hubris, prudence and pretentiousness, but never cowardice or dereliction of duty. Of course, conceding that Frank Jones was human is no grand revelation. He lived a personal life outside the Texas Rangers. Excavating the gems of that part of his narrative is also illuminating. Did devotion to duty trump tragedy on the home front? Was Captain Frank Jones' workaholic outlook, in truth, attentiveness or avoidance? Was he, in the best sense of the word, domesticated? Or did he vicariously sate the streak of wildness coursing through his bloodstream by shortstopping the meanness of ne'er-do-wells? Had Captain Frank Jones' life story bled into the twentieth-century would his name have been added to that capriciously drawn list of great Ranger captains?

Highlighting with microscopic and genealogical specificity the numerous accomplishments of Frank Jones' antecedents would make—and really has made—a fine Republic of Texas story. Pointedly though, *Six-Shooters and Shifting Sands* is the fleeting biographical tale of but one man. All encompassing genealogical enumerations are real meaningful—primarily to family members. The life of Frank Jones will herein be pared to the bone—but not gutted—regarding threads of genealogical minutiae. There is, however, permissible and logical relevance to mentioning his parents and siblings and love interests; they all rightfully play into his thrilling Wild West story.

Aside from valued genealogical treatments, drowning an otherwise good story with a torrential downpour of names and birthdays as sometimes writers do, is more often than not downright confusing and for the most part unnecessary. Dousing general readers with such an unremitting flood may somewhat satisfy nonfiction writers' basic itch to showcase his/her research thoroughness, but often it actually dampens readers enthusiasm, sluicing them into flipping and skipping pages. Detailing personal histories of collateral players jumping into and out of this story, sidestepping any semblance of chronological sequence, will be shelved.

For sure Frank Jones' biography will not be misleadingly corrupted by wittingly altering what he is known to have written simply to placate one-dimensional religious sensitivities. Shamelessly imposing pious personal beliefs on readers within the historical framework is wrongheaded and in the case of *Six-Shooters and Shifting Sands* sidestepped in lieu of truthfulness. Proselytizing is best reserved for the pulpit.

What will not play into the story is atonement. Apologetically skirting around sensitivities is as inappropriate as gratuitously exploiting those sensitivities. Frank Jones was but a mere mortal, a product of place and time—as well as genetic makeup. During part of that time and in some of those places not all was real nice. Thematically *Six-Shooters & Shifting Sands* does not pander to political correctness, prostituting the story just for the sake of political correctness, appeasing idealists. Perhaps, in keeping with a wide awake spirit of just sticking with the truth, it's best to simply settle for correctness. Luckily, in Frank Jones' case there is no dearth of correspondence revealing the mindset of a man. Perusing that pile of archived paperwork exposes a real-time reality: Good and bad. Throwing stones backward into time from an armchair is not risky. Decision making in real time was/is for lawmen and law enforcing women. By the very nature of a preferred career choice Frank Jones had embraced excitement, but had also invited no little controversy into his life. Thankfully, too, while studying Frank Jones' allotted Texas Ranger time there will be no shortage of on-the-ground episodes to reinforce or shatter notions about the suitability and viability of his managerial brilliance—or the lack thereof. In the end, judgments will be the reader's call.

Quite often the published works dealing with Texas Rangers are worshipful chronicles, particularly treatments penned a half-century or more ago. Searching for heroes with haloes was not rare. Simply inventing them was not uncommon. More recently, though, the bent seems more attuned to panning Texas Rangers as an institution and excoriating particular Texas Rangers as loathsome thugs and hardhearted terrorists sans even a dash of morality. Blindly venerating histories are dead wrong, as is a madcap journalistic lynching. Every now and then, dredging up a manipulative guise of scholarship to press an agenda is transparent. Perhaps much to the chagrin of folks idolizing Texas Rangers and much to the mortification of others intent on vilifying Texas Rangers, *Six-Shooters and Shifting Sands* will rest across the fulcrum of evidence and logic. Relying on commonsense and facts might prove especially troubling for a cadre of agenda-driven proponents. Dispassionately watching their advocacy crumble beneath the weight of substantiation is not gratifying, but wobbly platforms of supposition, in the end, customarily collapse. Predisposed revisionists sometimes get it wrong. Recklessly exposing bigotry with bigotry is a puzzling phenomenon, though not infrequently spitting forth from certain dogmatic quarters. Haphazardly sensationalizing acts of brutality handed out by one crowd while, at the same time, ingloriously ignoring parallel brutality issued by a competing subset is a baffling trend—trying to bamboozle readers—but, at this late date, is not necessarily an irregular device. In particular cases the tricksters' lame excuse-making is more than dishonest—it is dreadful. History is best repeated with honesty. Frank Jones and Rangers of his day—and this day for that matter—were not then or are they now perfect. Shortcomings are omnipresent. Flawlessness is a worthy target, but no one scores hits in the bull's-eye every time. As nonfiction pages of *Six-Shooters and Shifting Sands* turn, the reader will not be splashed with idolizing whitewash, nor will he/she be indelibly stained by suppositional dirty black ink. What follows is, hopefully, unvarnished and unapologetic Old West history. Plainly resorting to everyday speak: "What it is, is what it is!"

What *Six-Shooters and Shifting Sands* is not, is an end product absent contribution of others. Nonfiction work is never unaided. Researchers and writers must rely on help and, too, shed any timidity about seeking or asking for that help. Perhaps surprising for the general reader is the fact that—in most cases—helpmates willingly and gladly give of their time and from their jam-packed storehouses of resources, selflessly assist one another. Simply exchanging ideas and interpretations is important too. Mentioning those gifts is always a pleasure.

First and foremost a genial vote of thanks must be extended to Kirby W. Dendy, Chief of the Texas Rangers, and a good friend of many years. Chief Dendy's managerial and law enforcing responsibilities are near unfathomable. He has devoted his life to serving the people of Texas. Likewise that same devotion to principle and duty, as headman of the Texas Rangers, carries over to maintaining the institution's outstanding level of professionalism and investigative profiency. Advantaging themselves of the very latest advances in technology and constantly undergoing training to keep abreast of techniques necessary for perfecting quality felony investigations and/or apprehending dangerous violators, the Texas Rangers of today, as were their predecessors, are wrapped in an ever evolving transitional progression. Attentive Texans are well aware when they read newspaper or scan internet accounts or watch TV reports by on-air correspondents regarding a major act of Lone Star State criminality, a Ranger will be there, either leading the investigation or lending a helping hand with his/her expertise. There is another hard bottom line. Should circumstances turn "Western," today's Texas Ranger, as a last resort, will be a warrior. In the far-flung Panhandle or along the challenging Rio Grande, the Texas Rangers were there then, and are there now. Chief Dendy's supervisory duties—as can readily be deduced—are awesome. As well as his rock-solid commitment to the contemporary law enforcement issues, Chief Dendy is an ardent advocate of preserving legitimate Ranger history for future generations. He passionately believes modern-era Texas Rangers must do their part as caretakers and stewards of that heritage. There could be no honor greater for *Six-Shooters and Shifting Sands* than a Foreword penned by Chief Kirby W. Dendy.

This biographical project and any others dealing with Rangers are dependent on materials archived at the Texas State Library & Archives Commission at Austin. The files are voluminous. Accessing that data would seem like a daunting and overwhelming job. Donaly E. Brice eases that pressure. Assuredly his tenure as a veteran archivist with years of service figured by decades is impressive, but everyone in the field of researching and writing Texas history is appreciative of Donaly's genuine—heartfelt—sincerity and affability. How he manages to never be too busy to assist others creates its own mystery: Where does he find any time to research for his own catalogue of published works—which are quite extraordinary? Thank you, my friend.

Pulling in tandem with Donaly is another team of outstanding professionals. When compiling biographical and/or genealogical background material involving specific Rangers or richly delving into episodes involving them necessitates a visit—or numerous visits—to the Texas Ranger Hall of Fame & Museum at Waco, TX. This outstanding institution, by act of the state legislature, has been dedicated as the official Historical Center and Repository for the Texas Rangers, a stellar and foremost achievement. Adding to those laurels was the recent and well deserved endorsement by the Texas Department of Public Safety Commission, formally naming TRHF&M as the steward for the upcoming Texas Ranger Bicentennial, a most fitting tribute Executive Director Byron Johnson was delighted to accept: Preserving and promoting Ranger history and, by extrapolation Texas history, is his overriding goal. Particularly for writers or genealogists or movie and television documentary producers the place to be at this first-class facility is the Tobin and Anne Armstrong Texas Ranger Research Center, under the most capable management and leadership of Deputy Directory Christina Stopka. She, along with Research Librarian Amanda Crowley, did magnificent work in helping bring Captain Frank Jones' compelling life story to fruition.

Also helpfully stepping to the mark was Doug Dukes, Liberty Hill, TX. *Six-Shooters and Shifting Sands* was made whole by his utterly tireless technological input and sound counseling. An accomplished researcher and published author in his own right, Doug unflaggingly and smilingly trudged forward filling in the blank spots and making up for modern-age inadequacies owned by this writer. Doug's friendship is valued, his support never unappreciated.

For this particular project—as well as many others in the past—particularly focused inquiries or standing as sounding boards for theoretical as well as historically relevant questions were two esteemed friends and writing *amigos*, each with a string of nonfiction books about the Old West to their credit: the award-winning Rick Miller, Harker Heights, TX, and the recognized authority on Texas feudists, Dave Johnson, Zionsville, IN. They unselfishly laid aside their writing projects, evaluating the Frank Jones' manuscript for completeness and readability—and thoughtfully tagging typographical errors, as well as proffering positive suggestions. Commendably and graciously they each stepped to the plate as men, not corrupting the review process into a self-aggrandizing platform. *Six-Shooters and Shifting Sands* is an improved product thanks to their capable and competent input.

Thanks also must be extended to Texas Ranger researcher extraordinaire Robert W. Stephens, formerly from Dallas, but now Dunwoody, GA. He's been at the game near half a century, turning out many works highlighting Texas Rangers and those choosing to challenge them with belligerence, bullets, and/or buckshot. For this project his help was invaluable, but that comes as no surprise. Robert Stephens is always at the starting-gate, ready to go, when it comes to sharing his knowledge or opening his personal historical files for perusal.

Especial appreciation must also be passed to Candice DuCoin, Round Rock, TX. Candice is not only a bloodline relative of Frank Jones, but has also authored a fascinating book about other law enforcing branches of the Jones' family-tree, *Lawmen on the Texas Frontier: Rangers and Sheriffs*. Aside from the wealth of historical and genealogical data at her fingertips, for the book in hand she has most graciously shared photographic images from her personal archives, some never before published. Candice is committed to preserving history—good history—and readers will profit from her contributions to the biography herein. Many thanks, my friend.

Another good friend putting his inimitable touch on *Six-Shooters and Shifting Sands* is Western artist extraordinaire Donald M. Yena. Again he has kindly tendered the go-ahead for this writer to grace a book's cover with his artwork. Don's paintbrush Old West storytelling is matchless. Dying embers, ashes growing cold, and a Colt's six-shooter safely holstered are symbolic of a frontier life once raging with passion and a spirit of adventure but, too, emblematic of life overtaken by time and eternal quietness while flickering light surrenders to darkness—as it must. Painstaking historical accuracy and authenticity are the hallmarks of Don Yena's canvas masterpieces. The visual imagery of his painting is always thought provoking and appreciated. *Muchas Gracias*, Don Yena!

As would be expected there were many others adding their brand of expertise to making this project round, such as Jan Appleby, Mason County Historical Commission, Mason, TX; James Baird, San Francisco, CA; Michael Barr, Gatesville, TX; Melleta R. Bell, Archives of the Big Bend, Sul Ross University, Alpine, TX; Lynn Blankenship, San Saba Historical Commission, San Saba, TX; David Braeutigam, Arlington, TX; the late Jeff Burton, England; Clifford R. Caldwell, Mountain Home, TX; Clarissa Chavira, Texana & Genealogy, San Antonio Public Library, San Antonio, TX; Les Cotten, former Navarro County Sheriff, Corsicana, TX; Mike Cox, Austin, TX; Ronald G. DeLord, Georgetown, TX; Jan Devereaux, Maypearl, TX; Robert Ernst, Perkins, OK; Suzanne Giffin-Garcia, San Francisco, CA; West Gilbreath, Sanger, TX; Shannon Gillette, Saint Jo, TX; Charles H. Harris III, Las Cruces, NM; Jane Hoerster, Mason County Historical Commission, Mason, TX; Kurt House, San Antonio, TX; Harold E. Jobes, Cedar Park, TX; Josh Lehew, Waxahachie, TX; Nell Ann McBroom, Director, Tales 'N' Trails Museum, Nocona, TX; J.P. "Pat" McDaniel, Director, Nita Stewart Haley Memorial Library & History Center, Midland, TX; Phyllis Poehliman, Lometa, TX; Gary Boyce Radder and Jeri Radder, Alamo, CA; Shirley Aten Roberts, Amarillo, TX; Clay Riley, Brownwood, TX; Louis R. Sadler, Las Cruces, NM; Cathy Smith, Nita Stewart Memorial Library & History Center, Midland, TX; Paul N. Spellman, Wharton Junior College, Wharton, TX; Michael L. Toon, Associate Professor and Librarian, Ret., The Texas Collection, Baylor University, Waco, TX; Joseph H. Troubaugh II, Carlisle, PA; David Turk, Historian, U.S. Marshal's Service, Washington, D.C.; Deen Underwood, El Paso, TX; Lexie Van Tassel, Clifton, TX; Sally Walker, Shallowater, TX; Harold J. Weiss, Jr., Leander, TX; Jim Willett, Director, Texas Prison

Museum, Huntsville, TX; Charles Wright, U.S. Customs and Border Enforcement, Las Cruces, NM; James Wright, Whitney, TX; Donald M. and Louise Yena, San Antonio, TX.

Although mentioned last, their role really is first-place—The University of North Texas Press. Absent committed publishers there are no books. As far as commitment to first-rate products go these folks know how to get the job done—and get it done right! Literary awards, positive book reviews—though subjective—and many, many history association accolades accrued by their wide-array of Wild West era authors would forestall any argument to the contrary. Proof, as they say, is in the pudding and for those aficionados addicted to true Western tales UNT Press has perfected the recipe—down pat. Therefore, while casually perusing or seriously scrutinizing pages of *Six-Shooters and Shifting Sands*—or any UNT Press book—the reader should not neglect to notice the duality—writer and publisher—and the number of hands effectively stirring the pot. In this case the product was enhanced—made better—and actually possible through the hard and ceaseless dedication of Administrative Assistant Lori Belew, Director of Marketing Paula Oates, Assistant Director/Managing Editor Karen DeVinney, and Director Ron Chrisman.

CHAPTER 1

"Dragged to the Ground Lanced and Scalped"

AT THE TIME FRANK JONES CAME INTO a Texas world the place could still be legitimately characterized as the wild and woolly West. The Lone Star State was a hotbed for Indians with ideas of raiding and revenge on their minds.[1] Widespread lawlessness had not yet gained its post-Civil War notoriety—that was a few years into the future—but scattered settlements were still in need of sheriffs and town marshals. Even tenderfoot voyagers were counseled about the wisdom of traveling armed, at least with a revolver, preferably with a rifle or shotgun, too! Though it may ring of the melodramatic, if a mid-nineteenth-century player was desirous of finding some genuine blood and thunder adventure, frontier Texas was an ideal piece of real estate.

Texas was tough ground to cover, not only in the countryside but nearer in, say in a burgeoning municipality like Central Texas' Austin. The county of Travis was named after the fallen Alamo commander William Barret Travis, and was pleasantly situated at the eastern edge of the picturesque Texas Hill Country—with her seemingly endless springtime carpet of Bluebonnets. Fledgling as she was, the city of Austin would lay claim to being both a county seat and state capital. She was a town on the make. Created from historically prosperous Bastrop County during 1840, the year of the Great Comanche

Raid, Travis County wasn't officially organized until three years later on the eighth day of April 1843.[2] One should not be naively misled: The formal county organization was no overnight and magic guarantee that horseback marauders wearing war-paint automatically placed the city off limits. Industrious warriors prospected for a gainful break—anywhere.

In fact, right there in Austin on Sunday afternoon 3 November 1844, just 400 yards from the widow Nancy Simpson's West Pecan Street log residence, Indians lay in wait. The planned abduction was near a pushover for lurking raiders. When Mrs. Simpson dispatched her fourteen-year-old daughter Jane and son William, age twelve, to fetch milk cows, the trap sprung shut. Merciless Indians captured for the short term, but later coldly murdered and scalped Jane. Afterward, subsequent to a tortuous spell of captivity, William was ransomed for $137 worth of "tobacco, salt, clothing, blankets, coffee, sugar, powder, and lead."[3]

Scratching for economic survival in early day Texas prompted pioneering folks to examine opportunity wherever it might be lurking. Precisely tracing the entirety of movements and motives for William Early Jones and his second wife, a widow, Keziah (Rector) Baxter Jones, relocating from Seguin, Guadalupe County, to alluring Comal County (county seat New Braunfels) and then to the Curry Creek settlement is not mandatory, but the repeated repositioning is an integral part of the story at hand. Too, at this point it is but appropriate to nip any anticipated puzzlement in the bud. Though for a time period the delightful Curry Creek area could rightfully call Comal County home, such would not always be the case. Simplicity was foreign to the ways Texans do things and in this instance made more knotty by headstrong intrastate squabbles regarding aligning with the anticipated Confederacy. Blanco County (county seat Johnson City) was lopped off of Comal County during 1858, and Kendall County (county seat Boerne) was chiseled from western Blanco and southeastern Kerr (Kerrville) Counties during the first month of 1862. After the surveys and splits and nitpicking about boundary lines Kendall County owned the delightful—but yet perilous—setting of Curry Creek.[4] The enchanting spot was sited north and a touch west of the Alamo City and not too terribly far southwest of Austin. And there, along Upper Curry Creek, William E. and Keziah established their ranch—a homestead—and the base for the raising of livestock for their larder and the marketplace.

William Early Jones, a Georgian by birth, had bathed in the troubled waters of Texas history.[5] Sometimes referred to as "Fiery Jones" the well-educated patriarch was a lawyer, judge, journalist, legislator, political activist and, regrettably in one sense, but not sadly in another, an exultant surviving prisoner of Mexico's infamous Perote Prison.[6] For a spell he partnered with iconic Texas personality John Salmon "Rip" Ford in the newspaper business, publishing the *State Times*.[7] The fits and starts of city life—if it could really be called that—defending editorial stances, hunting for advertisers and subscribers to keep things afloat, and those tedious days of listening to haranguing lawyers litigate on behalf of this defendant or that plaintiff had worn thin. Taking a respite from much of that nonsense sounded good. Judge Jones had constructed a saw mill and shingle making facility at the confluence of Curry Creek and the Guadalupe River, southeast of the ranch.[8] The fact that such an operation was somewhat labor intensive was of no major concern for Judge Jones: Tax records enumerated "7 Negroes" as a part of his net worth.[9]

With the saws buzzing and livestock wandering across the more than 2,400-acre ranch, William and Keziah began planning for new arrivals to join the twins, William Kenner and James Russell, who had made their initial appearance the year before on June 4, 1849, at Seguin. At what was then Comal County, but now Kendall County, birth of the twins was followed by the arrival of Gerry "Dood" Jones on 24 May 1852 and Pinckney "Pink" Jones on the twenty-first day of March 1854.[10] The births, as would be expected, were greeted with joy.

Other folks were planning their arrival at the Curry Creek ranch—and they wouldn't be welcome visitors. Judge Jones, penning an explanation for the *Seguin Mercury* of July 21, 1855, introduces readers to the uninvited company: "It is a painful duty devolving upon me to communicate to you the particulars of an Indian outrage just committed in this neighborhood. On Saturday morning last Mr.

Jesse Lawhon, who has been living with me for nearly two years in the capacity of overseer and manager of my farm and stock, went out accompanied by one of my negro men to drive up some oxen. About 11 o'clock the negro boy ran home afoot and barefooted and wet to the hips, and told me he feared that Mr. Lawhon had been killed by the Indians; that Mr. Lawhon and himself were riding together in search of cattle, and when descending a hill into the valley of one of the branches of Curry's Creek, near the foot of the mountains, they were attacked by five Indians who emerged from the bed of the creek and rushed upon them at full speed."[11] According to Judge Jones the quintet of attackers were not all ethnic brothers: Four were Indians "naked and armed with guns," and the other, a "white man dressed in dark clothes with a fur hat."[12]

Luckily the "negro boy" made good his getaway and was able to sound an alarm. Unluckily, twenty-five-year-old Jesse Lawhon was not, leaving behind a young crying wife, Lavonia, and two small children to mourn the heartbreaking loss of "an industrious and most worthy citizen, sober, moral, and of unimpeachable integrity, universally esteemed by all neighbors and acquaintances."[13] A grieving community assembled, and with "stricken hearts" reverently placed Jesse Lawhon in his final resting place—but the Curry Creek settlement was not at rest.[14]

Making a general statement—sometimes dangerous in a historic context—in this instance is a safe call: "in the summer of 1855, Indian depredations fell with mounting frequency on the settlers of the Guadalupe and Blanco Rivers in the Hill Country north of San Antonio."[15] During the month of June warriors had plagued the western portion of Guadalupe County, stealing horses and killing "a negro belonging to Mr. Elam." Then they charged after Pendleton Rector and Doc McKee (McGee ?), the son of a popular Methodist minister, Reverend John S. McKee. Rector, though thrown from his horse, managed to scamper into a thicket and somehow avoid calamity. Doc McKee, riding a plodding mule, wasn't so fortunate: "He was roped, dragged to the ground, lanced and scalped."[16] From the settlers' perspective the forays were epidemic, prompting Comal County's distressed residents to rally at a public meeting at New

Braunfels on 12 September 1855 eyeing limited options regarding self-defense: "Despite their location almost a hundred miles behind the so-called frontier, they were being raided."[17] Sadly, more horrifying news would break for the William E. Jones' family during that wearisome year.

Expending effort defending or condemning the actions of James Hughes Callahan, commander of a company of provisionally tenured Rangers—temporary enlistments—is not compulsory. Governor Elisha M. Pease, wholly overwrought with pleas and petitions, pressed the veteran frontiersman and Indian fighter into service.[18] Judge William E. Jones had been sounding the drumbeat for an unrestricted search and destroy mission.[19] The task was plainspoken: There was no money in the state's coffers for salaries, but chastise any marauding Indians with an unbending vengeance. Chase them to the gates of Hell if needed—into Old Mexico if they went there first.[20] Pay, if it came at all, would come later. The problem needed a fix, right now—immediately! Supporters would defend Callahan's sortie, detractors would assert the actual purpose was to recapture runaway slaves seeking refuge south of the Rio Grande.[21] Others, William Robertson "Big" Henry, being one, were championing for splashing across the Río Bravo and interjecting an armed Texas contingent into raging political and revolutionary turmoil then underway, explicitly declaring: "War to the death against Santa Anna and his government."[22] Callahan's and Henry's calls for saddle-hardened volunteers did not go unanswered: Texans were fighters. All they needed was a good reason—at least in their minds—to punish Mexicans for past atrocities or Indians for blood-spattered episodes more recent.

In particular Henry's message struck a note with twenty-four-year-old Willis H. Jones, the first-born son of William Early Jones during his earlier marriage to Caroline (Randle) Jones.[23] Unscrambling motives for his move—with precision—is unworkable: Was he holding a grudge, fostering a hatred for his dad's imprisonment by Mexicans at Perote or did a simple spirit for adventure force his hand? Did he want to even a score for butchery of Lawhon at Curry Creek? At San Antonio on 10 September

1855, riding a high-dollar horse valued at $125 and carrying arms worth $60, Willis enlisted in Captain Henry's company of would-be Lone Star warriors.[24] In any event and despite any controversy that would ensue, and there would be plenty, Private Willis Jones was far removed from any policy making or command decisions.

Shortly Callahan's men, Henry's volunteers, and a third company answering to Nathaniel "Nat" Benton, merged into one in-the-field corps, James Hughes Callahan battalion commander, Henry and Benton, company captains.[25] Now, Willis H. Jones was voluntarily and dutifully riding as one of Commander Callahan's unpaid Texas Rangers. Nineteen days later, Private Willis H. Jones was perched atop his horse four miles north of Eagle Pass, Maverick County, looking at the winding Texas boundary below: The Rio Grande waters were swollen by an unremitting rainfall upriver. There is dispute as to whether these Texas Rangers crossed by invitation as asserted by Callahan, or by force and at gunpoint as proffered by witness Emilio Langberg, military commander of the Mexican State of Coahuila.[26] But cross they did.

On 3 October 1855, twenty-odd miles south of Piedras Negras, near Río Escondido—really a creek—the 110 Texas Rangers and a greatly superior mixed contingent of Mexican soldiers and Indians collided. Fittingly, maintaining Texas Ranger tradition, it may be reported that these no-nonsense Texas Rangers inflicted heavy causalities. A scorecard of dead and wounded enemy combatants—Mexican and Indian—was significantly lopsided, at least so said James Callahan. There is, however, another hard and undisputed truth regardless of the first one: Willis H. Jones and three other Texas Rangers were left dead on the battlefield, while their colleagues whipped around, making fast tracks for the border before enemy reinforcements made a show and doled out big-time payback.[27] Positively the lifeless Ranger Private Willis H. Jones did not witness the sacking and burning of Piedras Negras before James H. Callahan's Rangers sought safety, splashing back across the Rio Grande. Governor Pease was not pleased at all regarding the tactic of torching of Piedras Negras, even if at least part of the raging inferno was the result of Seminole Negroes shooting flaming arrows into town in an effort to dislodge Rangers.[28] Governor Pease was not any too happy, but political expediency tempered his written remarks to Commander James Hughes Callahan—still in the field:

> When you got on the trail in pursuit of the Indians who had been committing depredations upon our settlements, and found that they had crossed the Rio Grande, you were justified in following them there for the purpose of recapturing the property stolen by them and punishing them, but you had not the right to take possession of or to occupy Piedras Negras or any other village or property of Mexican Citizens; After the termination of your engagement with the Indians you should have returned immediately to this side of the Rio Grande, and I trust that you have already done so.[29]

Having covered his gubernatorial fanny with the foregoing admonishment, the state's chief executive knew where much of the general public's sympathy would lay, and it was not with Mexicans or Indians or mealy-mouthed sympathizers. The second half of the letter to Callahan was effusively praiseworthy, but even then Governor Pease couldn't let go of worry:

> Your encounter with and defeat of such a large body of Indians reflects great credit upon yourself and the brave men under your command, and I trust that no acts have been committed by your command against the Citizens of Mexico which will give them any just cause of complaint against you.[30]

Taking a deep breath, Governor Pease had much more to say, this time to the U.S. Military. Repeating a portion of it now will be meaningful for its impact on Frank Jones' story later. In a missive dated 13 October 1855, to the Commanding General of the U.S. Army in Texas, Persifor F. Smith, Governor Pease had this to say, in part:

> You will perceive that I made no objection to his [Callahan's] pursuit of the Indians across the Rio Grande, and that I only objected to his occupation of the territory of Mexico after the termination of his engagement with the Indians. That he was justified in pursuing the Indians across the Rio Grande on their retreat from this

> state, where they had been committing depredations upon our citizens, I presume will not for a moment be questioned, and if this leads to a border warfare between the citizens of this state and the Mexicans and Indians no one will regret it more than myself, but the fault lies with the United States government, whose neglect to furnish protection to our settlements against the repeated depredations of these Indians during the past year, rendered it necessary to call into service Volunteers of this State for our protection.[31]

James Hughes Callahan's Rangers retuned to the Leona River country west of San Antonio where they were to be mustered out of service. They had come home to the cheering adulation of some contemporaries then, but discordant denigration later from U.S. military brass, distraught diplomats, and annoyed abolitionists, as well as succeeding generations of armchair thinkers.[32] William Early Jones, at the time, would hear none of that negativity. He was heartbroken! He, too, was mad, thoroughly angry. Mad enough to raise a crowd of leathery volunteers to invade Mexico and extract revenge on the Mexicans and their understood Indian allies.[33] Although the jingoistic ranting was in one way or another emotionally fulfilling, such venting about a punitive invasion came to naught.

When the midnight hour finally passed, allowing Father Time to surrender 1855 and begin marking a new year, two newsy issues would be of interest and importance to William E. Jones and his ranch-raised boys: Keziah was pregnant. The new baby brother/sister was scheduled—if everything went right—to arrive during early summer. Others hadn't waited for summer. The incessant Indian raids had not abated. That year following the murder of Jesse Lawhon and the Callahan expedition would notch several landmark clashes between the U.S. Army and Indians in and around the Texas Hill Country—all too close for the Jones clan on Curry Creek to find any comfort.

Riding hard out of Fort Mason on February 14, 1856, Captain James Oakes, at the head of Company C, 2nd U.S. Cavalry, was in pursuit of a band of Waco Indians who had been on the warpath, raiding settlements throughout the region. After six grueling days the soldiers and tribesmen locked up: An Indian died and two troopers were wounded. It was, according to military records, the first time a 2nd Cavalryman killed an Indian.[34] William E. and Keziah Jones took notice, as did most Hill Country folks.

The wait for like news was but short. The following month, on the eighth day of March, Captain Albert G. Brackett in command of Company I, 2nd Cavalry, detected the camp of Lipan Apaches on the Guadalupe River in Kerr County, Kendall County's immediate western neighbor. These raiders had been returning from an incursion near San Antonio, and were guilty of killing settlers, looting cabins, and stealing livestock. During a dismounted charge Sergeant Henry Gordon and his soldiers "killed three of the Indians, and recovered stolen horses, mules, and a bank draft for 1,000 British pounds."[35] Mrs. Keziah Jones was suffering morning sickness and, rightly so, the jitters.

Although the exact time and date is hazy and the foundation is oral history, there's no reason to doubt it. Purportedly, on one occasion—and this is about the correct timeframe—William E. Jones was absent from the Curry Creek ranch, away on business. Keziah was home alone, the sole caretaker and guardian for young kiddos. As good luck would have it, Keziah spied three Indians lurking nearby, sneakily reconnoitering and drawing the blueprint for attacking a defenseless woman and her little brood. Grabbing a handy rifle she climbed stairs, pushing through an emergency trapdoor and onto the house's roof. Carefully aligning the rifle's front sight the lively lady touched the trigger, letting a bullet fly. The heavy projectile thumped into red meat and gristle, knocking the surprised warrior off of his feet and into eternity. His two cohorts not knowing just how to predict the outcome of tangling with a tigress, hightailed for safety elsewhere.[36] Keziah breathed a sigh of relief. She was worried, though.

Again, during the spring of 1856, U.S. Army fellows and Lipan Apache went to war, not too far from Kendall County and the Jones' ranch. On April 13, 1856, Captain Thomas Claiborne Jr. and his joint command of Companies B and D, Mounted Rifles and Company F, 1st Artillery, riding out of Forts McIntosh and Duncan and a posse of twenty-five citizens from Laredo, overhauled the band after an exhausting and roundabout 300 mile chase. On Turkey Branch of the sparkling Nueces River, in the beautiful country west of Uvalde, the pursuers killed one Indian, wounded another, and made prisoners of four.[37]

What had not been killed was the growing uneasiness felt by Keziah, now heavy with child. During the intervening thirteen-year timeframe, between Travis County's organization and the projected birthday of another precious baby for the Jones household, the city of Austin had blossomed. The municipality was, if an analogy is permitted, an island paradise: Within confines of the city it was a dreamscape utopia, but one wholly surrounded by deep waters and predators. Realistically, were folks to avoid barrooms and bordellos and betting dens there was little worry of meeting mayhem. Though, too, it was not unwise at times to steer clear of the cockamamie shenanigans unwinding at the statehouse on Congress Avenue—not just a few legislators stirred their neat whiskey with the barrels of Colt's six-shooters or sported a timepiece in one vest pocket, a Derringer in the other. The asinine comedy of their chronic foolishness continually held potential for tragedy. For the heart of Austin and her close-in suburbs the threat of raiding Indians was but a phantom of the past. Keziah Jones—undoubtedly with the selfless support of William E.—had made the decision she would give birth at Austin, not on the isolated ranch at Curry Creek. Why chance birthing a baby to the sounds of earsplitting war whoops and echoing bombardment from Colt's percussion pistols and fire belching shoulder guns? Babies' first gulps of air, those welcoming them into the world, should be unpolluted: Not tiny lungs inhaling and choking down gunsmoke and minuscule particles of unspent black powder. Keziah's next baby's birthplace—girl or boy—would be in the Capitol City, not Curry Creek.[38] She was adamant!

And so it was. During the waning hours of June 12, 1856, the subject of this vignette, baby Frank Jones bleated his way to his mother's reassuring bosom at Austin.[39] Perhaps particularly poignant for William Early Jones, the following month on the twenty-first day of July, it was approved that acting in lieu of his dead son Willis, as administrator of the estate, he would be allowed to accept the state's reimbursement for the loss of his son's horse and arms during the cross-border battle at Río Escondido.[40] Keziah Jones' premonitions regarding the very real possibilities of rampaging Indians chancing a raid into her neighborhood had not been grounded in misplaced hysteria. Before Frank Jones celebrated his first birthday Comanches hit hard in Kerr County, stealing horses and scaring settlers.[41]

Commanding at nearby Camp Verde was the U.S. 2nd Cavalry's Captain Innis R. Palmer. Quickly acceding to petitions of panicky Hill Country citizens, Captain Palmer ordered Sergeant Walter McDonald and fourteen cavalrymen to act as bloodhounds: Overhaul, severely punish raiders and recapture horses the Indian thieves had stolen. Riding with the soldiers, acting as a guide, was José "Polly" Rodriguez. Also accompanying the squad were Dr. James Crispin Nowlin, who would (in 1859) become a close neighbor of the Jones family on Curry Creek, and his nephew, Henry Moore. The pursuers crossed the Guadalupe River. At the headwaters of Kickapoo Creek in what is now Tom Green County (county seat San Angelo) Dr. Nowlin espied the Indians and drew first blood, blasting a charging marauder with buckshot from his shotgun. The good doctor's second barrel misfired, forcing Nowlin to speedily dismount his gyrating horse in order to repair and recharge the scattergun. While thus afoot he was wounded, an arrow's shaft protruding from his upper leg. Then, a slug from "an old flintlock musket" struck the physician's horse near the throatlatch and dropped the gelding doornail-dead. With an empty Colt's six-shooter in hand Dr. Nowlin "kept the wolf off" by brazenly pointing its muzzle at advancing Indians—a nervy but effective bluff. Two troopers weren't as fortunate, dying on the battlefield. Another, Private John Martin, would mortally succumb to his wounds subsequent to being transported thirty-odd miles to Fort McKavett. The Comanches quite expectedly had several wounded, but none—not a warrior—was left to be scalped or made prisoner. During their retreat the Indians abandoned five horses and two mules. Since the brands didn't match livestock they were looking for, the very real likelihood was that the soldiers engaged in combat with a different party of Comanches than they had been sent to chase and chastise.[42] Such a distinction was entirely inconsequential to Keziah and unnoticed by Frank; he was yet in diapers.

Tracing with tedium the maturation of Frank Jones is not necessary for forwarding his story. As already pointed out and can be deduced from his father's professionalism, and as will be drawn later from the employment landscapes of his older brothers, Frank Jones was born into an educated and reasonably affluent family. Certainly he or they were not eking a hardscrabble living from the land, as were so many Texans of the pre-Civil War era. Education mattered to the elder Jones: "He was a fine scholar and writer and an impressive orator, always conservative and logical."[43] Judge William Early Jones held dear his philosophy about the value of academia, and vigorously passed those beliefs to his boys—in no uncertain terms. There was no shame in wearing hand-me-downs, but poor grades and laziness were not to be tolerated in the William E. Jones household. Thus far his report cards have not surfaced, but it will prove crystal clear—whether in the classroom or homeschooled or both—Frank Jones learned well the ABCs of reading and writing and arithmetic.

There were other lessons to be learned too, those not taught in the classroom. There were technical skills and social skills to be accomplished by Texas boys on the march to manhood. The Lone Star State was, without exaggeration, yet wild and woolly. Transportation was for the most part accomplished horseback or slapping leathers across the trudging rumps of mules while atop a wagon's splintery wooden seat, all the while keeping a sharp watch for a Comanche or Apache planning an ambush. At an early age boys were expected to saddle and ride their own horses, even those with a hump in their back on cold mornings. Ranch boys learned the fine art of tattooing a catch-rope's loop around the horns, pitching slack to the cow critter's off side, turning obliquely and spurring hard away from the near side—tightening the rope—and throwing the creature to the ground for branding or doctoring or robbing its manhood with a sharp blade. Calves still on the teat were roped by the neck or hind legs and dragged bawling toward the white-hot embers and red-hot irons, gluey slobber clinging to their milk-splashed gums. At the catch-pen it was stinky, an odorous world of sweat, scorched hair, burnt hide, and cow shit.[44] Farm boys could—near blindfolded—progress through the steps of harnessing teams without getting kicked, or stepped on, or having a plug removed from a forearm by an insolent teeth-gnashing mule, before repairing to the field in breaking light and thence commit to breaking more ground, tilling the soil—day after day. A sodbuster's life was weary.

Another mechanical skill to be incorporated during that learning curve between adolescence and adulthood was a familiarity with firearms. Most boys are fascinated with guns. Earning the trust attendant to being turned loose with a rifle or shotgun was a rite of passage for Texas boys—it moved them from a station wherein childish mischief was sometimes stomached to a place on the pathway to responsibility where it wasn't. Early in life on the Texas frontier boys morphed to men—at least in their minds—when allowed parental permission to have their very own "gun"—which meant rifle or shotgun—handguns being generically referred to as their Colt's or simply as six-shooters.

Handiness with a gun could put meat on the table, or keep an enemy on the warpath from inflicting harm, or in lawful hands encourage *mal hombres* to admit defeat. Particular to the William E. Jones' household, by age twelve the boys were habitually going about their chores armed, six-shooters buckled around their waists.[45] At the ranch boys turned into men real fast. When he was but fifteen years old, an armed Pink Jones was placed on a nighttime stakeout at the Curry Creek ranch due to Indians raiding in the area. Beneath the moonlit sky Pink was involved in the shooting wherein interloping Indians were caught sneaking about, eyeing chances for murder and/or livestock theft. One of the ill-omened raiders was critically wounded, later found dead.[46] Papa Jones was elated that Pink had stepped up, making mention of the episode in a personal letter to the governor:

> One Indian was shot & wounded here at my place—from the blood we think, badly—it was done in the night—one of my younger sons & a Mexican in my employ were watching & both fired at them.[47]

Cowboys and Indians was no silly kid's game. It was played hard and for keeps at Curry Creek. As he matured, Frank Jones was an adept student of such serious business, mastering an uncanny knack for marksmanship. One gunfighter gentleman who in fact witnessed Frank Jones' sharpshooting talent later extolled: "He really was in a class with Carver or Buffalo Bill. I've seen him shoot an empty cartridge or piece of money thrown into the air, and he never missed the bull's eye when shooting with a Winchester."[48] Such exaltation may seem buttery, but that doesn't necessarily render it untrue.

What was true was another lesson, a tutorial of great consequence: More than ever critical at a place and time where the possession of weapons was ubiquitous. Although undercarriage of the adage may be trite, yet, even at this late date, the implication is not hollow: "In Texas if God had wanted men to fight like cats and dogs, He'd given 'em claws and paws." The translation is easy. It's better to bust a cap than a knuckle. Though that hyperbole is rich, the interpersonal doings among grown men are fraught with implicit rules. Vulgarly labeling—in jest with a wink and a smile—one's good friend a "sorry son-of-a-bitch" may casually or jokingly be brushed aside. Those same words spoken to a stranger or in anger would likely prove humorless—and maybe even harmful to the speaker's good health and well being. Then—or now—learning how to differentiate between slurred and drunken utterances which were/are just harmless fun, and prickly challenges more sinister is vital. All so soon young Frank Jones will find himself in a hard world where book learning was okay, but there also was that other classroom: a college of hard-knocks, long standing customs, traditions, unwritten conventions, and even some very real and undisputed cow camp etiquette. Imprudent little boys jabbered rather than listened or looked or learned. Smart boys paid attention. Frank Jones was smart.

Intelligent as he was, dissecting the dichotomy of his father's decisions on two relevant Texas issues was puzzlement for Frank. In those earlier days, before Frank came along, William E. Jones was a zealous opponent of Texas relinquishing her standing as a sovereign Republic and suffering Annexation, christened with statehood. Texas should stand on her own—in his mind. Fifteen years later, after Frank was born, at the brink of a Civil War, when it was time to fish or cut bait—secede from the United States or not—Judge Jones fervently propounded the wisdom of staying whole, a part of the Union. Nevertheless Texas voted in favor of the Confederacy, and William E. Jones—above all else—was now a dyed-in-the-wool loyal Texan.[49]

Of the many unwelcome sociological offshoots from the Civil War, rampant lawlessness was drawing no little attention. And for this survey, the throbbing heartbeat of violence was running unchecked in the Texas Hill Country—the bailiwick for the William Early Jones family. Truly, Comanche and Lipan Apache had not taken a holiday, but the likelihood of being punctured with arrows or scalped had been augmented with the potential for being lynched or bushwhacked. Loosely organized bands of outlaws, desperadoes, and deserters were roaming the countryside. With an eye to orchestrating a workable and effective model for cutting-edge defense, Texas was subdivided into Frontier Districts. The Jones' ranch on Curry Creek, where school age Frank was growing up, was a part of the Third Frontier District, headquartered at the quaint German community of Fredericksburg, Gillespie County.[50]

Regrettably, numerous were the killings in the Third Frontier District. During one month alone, twelve hapless men were gunned down, "including two soldiers, six settlers, and four bushwhackers." In the picturesque country of the Pedernales River, company commander Captain Christian Dorbandt daringly but unproductively attempted to apprehend or kill a coldhearted set of "renegades." During one six-shooter confrontation, Christian's fighters did manage to kill two "deserters" who had resisted arrest with a gunplay of their own. Ruefully, Captain Dorbandt characterized Blanco County as being in "a pitiable condition." At the time, there were many at-odds allegiances: not everyone was an especially nice guy. "A series of murders, robberies, and outrages perpetrated by bushwhackers, state troops of the Third district, and men of the Frontier Regiment excited the populace of Gillespie and Kendall counties into a frenzy." Inmates were unsympathetically mobbed at the Gillespie County jail, where the gatecrashers murdered three prisoners and wounded three others.[51] Opportunistic Indians had not been asleep. A party of Comanche, apparently on a horse-stealing foray, had been spotted in that very same Pedernales River region twenty-odd miles west of Fredericksburg. Shortly, eleven provisional Rangers and eleven pedestrian Comanche went to war: Six Indians were killed, one Texan, John Benson, was wounded when the point of an arrow "curled around the [hip] bone like a fishhook."[52] At the time it was supposed that the Rangers could have killed more Comanche had they not been using inferior "Confederate powder" in their second-rate single-shot rifles.[53] By any man's calculation, Texas was a bloody mess!

By any woman's measure childbirth was a bloody mess too: Positively traumatic and painful. Keziah was with child, again. This time safety at Austin was out of the question, her condition delicate. She would give birth at the Curry Creek ranch. While Comanche and Kiowa and Lipan Apache were jumping back and forth, and soldiers decked out in blue or gray were ramping up to kill each other by the thousands, Keziah writhed in agony, clinched her teeth, producing what she hoped would not be cannon fodder for someone else's senseless war. Emmett "Spunk" Jones, on the twenty-fifth day of March 1861, came crying into the world of frontier Texas, the last of William's and Keziah's half-dozen surviving sons.[54]

With the undaunted spirit of an old warrior, it was not in William Early Jones' makeup to nonchalantly sit on the sidelines while his Texas compatriots were sacrificing blood and treasure: On two separate occasions Judge Jones volunteered for service defending the Texas Frontier during wartime. For a time—ten days—in 1861 he enlisted as a private with Captain William A. Blackwell's company of makeshift Rangers—Minutemen—from Blanco City, Blanco County. During a second protective and proactive tour, 1864, Judge Jones was commissioned the captain for a company of Texas Rangers' short-lived assignment to Kendall County, 3rd Frontier District of Texas, under the chain-of-command leadership of the district's senior officer, Brigadier General of Texas State Troops, John D. McAdoo.[55] Subsequent to an in-the-field inspection circuit and returning to his base at Fredericksburg, General McAdoo reported on the utterly appalling state of affairs within his Third Frontier District:

> I found almost the entire population of a large portion of the District laboring under the greatest excitement. Within a few months, twenty men had perished by violence. Some had been waylaid and shot; others taken from their homes at the dead hour of midnight and hung, and their homes robbed; and some had been mobbed and murdered in jail and in irons. No man felt secure—even at home. The Indians seemed to be the least talked of, the least thought of, and the least dreaded of all the evils that threatened and afflicted the Frontier.[56]

Auspiciously moving Frank Jones' story does not necessitate step by step recitals of every act of criminality or Comanche and/or Kiowa sortie wrecking havoc in the Texas Hill Country during and after the pitiless Civil War. Robert E. Lee's surrender at Appomattox did not assuage the troublesome times in frontier Texas. Recalcitrant Indians hadn't surrendered their propensity for raiding and revenge directed at defenseless Texas settlers or scavenging their susceptible herds. The 1860s "was the bloodiest decade in the Western Indian wars."[57] Judge William E. Jones concurred, so informing Governor E. M. Pease: "The Indians are worse now than at any previous period, their inroads are more frequent and they are more successful in getting off—."[58] For the retelling of Frank Jones' riveting story, highlighting a couple of particular Comanche forays is appropriate: The first of these bloody 1868 episodes unfolded in Legion Valley along Legion Creek, a dependable water source feeding into Sandy Creek, a Colorado River tributary about fifteen miles south of Llano, not too far removed north of the William Early Jones' homestead and ranch on Curry Creek.[59]

Massaging the story to make it nice is wrong. On the fifth day of February 1868, near sundown, Comanches struck the homestead of John S. Friend, a farmer and rancher, though absent at the time. Unfortunately, however, the house was full of family and friends, mostly women and little children. Laying siege to the house was not necessary; fifteen Comanche, two of whom were women, and perhaps "one negro" gained entry.[60] The coldhearted brutality then, and later, would measure horrendous and hideous. One or more of the gruesome raiders drove three arrows into Matilda Jane Friend, who smartly feigned death: "Matilda lay where she fell, with face to the floor. A warrior bent down and severely slashed her left hand three times, cutting the nerves. He jerked the arrow in her side up and down several times to make sure she was dead, then cut a two- by four-inch 'scalp' from the right side of her head, and a two- by three-inch patch from the middle back of her head. The pain was intense, but Matilda still played dead."[61]

After plundering the house, the Comanche made prisoners of adults and children, and then vamoosed. Less than a mile from the scene, for a reason unknown, a warrior choked to death one-year-old Fielty Johnson. Her mother, also a prisoner, was understandably horrified. She vainly attempted to try to take the baby away from the kidnapper, "but the angered Indian smashed its head in."[62] After traveling another mile the Comanche murdered three-year-old Nancy Elizabeth Johnson, cutting her throat and holding her upside down in front of her mother Rebecca, laughing, while allowing blood to puddle at the heartbroken lady's feet. Mrs. Johnson fainted.[63] Indians scalped little Nancy, "leaving one small tuft of hair near her neck."[64] Making camp for the night at Cedar Mountain, the Comanche "built a fire, roasted some meat and gang raped the women."[65] Sometime during the night or early next morning an executioner speared a lance into the pregnant Samantha Johnson, cut her throat and scalped her, leaving her sitting in an upright position, horribly mutilated and dead. Later near the homestead of J. C. Tally, Indians raped and murdered Rebecca Johnson. Near Hell's Half Acre also referred to locally as Cut Off Gap, about four miles from Cedar Mountain, the Indians stopped again, slaughtering Amanda Townsend, eighteen. An on-scene eyewitness to the macabre discovery would later recall and write:

> She had been tied down upon the cold ground, which was covered with snow, and from all appearances, had been outraged in the most brutal manner. She was then killed, and her body mutilated almost beyond recognition. [She had been] tied in a position so that the fiends could satisfy their brutal lusts.[66]

Resorting to every practicable means at his disposal, even within pages of the widely circulated *San Antonio Express*, John Friend pled, begging Indian Agents or traders to rescue the kidnapped children, "who had been taken from my house by Indians." The distraught father was promising—publicly—that upon recovery of the children the liberator would be "liberally remunerated."[67] Eventually, if there ever could be a happy ending to what turned out to be "the bloodiest tragedy in Llano County" it may be reported that youngsters Lee Temple Friend and Malinda "Minnie" Caudle would be bargained for, ransomed and repatriated.[68]

During the same year, 1868, that the ferocious raid on John Friend's ranch was carried out, Comanche were back on the scene at Curry Creek on the twenty-eighth day of October. The Indians had "divided and scattered all over the country, being at the ranches of Sansom, Calahan, Reese, and Judge Jones on the same night, and two at each place had succeeded at getting off with some stock."[69] In fact, three Indians had been caught unawares at Dr. Nowlin's ranch. Marksmanship killed one raider outright. Another, suffering a bullet wound, was knocked to the ground on his hands and knees, then mortally dispatched with arcing blows from a hoe-handle wielded by the infuriated and vengeful—and apparently run amok physician. The other prowler, who had been wearing a cap made from a polecat, escaped.[70] Naturally such an episode was big doings for the Curry Creek neighborhood, Doc Nowlin's place being but a mile from Judge W. E. Jones' home. The morning after the fight, as then seven-year-old Emmett Jones as an elderly man recalled for an inquisitive newspaperman, "my father, two brothers [Frank?] and myself visited the scene and looked at the dead Indian. It was a gruesome sight and one I cared not to ever see again. 'Here is where I spiled [*sic*] him with the grubbing hoe' said Dr. Nowlin showing us where he had hit him."[71] Whether he saw the dead Indian or not, there's little doubt that adolescent Frank Jones, yet living at home on Curry Creek, would have been intrigued and repulsed by another turn of events.

Perhaps he shouldn't have been and maybe he wasn't surprised: After all, Blanco County and her sister counties were, at the time, and for years had been the scene of many Indian attacks. Cicero Rufus

"Rufe" Perry, a grizzled Indian fighter and battle-scarred frontiersman, in his own way, with his own brand of grammar, highlighted:

> I then moved to Blanco Co whar I have remained ever Since. When I first wint thair was Indions nearly evry light moon. I was oute very often but never caught up with them but once thair was but 2 of us and 40 of them So wee dun the running.[72]

Eager-beaver Frank Jones soon learned that a band of Comanche had quit their buffalo-hide teepees for another speedy trip into the Texas Hill Country, his neck of the woods. On the twenty-second day of July 1869, along pretty Cypress Creek in Blanco County, the warriors cunningly stalked opportunity. Taking a welcome—and rare—day off from the rough routine of ranching chores and housekeeping drudgery, Thomas C. Felps (sometimes Phelps) twenty-seven, and his nineteen-year-old wife, Eliza, grabbed cane poles and headed for the creek, a little fishing beneath the awning of shade trees would be a most welcome break from a scorching sun. Without doubt they carried some sort of live bait to the creek, but Mr. and Mrs. Felps, though they certainly knew naught at the time, were the bait.[73]

The enjoyable picnic and hook-wetting excursion—in a split second, spun from pleasure to pandemonium. The Comanche struck fast and the Comanche struck hard. Tom Felps was felled by bullets—dead—but he was lucky. Eliza, struggling mightily and fearfully fought for her life no doubt. Comanche, now, were not forced to waste a precious charge of powder and ball or too much labor. Eliza failed in warding off the hard blows to her arms and face "with a club" before she was speared in the breast, extinguishing her life. Whether the scalping of Eliza came before or after she and Tom were stripped of their clothing goes unsaid, but scalped she was.[74] There is no mention of Eliza being sexually assaulted, and there is no reason to suggest this pack of warriors suffered any penalty for the murders. In fact, according to Daniel Webster Roberts, who resided in the section, a chase after the marauders was futile: "The Indians then had a start of several hours, which was too big a lead to overcome, even if an armed posse had been ready to take the trail."[75] Whether or not aftermath of this raid was the one that led to a council of war on the part of settlers is iffy, but their outcry was painfully real—and not unnoticed.

Another old-time raconteur contends—maybe correctly—that straight away after Tom and Eliza Felps were brutally dispatched, the twenty-odd warriors scooted to the nearby ranch house of Benjamin Felps, where they rounded up a herd of grazing saddle-horses. Then it was off to the Johnson place, where quite effortlessly they slaughtered one of the Johnson brothers and captured the other, a terrified twelve-year-old. Nearing Fort Mason—deliberately—the fleeing raiders cut some horses from the herd and turned the young Johnson boy loose, a tactically sound move. History bears witness the Comanche could be fierce and dangerous adversaries, but for this instance fast flight outweighed a hard fight. For the moment, struggling and straggling pursuers—this time took the bait—and were more-or-less content to round up a few horses after recovering the kidnapped boy. If the scampering Comanche took heart in the settlers' seemingly lackluster pursuit it was wrongheaded—a colossal mistake. These murders in particular had galvanized the resolve of area residents—a head of steam was building.[76]

As bad as the threat from marauding Indians was, Frank Jones—it may be supposed—had also taken note of another harsh and very true frontier reality. Wayward Comanche warriors had not cornered the market on meanness and murder and misappropriating.

Scores of native and/or transplanted Texans returning from the eastern battlefronts were anything but reconstructed, although they were being overseen—seemingly overrun in their minds—by a heinously radical Reconstruction bureaucracy. Lawlessness, in every sense of the word, was truly widespread: Pandemic in places. By 1870 Texas was leading the nation in the number of homicides, just shy of 200 ahead of her nearest competitor: An honor of less than admirable distinction, to be sure. That same year, local lawmen from 108 organized counties reported that in the aggregate there were 2,700 wanted criminals at large. Of those fugitives more than 1100 were charged with either Murder or Assault to Murder. Only half of the organized counties had jailhouses, and in the whole state but twenty-four were deemed secure enough to guarantee confinement.[77] Local law enforcement in the post-Civil War/Reconstruction era was—to put it mildly—lax. Pleasing constituents was the pathway to repeatedly holding elected office. In many frontier burgs those folks finding themselves with an overly aggressive or politically insensitive sheriff or town marshal would do with ballots what the law frowned on them doing with a bullet. Then or today sheriffs walk a fine line. None are anointed, all are elected.

Somewhat surprisingly on one hand, not so much on the other, William E. Jones was tagged for another judicial assignment: Reconstruction Governor Edmund J. Davis appointed him Judge of the 32nd Judicial District of Texas, a state jurisdictional territory covering the counties of Williamson, Burnet, Lampasas, San Saba, Llano, Brown, and Mason. Though the move would take a little doing and require time, Judge Jones relocated his family—at least on a temporary basis—to acreage a few miles west of Georgetown, Williamson County.[78] Texas was in dire need of a big dose of judicial oversight.

Texans were imbued with birthrights—a pigheaded spirit of independence and an entitlement to sport Colt's six-shooters and Bowie knives. Not too far from the Plantation Country settlement of Millican Crossroads, Brazos County, a smoldering hotbed of racial radicalism, a young man from Leon County was taken into custody. Newspaper coverage in the *Cleburne Chronicle*—as meant to be—was amusing, but substantially indicative of not just a few hard-edged Texans' deep-rooted and dearly held deportment:

> On his person was found the following side arms: two six-shooters, one derringer, a pair of brass knuckles, a poker "full"—three tens and a pair of sevens—a large knife and seven or eight morphine powders. He was prepared to either kill or cure.[79]

Edmund J. Davis, Radical Republican Governor of Texas, had in his mind a cure for eradicating widespread lawlessness. The judicious diagnosis was undeniable; the prescription was—and would be—ever so contentious. The governor's medicine was creation of the Texas State Police. The shenanigans brought into play as insurance for passage of the bill birthing a statewide civilian police force makes for an entertainingly amusing tale—an example of typical comedic Texas politics—Republican or Democrat.[80] The Texas State Police were to be comprised of 257 appointments, under the direct supervision of the state's adjutant general, who would also serve as the organization's chief of police. Recruits were to supply their own arms and horses. And, rather progressively for the times, the salary was not too shabby: 225 privates $60 per month, 20 sergeants $75 per month, 8 lieutenants $100 per month and 4 captains $125 per month.[81] Uncontrolled desperadoes plaguing communities wherein local authorities were crippled or corrupt or complacent were to—at last—receive their overdue comeuppance. Since recruiting standards were flexible—ahead of the times—it would be perfectly permissible if some of those policemen issuing that dose of just deserts were freedmen. Such a progressive remedy sounded good—on paper. Black men carrying legal authority to make arrests and go about armed with Colt's six-shooters was an oversized and sour pill to swallow for many—most—inflexible white Texans: Way too big and way too bitter! Republicans had managed the treatment—at least in the short term—and now they could figuratively live or die by the cure. The state's chief executive signed the enabling legislation on July 1, 1870.[82] Frank Jones had just turned fourteen, old enough to think about his future, sharp enough to muddle through comments he was hearing about the Texas State Police: Some of those musings were troubling. Those reflections, however, could be put on momentary hold: Raiding Indians were again newsmakers of the day.

Although lacking a formal education, Cicero Rufus Perry had earned graduate degrees in the science of survival and Indian fighting on the Texas Frontier. Subsequently he was named the first Texas Ranger captain of Company D during the Frontier Battalion era. *Courtesy Armstrong Ranger Research Center, Texas Ranger Hall of Fame & Museum.*

Malinda "Minnie" Caudle, also kidnapped during the raid in Legion Valley, was given the doll she was holding by a sympathetic soldier, subsequent to being ransomed at Fort Sill from her Comanche captors. *COURTESY DAVE JOHNSON.*

The modern-era headstone of Jesse Lawhon killed by raiding Indians while employed gathering cattle at the William E. and Keziah Rector Jones ranch on Curry Creek in what is now Kendall County, but earlier part of Comal County. *COURTESY CANDICE DUCOIN.*

Seated at right is Guadalupe County Sheriff Adam Seidemann. Earlier, when a young Frank Jones would have known him—and looked up to him—Seidemann was a six-shooter-wearing and courageous deputy sheriff at cutting edge New Braunfels, Comal County. *COURTESY ARMSTRONG RANGER RESEARCH CENTER, TEXAS RANGER HALL OF FAME & MUSEUM.*

Be it legitimate fact or puffed folklore much of the early-day and legendary Texas Rangers' reputation as fearless revolver shooting horseback cavaliers may be attributed to the real life dramas and death defying feats of the courageous and capable John Coffee "Jack" Hays. *Courtesy Suzanne Giffin-Garcia.*

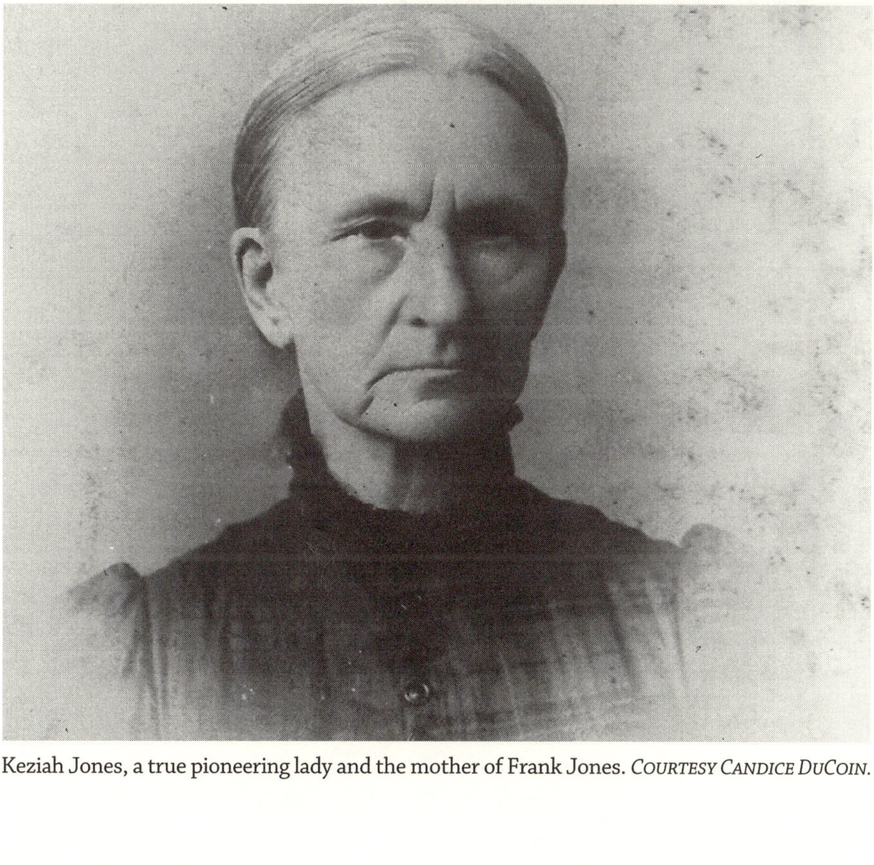

Keziah Jones, a true pioneering lady and the mother of Frank Jones. *Courtesy Candice DuCoin.*

Captured by Indians during the Legion Valley atrocity, young Lee Temple Friend, seated at left, was eventually bought from Comanches at the Fort Sill Reservation. *Courtesy Dave Johnson.*

Governor Elisha M. Pease lauded Ranger Commander James Hughes Callahan and his men for their tenacity and bravery for crossing the Rio Grande and engaging the enemy, but chastised them for after-action occupation and destruction of the Mexican village of Piedras Negras. Frank Jones' half-brother Willis Jones was a mortal casualty of the battle taking place in Mexico. FROM *INDIAN WARS AND PIONEERS OF TEXAS* BY JOHN HENRY BROWN.

Another iconic frontier-era Texas Ranger was John Salmon "Rip" Ford. Frank Jones' father William Early Jones and Rip Ford partnered in the Lone Star State newspaper business for awhile. *COURTESY ARMSTRONG RANGER RESEARCH CENTER, TEXAS RANGER HALL OF FAME & MUSEUM.*

Comanche Indians: Whether or not it is war-paint daubed on their faces is assuredly indeterminate. FROM *THE INDIAN WARS AND PIONEERS OF TEXAS* BY JOHN HENRY BROWN.

CHAPTER 2

"Beneath the Heel of an Indignant Legislature"

THE U.S. ARMY, ACCORDING TO MOST Lone Star settlers, was near useless—a belief not a fact. Comanche and Kiowa had treated to a tentative peace with the United States and were for the most part residents of the Fort Sill Indian Reservation, though several tribal bands yet roamed and hunted the unsettled Llano Estacado when not treading the warpath. Many self-confident warriors made a distinction between white folks south of the Red River and mid-Westerners or Easterners, seeing them as differing people, thinking there was "no inconsistency in signing treaties with the Americans while continuing to war on the Texans."[1] Not at all inaccurately, as many grumbling Texans were perceptively claiming, the mismanaged Indian reservation was but "a city of refuge where warriors received government supplies and protection while resting between raids."[2]

From many frightened settlers' perspective it seemed the raiding Indians never took a holiday. Two lightning raids into the Texas Hill Country are illustrative—both involve kidnapping kids. On New Year's Day 1870, near Castell, Llano County, ten-year-old Adolph Korn was abducted by Apaches and spirited away to the Fort Sill Reservation. There, with the dealing acumen of a tightfisted slave-trader, a Comanche bought Adolph at a bargain-basement price: "a sorrel horse, a pistol and ammunition, a blanket, and some other trinkets."[3] That same year, about the time bluebonnets started dotting the hillsides, ten-year-old Herman and eight-year-old Willie Lehmann were snatched from their parents' farm by Indians in Loyal Valley, southwest of Castell. Eventually Willie escaped after falling off of a horse, the Apache fearing to turnabout and retake him. Herman, after suffering many hardships and shedding his ancestral roots, eventually became an adept warrior, a "white Indian." In the end both Adolph Korn and Herman Lehmann would be sent back to "white society."[4] Understandably, though, at the time the young boys were shamelessly abducted—within months of each other—the crimes were sensational newsmakers. Citizens were outraged: Calling for action!

By mid-year 1870, Governor E. J. Davis, accepting the federal military's shortcomings and bending to public pressure, was poised to leap. And part of that building pressure was coming from Judge Jones: "I am requested by my neighbors to post you of those occurrences & request you to put the Rangers on the war path as soon as it is in your power to do so. . . ."[5] Shortly, with approval of the state's legislature, Governor Davis called into service for a twelve-month stint twenty provisional companies of Texas Rangers, Indian fighting Rangers.[6]

The legislation formally doubled down on making sure these Rangers and their commanders answered only to the governor of Texas. Under no circumstances would they report to governmental bureaucrats or politicians or generals in the nation's capital at Washington. Somewhat ironically, however, the outfit was and would be patterned after the United States Army.[7] Each of the companies would be commanded by a captain, who in turn would oversee the day by day activities of a lieutenant, a medical officer, three sergeants, four corporals, one bugler, a farrier, and fifty privates. The monthly pay scale would range downward from $100 at the top, to $50 at the bottom—there being a $2 differential between sergeants and corporals, and a $2 differential for corporals and the farrier, with regard to pay for the bugler and privates.[8]

Each recruit volunteering for service on the frontier was "required to furnish himself with a suitable horse, six-shooting pistol (army size), and all necessary accoutrements and camp equipage. . . ." The State of Texas would reimburse the Rangers for any horses killed and provide gratis rations and ammunition (at cost) for the men, hay and grain for the horses.[9] Clearly cognizant of advantages associated with troops on the battlefield being armed with like weapons the Lone Star State—with a stipulation—would spring for the initial cash outlay:

> Said men shall be furnished by the State with the most effective and approved breach-loading cavalry arms, and for this purpose the Governor is hereby authorized, on the passage of this act, to contract, in behalf of the State, for fifteen hundred stands of arms, together with a full supply of ammunition; each company, on its organization, to be supplied with its full quota of arms and ammunition. The same so furnished to be all of the same make and caliber, and each member of the company to be furnished with the arms to be used by him, at the price the same shall cost the State, which sum shall be retained out of the first moneys due him.[10]

Historically these hastily mustered Texas Ranger companies, only fourteen due to budgetary constraints, would be broadly dubbed the Frontier Force. Following family tradition, Frank Jones' older brother—one of the twins—James Russell Jones enlisted on August 25, 1870 in one of these hurriedly shaped Ranger units, Company C, the one captained by a real campaigner, a veteran of the Callahan Expedition and first sheriff of Kendall County, John William Sansom,[11]

By most accounts Captain Sansom was a hard-charger, fearless, and a seasoned leader proven "capable and energetic."[12] Apparently, so too was twenty-one-year-old James Russell Jones. Riding a $90 horse, Jones reported for duty. Thereupon he was quickly issued a Winchester carbine ($30) and 80 cartridges ($3.20), the no-nonsense accountability meticulous.[13] Either due to geographical familiarity or personal friendship or recognition of James Russell Jones' practical knowhow as a cutting-edge Texas frontiersman, Captain Sansom enrolled him as Company C's 3rd Sergeant.[14] Subject to swearing in and the issuance of arms, half of the recruits were armed with state-issued rifles, the other half only with six-shooters, Company C set off for its Texas Hill Country headquarters, Old Camp Verde in Kerr County. Upon arrival enlisted men and noncoms piled their gear into tents, the officers ostentatiously quartering themselves in an abandoned private residence.[15]

Not to be inadvertently confused with Frank Jones, the subject of this narrative, but former Comanche captive Franklin Jones, now commanding Company A, Frontier Force, had arrived in Austin with his men on August 18, 1870. They were to be mustered into Indian fighting service, stationed at Fort Mason northwest of teenager Frank Jones' Curry Creek homeplace and Company C's installation at Camp Verde.[16] The *Daily State Journal* quickly explained their urgency: "The counties of Llano, Mason, and Gillespie, swarm with savages. The farmers are shot down in their fields and their stock stolen before their eyes in open day. Not for twenty years back have the Indians been so bold, well armed and numerous as now. At Llano the frontier is breaking up in consequence of these incessant and ferocious raids. We learn with pleasure that the frontier company now being mustered in here, under Captain Franklin Jones, are daily expecting the arrival of their Winchester guns from Brenham, and that they will take a bee line for Mr. Lo [Indians] as soon as armed."[17] Less than two months later an effusive newspaperman for the *Daily State Journal*—maybe the same one—was notifying and warning:

> Indians have been swarming this month on the frontier. On the upper Colorado, in Brown county, they attacked a store in force, but were repulsed. On the San Saba, Cypress creek, and the little Llano, they have been stealing horses. Captain Jones, whose company of Rangers is stationed at Fort Mason, has sent out a scout of twenty men with rations for twenty days. There are now three mounted scouts in pursuit of these depredators, and it is likely that some of them will find the game.[18]

Before the leaves began turning their golden hue and crisp October nights activated the heralding of an overdue death for 1870's sweltering summer, Captains John Sansom's and Franklin Jones' companies were on scout—looking for Indians—joined by the ever industrious Captain Henry Joseph Richarz's Company E sallying forth from their headquarters at old Fort Inge near scenic Uvalde.[19] Thankfully for historians, the Scouting Reports—at least part of them—are available, and they are revealing about the arduous days and tortuous miles the men, including Sergeant James Russell Jones, expended while on the one hand hunting for Indians, and the other making known their presence—interdicting the bona fide viability of Comanche or Kiowa or Lipan Apache even making an incursion into the Texas Hill Country settlements. Reliving their day by day activities would prove fascinating—and is doable—but word count limitations push the narrative: This is Frank Jones' story. Momentarily highlighting an excerpt from one of Captain Sansom's letters to the state's adjutant general is representative:

> . . . I am very glad as yet that I can report to you that there has been no horses Stolen from the District of Country that I am assigned to Guard. And I assure you that ever Since the war among our Selves Closed[,] Say 1865 the Indians have been very bad in Kendall, Kerr, Blanco and Bandera Counties and not a horse has been taken from the above counties Since my Co. has been in the field—They May Come; first I will try to beat them at their game before they start out. Hoping that this report is sufficient. . . . [20]

The tireless work of these Texas Rangers may be and has been summed up succinctly: "Thanks largely to the drive of these captains, the frontier from the mouth of the Pecos to Laredo came under closer scrutiny than ever before. Constant and thorough scouting curtailed Indian raids and gave stockmen of the Nueces and Frio ranges a new sense of security."[21] Briefly!

Safe havens—on this earth—even in Texas are but fleeting asylums. Sad news broke from enchanting Llano in the Texas Hill Country. On the eighteenth day of April 1871 while on the bench hearing a case, Judge William E. Jones suffered a devastating stroke and died.[22] The family was stunned, absolutely overwhelmed. A pioneering Texan was gone. Governor Davis was shocked with the breaking news, but any time exhausted whining or crying or idly mourning was wasted. His administrative woes were mounting.

The periodic activations of Texans for service in outfits akin to the Frontier Force were but stopgap measures. Minute Companies had been called up after formalized authorization in 1871, organized during 1872, and then reorganized the following year. Even later so-called Ranging Companies had been called out—for a four-month lifespan during 1873.[23] One of these reconstituted units is particularly germane for recounting the life story of Frank Jones. Charles A. Patton captained Minute Company C—the Kendall County Mounted Minutemen—a reorganized command with James Russell Jones as corporal, and his younger brother Frank, sixteen, as an eager private.[24] Later, brother Gerry Jones' name would appear on the Muster and Payroll for the Kendall County Minutemen.[25] Frank's enlistment—a provisional Texas Ranger of sorts—was a life-changing experience for young Mr. Jones. The whirlwind of activity and promise of excitement was much to his liking. Apples and acorns don't fall far from the tree, and just like his father William Early Jones, Frank was not content to be a sideline spectator. He wanted a position on the field of action—an active part in the dramatic theater of Indian War. Of this enlistment of less than a year, it would not be barbarous warriors bringing it to a close for young Frank Jones. Ugly partisan politics would be the disagreeable culprit. Until he mustered out there's not room for too much doubt, as best he could, Frank Jones was keeping up with the adventuresome life of hunting for Comanche and Kiowa and Lipan Apache, or as the tactless newspapermen typically phrased it, finding his "game!"

East of the frontier line—the interior counties—members of the Texas State Police were finding their game too—alleged lawbreakers—arresting most, killing a few. The outfit's first six months scorecard is quantifiable: 978 arrests, of which 109 were suspected murderers, 130 charged with assault to murder, and 394 supposed violators of other felonies. They, too, propitiously recovered approximately $30,000 worth of stolen property.[26] The following year, 1871, the Texas State Police tally for arrests came in at 3,260.[27] It would seem the outfit was doing some pretty good work—clearing brigands from the bush, brush, and brambles—and the saloons and whorehouses.

Striking as the numbers seem, not everyone was happy and electrified with performance of the Texas State Police—particularly Democrats.[28] There was the natural antipathy between rival political parties striving for power and domination. Jockeying for statehouse supremacy was an interminable struggle—then or today—preposterously pathetic, but real. Not just a few Lone Star folks thought empowering the Texas State Police usurped the muscle of legally and locally elected county sheriffs and town marshals. The majority population had no truck with blacks wearing badges, sometimes not even their white supervisors: "I think we ought to have at least twenty five good men (all white)," said Texas State Police Sergeant J. M. Redmon, posted in Lampasas County. He feared, and conceivably rightly so, that black policemen could and would be coldly bushwhacked "any night."[29] Although it's been written and generally believed, the white/black ratio was 60 percent to 40 percent within ranks of the Texas State Police. It's a debatable computation and the actual number of black policemen should be—somewhat—ratcheted downward.[30] However, regardless the fine-tuning of roster roll numbers by modern-era scholars, futilely arguing over percentage points was of no real consequence, then. Not to mulishly hardcore southern Democrats and indecisive moderate Republicans and dithering Independents: One damn black policeman was, well, just one too many.

Much to the chagrin of Texas State Police sponsors and supporters, the organization, much to the delight of Democrats and detractors, did own an overflowing bag of dirty laundry. And it was aired in public. Most of the appointments—patronage appointments—were being handed out to Republicans or guys, black and white, avowing that they were steadfast in their core and demonstrated beliefs—unconditionally loyal and devoted Republicans. Somehow, one of the initial captain's positions went to John Marshall "Jack" Helm, "the most noted brigand since the days of Quantrell [*sic*]," a true dead-game *mal hombre* with an authentic man-killing record.[31] Jack Helm's translucent justification for shooting down "escaping" prisoners was derisorily wretched. Helm was booted out of the Texas State Police—but prosecutors forwent the filing of criminal charges for the evident murders.[32] Did they stand in fear of Helm?

Adding to the din of criticism was the declaration of Martial Law in several counties, perhaps justifiably so, but Texas State Police cynics thought it was an overreach and misguided, an abject abuse of power: Using the outfit like an occupation army! That disgruntlement was compounded by another turn of events, one surrounded in supposition, but substantially suspicious nonetheless. Texas Adjutant General and Chief of the Texas State Police James Davidson went missing in action, never to return to the Lone Star State, as was $37,454.67 of the public's cash.[33] Though his travel plans had been kept secret then, now it may be reported—by the best evidence at hand—that Davidson ended up in New Zealand, where he—somewhat later—committed suicide.[34] Though no dispersions are cast at Davidson's replacement personally, but the governor's personnel selection was dubious. The Texas State Police had a brand new chief, twenty-five-year-old Francis L. "Frank" Britton, who by sheer coincidence just happened to be a cousin of Governor Davis' wife, Anne Elizabeth. Too young for Civil War combat and wholly a tenderfoot in the tough law enforcing game, Frank Britton's appointment was doubtful at best, heavy-handed malfeasance and ineptness at worst.[35]

For Governor Davis and the Texas State Police things did get worse. During what may be rightly labeled a bungled arrest attempt inside and outside of Jerry Scott's Saloon at Lampasas, the Grim Reaper reaped. Captain Thomas G. Williams, James Monroe Daniels, Wesley Cherry, and Andrew Melville did what some lawmen shied away from doing, locking horns with the notorious Horrell brothers "who were raised to horses, cattle, whiskey and guns" and their pals by blood or marriage—or a blindly trusting friendship.[36] On 14 March 1873 they, the state policemen, forfeited their lives: Outfoxed and outgunned during the crescendo of gunfire beneath a canopy of blue haze and burnt powder.[37] Timing of the officers' murders was fortuitous.

What is an interesting story in itself—with several intriguing sidebars—will have to be left in the backwaters of moving Frank Jones' compelling story. Cut to the nub, it may be reported that through an electoral process the highly unpopular Governor

Edmund J. Davis was turned out by voters, replaced by Richard Coke and a majority Democrat legislature. Absent a crystal ball or Tarot cards, little could seventeen-year-old Frank Jones have even comprehended it then, but musical chairs at the statehouse would prove momentous. There was, however, a priority item on lawmakers' agenda: Formal elimination of the detested Texas State Police. On April 22, 1873, a plurality of politicos and not just a few joyful citizens had their way, the outfit was no more.

Bold print for an insert in the *Dallas Daily Herald* eulogized: **The Scepter of the Tyrant Broken! The Chains Shattered! The People Free!** Followed by some snappy verbiage:

> The people of the State of Texas are to-day delivered of as infernal an engine of oppression as ever crushed any people beneath the heel of God's sunlight. The damnable Police Bill is ground beneath the heel of an indignant legislature.[38]

Unfortunately, as unconstrained Texans would soon come to realize, unfriendly Indians and unsympathetic desperadoes and unwelcome Mexican bandits and a number of feuding nitwits could have cared less what some whacky politicians at Austin were doing about peace keeping and policing matters.

Seventeen-year-old Frank Jones may or may not have been paying close attention to the commotion unfolding at the statehouse. That damnable Police Bill may have been ground under the heel of politicos pleasing the predominate population, but the Lone Star State was now strategically defenseless—in the eyes of most Texans. For them the understaffed and ineffective U.S. Army was but a weak-kneed step-sister. Reconstruction was dead. And, so too, were not just a few Texas settlers and townsmen suffering at the bloody hands of depredating Indians and brown-eyed border jumping bandits and/or blue-eyed desperadoes disregarding legality—and civility. Criminality is not—was not—racially or culturally biased: No one owns exclusivity.

During the first week of August 1872 the folks in Llano County were aghast. A band of Indians had been crisscrossing though the country, chasing J. P. Mullins to the outskirts of Llano itself, causing him to "lose his saddle-bags and law books in the race." Then, undaunted and unchallenged it seemed, the Indians skirted Riley Mountain and chased after a youngster named Watson, "shooting through his clothes." A day or two later they attacked a ranch on Sandy Creek, just above the Blanco County line, stealing a herd of horses and driving them to the vicinity of Buffalo Peak.[39] Although the previously mentioned Dan Roberts attributes the below cited post Indian raid meeting to the time Tom and Eliza Felps had been pitilessly murdered, in 1869, the most probable scenario—adhering to documentable chronology—would spot the meeting in response to this 1872 raid through Llano County and the surrounding neighborhood. At any rate, Dan Roberts said:

> On the following Sunday several of the young men of the neighborhood gathered at the home of my father, Alexander (Buck) Roberts. Repairing to the shade of a little grove nearby, we held a council of war. The situation was too plain to admit of a misunderstanding. The issue involved a matter of life and death and we faced it fairly and squarely. The one resolution introduced and unanimously carried was that the next time the Indians came into our neighborhood, we would follow and fight. There was nothing heroic in our resolution; on the contrary, we were simply governed by the law of self-preservation. If we remained at home and permitted the Indians to continue unmolested in their raids, there was a strong probability that, family by family, nearly all of us would be butchered; while if we engaged them in battle there was a least a fighting chance that we could "get" some of them. We could do no worse than be killed in the fight and that was better prospect than being butchered as we slept.[40]

Less than a week later, on August 13, 1872, news of Indians on the prowl broke in the area again.[41] Saddling up to chase and destroy were the aforementioned Dan Roberts and his brother George Travis Roberts, John O. Biggs, C. Stanton Jolley, and the Bird brothers, James Thomas and Joseph Dorriss. Along Hickory Creek the leaderless band of Blanco County boys found what they had been sorely hunting, the Comanches' trail. And, here too, they were joined by local and visiting reinforcements: William E. and James Ingram, T. S. "Frank" Waldrip, Sanford Backness. J. W. Hogg, George W. Stevens, Creed Roberts, James Buckner "Buck" Barry, and J. C. "Cam" Davidson. A few members of the Indian chasing platoon were grizzled—proven fighters—some, though tough, had barely left boyhood on the back trail. Not a one of the civilian cavalrymen were adequately armed, some only with nearly worn out Colt's six-shooters and Dan Roberts having but "an old Spencer saddle-gun which had been in the army service. It was a big caliber rifle, with a magazine holding seven shells, and perhaps the best gun in the squad. . . . The equipment of arms of our squad was very poor, probably inferior to the equipment of the Indians."[42] It was not a good day to be outgunned.

Reading sign revealed this war party of Indians tallied about thirty-eight, not three or four.[43] By marauding standards for the place and time, the count was not trivial—it was a major raid. Throttling forward the eager Indian hunters finally got their chance to bite at the plug—and it proved a hard chew. At Deer Creek—near present-day Kingsland, Llano County—the hunt ended. From their smartly concealed lair in a "little draw or shallow ravine" the Comanches poured hellfire into the lesser numbered posse. Before dismounting the Texans cut loose with a volley, and then jumped—scrambling for cover. The clever Comanches had planned the ambush expertly. Any advantage of terrain and timing went to them. The Texans were "seasoned" and determined. Just days before at Buck Roberts' house, they had vowed to fight—to the last man if necessary. Pride prevented them from tucking tail. Practicality precluded their dashing across open ground. And moreover, George Travis Roberts was already a casualty, not mortally, but wounded in the face, the bullet having clipped "the cheekbone just under the eye, passing through the nose and grazing the left cheek bone as it passed out." Blood was spurting or dripping or oozing and blinding young Roberts—who in turn required medical attention, which depleted the Texans' gun shooting ranks by two. The firefight was intense, each side peppering the other, neither side able to compute the damage they were doing, only the damage being done inside their lines. Thoughtlessly,

Dan Roberts exposed himself at a most inopportune time and took a Comanche's bullet in his left thigh, "missing the bone and passing entirely through my [his] limb."[44] Although the wounds would not prove disastrous, Joe Bird caught bullets—at different times—in both shoulders. With two more wounded Texans, each requiring a stabilizing medical helpmate, prudence overtook bravado and/or bravery. The Blanco County Comanche chasers struck out for a doctor's help—and home.[45]

Catching wind of the hubbub on Deer Creek, Rufe Perry rounded up some neighbors, striking out to give the Comanches a thrashing. Fortunately for somebody, the fleeing Indians managed to outdistance Perry, escaping, but apparently not unscathed. Reportedly, the Indians left several horses dead on the battleground, and Perry's posse purportedly found "the graves of four of the braves who had been consigned to the happy hunting ground as the result of the fight. . . ."[46]

The surviving Comanche—racing for the Llano Estacado or the Fort Sill Reservation—to find sanctuary could not have been any too happy, but some of those pot-bellied cigar-smoking lawmaking guys sitting behind glossy maple desks on Congress Avenue were extraordinarily happy—ecstatic. They were puffing to show their gratitude for those Blanco County boys setting those damn wayward Comanche to flight. Upon introduction of a formal resolution by Texas State Senator H. C. King, and its subsequent legislative approval, state funds were earmarked for purchasing spanking new .44 caliber Winchesters, the improved 1873 model soon to be released, as a commemorative act of appreciation for participants of the Deer Creek Fight.[47] The state's grateful legislators weren't simply vicariously fantasizing about doing war with threatening and dangerous Comanche warriors, they were sincere, but, for sure, out of harm's way.

Close by some Texas guys weren't daydreaming about thrills, the fun was already underway. At the top of Llano County's Packsaddle Mountain rancher James R. Moss and seven of his fellow countrymen surprised a band of Comanche that had been stealing horses and cattle in the area. Because of their elevated vantage point the

Indians had felt secure, but their sentry went to sleep on the job—and got killed by wide-awake Texans. Then, the fight became general and desperate. On the one hand the ranchers were trying to cut out and recover their stolen horses, on the other, the Comanche, riding hell-bent-for-leather charged—twice! They were repulsed during the close contact mêlée but four Texans were wounded, and Indians left two dead on the battlefield. The Llano County boys—after warriors fell back—thought the big doings were done. Not so! All at once, simultaneously exhibiting fearlessness and foolhardiness the Comanche chief—headman for these raiders—Winchester in hand and alone defiantly carried battle to the taken aback Texans. Whether he was afoot or horseback is hazy, but six bullets tore into his torso, toppling him to the rocky ground—dead. The other warriors skedaddled down the off side of Packsaddle Mountain making good their getaway. The Indians' abandoned camp revealed they had made a home away from home—a rendezvous—as Texans recovered horses, buffalo robes, jerked meat, Navajo blankets, silver-mounted saddles and bridles, along with a few Winchester and Henry rifles.[48]

On December 10, Lieutenant Charles L. Hudson, 4th Cavalry, U.S. Army, with forty-one troopers from Companies A, B, C, and I, working out of Fort Clark at Brackettville (Kinney County), were on a routine patrol in the vicinity of South Kickapoo Springs, Edwards County. At the crucial watering site, by the West Fork of the Nueces River, one of his scouts located a "hidden remuda of Indian horses." Lieutenant Hudson forthwith secreted his troopers. Subsequent to murdering fourteen Mexicans and a couple of Texans and taking three Mexican hostages, the mixed contingent of nine Kiowa and twenty-one Comanche splashed across the meandering Rio Grande into Mexico for a time-out. Somehow, two of the raiders' prisoners escaped—and, eventually, sounded the alarm. A messenger overtook Lieutenant Hudson informing him of the carnage and presumed whereabouts of the bronco warriors. Knowing exactly where the Indians would likely be coming to, but obliquely reconnoitering, Lieutenant Hudson interdicted their attempt at recovering the rested horses, finding the war party atop the crest of a ridge on the Texas side of the Río Bravo. Tactically smart, Lieutenant Hudson dismounted his men—their aim would be truer—and charged the startled Indians, opening a blistering fire at seventy-five yards. Though they tried to fight, after ten minutes the Kiowa/Comanche marauders could stand it no more. Like a covey of quail, they broke and ran, but couldn't fly. Smelling blood on the rocky desert floor, Hudson ordered his cavalrymen to remount and give chase. What transpired was a "rout." His troopers, though suffering a wounded colleague, killed nine Indians, one being Tau-ankia, son of the fierce Lone Wolf, killed with a pistol ball from the lieutenant's Colt's revolver. Troopers and Texans were jubilant—especially after recovering eighty-one horses—but news at that city of refuge, the Fort Sill Indian Reservation, wasn't amenable: "Lone Wolf vowed revenge on all whites."[49]

By chance, timing for the Indians' brutal raid and Lone Wolf's ranting threats of retaliation, meshed splendidly with ideas swirling in Governor Richard Coke's brain. Hardly more than a month after the episode, Governor Coke made an Inaugural Address, to be picked up by the masses of concerned Texas citizens. Wherein the strong-minded Democrat governor pledged—promised—to "add a system which will supplement the efforts of the Federal government for the protection of our suffering frontier. . . ."[50] The "system" the governor had in mind would evermore impact the annals of Texas—adding to the state's illustrious history and legend, its mystique and mythos, but it, too, would be a pivotal—truthfully one of the defining moments—in the Wild West life of Frank Jones, now eighteen years old.

Laying aside the specific nomenclature of the several militia units to be held in reserve—not called up—excepting for extreme emergencies, Governor Coke had it in his head that Texas in general and the Texas frontier in particular, were in dire need of a permanent body of saddle-toughened men multi-tasked with doing what the beleaguered U.S. Army had thus far not done: Protect the front line. His proposal to the Democrat controlled legislature was blunt. Governor Coke wrangled that the Fourteenth Legislative Session should pass into law:

> An act to provide for the protection of the Frontier of the State of Texas against the invasion of hostile Indians, Mexicans, or other marauding or thieving parties.[51]

Officially—on paper—the outfit was to be the Frontier Battalion; informally the officers and enlisted men would be known throughout the state—and world—and to history—as Rangers, Texas Rangers. Tearing a page from the defunct Frontier Force of Governor Davis' bygone days, the Frontier Battalion would be based on a military model, but Governor Coke had several amplifications and alterations in mind. Primarily, recognizing that due to local politics, inadequate funding, dishonesty, deleterious personnel selections, and being hemmed in by that jurisdictional nightmare, the county line, sheriffs and constables and city marshals were—at times—wholly ineffective. Governor Richard Coke wanted a remedy. He made sure the Frontier Battalion was legally sanctioned to flex the state's law-enforcing arm. Specifically, that "Each officer of the battalion and of the companies herein provided for, shall have all the powers of a peace officer."[52]

The staffing sculpting was straightforward: Six seventy-five-man companies, A-F, deployed on a fluid north/south line along the Texas frontier—from the Rio Grande to the Red River. Each company would be commanded by a captain, who in turn would supervise two lieutenants, who would look after and be responsible for the noncoms competently doing their jobs: maintaining discipline and seeing that buck privates followed orders and completed assignments. Heading up the Frontier Battalion would be a battalion major, answering directly to Texas Adjutant General William H. Steele, a high-ranking Confederate veteran with notable leadership credentials.[53]

Governor Coke and AG Steele would select the battalion's senior officers; company captains would be allowed the satisfaction of hand-picking their lieutenants, sergeants, corporals, and rookie recruits. As with earlier state units, enlistees would furnish their own horse, a gelding. There would be no uniforms, just high-top boots and a wide-brimmed hat. The State of Texas would furnish the beans and bacon and bullets free of charge. Horse feed was gratis, as was the distinct pleasure of being allowed to live with Mother Nature—outside—twenty-four and seven. Predictably, the firearms would be issued—not gifted—by the forever munificent State of Texas: In this particular case, for the Frontier Battalion, a single-shot Sharps carbine—a gun with "a bore big enough for a gopher to crawl through."[54] Yes, the Rangers this time around would still pay for the gun out-of-pocket so to speak, $16 deducted from their first quarterly pay warrants, figured at $40 per month. Rangers not having a working six-shooter would be issued one under the payroll deduction plan: $15 for a New Model Army Metallic Cartridge Revolving Pistol, popularly nicknamed the Colt's Peacemaker, chambered for the .45 Colt, a sure enough man-stopping cartridge—most of the time.[55]

Since it was anticipated these Texas Rangers would be "Kept actively employed during their term of Service only young men without families and with good horses" would be recruited. There was not any need for a persnickety translation: Married men need not apply.[56] Again, somewhat predictably, such a stricture didn't affect officers: Captains and lieutenants could be married. Deadbeats need not apply either: "Persons under indictment or of Known bad character or habitual drunkards will be rejected."[57] Freedmen and/or black men could look elsewhere for a state job: There would be no place for them in the Rangers for the next hundred-plus years.[58]

Was there a sane rationale for enlisting, living a hard camp life, days and nights in the saddle chasing phantoms and sometimes dodging an arrow or sidestepping the thrust of a lance? Penning an explanatory 1874 letter to the *Waco Daily Examiner*, an old-time Texas Indian fighter prophetically guessed filling the Frontier Battalion's ranks would not be too difficult: "Much is said about the amount to be paid rangers for the protection of the frontier. In old times in Texas, when men were needed for the like purpose, wages was not questioned. . . . The intermission of eight or nine years since the [Civil] war has made plenty anxious for adventure on the Plains. To kill buffalo and other game, men who might make much more at home would be easily found to go in an expedition of six months for very little pay, and well satisfied. With the expense of an outfit, balanced with what they get for wages, one or two thousand men would take the field for amusement to join in privations and dangers for the sake of romance, and to have the enjoyment in future days to tell their friends and strangers, who never got the same chance of being heroes. . . . that they have seen the same extraordinary sights depicted in such glowing manner, as they will be by the writers in subsequent generations."[59]

Chosen to lead the Frontier Battalion into battle—and in due course the history books—was John B. Jones, a highly educated Confederate veteran calling Navarro County home. Jones was a man imbued with ethics and integrity. His leadership and administrative talents were hammered from hard steel. His personal courage was unflinching, none could question that. He, too, like all folks on earth, was merely a mortal man and not 100 percent mistake-proof or always right. Some jealous folks, however, did query his selection as the Frontier Battalion's Major. The battalion's primary mission was to protect the frontier's line and chastise Indians who breached it. As an Indian fighter what did Major John B. Jones' résumé say? It was a blank page! John B. Jones—of whatever else may be said—was altogether untested in the arena of Indian warfare: He had no practical familiarity, none whatsoever. Despite criticisms and petitions coming from certain quarters, recommending first one candidate, then another to fill the top spot, an inflexible Governor Coke and the immovable Adjutant General Steele stood by their man.[60]

Not wasting much time after passage of the legislation, captains for the Frontier Battalion's six companies were appointed and their PO (Post Office) assignments specified: Company A, John R. Waller, PO Stephenville, Erath County; Company B, George W. Stevens, PO Jacksboro, Jack County; Company C, Elisha Floyd Ikard, PO Henrietta, Clay County; Company D, the aforementioned Rufe Perry, PO Mason, Mason County; Company E, William Jeff Maltby, PO Brownwood, Brown County; and Company F, Neal Coldwell, PO Bandera, Bandera County.[61]

At the ranch on Curry Creek, the Jones brothers were giving that old-timer's reflections—the one who wrote the *Waco Daily Examiner*—some very serious thought. William Kenner Jones, who had earlier "read" for the law under the tutorship of the Hughes &

Montgomery partnership at Georgetown, Williamson County, was allocating consideration to the Frontier Battalion, even though by now he was already a well-regarded member in good standing with the Texas bar.[62] Gerry and Pinckney who, too, had big-time legal careers in their futures, were eyeing with envy the chance for tasting adventure as hard-charging Texas Rangers with the Frontier Battalion. Spunk Jones, the youngest brother, was interested in chasing and clashing with a few Indians before that contest shut down for keeps, as perceptive Texans knew sooner or later it likely would. And then, there was teenager Frank. Unlike his father and several brothers, young Frank's spirit for breath-taking excitement was stirring from deeper within. Frank's siblings were good men—damn good men to be sure—but his ultimate challenges and satisfactions would not come atop a mountain of wordy law books or deferentially standing and debating before the Blind Mistress of Justice. Frank Jones was at the precipice of making a big decision.

Governor Richard Coke. Subsequent to disbanding the Texas State Police, he was personally responsible for blueprinting the Frontier Battalion—Texas Rangers. *Courtesy Dave Johnson.*

Prior to formation of the Frontier Battalion there was for a time the Frontier Force. Here is a wonderful tintype showcasing three of that outfit's Indian fighters. Standing, Joseph Beck: Seated from L to R: Jacob Haby and Joseph Burrell. *Courtesy Donald M. and Louise Yena.*

Gui-päh-go (Lone Wolf) the Kiowa leader vowing revenge for Texans after his son and nephew were killed when returning from a murderous raid into Mexico. Lone Wolf kept his promise in Lost Valley. *Courtesy Nita Stewart Haley Memorial Library & J. Evetts Haley History Center in Midland, Texas.*

Major John B. Jones, Commander of the Frontier Battalion. *COURTESY ARMSTRONG RANGER RESEARCH CENTER, TEXAS RANGER HALL OF FAME & MUSEUM.*

Frank Jones' twin brothers. L to R: James Russell Jones and William Kenner "W. K." Jones. For a period of time both banked service as Rangers. *Courtesy Candice DuCoin.*

Chapter 3

"We Fought under the Black Flag"

THE FIRST OF THE JONES BROTHERS to become Frontier Battalion Texas Rangers were William Kenner and Pinckney. Both enlisted in Neal Coldwell's Company F in Kerr County on June 4, 1874. Following the footprints they laid down hunting for Indians in the Texas Hill Country and later chasing bandits in South Texas below the Nueces Strip—The Wild Horse Desert—is achievable but only serves, in this narrative, to sidetrack their brother Frank's story. Though, before they mustered out during the summer of 1875, William had made the rank of lieutenant and Pinckney figuratively wore sergeant's stripes.[1] The bottom line is not blurred—Will and Pink Jones were lawyers—not lawmen.

The daring Jones boys were not participants at the time, but episodes of historic proportion transpired in North Texas and the Panhandle during 1874, subsequent to charter formation of the famed Frontier Battalion. The exhilarating events, scores of miles removed from Curry Creek, would have considerable bearing on the future of Frank Jones.

Hardly a month after young men began pledging their time and allegiance to the Frontier Battalion, hot news broke from the Llano Estacado. In what is now Hutchinson County (county seat Borger), cut by the Canadian River, reposed a little out-of-the-way settlement of hovels built with mud bricks. Buffalo hunters and traders and teamsters knew the rude configuration of buildings as Adobe Walls. At the tail-end of June 1874, a mixed force of Plains Indians knew it as a target. Several hundred—estimates vary—Comanche, Cheyenne, and Kiowa tried to massacre the twenty-eight men and one lady at Adobe Walls. Under siege, the buffalo hunters with their long-range Sharps rifles (not carbines) managed to kill seven Cheyennes and six Comanches, seriously wounding perhaps as many as twenty. The hunters held the attackers at bay. Eventually catching good sense, that they could not dislodge their foes and were not impervious to big .50 caliber bullets as a medicine-man had claimed, the Indians retreated and rode away to fight another day. The upshot of the Indian assault at remote Adobe Walls was quantifiably measurable and theoretically earth-shattering. The Indians left three dead whites in their wake and managed to wake up a heretofore sometimes sleeping giant—the U.S. Army.[2]

The following month, closer in, and directly striking home for Major John B. Jones and Texas Rangers of the Frontier Battalion was another hair-raising clash with 100-plus maddened warriors: Kiowa more-or-less captained by the ever formidable and revenge-seeking Lone Wolf. In the broken country—some say mountainous—recesses of Jack County northwest of Fort Worth, Major Jones' Texas Rangers and Lone Wolf's men went to war in Lost Valley. The Rangers had ridden into a trap—and the Kiowa had tripped the jaws, forcing Major Jones' men to ride pell-mell for refuge in a shallow ravine, one not deep enough to offer protection for the horses, which were whinnying and snorting and stomping—spiders in their minds, panic in whites of their eyes.

Though clearly in an untenable position, Major Jones did not vulnerably become unnerved. Courageously exposing himself to enemy fire, he resolutely maintained a field-of-fire discipline. Sadly, Ranger William A. "Billy" Glass had been cut down before reaching scant shelter of the gully, later dying as a consequence of his five bullet wounds. He was the Frontier Battalion's first Ranger to die in the line of duty—a truly notable but less than inspirational distinction. Other Texas Rangers would suffer wounds, disabling, but not mortal—that is until Private D. W. H. "Dave" Bailey fell into Kiowa hands while making a madcap dash to fill canteens for his thirsty and fast dehydrating comrades. It was summertime in Texas—always hot. The overhead sun was unmercifully hurling her blistering spears from above. Atop a sweltering Mother Earth the Kiowa—in plain sight of the hopelessly pinned down Rangers—were hurling their spears too: Straight into terrified and helpless Ranger Dave Bailey. Texas Ranger William A. "Billy" Callicott described the repulsion blazed into Rangers' memories, powerlessly looking on as Indians "scalped him, carving him up like a beef steak, and then taking the butt end of their guns and stamping his skull and brains in the ground in sight of the Major and the boys in the creek."[3] Utterly mortified Texas Rangers were, quite expectedly, not the only witnesses on the battlefield. Afterward, one of the Indians didn't pull any punches, bending to insipid political correctness. Hunting Horse simply told the truth, ugly and incriminating as it was:

> When I got to the place where they had killed the other ranger, I learned that Dohausen had thrust him off his horse with a spear, but that Mamaday-te had made first coup by touching him with his hand. Lone Wolf and Maman-ti and everybody was there. Lone Wolf got off his horse and chopped the man's head to pieces with his brass hatchet-pipe. Then he took out his butcher knife and cut open the man's bowels. Everyone who wanted to shot arrows into it or poked at it with their lances.[4]

Later, unapologetically a Texas Ranger would spend his two cents worth about real time reality in the combat zone. Much like his Indian adversary, he was not mush-mouthed regarding ethnic and/or cultural morality. Nor was he—and would not be—tortured by latter day idealists' notions of selective sensitivities or a quixotic idea of what was or was not fair play, not at a time steel-tipped arrows were flying and lead bullets were zinging—and spilt blood was painting the dirt: Everyone bled red!

> We rangers, as well as Indians, fought under the black flag. We asked no quarter and gave none. Whenever we met it was simply a case of outfight or outrun 'em, which ever could be done the best.

> When we fell into their hands they scalped us and frightfully mutilated our bodies, frequently cutting and hacking us to pieces. We didn't do as bad as that but scalped them just the same.[5]

There is a final act to the Lost Valley drama: Kiowa eventually retreated and Rangers escaped. There is also a degree of irony. Subsequent to the siege being broken, Major Jones and the U.S. Army's Captain T. A. Baldwin, along with 100 hard-riding and hard-charging troopers of the Tenth Cavalry Regiment's Companies I and L, poked around for a few days trying to pick up the trail of Lone Wolf and his lusty followers. Texans and provisional Rangers had earlier fussed incessantly about freedmen being a part of the detested Texas State Police. The 10th Cavalry, excepting for officers, was a black regiment, Buffalo Soldiers. Now—it seems—those fortunate Lost Valley surviving Texas Rangers were glad—damn glad—to have the company of blacks decked out in brass-buttoned blue-coats.[6] Black men's blood ran red, too!

News of the fight at Lost Valley splashed across the pages of Texas newspapers, as faraway as the Lone Star's Gulf Coast in the *Corpus Christi Gazette* and the *Galveston Daily News* and in North Texas papers such as the *Dallas Daily Herald*.[7] Generally Major Jones received good press. He did however, later and somewhat preposterously intimate in an annual report to Adjutant General Steele that he had participated in ". . . an engagement of several hours duration, defeated them and forced them to take their back track in the direction of the reservation."[8] Charitably it's been proffered Major Jones may have thought he had driven Kiowa from the field, a belief buttressed by his being a total "neophyte at Indian warfare."[9] Texans would hear none of such nonsense. Analytical pundits may grade—rightly so—the fight at Lost Valley as a "bad start for the Frontier Battalion."[10] However on-the-ground folks in the Lone Star State were right happy with Major John B. Jones and his strapping cadre of boys willing to do battle, even if some of them were but whippersnappers, yet wet behind the ears and strangers to a straight razor. Frank Jones was teetering—watching—waiting—about to jump.

The following year, 1875, Major Jones and Frontier Battalion Rangers were able to put a new face on their Indian fighting knowhow, again in the vicinity of Lost Valley. During the first days of May, seven Comanches bolted or left with permission (there are competing versions) the Fort Sill Reservation. Under the nominal leadership of Isa-toho (Black Coyote) the Indians were intent on stealing horses, not revenge. After reasonable success at the Jack County ranch of the Loving family, the band of wily raiders—now well mounted on stolen horses—were strategically spotted by Rangers from their appropriately named vantage point, Spy Knob, in the neighborhood north of present day Jermyn, Texas.[11] The Indians, according to Major John B. Jones' account, "were armed with breach loading shot guns and six-shooters."[12] During a running battle on the eighth day of May the twenty Rangers overtook and killed five Indians, three having fought fearlessly even after being dethroned from saddles, one of which "had the scalp of a white woman fastened to his shield."[13] As it turned out, one of the warriors was a woman, the wife of Black Coyote, a female combatant "young, good-looking, and evidently part white," who discharged all the loads in a pair of Colt's revolvers at Rangers. Major Jones somewhat in awe remarked that she "handled her six-shooters quite as dexterously as did the bucks."[14] With her weapons useless but for clubs, the frightened woman now seeking some turnabout compassion opened her blouse exposing her breasts and painfully stated the obvious: "Me squaw, me squaw!" Her pleas for mercy went unheeded. A Ranger's bullet eternally quieted her appeal.[15]

To hardened Texans—and no defense is being proffered—such last-minute remonstrations on the battlefield, if not commonplace, were not unheard of and seldom bought benevolence. Women could be—and sometimes were—pitiless warriors. Mrs. Mary Melisa (Phillips) Haynes summarized a similar situation involving her brother Montgomery Wright "Gum" Phillips during an earlier bloody Blanco County clash with raiding Indians:

> At that moment my brother had gained ground and run up between them, and as quickly as a flash my brother had his pistol up against the Indian's head. At the same time the Indian jerked open her blanket baring her breast, and saying: "Me Squaw." But

> with an oath he Said, "What do I care?" so "Me Squaw" went to the happy hunting ground which was all said and done in the twinkling of an eye. Gum's pistol just naturally went off. "Me Squaw" had no effect when they killed and scalped our people; if anything our women were the most horribly treated.[16]

Another of the Comanche killed during the confrontation with Major Jones and his Rangers was Ay-cufty (Reddish), a curly-headed fighter with a shock of auburn hair, no doubt a warrior of mixed ancestry.[17] Were the raiders Indians or whites masquerading as Indians? Shoring up any suppositional beliefs concerning tribal identity, "Rangers [soldiers] cut off the heads of the dead and sent them to Washington, where it was confirmed that they were in fact Comanches."[18]

What was of real doubt, however, was the dead Indians' reason for being "off reservation" in the first place. There was an assertion that the Indians had been issued "hunting passes." The perplexed Indian Agent J. M. Haworth was appreciably angered; the inoffensive Indians had been needlessly and ruthlessly attacked—to his way of thinking.[19] Texans, in general, were of one mind: Comanche in Indian Territory weren't issued passes to cross the Red River and hunt horses or cattle or homesteading ranchers or kids to be ransomed. Just months before Mohecut (Black Beard) a Comanche chief leading a sortie into the vicinity of Rocksprings, Edwards County, running ahead of a maddened posse of settlers had dropped his "certificate of good conduct," issued by Agent Haworth the previous year.[20] If anyone in the Lone Star State possessed the legality for hunting—it was Rangers. Texas lawmakers had made that quite clear. Part of the Rangers' job description was to hunt for Indians—and kill them.

Flamboyant legislators promising to gift veterans of that taxing 1872 Deer Creek Fight with the latest model Winchesters had not been regurgitating self-aggrandizing hooey designed to catch a favorable headline: The fancy rifles—with engraved silver shields painstakingly inlaid into the hand-selected and highly polished walnut stocks—were actually, finally, shipped to the Texas statehouse.

It was dynamite news for the whole capital city and for the named recipients: The *Austin Daily Democratic Statesmen* swanked—proudly—that the improved Winchesters "were beauties, and will no doubt be preserved through generations as heirlooms."[21] The customized Winchesters were appropriately and appreciatively awarded.[22] Particularizing nineteen-year-old Frank Jones' thoughts about Texas Hill Country fellows from his general neighborhood earning a first rate fresh-on-the-market improved Winchester for fighting some merciless Indians is not doable. Reasonableness would, however, suggest it was real heady stuff for a young man savoring a taste for adventure. Timing is tempting—for asking rhetorical questions that cannot be answered with firmness. Mention of those fancy Winchesters being handed out appeared in the newspaper edition of August 25, 1875.[23]

Within a week Frank Jones was a Texas Ranger. At Austin, on 1 September 1875 he enlisted as a private in the Frontier Battalion's Company A. The unit was then commanded by Lieutenant Ira Long, a junior officer who had handled himself exceptionally well in the heat of battle during that second skirmish with raiding Indians near Lost Valley.[24] Why they didn't join the same troop is unknown, but on the same day brother Gerry "Dood" Jones signed on as a Ranger with Company F in Gillespie County.[25] Because of budgetary concerns the battalion had undergone several manpower readjustments and a realignment tweaking—for the interim—lieutenants were, now, top dogs at the company level.[26] Frank reported for duty sans a six-shooter, and one was issued, the $15 to be deducted from his quarterly pay.[27] At the time of enlistment Lieutenant Long was in process of relocating himself and some of the rehires from Wise County (county seat Decatur) to Mason, Mason County, scene of the then ongoing and bizarrely fractious and inane Mason County "Hoo Doo" War, a transitional challenge for Texas Rangers of the Frontier Battalion.

In truth, by the time Frank Jones became a Frontier Battalion member, the Red River War, as it came to be known, was winding down and mopping up operations underway. Although it somewhat knocks legend askew—and is near blasphemy to assert—it was not indestructible Rangers ten feet tall and bulletproof that finally broke the back of Plains Indians raiding into Texas. That distinction could jointly be awarded to two allies: Old Man Winter and Uncle Sam. After U.S. Army headquarters mapped the strategy and field officers implemented the tactics of chasing Comanche and Kiowa and a few Cheyenne to the ends of the earth in Texas—and the Palo Duro Canyon—destroying their lodges, commissary, horses, and putting them afoot hungry, destitute, and disillusioned, for the most part and for most warriors the game was over.[28]

On the other hand, the game playing out in Mason County was stormy: Raining bullets and flooding blood. A feud was underway.[29] Cattleman Tim Williamson had been murdered while in custody of a sheriff's posse, deputy Johann Anton Wohrle having killed the prisoner's horse beneath him, preventing his escape and allowing triggermen to do their "duty." As luck would have it, former Company D Texas Ranger William Scott Cooley was an extraordinarily close personal friend of Williamson. Cooley could sate his taste for sweet revenge only by repaying the kindness: He gunned down Wohrle while the unsuspecting fellow was cleaning out a well on the outskirts of Mason. Then, if most reports are anywhere close to accurate, Scott Cooley jumped from his horse, stabbed the victim several times and took his scalp for a trophy.[30] The thunderclouds of turmoil lingered over Mason County, bolts of lightening knocking men out of the saddle time and again—obliging newsmen to write obituaries while preachers eulogized and the highly partisan and corruptible sheriff of Mason County, John E. Clark, looked the other way.

Probably unbeknownst to Frank at the time of his enlistment, but during the following week gunfire from feudists had spit its venom killing Moses B. Baird and seriously wounding George W. Gladden.[31] Clearly Major Jones was in the dark—or wasn't any too concerned about putting any law enforcing duties on the agenda. Subsequent to his resounding triumph during the second Lost Valley doings, Jones was planning an important battalion offensive aimed at eradicating any residual Indian raids spilling over from the Red River War or Apache crossing the murky Rio Grande and using Mexico as a nifty shield. And, yes, there was a practical side for the major's rationale, and it was but matter-of-fact logic. In a letter to Lieutenant G. W. Stevens, Company B, among other items, Major Jones pleadingly penned: "We must if possible have some scalps to show for our work this Fall or the next Legislature may stop our pay."[32] Perhaps the major readjusted his wording for another letter that same day, but the clear message was aboveboard. He emphasized to Company E's Lieutenant B. S. Foster the urgency for measurable outcome: "We must if possible have something to show for our Fall work or the next Legislature will think there is no longer any necessity for us on the frontier and Stop our pay."[33]

What was stopped was Major Jones' blueprinted Indian campaign. Though written with an astute politician's flair, there was core truth in the governor's words, carried by the adjutant general for coaching Major Jones: "Whilst you may find Indians on Devils River, you will be sure to find devils in Mason."[34] Major Jones was forthwith, by executive command from Texas hierarchy, instructed to send a company of Texas Rangers to Mason. Many of the major's freshly recruited Rangers were yet untested young men, like Frank Jones. To make a show of force in Mason—a believable show of force—would require highly competent and gutsy leadership. Major Jones would scrap the battalion's Indian hunting operation and strike the road for Mason. Negative newspaper reports and petitions from distraught Mason County residents had caught Governor Richard Coke's ear. Politicos listened: Rangers followed orders.[35]

There was no order in Mason County. On 25 September 1875 several days before any Rangers were onsite, hell popped again. Thinking James "Jim" Cheyney was the bell-mare surreptitiously leading Moses Baird to his death, revenge minded feudists moved his name to the number one spot on their "hit" list. Whether or not anyone drew straws is moot; the murderous task fell to a fellow identified only as Williams and John Peters Ringo, who already owned a tough reputation and would double-down on that unbending posture several years later at Tombstone, Arizona Territory. On Comanche Creek at Cheyney's home the two cool executioners with smiles on their faces and taking breakfast as an excuse smoothly bamboozled their host. From the front porch Jim Cheyney told the boys to step down and wash up, and he turned to the soapy basin, towel in hand. The bad boys jumped down, but instead of swabbing their hands with suds, vehemently showered Cheyney with lead balls—.45 caliber. Thoroughly satisfied that they had "made fresh meat" out of the supposed snitching Cheyney, gunmen Williams and Ringo reunited with their coconspirators at raucous Mason. There, exhibiting an appalling spirit of machismo, and assuring that their killing would gain "public notoriety," murderers Ringo and Williams boasted that "if somebody did not bury him he would stink." Afterwards, absent a hint of hurry, the murderous yahoos unflappably rode southeast out of a terrified town toward Willow Creek. Their departure caught notice, but not pursuit.[36]

The trip to Mason County would be an eye-opener for Major Jones: "In passing Keller's [Store], on the Llano en route for Mason I was surprised to see fifteen or twenty men armed with Winchester Carbines and six shooters, rise up behind a stone fence in a fighting attitude. . . . They were headed by Mr. Clark, the Sheriff of the county, were well armed and had a strong position in the angle of a stone fence commanding the ford of the Llano and the approach from two directions for four or five hundred yards."[37] This crowd, as Major Jones learned, were planning to ambush their adversaries, who it was reported were supposed to be in the county with intent to "burn out the Dutch [Germans]."[38] Perhaps by mere fluky happenstance tragedy was averted.

Thinking he might intercept the other party, Major Jones somewhat backtracked to Loyal Valley. What he found was disturbing and disheartening: "I find the homes closed a death like stillness in this place and an evident suspicion if not dread in the minds of the inhabitants. Every man is armed but so far as I have been able to ascertain there is no body of armed men in or near this place, at present."[39] Overnight, Major Jones camped at Cold Springs (Loyal Valley) and penned a hasty report to Adjutant General Steele. His next report to the AG would substantiate the worst and be a harbinger of the six-shootin' future in and around Mason.

Arriving in Mason ahead of Major Jones and his contingent of Rangers were a trio of hardened Texas characters. On the twenty-ninth day of September, during the morning, the now infamous Scott Cooley, the ex-Texas Ranger, John Baird from Burnet County, and George Gladden, who had recovered from his wounds, made an appearance in Mason. It was not a friendly social call. Staked out behind a local barber shop the gang of three waited—waylaying written on their program. Daniel Hoerster, Peter Jordan, and Heinrich "Henry" Pluenneke leisurely rode into the ambush. Providentially, the unwary Pluenneke and Jordan evaded the hurried bombardment unscathed—well, nearly: A bullet zinged past Pete Jordan, leaving its grazing and burning marker on the side of his head. Hoerster was not near so lucky, the shotgun in Baird's hand had allowed him to get his "meat." Four 00 buckshot ripped into Daniel's throat, knocking him from the saddle—a dead man falling. Understandably the town was in "a State of terrible excitement and alarm caused by the killing of Dan Hoerster, a German. . . ."[40]

Frank Jones and twenty-two other freshly enlisted Rangers traveled with Major Jones, rendezvousing with Lieutenant Long at Mason on September 29, 1875, before sundown.[41] Although not actually named in the report it is not unreasonable to presume—and it's highly likely—that Private Frank Jones, two days after arriving at Mason, was a member of one of the units away from camp, in the field "scouting in search of Out-laws."[42] Frank Jones' life as a rookie lawman was underway. And, it's not inappropriate to note policing matters would prove to be his forte, not following, finding, and fighting Comanche and Kiowa who'd skipped the agency headcount for a bleeding foray south of the Red River.

Distilling a 100 percent list of the causative factors for the Hoo Doo War is not practicably workable: Cultural divides and personality, egos and excuse making embargo such simplicity. There are, however, several ingredients stirred into the recipe for a fiery feud—and its funerals. A scattered—incomplete—recap is but fitting.

Many of the Mason County residents, in fact much of the Texas Hill Country population, was comprised of German immigrants or the sons and daughters of German immigrants. Most of the German settlers arriving through ports of the Texas Gulf Coast and choosing to homestead in that general neighborhood fit in rather handily, adopting an Anglo-American culture, and perhaps most importantly to Texans, English as their primary—and soon—their only language. They graciously assimilated—conformed—to a new way of life in a new land—rather quickly. For the most part German pioneers venturing further inland did not: In the Texas Hill County they held strongly to their ethnicity, continuing to speak only German, think only German, eat German food, make German wine, and sit through Sunday sermons preached in German, always praying to God Almighty in German. To their unpretentious way of thinking, non-German folks in their genially planned old-world villages could just learn to speak German—not vice-versa.[43] Now what good rough and tough Texan would bend to such preposterous asininity?

There was another rub, and it was a whopper. By an overwhelming majority—not all—of the German folks of Mason County boldly chose to align themselves with the Union rather than the Confederacy when the call for Secession went to a vote. What good Texan could abide by that? Tolerance for any diverging opinions during a time of war—or while building a head of steam for an upcoming war—was/is always in short supply.[44] Right or wrong, Texans were fighters! Statewide, many hardcore supporters of the Southern Cause figured those damn pacifist Germans were traitors—pure and simple, cut and dried.

After the Civil War the competition to burn brands of ownership into wandering herds of unmarked cattle was widespread and fierce. Too, though it's sometimes overlooked, there was much wealth to be had by merely trafficking in cow-hides.[45] Midnight skinning was ubiquitous. There were hard truisms spoken by old-timers, maybe not eloquently, but true nevertheless. Such as a snippet in the *San Antonio Daily Herald*: "There are men in the country who never bought a cow in their lives who now have large stocks, and they get them by branding other peoples stock entirely, and if you will show me a man who cow hunts or lives in the country away from a butcher shop who does not brand calves or eat meat not his own and contrary to law, I will show you nine men to one that does do it."[46] Ike Pryor, a bona fide and tough Texas Hill Country cattleman, coughed up reality by suggesting that any cowman of open range days who claimed never to have put his brand on somebody else's animal was either a damn liar—or a damn sorry roper.[47] Explicitly zeroed on Hoo Doo War territory, a plain spoken chronicler didn't cherry-pick truths: ". . . if we should send every man to the penitentiary that ever stole a cow, there wouldn't be any citizens in Mason County."[48] Under the circumstances of an Open Range philosophy, where cattle could drift at leisure—irrespective of county lines—truly: "A man who could keep his hands entirely clean under such conditions would have been a little eccentric."[49]

The bottom line is plain. Texans, especially frontier Texans who now also expediently considered themselves simply as "Americans," held sacrosanct in their hearts a dogmatic antipathy for a differing culture. The Germans, who thought of themselves as Americans too, but still manifestly as "Germans," were equally entrenched. In fact—an indisputable fact—while many of the Texas Hill County's Germans maintained their ethnicity and native language, they had clearly made a concession to "one American custom: the use of rope, steel and lead to maintain peace and property rights."[50] Discord from both camps was dangerously mean-spirited. Disputes—deadly disputes—with regards to the ownership of wandering cattle in days before barbed-wire were commonplace and more times than not final resolution was sought touching hair-triggers. Courtroom justice was fleeting, six-shooter justice was final. At the time, feud mentality was pervasive: There was always payback. Family and friends were obligated to even the score, settle the hash of anyone killing or insulting blood relatives and/or in-laws and/or *bueno amigos*. The vengeance was cyclical; unyieldingly the dead bodies piled up while gravediggers hustled—and widows wept.

By the time rookie Texas Ranger Frank Jones made an appearance in Mason County the lid had already come off. There had been many murders, retaliatory murders, and the county jail had been mobbed by a lynch-minded crowd, while a lonesome Texas Ranger watched in outrage but—somewhat understandably—wordlessly and safely kept his own counsel in the face of overwhelming odds. That storybook One Riot, One Ranger hokum was just that, hokum![51]

Near immediately after the death of Dan Hoerster and the Rangers' arrival in Mason, Major Jones was dunked into the cold torrent of Texas Hill Country reality, admitting:

> The National prejudice is so very bitter here, Americans against Germans and vice versa, that I find it impossible to get a consistent or reliable account of the troubles and am sorry to have to report that very few of the Americans whom I have met yet manifest any disposition to assist in the arrest of the perpetrators of yesterdays deed or any particular desire to have them arrested.[52]

After what was interpreted as roughshod treatment by an "armed force of 30 to 40 men," that had blistered into Loyal Valley, searching "nearly every house, cabin & stable," a number of residents petitioned Major Jones, pleading that a detachment of Rangers be stationed there. Furthermore, they had gladly "selected a committee of old quiet men, not being implicated in any party strife or feeling" to meet with the major.[53] Bending to their appeal, two days later Major Jones directed Lieutenant Long to detail Company A's Corporal Nelson and seven men to the area and to remain there—preserving the peace—until receiving further orders.[54]

There was another meeting on the mind of Major John B. Jones. He was not happy, nor should he have been. The previously mentioned ex-Ranger Scott Cooley was a wanted man; a known murderer legally charged with a $300 price on his head—to be paid by the governor. Several—though it's scandalous—Texas Rangers were refusing to hunt for and arrest their friend of bygone days, and in fact many of the Company D Rangers were not even slyly inconspicuous. Their sympathies were with the "Americans" not the "Dutch." At an earlier point in time, even the Company D commander, Daniel W. Roberts, had downplayed one coldhearted execution. Candidly, but tastelessly for a lawman, pronouncing: "The mob has been operating some in Llano County lately. Killed one man named Wages—ordered several more to leave the county. As yet they've harmed no good men."[55] Weird talk for a lawman, no? Each faction wanted Rangers on their team. Good man or bad man, Major John B. Jones wanted Mr. Scott Cooley in a pine box or handcuffs. Rangers refusing to do their duty were downright expendable. As Private Frank Jones no doubt stood by in stark disbelief, three Texas Rangers openly declared that they positively would not and "could not conscientiously discharge the duty to which they have been assigned." Undaunted and forthrightly the major discharged all three Rangers, Sergeant N. O. Reynolds, along with Privates James P. Day and Paul Durham of Company D.[56]

The remaining Rangers rambling throughout Mason County were doing their jobs—if primary source documents are meaningful, especially the hard-charging boys in Lieutenant Long's Company A, Private Frank Jones' outfit. Seldom are rookie Rangers actually mentioned by name—unless in trouble—during their first few months of service. And so it is with Frank Jones. The generic statement in Monthly Returns and correspondence to headquarters normally is name specific for the Ranger in charge of a scout, followed by something similar to "with ten men" or "eight men and the 1st Sergeant scouted to. . . ." Before his service to the Lone Star State is ended Frank Jones' name and signature will mark hundreds of pages of bureaucratic reports and responses. But for the short term—in and around Mason—it must register as but supposition that Private Jones participated in some, not all, of the twenty-two arrests attributed to Major Jones and the Frontier Battalion.[57] Provably, at least to this point, Major Jones could say and was saying "that there has been no blood shed since I came here."[58] Vigilantly reconstructing Company A's across-the-board movements with painstaking meticulousness is plainly doable but not requisite. The boys were busy.[59] History will stand as the witness, enforcing the law was to Frank Jones' liking. Not to Major Jones' liking was the abrasiveness of pigheaded partisans.

Rumors wafted back to Austin charging that Major Jones was not doing his job impartially. It was a stinging accusation made to Governor Coke, then forwarded to Adjutant General Steele: Then rolled downhill to Major Jones. The bitch was tactless and unfounded. One crying for response and Major Jones snapped back, politely but vigorously:

> In reply to your comment of the 14th inst. I have to say that I am not surprised that reports have gone to the Governor that I had taken sides with one or the other party to the terrible feud in this county, but am surprised that he should have taken any notice of it. . . . I knew the difficulty of steering clear of interpretations of partiality when I came here and consequently was as careful as possible from the first to act in such a manner as to give no cause for such a suspicion ever. With this object in view I avoided any particular personal or social intercourse with either party, fearing that if I was known to be often with one party the other would think I was taking sides. Notwithstanding this I had not been here more than ten days before each party accused me of taking sides with the other and for that reason I am at a loss to form an opinion as to which party, if either, has made the complaint to the Governor. . . . [60]

Major Jones' missive seems to communicate a pristine aura of nonpartisanship and, for him personally, it was probably true. He was, however, forced to acknowledge that not just a few Texas Rangers from Company D were anything but neutral. As major of the six-company battalion Jones could not tarry too long in any one spot, the work elsewhere was ongoing and demanding administrative attention. The Rangers' behavior at Mason prompted him to identify truth and alter his plans. He was not hesitant or subtle:

> I brought with me Lt. Long's Co. and eight men of Lt. Roberts Co., the latter for the reason that they had been here before and were well acquainted with the country, intending to remain here only a few days however and then station Lt. Roberts company here and leave it here for some time to come. Within a few days however I became convinced that it would only aggravate the trouble to leave Lt. Roberts company here for the reason that the sympathies of his men were entirely with one of the parties to the feud. That the notorious Scott Cooley having at one time been a member of the company had many friends among the men who were in sympathy with him and his party and entertained a violent prejudice against the Sheriff Clark and the German population.[61]

Showing the utmost confidence in Lieutenant Long because Major Jones honestly judged Ira as "a very discreet officer [and] will be able to keep things quiet" the battalion commander resumed his customary inspection tours: Visiting the various companies in the field, not simply hosting grandiose and self-aggrandizing staff meetings at Austin. Lieutenant Long, along with Private Frank Jones and other rookies "lately recruited in the interior counties who have no personal acquaintance with the people here, no Knowledge of the troubles heretofore and no prejudice for or against either party" would handle the peace keeping mission at Mason.[62] For a reason as yet solidly locked tight, Dood Jones opted to not saddle himself with any policing business: He discharged from Company F on the 30th day of November 1875 in Edwards County. Assuredly the resignation did not carry any undue negativity—his Texas Ranger service was yet far removed from measuring as an impetuous three month lark.[63]

Lieutenant Dan Roberts and Company D's obviously less than stellar performance during the Hoo Doo War turmoil, while justly earning harsh criticism, is somewhat understandable and to some extent explainable. Institutionally the Texas Rangers—and little did they actually realize it at the time—were fast morphing from military-like Indian fighters to civil law enforcement officers. Therefore it is not unreasonable to suggest that hardly any charter member of the Frontier Battalion envisioned—at time of enlistment—that chasing after Comanches and/or Apaches would take a backseat to hunting and hamstringing desperadoes. The transition was taking place fast. Seldom is big change free of snags.

If tiring days spent in the saddle equated to success, certainly the Rangers in Company A stationed at Mason during 1875 were superstars: Like a comforting blanket they were all over the county and surrounding neighborhoods. The first time Frank Jones is mentioned by name in official Frontier Battalion correspondence—as thus far is known—was during latter December. As product of periodic sweeps through the countryside Company A Rangers nabbed a fugitive.

It seems that Mr. C. C. Rush had switched sides. He had tarnished the badge he once wore as a Wise County deputy sheriff—Ira Long's original bailiwick. Though details are skimpy it seems that Deputy Rush "Stoled a horse and several hundred dollars of Public Money" and departed Decatur, hitting the Owl-Hoot Trail. Whether or not Lieutenant Long knew him beforehand is indeterminate, but what is not vague is the fact Company A Rangers had to make disposition of a prisoner. Handpicking trustworthy Texas Rangers for the assignment, Lieutenant Ira Long detailed Corporal J. D. Nelson and Privates Charles Walsh and Frank Jones to transport the prisoner—horseback—to the county seat at Decatur and turn him over to a most pleased sheriff, Robert G. Cates. Though there's no paper trail particularly identifying Frank Jones' mindset, it's not unreasonable to postulate that this, sitting tall in the saddle with a Winchester in the scabbard and a Colt's .45 strapped to his hip, on an important mission, was exhilarating for a Ranger but nineteen years old. The prisoner was transported back to Wise County absent incident or fanfare. The cold-weather roundtrip, in excess of half a thousand miles, had taken Private Frank Jones and his cohorts twenty-two days, arriving back at Mason on the twenty-fourth day of January 1876.[64]

During this time frame—December 1875/January 1876—there was a frenzied flurry of activity concerning Company A's manpower strength and geographical positioning. G. W. Todd in a letter to Major Jones was figuratively crying for attention, begging: "But for God Sake don't take the Rangers away, but send more for I know they are needed worse here than anywhere else. . . . Lieut. Long is the right man and in the right place but he has not force sufficient to do what the emergency of the Case demands. He has now out 2 scouts and has only a few men in Town, not enough to cope with the 11 outlaws which were in Town last night." Todd was predicting, because "Cooley and party" were "becoming more bold everyday" that times in and around Mason were steadily becoming "more dangerous." He also chimed in that a liquor dealer named McDonald based in Austin was sometimes the headquarters for Scott Cooley and boys when they were in the Capitol City.[65]

In the face of administrative orders—which were not secret—the Company A staffing pattern was to be reduced to but two sergeants, one corporal, and seventeen privates.[66] Lieutenant Long was thunderstruck with front office management's jaded recognition of his on-the-ground reality: "I asked in a previous letter [to] retain all the men that I had in the service and for fear the letter has not reached you I mention subject again. I would not ask as much but I need all the men that I have." More than anyone else the Company A commander knew that outlawed fugitives "Cooley, Gladden & Beard [*sic*] were Still in the Country."[67] Lieutenant Long's appeal did not fall on deaf ears. Long updated Major Jones: "I recd. to-day: an order from General Steele to keep the Company at its present strength. . . ."[68] The news about retaining Company A in Mason County meshed perfectly with the entreaty from a meeting of concerned citizens:

> Resolved that we hereby tender our thanks to Lieut. Long and the men of the frontier Battalion now Stationed amongst us for the prompt and efficient discharge of their duties under the trying situation in which they have been placed and we desire to put on record our appreciation of their uniformly Excellent conduct and the Sprit shown by their commander of being guided by the law of our common Country and that only.[69]

Company A remained assigned to Mason County, although their scouts took them hither and yon throughout the entire region—and beyond. Though yet a young man Private Frank Jones was a busy fellow but had thus far escaped an exchange of gunfire—such would not always be the case, but would hold true for this term of enlistment. However there was a Company A casualty. Somehow while on guard duty Private W. P. Raynor accidently—inappropriately tinkering with his Colt's six-shooter—suffered a self-inflicted wound. Lieutenant Long's prognosis was short and stubby, about like the first finger of Raynor's left hand after it was "amputated."[70]

Such negligence was not the only accident obligating a report from Lieutenant Long. This time, however, the blame or responsibility could not be laid at the doorstep of a Texas Ranger. Somewhat unfortunately sixteen Springfield .45-70 carbines earmarked for the battalion and stored at David Doole's hardware store in Mason were totally destroyed by fire. According to Major Jones, the conflagration was "the result of accident, or rather carelessness, on the part of Mr. D's clerk."[71] Lady Luck was winking—or smirking—at Rangers assigned to Mason.

Another malady overtook some of the Company A boys with a vengeance—the Measles. Lieutenant Long was at a loss to explain where his speckled-faced warriors had acquired the disease, noting: "None of us are able to tell where they come from. Within the last two or three days many of the citizens taken them and in fact—they seem to be well scattered over the country."[72] Whether or not Private Frank Jones was one of the men cared for in a "private house" goes unrecorded—name specifics were not a part of the official reporting.

What was officially reported was the expenditure of a sizable quantity of ammunition. Recognizing the value of close quarter firearms proficiency now that the Frontier Battalion troops were moving more and more into a law enforcing posture, Major Jones had authorized the Rangers of Company A considerable leeway with what was deemed—evidently—surplus ammo. On a wide-ranging scout through Throckmorton and Shackelford Counties, a reconnaissance covering 300 miles during the month of May, Company A stalwarts were given ample opportunity for firearms familiarity: Discharging 700 rounds of carbine ammo, and firing 1300 pistol cartridges.[73]

Perpetually mobile, Major Jones, always in need of an armed escort so his response to this or that catastrophe could be decisive and overwhelming, had drafted Company A as the arm holding his hammer of physical supremacy. Accordingly the men—and boys—assigned to Company A were forever on the move.

As the summer of 1876 opened, the opportunity for clear weather, the Frontier Battalion's commander notified Lieutenant Long to marshal his manpower in readiness for a major scout. The lieutenant was ordered to ensure each man would travel light, carrying "no baggage except one blanket." They were, however, to be weighted with ammunition: "one hundred rounds each of pistol and Carbine Cartridges." Cooking utensils were to be kept at the minimum. On the other hand, the company was to take for their horses, "as much corn as you can haul."[74]

Acting as Major Jones' escort, Company A in its entirety, Private Frank Jones included, pushed a grueling schedule as evidenced by Lieutenant Long's retracing:

> The Company continued its march from San Felipe in the Rio Grande on the first of the month to Devils River up its entire length and across the country to Live Oak creek. Down that to the Pecos River thence back up Live Oak creek across the plains to head of Lipan creek thence to the South Concho to Kickapoo Springs to Co. D. at Menardville thence to Co. E. on the head of the Jim Ned [Creek] thence across to the head of Elm creek a tributary of the Clear Fork of the Brazos by Mustang Springs [thence] to Yellow Wolf Creek to Champion creek to the source about 60 Miles West of the East Line of Tom Green County.[75]

The tortuous schedule was no less demanding the following month as Major Jones and his escort inched their way north and south, east and west, but eventually into Kerr County at the end of August 1876.[76]

And it was there and at that time, back in the Texas Hill Country west of San Antonio, when Private Frank Jones, after a year away from home, voluntarily discharged from the Rangers; the agreed to one-year period of enlistment having expired. His service to the State of Texas was far short of extinction. Rest and relaxation and reuniting with his mother and brothers were at the top of Frank's near term agenda.[77] That persistently exhilarating Texas Ranger business was to his liking, though. Smart as he was he had taken due mental note. Those incessant comings and goings for Rangers of the Frontier Battalion was but a seesawing and merry-go-round state of affairs. When the time was right, he could just jump back on the bandwagon—filling a blank slot on the battalion's Muster & Payroll.

Texas Ranger Frank Jones would rise through Frontier Battalion ranks, making transitions from private to corporal to sergeant to lieutenant to captain: His sincere devotion to duty unquestioned and unfaltering. Contrary to hero worshiping idealists, the afterward revered Texas Ranger leaders were not born with captain's bars pinned to their diapers. Ascendency to the top—in most instances—was the positive result of hard work and demonstrated competency. PHOTO FROM *TEXAS RANGER SKETCHES* COURTESY THE AUTHOR, ROBERT W. STEPHENS.

John Peters Ringo of Hoo Doo War and Tombstone fame or infamy. Like a few of his most celebrated Arizona Territory adversaries Johnny Ringo did have a cut on the notch-stick for coldblooded murder. Also like them, his characterization as a Wild West gunfighter was/is overblown if hardcore factuality is the benchmark. *Courtesy Dave Johnson*.

Daniel Webster Roberts. He and others were awarded an Improved Winchester by the Texas State Legislature for their participation in a Texas Hill Country fight with raiding Indians. Later he would see Texas Ranger service as captain of Company D, Frontier Battalion. *Courtesy Dave Johnson.*

Quanah Parker, son of Comanche captive Cynthia Ann Parker, was a prominent participant in the battle at Adobe Walls with buffalo hunters in the Texas Panhandle. *Courtesy Tales 'N' Trails Museum from the Benton Collection.*

When Texas Ranger N.O. "Mage" Reynolds was called on to hunt for and arrest former Texas Ranger and murderer Scott Cooley, he chose resignation over obeying official orders. *Courtesy Dave Johnson.*

Dan Hoerster met his Maker and a mortician at Mason, assassinated by feudists lurking behind the town's barbershop, another victim of the bloody mess Texas history knows as the Hoo Doo War. *Courtesy Dave Johnson.*

Ira Long, photographed during twilight years. He, too, was a veteran of hard-fought Indian campaigns, earning praise for heroism and bulldog tenacity. During the Mason County "Hoo Doo" War, Lieutenant Long commanded Company A of the Frontier Battalion wherein Private Frank Jones was positioned as a rookie Ranger. *Courtesy Armstrong Ranger Research Center, Texas Ranger Hall of Fame & Museum.*

A wonderful photograph of Kiowa Chief Ahpeahtone. Unfortunately the Indian woman is not identified. *Courtesy Tales 'N' Trails Museum from the Benton Collection.*

Another striking photograph is the studio portrait of the attractive Hattie, sometimes Indian interpreter: Always a Kiowa. *Courtesy Tales 'N' Trails Museum from the Benton Collection.*

Tried and true, Henry Clay "Hank" Smith was a hearty Texas pioneer. Roaming the American Southwest, Hank established his plucky reputation as an Indian fighter, hunter, hotel and wagon yard proprietor, an all around entrepreneur. He was the Real Deal! *Courtesy Nita Stewart Haley Memorial Library & J. Evetts Haley History Center in Midland, Texas.*

Stockman Timothy P. Williamson and wife Mary. Prisoner of a partisan Mason County deputy sheriff, Tim had his horse killed beneath him, insuring that the mob's handiwork with six-shooters and indifference would introduce him to the undertaker and the hereafter. *Courtesy Dave Johnson.*

The trio posing for this shutterbug were, by most accounts, Frontier Battalion-era Texas Rangers: Charter members of Company D. The preeminent authority on the Mason County "Hoo Doo" War is of the learned opinion that the guy seated on the left is the notorious Scott Cooley. *Courtesy Dave Johnson.*

CHAPTER 4

"Several Shots and Run Him into the River"

SUBSEQUENT TO THE ANNUAL reshufflings and readjustments and more readjustments mandated by budgetary constraints and unremitting administrative tinkering, the Frontier Battalion's Company F was strategically positioned at Camp Wood in the northwestern corner of what was at times wrongly referred to as Uvalde County, but was then Edwards County (county seat Rocksprings), and is now guaranteed to be spotted in southwestern Real County (Leakey).[1] The unit's commander, Lieutenant Pat Dolan, was a veteran frontline settler, survivor of a shoot-out with Mexican bandits, Indian chaser, a tried and true Ranger, the former sheriff of Uvalde County and the future sheriff of another county.[2] Pat Dolan was legit!

Probing the mindset of Frank Jones, now a civilian Kendall County farmer and a sideline spectator of the Frontier Battalion's doings would be an unworkable exercise—at least for the short go. Such would not be the case with one of Frank's older brothers. Subsequent to his earlier enlistment of but three months service with the Texas Rangers, Dood Jones opted to give law enforcing and Indian hunting another try. On the first day of September 1876 he signed on with Lieutenant Dolan's Company F.[3]

Whether or not Dood Jones was in fact an actual participant as one of "the 12 men" scouting for fresh sign of purported Indian raiders along the West Fork of the Nueces River is indeterminate. Involving Dood Jones in the unproductive arrest attempt when Company F's Sergeant T. J. Frazer and "4 men" left camp hunting for Mr. Holmes and Mr. Ellis after their alleged shooting affray is, likewise, but guesswork. Similarly, when Lieutenant Dolan ordered the sergeant and "4 men" to search for and arrest a couple of fellows responsible for stealing horses along a tributary of the Nueces, Private Dood Jones may or may not have participated.[4] Though but theory—not owning specifics—it's not irrational to suggest Dood Jones was active.

What is not conjectural is Frank Jones' next move—he could stand life on the farm no more. On November 25, 1876, he became a Texas Ranger once again, enlisting with Lieutenant Dolan, at the Camp Wood site, filling an open vacancy on the unit's roster as a private in Company F.[5] Spine tingling excitement was in his near future. There, however, would be a few false starts.

As when Company F Rangers hit the trail looking for "twenty to sixty" Indians reported to be prowling Turkey Creek and the West Fork of the Nueces. After grueling time in the saddle and sagacious interviews Lieutenant Dolan reached a disappointing but at the same time reassuring conclusion. The group of game hunters from San Antonio, were "getting Scared at a bunch of Deer or Cattle at Mustang Pond on the Nueces' West Fork" thinking they were hostile Indians on the warpath. The scouting Rangers returned to Camp Wood.[6] And there, before the end of December a new face was loafing about the company's makeshift headquarters and campfires, Private R. H. Kingsbury had transferred from Company A into Company F.[7]

Absent documentation that the Jones brothers furloughed for the holidays it's but safe to assume that Frank and Dood celebrated Christmas 1876 and New Year's Day 1877 gobbling down helpings of wild turkey and cathead biscuits and hot coffee in the Rangers' Company F nerve center at Camp Wood. Texas Rangers like good grub—and holidays, too.

Hardly had the new month begun before Lieutenant Pat Dolan was noting a personnel problem—the march to professionalism was slow but underway. Dolan asked for authority to terminate Private

Kingsbury's state service because he believed "as a Ranger he is a total failure and from what I have seen of him I am inclined to believe he sometimes allows that tongue of his to wag too freely and not in the path of truth within."[8] Later, Lieutenant Dolan noticed that Kingsbury was malingering when it came to routine camp chores and/or cleaning up: Such work seemed to "grate on his sense of honor. . . . to have to help to do anything in that line."[9] Lieutenant Dolan in assuring Major Jones that his attitude regarding Private Kingsbury was not a simple conflict of personalities unequivocally graded his slacking subordinate as "a Kind of Pest to all the men."[10] A discharge was forthcoming.[11]

Other Company F Rangers were skating on thin ice—real thin. On the fifteenth day of January 1877 Sergeant Richard "Dick" Jones (no known relationship to Frank Jones or John B. Jones) and private H. S. Joines were on a spree at Uvalde. According to Dolan the pair "got very drunk." During the "drunken row" over a game of cards, Joines accused some of the players of stealing his wallet. Not surprisingly—for Rangers—both the sergeant and the private jerked out their Colt's six-shooters demanding satisfaction—a return of the "Pocket Book." Beneath dim candlelight the Rangers and the suspects searched diligently but to no avail for the missing billfold. Upon sensing a squinch of figurative daylight the supposed cheating malefactors made a break for liberty. A thoroughly miffed Lieutenant Dolan picks up the story: ". . . Jones and Joines discharged their Pistols several times. I cannot say if they shot at the men or not. . . . they [the Rangers] were both arrested and are now under Bond for their appearance before the Grand Jury in April next, charged with Assault with intent to Murder." The stupidity of the misbehavior was ludicrously compounded: Private Joines' wallet had never been lost—having been in his pocket "all this time."[12]

Upon sobering up, Sergeant Jones was embarrassed and remorseful. Private Joines was not. Unashamedly—more or less—Private Joines had "manifested imprudence" and was "in a goodly stock" of same. Pat Dolan could be forgiving—but offenders must at least show a tinge of regret. In fact, reading between the lines is not necessary. The irked lieutenant updated Major Jones: "Richard

Jones heretofore has been a very good man in every sense of the word but I shall leave his case entirely to you. . . . In Joines case it is different. . . . he has shown me all the disrespect and imprudence he safely could for which I Respectfully ask that he be Discharged. . . ."[13] They may have maintained the company headquarters at Camp Wood, but Dolan was not a happy camper. The Company F lieutenant's not subtle use of the word "safely" should not been underplayed: Gritty and gutsy Pat Dolan was not a man to trifle with.

Standing strong in support of their sergeant, many of the Company F Rangers signed a petition asking that Dick Jones be retained, perhaps punished, but not dishonorably discharged. Private Dood Jones was one of the signatories. Private Frank Jones was not. Whether he was away from camp at the time the petition was circulated or chose not to interject himself in the business of the outfit's top brass is nebulous.[14] Ultimately Sergeant Jones was temporarily reduced in rank, and H. S. Joines' service with the Rangers was terminated—dishonorably.[15]

During that first month of 1877 not all the boys of Company F had been misbehaving. Most were busy scouting southwest to the vicinity of Fort Clark, Kinney County (county seat Bracketville) looking for Indians—unsuccessfully. Later during the month they marched into surveyed but yet to be organized Zavala County (Crystal City). Lieutenant Dolan had garnered actionable intelligence that it was highly likely there was to be big "trouble between the cattlemen."[16]

Specifically it was being hotly alleged that certain parties were altering brands. With a red-hot running-iron it was relatively simple handiwork to change a **POL** brand into a **BOE**, as was being alleged. At a Zavala County roundup of suspect cattle, the owner claiming title refused Texas Rangers the right to inspect the animals. "At first he was obstinate and talked fight—but when it came [time] to test the matter he consented that the herd be cut. . . ."[17] Showing the figurative Ranger flag and sitting big stout horses while heavily armed with Winchesters and Colt's .45's the Company F response had been predictably effective: After a few days the cowmen and cowboys' ardor for six-shooter fireworks was cooled.[18]

On another front sharp blades were busy. The illicit commerce in what amounted to stolen hides was exceptionally brisk and very profitable.[19] Whether or not leeway is built in for a touch of exaggeration, earlier reports by both the *San Antonio Daily Herald* and the Alamo City's *Daily Express* had made note of the high volume traffic. The latter newspaper calculating that in just one year 800,000 hides had been exported from the Lone Star State and "that at least 500,000 of those were the product of hide rustling." San Antonio was and had been the center of operations for the illicit business, with much of the actual killing and skinning taking place in the countryside west and northwest of town. In fact, for awhile "Merchants from San Antonio, 'abandoning legitimate business,' thronged to the scene of 'shocking devastation' to purchase the ill-gotten hides." In selected sections of the Texas Hill Country and Edwards Plateau rounding up cattle and then slaughtering them just for their hides was rampant—and for the most part unchecked. Near Mason one trafficker dealing and disposing of illegal hides was so bold and unworried that the stench emanating from his ranch almost made the roadway impossible to pass. A few nitwits were rounding up their neighbors' unbranded cattle and honest mavericks, driving them into a hastily built brush pen, speedily putting a brand on them—and then slaughtering the animals, leaving all except the hides and a few choice cuts to rot.[20]

Conceivably the illicit trade in stolen hides had somewhat abated by 1877, but it was still a major concern for Lieutenant Dolan and the troops of Company F. In this regard the Rangers were zealous—not zealots—but energetically searching for midnight skinners and clandestine purveyors of stolen hides. February would be an active month. In one instance a peddler named Barton was arrested, his wagon containing "30 hides for which he can show no Bill of Sale or title of any kind whatsoever." Peddler Barton did, however, spill the beans, naming names and giving particulars about his acquiring questionable hides.[21] Another fellow, R. L. Brandon, was arrested with four hides, all suspiciously absent a hint of identifying marks or Bills of Sale. E. Hatch was caught with but one hide, but could not prove even an inkling of ownership and, ultimately, "admitted to having Killed the animal the same day." Thinking a small-time crime ring was operating in a big-time way, Lieutenant Dolan divided his meager forces, dispatching four three-man scouts to scoop up other suspected stolen hide traffickers.[22] For the biographical subject of this narrative the roundup would prove noteworthy.

Particularly the Rangers had been tasked with arresting three fellows: Allan A. McDonald (sometimes McDonnel), Sam B. Raney, and Jim Goodman. They were suspected of "selling stolen hides." Soon the fellows were in custody thanks to the exceptional labors of another Company F sergeant, J. J. O'Reilly and his crew.[23] Later, Rangers arrested Ed Hill and Steve McLane on similar charges. With prisoners in detention the Rangers traveled to Uvalde with purpose of placing their charges in the county jail. There, Sheriff George Johnson declined to accept all of the prisoners. He would only take two, Brandon and Hatch, perhaps correctly asserting that rightful jurisdiction for the others' arrests actually lay in Kerr County where they were wanted. Undaunted, Lieutenant Dolan and his Texas Rangers struck the road to Kerrville, by way of Camp Wood, prisoners Barton, Goodman, McDonald, Raney, and Hill in tow. At the Ranger camp Jim Goodman complained of an illness, too sick to travel next day.[24] At sunup the tireless Lieutenant Dolan accompanied by a strong guard left for Kerrville with his remaining four prisoners, leaving Goodman under the supposed watchful eyes of Privates S. C. Bowman and Richard Chute, who were theoretically following shortly behind with the company wagon and team—and the puking prisoner.[25]

Lieutenant Dolan had traveled less than mile and a half when he was overtaken by Private H. C. Gray, hard riding and near breathless. The news he bore was frightful. Jim Goodman had stabbed Private Bowman "with a Knife," stolen his horse and carbine, and was now a man on the dodge. Thankfully the wound would not prove mortal. Immediately Lieutenant Dolan sent the prisoners plodding toward camp under a heavy guard. A manhunt was called for and kicked into gear. While Lieutenant Dolan and Rangers were beating the bushes for Goodman, Private Gray—after catching his breath and letting his near jaded horse blow—made fast tracks for Camp Wood and reinforcements. Hurriedly urging men to saddle their horses, Private

Gray updated Sergeant O'Reilly about what had transpired on the road to Kerrville. The plan was simple: Race to Jim Goodman's Nueces Canyon house and arrest the knife-wielding yahoo. Riding hell-bent-for-leather were Sergeant O'Reilly, Corporal G. Morrow, and Privates W. Smedt, G. W. Forbes, H. C. Gray, and twenty-one-year-old Frank Jones.[26]

Unfortunately the Rangers arrived twenty minutes behind Goodman and failed to capture him outright. Abandoning his horse at the hitching-rail, the fugitive "took to a very heavy bottom of Timber." All night the Rangers remained out "chasing him around." On more than one occasion beneath the moonlight they—Frank Jones included—"shot several shots at him." Goodman's good luck would not hold: The Rangers "run him in the River and he finally froze out as it was very cold and they brought him to camp in the morning" after recovering Bowman's horse and gun.[27] They could not and did not recover Ranger Bowman's lost pride. As far as thus known this—popping caps at Goodman—had been Ranger Private Frank Jones' baptismal gunplay. There would be much more excitement scheduled for his career calendar. During this commotion Frank Jones and the other Rangers came through slick in the eyes of their commander, but two fellows did not near measure to that mark. Lieutenant Dolan was less than pleased with Privates Bowman's and Chute's due diligence—the lack thereof.[28]

At another turn of events the Company F Rangers were thunderstruck. Subsequent to delivering the "hide rustling" prisoners to Kerrville and turning them over to Kerr County Sheriff F. J. Hamer, the alleged offenders "were discharged, suffering only the inconvenience of being under Guard for fifteen days and the loss of 30 hides." Lieutenant Pat Dolan was flabbergasted, particularly noting that hides had been confiscated and he chaffed at the fact that "the Peddler admitted that he bought 12 of the hides from the other 3 Prisoners and they don't own a cow in the world." Lieutenant Dolan boiled it down to the nutshell: "So ends all our work in that case."[29]

Company F's hard work in the criminal arena was drawing praise in certain quarters, condemnation in others, and counter-surveillance from partisan spies and their crooked allies: "My camp is continually watched and all our movements are carefully noted by violators of the law or their friends," so reported Lieutenant Dolan.[30]

During the month following gunplay with Jim Goodman, March 1877, two episodes uncoiled which would be conspicuously telling concerning Private Jones' tenure as a Company F Ranger. It is highly likely—though not absolute—that Frank was one of the "ten men" accompanying Lieutenant Dolan on a dicey policing assignment: arresting a fugitive wanted in Blanco County for "shooting a man." On the Dry Frio, at the crack of dawn on the twenty-second day of the month, the tactical team rode up on the suspect's house. The Rangers well knew the purpose of their visit. So, too, did outlaw Smith. Ahead of the Rangers' approach Smith broke and ran from the cabin. The actual number of rounds expended by the Texas Rangers was not enumerated, other than "several shots." As far as is now known, the lawmen missed hitting the mark—where Smith's suspenders intersected on the back of his flannel shirt. Smith, if he did indeed shoot at Rangers also missed, but he did not miss out on making a clean getaway, smooth "getting into the Cedar." Their spirits downtrodden the Texas Rangers meandered back to home-base, Camp Wood. The message was perfectly clear whether spoken or not. In the business of enforcing the law and arresting bad guys, the presence of danger and possibility of death were ever near.[31]

With his head down and nose to the grindstone, Ranger Private Frank Jones was on the march to personal maturity and professional competency. His demonstrated levelheadedness and steel-nerved deportment was not going unnoticed. Before March was history Frank Jones made history, well, individual history: He was the lead Texas Ranger on an enforcement assignment: "On 27th inst. Pvt. F. Jones with four men started on Scout to Uvalde for the purpose of assisting the Sheriff to arrest parties near there who are charged with Horse stealing and Murder."[32] Records concerning the success or failure of the Rangers' supportive role are silent, but the gist of Frank's leadership dependability should not be overlooked. The eyes of upper-level Ranger management were focused on the young man from Kendall County.

Those same astute managerial type fellows were eyeballing some other folks. Desperadoes! Kimble County had been cut from the

Bexar Land District during 1858 but had not been formally organized until January 1876, the same year Frank Jones became a Company F Ranger. The first county seat was Kimbleville, then Junction City and soon thereafter simply Junction.[33] Cut by the Llano River and broken by rolling plains and a sometimes semi-mountainous terrain, Kimble County was/is pretty. In 1877 she was pretty damn tough, too!

Kimble County may not have been technically lawless on paper, but she was outright lawless. Major Jones had sent an undercover operative—Ranger H. B. Waddill, yet in his twenties—to snoop around and pinpoint the crooks. It was a dangerous assignment. Ranger Waddill was a whiz and in but short order had wormed his way into the evil environs. In truth very little got by the slippery little Ranger from Corsicana. He knew who was stealing, what they were stealing, where they hid what was stolen—and which county officials were in cahoots with the cow thieves and ne'er-do-wells. Within a clandestine report to Major Jones, young Waddill succinctly characterized Kimble County as "a thiafs stronghold, the two Llanos and all tributaries are lined with them. . . . Every one that is not known is looked on as the enemy. . . . the County is unsafe to travil through."[34]

Markedly stung by the Rangers' relative ineffectiveness in Mason County's Hoo Doo War, Major Jones—thoroughly committed to professionalism—engineered a plan for redemption. Success would be but morally and ethically fitting for Kimble County's honest citizens who were living in fear, and the anticipated triumph would likewise put the Frontier Battalion on the right road as peace officers. This time around, from the get-go, Major Jones would execute a hands-on approach, strategically and tactically.[35]

At the same time Private Waddill was covertly schmoozing and gathering valuable criminal intelligence, Lieutenant Frank Moore, Company D, through the efforts of a perfectly positioned helpmate, criminal informant Ben Anderson, crafted a list of names. On the sly Lieutenant Moore furnished Major Jones with his newly acquired info, data about the activities and whereabouts of thirty-nine known and/or suspected Kimble County outlaws and fugitives.[36]

On the eleventh day of April 1877, Major Jones revealed his game-plan to Lieutenant Moore with a cautionary note, which in part said: "Do not let any one know of my coming except the three men you send to Paint Rock and charge them not mention it to any one. I will bring Coldwell's and Dolan's Companies with me and will make a general 'roundup' of Kimble county but want it kept secret until we are ready to make the break."[37]

Major Jones' crusade against crookdom was to frame a coordinated raid—a sweep—waging war on brigands and bandits, cow thieves and brand blotchers, feudists and fugitives or anyone else not having a good reason for parking their fanny in Kimble County. Such fussy boundaries guaranteed in the U.S. Constitution regarding sufficient and reasonable Probable Cause were too pesky to worry about—Kimble County was, to this point, uncontrollable and unmanageable. Rights and wrongs of criminal procedure could—and would be—debated later.[38]

Initially Major Jones intended on calling the full-strength of Company F into play for the Kimble County Roundup. Interloping Indians, on foot, forestalled those plans. The presence of pedestrian warriors in the Nueces Canyon could lead to but one conclusion, one immediately relayed to Adjutant General Steele at Austin: "They will doubtless continue prowling about the country or concealed in the mountains for several days, probably until the full moon, then steal horses and make off with them."[39] Major Jones dared not take a chance:

> In view of this fact I deem it impolitic to take Lt. Dolan up the country with me, as I had designed doing but will take a detachment from his company which together with Coldwells' and Moore's Companies will be as many men as I will need in Kimble Co. although my last reports from there inform me that the desperadoes are in strong force, laying in large supply of ammunition and occupying a threatening attitude. . . . [40]

Unfortunately for the book in hand, whether Private Frank Jones was a part of the Rangers from Company F hunting for Indians with Lieutenant Dolan or a member of the thirteen-man detachment assigned to Major Jones' Kimble County Roundup is open-ended. In light of future correspondence between Major Jones and Frank Jones the latter seems the most probable, but it's not conclusive.[41]

Conclusiveness, however, does attach to the preplanned enforcement action commencing in Kimble County on April 19, 1877. Major Jones updated Adjutant General Steele:

> I sent out five detachments and in three days had scoured the county thoroughly. The southern and western push the first and the northern and eastern push the next two. My advance was a complete surprise to the entire community, only three persons in the county knew of my coming. . . . In three days I made twenty-three arrests. . . . I sent scouts out from time to time as I could learn the whereabouts of parties whom I wanted and have made forty-one arrests in all. Thirty-seven of them in Kimble County. . . . I have reason to believe I have caught every man who was in the county at the time of my arrival against whom I have charges except three, and two of those left the county before I knew of the charges against them. Four of the worst men in the county committed a murder three days before my arrival. Three of them left the county immediately. The other was the first man I arrested and is now in Jail. . . . [42]

Well, some of the prisoners did eventually make it to jail. Initially, though, since Kimble County had no lockup, the detainees were unceremoniously chained to a tree, like so many pet bears.[43] Others were kept in a temporary open-air enclosure commonly referred to as the "Bull Pen."[44]

The wheels of criminal justice sometimes grind slow but in this instance District Judge W. A. Blackburn bent to speedy imposition of the law. Since there was not yet a Kimble County courthouse, he opened for business beneath a shading post oak, "sitting on a log, the lawyers on exposed tree roots, and the grand jury on grass some fifty yards away so they couldn't be overheard. The prisoners, heavily guarded by Rangers, stood nearby."[45] Humorously—of a sorts—though really quite pathetic, twenty-five felony indictments had returned. Grand jurors having been privy to the evidence at hand were then disqualified from sitting in judgment and rendering verdicts. The upshot was stark. In the whole of Kimble County but nine qualified petit jurors could be summoned—trials had to be postponed and prisoners not posting bond were transported to jails in adjoining counties.[46] Besides a number of wholesale outlaws with hard reputations rounded up, also suffering severe legal headaches because of the Texas Rangers' aggressive operation was Kimble County Sheriff J. M. Reynolds, a surprised guy who was positively arrested and jailed at what was generically still called Menardville, but since 1871 had been christened with its present moniker, Menard in Menard County.[47] Soon thereafter the unprofessional sheriff resigned, thoroughly disgracing his tin star.[48] County Judge William "Will" Potter was certainly arrested but perhaps not actually handcuffed and incarcerated, pending his resignation from office.[49]

Thanks to the Frontier Battalion, for industrious and honest folks of Kimble County the yoke of despotism and despair had been—for the most part—thrown into the trash heap of vanquished corruption and crookedness. There was another edge to the mighty sword of justice. The Kimble County Roundup had tested the Texas Rangers' newfound transition into the field of civil law enforcement. It had been a watershed experience. They had, if statewide praise and adulation was factored into the equation, scored a resounding A+. Though Texans little realized at the time, positive news about the Kimble County Roundup would jump from regional to national notoriety during testimony before the Committee on Military Affairs, in relation to The Texas Border Troubles.[50] Particularly pleased, Major Jones was able to boast—which he couldn't about the Hoo Doo War—that his men had without firing a shot arrested an illustrious passel of bad men. Maybe more importantly, "Each man seems to take a personal interest and pride in catching every one he is ordered to arrest. . . . I must commend the men of my command for their conduct in this arduous and unpleasant work."[51] Newspaper editors seconded Major Jones' optimism, one later ingeniously writing for the *Galveston Daily News* about the turnaround in Kimble County:

> A Methodist revival is progressing up there, and the late evil-doers are doffing the six-shooter and getting themselves checked for a blessed immortality.[52]

There was yet plenty of grueling work in store for Private Frank Jones and the other Rangers. Were one to suppose Company F's enforcement actions in the province of arresting hide stealers had served as a deterrent, the erroneous thinking would quickly be dispelled by hardcore reality. Scarcely had the Rangers of Company F finished one case, before another jumped on the horizon of April's 1877 work. The Rangers had received reasonably good information that "there was a party of men camped on Live Oak [Creek] Killing cattle for their hides." Taking ten men with him, Lieutenant Dolan fished around until he found the owlhoots' camp—deserted. Scouting about, the Rangers discovered "Several carcasses of cattle that had been skinned" but they could not locate any staked out green hides or other items of evidentiary value. It was a dry run. Downhearted the Ranges returned to Camp Wood.[53]

Owing to advancing technological developments, near half of the Company F Rangers were clamoring to be armed with the latest improved Winchester carbines. They would willingly trade the long-range capability of .45-70 Springfield's—that they were now being issued—for the markedly increased firepower of the .44-40 lever-action carbines. These eager-beaver Texas Rangers would gladly buy the weapons—as long as the charges could be deducted from their quarterly pay warrants, even though normally converted to hard money at a discounted rate.[54] Typically the State of Texas was broke—strapped for cash. Major John B Jones ruefully replied: "The state has no improved Winchester Carbines & no appropriation to pay for any." Proactively Texas Rangers could skin cats—one way or the other: "I can purchase them for your men from private parties at $28 & can bring some up to them in April if they wish me to do so."[55] Lieutenant Dolan and the Company F Rangers in want of new weapons were pleased as punch: "If the carbines can be charged on the men's accounts and deducted out of their next pay at the rate of $28 in certificates you might bring ten for this Company."[56]

Something else was being brought to Company F—harassment, notably for Lieutenant Dolan. A complaint had reached the governor that under Dolan's leadership the Company F boys were somewhat lackadaisical in regards to scouting for signs of prowling Indians and had mistreated prisoners in their custody. In policing lingo there is an old saw: "If you're working, doing your job, somebody somewhere will be bitching about it." Some of the "hide rustlers" had a gripe and they were whining, hoping beyond hope that Company F and their boss would be transferred away from the Nueces Canyon country. Naturally, there always is a reverse side to coins of contention. A flood of counter-petitions poured into battalion headquarters pleading that Pat Dolan remain in charge and the company not be removed from their neck of the woods.[57] Surprisingly, even some of the fellows arrested during the February roundup of "hide rustlers" piped in, Ed Hatch, Allan A. McDonnell and Sam B. Raney proclaiming:

> We the undersigned hearing that charges have been made against Lieut. Dolan that Prisoners while in his custody have met with severe and harsh treatment, We of our own free will and accord wish publically to State that having experience as Prisoners in his camp have at all times received the greatest kindness and attention, both from him and the men under his Command.[58]

John C. Sullivan, the District Attorney for the 24th Judicial District of Texas, chimed in with his ringing endorsement of Lieutenant Dolan and the Rangers of Company F.[59] Cutting it down to the nub, Major Jones took stock of reality: "He [Pat Dolan] was formerly sheriff of Uvalde and made some bitter enemies in that section of country by the avidity and zeal which he manifested in pursuing and bringing to justice the violators of the law. I regard that of itself as an evidence of his qualification for much of the duty which is required of the frontier battalion now."[60]

For this time-frame particularizing the firearms utilized by Private Frank Jones may be accomplished by reasoned deduction: For the month of June he was not issued any Springfield carbine cartridges—as were several Company F Rangers—which would seem to suggest he was by this time armed with one of those improved Winchesters. Seemingly, however that was not the case. For another draw from company stores he was issued 20 .45-70 cartridges for his trap-door carbine. Frank was of course carrying the standard sidearm, a Colt's .45, generically tagged a "Peacemaker," drawing twenty cartridges for same during the June 1877 distribution and thirty-six rounds for the August draw. Ranger work dictated fellows be armed—at all times. Depriving folks of their liberty can be touchy. By any standard it may not on the surface be considered a major arrest, but Private Frank Jones continued to be individualized in the Monthly Returns and the Ranger Correspondence files, unmistakably a plus for any career-minded frontier lawman on the make: In this instance he arrested G. W. Keith, charged with Bigamy, and personally delivered him to Sheriff Hamer at Kerrville.[61]

Though the threat from raiding Indians had significantly declined, folks in the Nueces Canyon country were not totally immune from trouble. During late June, presumably Lipan Apache, struck: Stealing eight horses from the Wells' Ranch, two from Chalk's Ranch, and one from the Box Ranch. Not yet through, at the Johnson Ranch the Indians "attacked a man who was driving a Wagon in the pasture wounding him in the wrist [and] Killing one of his work animals," making off with the other, after cutting up the harness. Company F Rangers were brought up to speed. Sallying forth, Sergeant Richard Jones and eighteen men, which undoubtedly by the numbers included Private Frank Jones, pursued the raiders so closely that they "Killed all the horses but five head." At one point the Texas Rangers actually caught sight of the Indians, but, alas, "they traveled south of west from Camp Wood through one of the longest cedar brakes in the country [and] after they left the horses it was impossible to trail them there as they scattered in all directions." Even then, Sergeant Jones and his men stayed in the field two more days hunting for fresh sign and/or a workable trail—fruitlessly.[62]

What was productive, however, was Lieutenant Dolan's insight. During one of his scouts with five Rangers he reined up for a palaver with a horseback Pedro A. Valdez and three or four more exiled "Patriots from the Land of God and Liberty" who advised the company commander that Indians were about. According to the "Mexicans" they had actually seen seven Indians crossing the road halfway between Eagle Pass and Fort Clark with a large herd of rumored stolen horses. Pat Dolan was of the see-through impression he was being lied to, the ruse designed to divert his attention away from "their cutthroats." There were no whooping warriors, or trail thereof, and no sign of frightened horses driven before any Indian raiders.[63]

Assuredly all of the Company F Rangers were busy during June 1877, the outfit making numerous scouts after real and supposed Indian sightings. Their criminal work had also been demanding—in the aggregate they had arrested fourteen fellows and attempted to locate several more. Part of that lot snagged by the Texas Rangers was the handiwork of a scout participated in by Private Frank Jones. At Frio Waterhole forty-five miles northwest of Kerrville, they scooped up another fellow wanted by the Kerr County sheriff. Frank was assigned to deliver the prisoner to Sheriff Hamer. Easily stopping by the Jones' homeplace Frank traded his jaded horse for a fresh one, and before reaching Kerrville arrested another fugitive, a fellow named Gibson wanted in Gonzales County. There had been three murders "in this immediate neighborhood and several offenses of lesser grades. . . ." Though it may seem braggadocio, Lieutenant Dolan passed on to Major Jones a tad of law enforcing actuality: "We have pretty well got rid of nearly all the offenders in this and Frio Canyons, the attraction now seems to be Eagle Pass."[64] Frontier Texas was yet still a piece of murderous real-estate.

Toppled from his wagon seat, a dead man falling, Robert Kimble (*sic:* Trimble) had been viciously murdered—shot and stabbed—during a brutal highway-robbery in Atascosa County the next county below Bexar County and her shiretown of San Antonio.[65] On top of the butchery, the murdered victim's lifeless corpse "had been thrown from his wagon, and a rope was then tied around his legs and the body was dragged through the cactus and brush."[66] With absoluteness it cannot be determined how the clues unfolded, but tenacious area lawmen were on the lookout for the killers; two riding horseback and two atop the murdered victim's stolen wagon, by brand name a White Water Wagon. During mid-July 1877 Lieutenant Dolan had been apprised that the killers were possibly heading for Uvalde, not too very far south of his Camp Wood headquarters' campground. He dispatched five Rangers under the leadership of Ranger G. K. Chinn to intercept and arrest the suspected murderers. By Pat Dolan's reasoning the orders were clear, damn specific: "To go down to the old Eagle Pass Road and take a fresh Wagon trail, follow it up and if said Wagon was a White Water Wagon to bring the wagon and every one with it and turn it and party over to Sheriff Johnson at Uvalde."[67] Enough said!

As good luck would have it, the squadron of Texas Rangers and four "Mexicans" met on the road outside of Uvalde. And just as prescribed beforehand two were in the wagon, a White Water Wagon, and the other two were straddling well-worn stock saddles. Too many cooks spoil the broth, and too many independently minded Rangers can mess up a good plan—or muddy orders. The squad of Rangers was—for an unexplainable reason—hesitant. Ranger Chinn was, despite his confidently bestowed leadership authority, vacillating. Subsequent to spur-of-the-moment but a decidedly mutual consultation, "they all agreed among themselves that this was not the proper party—but—he [Chinn] would send them in with Privates [Richard] Chute and [B. L.] Temple without searching them for arms."[68]

The blunder was stupid and costly. After separating from their fellow brothers of the badge, Privates Chute and Temple started for Uvalde, escorting the quartet of alleged or not so alleged suspects. Abruptly the two Texas Rangers' world turned upside down—horror in a heartbeat: "When one of the Mexicans shot him [Temple] in the back [and the other] Mexican jumped out of the Wagon and shot at Chute 3 times and Chute returned the fire and supposes he hit the Mexican. The Mexican Killed Chute's horse and 4 Mexicans made good their escape. . . ." Once again Lieutenant Dolan was dismayed at the seeming ineptitude: Charging that the Ranger in command "failed to obey orders and also because Temple neglected his duty. Chinn claims that some parties told him that there was another wagon on the road with white men which he supposed was the Murderers." Company F's fuming commander was peeved, but not speechless: "All I can say is that it is to say the least a shameful business as 4 Murderers got away by men not obeying orders—one of the party did not get away he is now in Uvalde Jail, the Wagon with its contents and 4 horses I tuned over to Sheriff of Uvalde. I made every effort to retake the Mexicans. . . . without success."[69]

Post the gunplay and escape it was somehow learned that the fellow who shot and wounded Ranger Temple was Jose Cordova (sometimes written as Cordoba). For Texas Rangers, that was all they needed to know. Running Cordova to ground was the work assigned to Texas Rangers Frank Jones and Richard Chute: Jones because he was reliably even-tempered and Chute to make the identification. Lieutenant Pat Dolan's remarks are not indistinct, not by a scratch: "the Mexican who wounded private B. L. Temple was followed to the Rio Grande by privates F. Jones and R. Chute who were joined by some citizens. . . ."[70] Absent from the lieutenant's report is a persnickety geographical detail: Determined Texas Rangers Jones and Chute were unhesitant and crossed the Rio Grande—with or without—permission from Mexican authorities and with the aid of citizens (Mexican or American?) "surrounded a house" where Cordova and cohorts were holed up. Historians are familiar with the brevity of Ranger reports:

> Joe Cordova made a break again coming out at the door where Chute was stationed. . . . he was ordered not to come out by Chute, his only reply was to cock his pistol and make a spring where Chute Shot him setting fire to his shirt . . . he returned Chute's fire when Chute shot him twice more leaving him <u>dead</u>. There were two other Mexicans wounded by citizens [and/or Frank Jones ?].[71]

Secondary writings suggest the Rangers had "received permission from Mexican authorities to pursue the gang on Mexican soil." After-the-fact it was by hook or by crook learned that the dead Mexican was "a half-brother of old man Jose Cordova." But a scant two years later, three days after Independence Day, convicted murderer Jose Cordova settled his debt with Texas for the premeditated murder of Robert Trimble by climbing thirteen steps to the top of the gallows inside the Bexar County Jail's compound.[72] Ironically it was exactly the two-year anniversary of Trimble's unprovoked murder. When given opportunity to speak his last words Cordova steadfastly held to his innocence, but even in the faraway *New York Times* it was not skeptically reported: "Notwithstanding this declaration, however, the belief in Cordova's guilt was general, and the evidence against him conclusive."[73] Cordova's trying to point the finger at Antonio

Garcia was not considered creditable—he was believed to be a "fictitious person," a phantom dancing across the Blind Mistress Justice's scales. Shortly after the proffer of innocence was coolly spoken before a crowd of fifty witnesses, Bexar County Deputy Sheriff Gleason presented the black hood and it was placed over Cordova's head.[74] But seconds later the trapdoor dropped from beneath his scuffed brogans. The condemned Jose Cordova—as newsmen of the time sometimes snipped—was jerked to Jesus!

On the ninth day of August 1877, Major John B. Jones was much more concerned with internal manpower levels than he was with any mean men haunting this or that canyon. In accord with legislative and administrative demands Frontier Battalion company commanders were to issue honorable discharges to the Rangers of their respective units on the last day of August. The following day, in compliance with reorganization orders, each captain was to recruit and enlist two sergeants, two corporals, and twenty privates for the next twelve month term of service. Particular attention was to be paid ensuring that character qualifications were strictly adhered to: No man under indictment and no habitual drunkards were to be placed on the Muster & Pay Roll. Since the job was challenging, outside work hunting down and capturing or killing raiding Indians and/or Mexican bandits and/or white outlaws, there was one more caveat; "the men received must be mounted on good horses."[75]

Clearly with anticipation of the reorganization, Company F work took a noticeable downturn. In fact, examination of the Monthly Return particularizes no scouts or arrests after the middle of August. Whether either of the two Jones brothers participated in the company's last 1877 scout "up the country on the look out for Indians and cattle thieves" is indeterminate. Those Rangers found no sign of either, returning to Camp Wood on August 15. Three days later, though, both Frank's and Dood's names appear in the official paperwork: On the eighteenth of August both voluntarily discharged from the Frontier Battalion.[76]

Gerry "Dood" Jones, a Texas Ranger and brother of Frank Jones. *Courtesy Candice DuCoin.*

Texas Rangers were issued the Colt's .45 Single Action Army model, sometimes referred to as the Peacemaker. As with state-issued carbines, there was a payroll deduction plan. *COURTESY TEXAS RANGER HALL OF FAME & MUSEUM.*

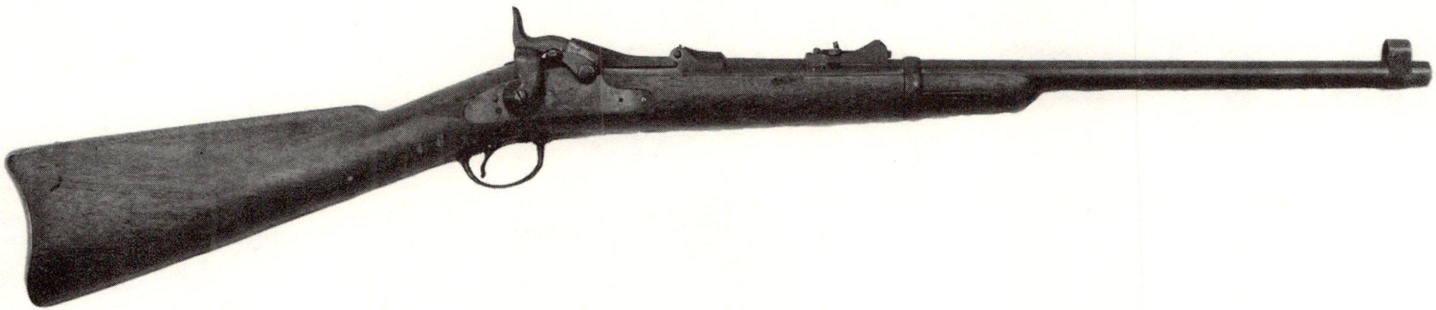

For awhile, before all Texas Rangers acquired Improved Winchester carbines, Frontier Battalion personnel were issued either a single-shot Sharp's carbine or trap-door Springfield carbine, both chambered for the whopping .45-70 caliber, guns with—as one Ranger remarked—a bore big enough for a gopher to crawl through. Rangers would reimburse the state by having funds deducted from their quarterly pay warrants. Until buying a Winchester repeater, Frank Jones was armed with a Springfield as pictured above. *Courtesy Texas Ranger Hall of Fame & Museum.*

Lieutenant Pat Dolan, Company F Frontier Battalion, the former sheriff of Uvalde County and the future sheriff of Jeff Davis County. Frank Jones' acquisition of practical law-enforcing skills blossomed under Dolan's tutelage. *COURTESY ARMSTRONG RANGER RESEARCH CENTER, TEXAS RANGER HALL OF FAME & MUSEUM.*

Outlaws supreme. From L to R: Roll and Del Dublin. *COURTESY DAVE JOHNSON.*

CHAPTER 5

"Sworn Enemy to Rangers and Sheriffs"

INCESSANT COMINGS AND GOINGS OF fellows jumping back and forth, into and out of the Frontier Battalion makes for a mindboggling task. Thanks to Major Jones' bureaucratic leanings, paper trails are extant. Resultantly, while retaining their lines on the payroll, most Texas Rangers and their company's enforcement activities may be followed—even if loosely and from afar. When an impulsive fellow drops off the company books is when it sometimes turns foggy. Private citizen Frank Jones, at age twenty-one, is no exception.

For whatever reason young Frank wanted to give life on Curry Creek another try. Unlike so many rural raised youths and although he was handy with a gun and at home horseback, an ever vigorous Frank opted to forego the cowboy life and give farming a go.

Although no longer an active Texas Ranger, it is quite clear Frank Jones was somewhat still in the loop—and more than favorably recognized by Major John B. Jones. The Frontier Battalion's commander cut Frank Jones in on an alert: the Rangers were hunting for and looking to arrest John Gorman. Did the ex-Ranger know his whereabouts? In a December 17, 1877, letter Frank Jones responded: "I am told by a young man recently from the Llano that there is a man living somewhere above Junction City whose name is Gorman but he is living under an assumed name and that he had forgotten [the alias]."[1] Cementing the contention that Frank Jones and Major Jones were *bueno amigos*, despite the age difference, may be extrapolated from another portion of the revealing letter.

While yet a Company F Ranger Frank Jones was—on the sly—checking up on another Texas Ranger, based on disturbing information he had somehow stumbled upon:

> You are probably not aware that Jack Miller, who was a member of Capt. Coldwell's Co. the three months unappropriated time, had prior to his joining the company broke jail and fled from Limestone County for killing a man there. I tried while in Lt. Dolan's Company to ascertain if there was any indictment against him but never learnt definitely whether there was or not.[2]

Yet a private citizen, it seems the investigative bug wouldn't let go of Frank Jones' pant leg. Seemingly he was still checking up on the Millers, advising Major Jones: "Lum Miller (a brother of Jack) has a wife in Limestone County and one here. They are both living here and are bad men and the community would be glad to be rid of them."[3] Making sure Major Jones understood that just because he wasn't maintaining official law enforcement status, if he could, Frank would willingly—with pleasure—still supply any information that would or might lead to the arrest of "fugitives from justice." He was at this point, however, not ready to reenlist with the Frontier Battalion, mainly due to finances: "A private's pay would not induce me to join anymore."[4]

Postulating that Frank Jones, while tilling the soil facing the flatulent behinds of a team of mules, often daydreamed about past days with the Rangers is not irrational. Was he really going to trudge after mules' hind-ends forever? No doubt—when he could—Frank followed the latest gossip about his friends and their travels scouting after Indians and bad men while the battalion's companies were ginning headline copy for the newshounds and correspondents. If ever there was a period of carefree tranquility in Frank Jones' life it was now—farming at Curry Creek.

The whole clan was at homeland. Though aging, mama Keziah was there, feisty as ever! Brother Dood Jones was industriously studying for the law, but raising sheep in the meantime. Younger brother Emmett was farming alongside Frank. Pink was a talented area lawyer. And, besides being the U.S. Census Enumerator for Curry Creek, attorney brother William Kenner Jones, his wife Rosilla and their toddling daughter Elizabeth called the neighborhood home.[5] The other twin, James Russell Jones, was there also, along with his wife, Mollie, the daughter of that aforementioned Indian fighting Doctor James C. Nowlin, and their continually growing brood, which would in the end total ten, twin boys and eight precious girls.[6] And though he maintained Texas Ranger tradition by coming and going and going some more, Curry Creek was likewise the birthplace of the notable John Woodard "Wood" Saunders, a ring-tailed tooter on one stage and a sure enough plucky Ranger, "a forceful man devoid of fear" on the other.[7]

However others were living in dread. The family of John B. Jones, now the Texas Adjutant General, and troops of the Frontier Battalion were in fear of the worst. Their beloved kinsmen by blood, marriage, and workplace camaraderie was first slowly, then rapidly, succumbing to seriously advancing—racing—health issues. Namely Jones was suffering the deficiency of a hale and hearty functioning liver. Subsequent to treatment by a team of renowned and accomplished physicians, and several painful aspirations of his liver, the once hard-charging and hard-riding commander of the Frontier Battalion, now weighing but ninety-eight pounds, was at trail's end. At but forty-six years of age, on July 19, 1881, John B. Jones passed to the other side.[8] Deferentially the *Galveston Daily News*, in part, opined:

> for his active, earnest work, by his upright, manly and consistent bearing, and his noble efforts to secure the reign of law and the supremacy of order, he has won a name and a fame that will be enduring, and has secured for himself a warm place in the affectionate regards of all the people of Texas.[9]

For Frank Jones the hiatus at Curry Creek was just that—temporary—albeit a short multi-year stopover while he cleared his head.

Could the death of John B. Jones, his mentor and friend, have had a sledgehammer impact on Frank? At twenty-five it was time to step to the lick-log—make a decision—was he meant to be a farmer or fighter, plowman or peace officer? The choice was his. And he made it!

On the twenty-eighth day of July 1881, less than ten days after the death of Adjutant General Jones, Frank Jones enlisted in the Frontier Battalion's Company D, then commanded by the previously noted Daniel Webster "Dan" Roberts, and headquartered in Menard County.[10] Though not of imposing physical stature, the dark complected gray-eyed Private Frank Jones was already a known and proven product: cool under pressure and a dynamo in a scrap—a six-shooter scrap. Perhaps more importantly, though, Frank Jones had leadership potential, a quality not missed by the hierarchy. Frank Jones could now make or break his career as a Texas Ranger.

This time around, with experience under his belt, almost immediately Private Frank Jones' name is specified as the man in charge of an enforcement action: "Aug 26th. Pvts. [Frank] Jones, [T. H.] Hammer and [G. M.] Hughes made scout to Junction City to keep the peace by request of Dept Sheriff. Arrested 'Bill' Taylor. Charged with assault with intent to Murder (2 cases)."[11] That Private Frank Jones was the nominal leader of the Texas Ranger trio is drawn from Captain Dan Roberts' succinct summation of the apprehension, noting that Bill Taylor had been arrested by "Pvt. Jones & others" and that the wanted fellow had been transported to Menard and turned over to the sheriff, H. W. Merrill.[12]

During the standard motions of reorganizing battalion companies at the end of August the managerial career of Frank Jones was launched: As of September 1, 1881, he was promoted to the noncommissioned rank of corporal. He was at once thrust into supervisory duties: Traveling with three privates, Corporal Jones took up temporary station at San Saba, San Saba County, during a term of district court and then moved into Kendall County to "guard Kendall against violence." It was a twenty-one-day assignment. As the month closed, Corporal Jones was at Fredericksburg with four men assisting longtime sheriff John Walter.[13]

September 1 had also been meaningful for another of the brothers. Following Frank's lead, Emmett "Spunk" Jones had enlisted as a Texas Ranger private with Company D.[14] The following month Company D underwent a significant change: Captain Roberts resigned. Taking his place as commander of the company, Lamar Pemberton "Lam" Sieker was promoted from sergeant to lieutenant.[15]

A charter member of the Frontier Battalion, the thirty-four-year-old Lam Sieker was a splendid choice. Lam Sieker's influence on the Texas Rangers was profound. The Confederate veteran, aside from being personally gutsy, was wedded to an idea. One of his core beliefs was that a true Ranger—a good Ranger—should have fundamental principles, a doctrine of duty.[16] Lam Sieker desired Frontier Battalion service of only men who wanted to be there. For those that couldn't or wouldn't hack it and were bellyaching about being discharged—even predating their agreed terms of enlistment—well, by damn that was just fine by him. The guy looking for an early way out ceased "to be a good Ranger, for the reason he lacks interest and does only what he is compelled to do, and does not do his duty from a sense of duty as a good Ranger should." Sieker was not wishy-washy. Though his contribution to the Rangers is more-often-than-not overlooked and underplayed, Lam Sieker was one—maybe the one—that instilled ideas of upholding honorable tradition, commendable work ethics, and a stalwart spirit of camaraderie within the Frontier Battalion's lower-level ranks. The much ballyhooed and legitimate Ranger *esprit de corps* flowered by his example—and at his insistence.[17]

As fall ebbed toward winter and the closing of 1881, it was abundantly clear Corporal Frank Jones was on top of his game. During December, riding at the head of a four-man detail, besides ensuring peace during the district court session at Llano, which he thought was "very necessary to prevent violence," Corporal Jones also made a general sweep though the country. At Llano he arrested an alleged cattle thief. At Crabapple Creek the detachment latched on to Albert Smith, charged with Attempt to Murder, and before returning to camp, at or near Enchanted Rock took into custody a man accused of horse theft. The fifteen-day scout covering 360 miles put him in good stead with the Ranger front office.[18] Lieutenant Lam Sieker was not faring as well. The Rangers were morphing into topnotch crime-fighters—slowly but steadily—however the outfit was not impervious to bureaucratic nitpicking. The dumbfounded Company D commander was asked to justify his rationale for expending state funds on "stem matches."[19] Extravagance?

Though he was justifiably busy into the first two months of a new year, Corporal Jones was forced or chose by the hurdles of undisclosed family business to voluntarily discharge from the Frontier Battalion on the last day of February 1882.[20] In writing to the adjutant general regarding Frank Jones' resignation, Lieutenant Lam Sieker was decidedly complimentary: "Corpl. Jones is a good Ranger and although I hate to give him up, I recommend his discharge at his urgent request for the reason he states. He states his business is urgent and requests that it date from March 1st (or rather Feb. 28)."[21] The urgency of Frank's personal business is unclear.

Whether or not the willful separation from the Rangers interplayed in someway with one of his brother's political moves is up for grabs. William Kenner Jones, smart as a whip, had been holding down the elected position of county attorney for Kendall County, maintaining an office and home at Boerne, the county seat. In addition to his public service duties, William Kenner partnered with his brother Pinckney, also an attorney, in a general law practice and real-estate venture. William K. Jones' comment is short and sweet and markedly not too terribly revealing: "I resigned my office of County Attorney and in 1882 moved to Curry's Creek and bought some sheep and tried the stock raising business."[22] Precisely pinpointing private citizen Frank Jones' economic interests and/or personal family business and/or conflicted career aspirations during this period is for the most part not viable. There is broad leeway for speculation and abstract questions, but no solid answers.[23]

During February, besides Frank Jones and the Texas Rangers parting company, a couple of other personnel matters were disposed of. Corporal T. H. Hammer was reduced in rank for "being drunk and disorderly," and Private S. J. Rawls was handed a Dishonorable Discharge for "allowing a prisoner to escape through carelessness."

Lieutenant Sieker was no martinet, but he would not be bulldozed by misbehavior and sloppy inattention to duty.[24] On the other hand, the Company D commander was not an insensitive hard-liner if a man had been pulling his weight. The stricture about privates and noncoms being single men was yet in place. So, when Ranger S. D. Coalson asked to be discharged early "to get married" the lieutenant gave the okay, but only because the young man had "been a good and efficient ranger for several years. . . ."[25]

Hardly had Corporal Frank Jones' name been removed from the company books before his brother Spunk's name was in the book, well, a newspaper. Childishly interjecting himself into Frontier Battalion personnel matters, Spunk, not yet twenty-one, penned a letter to the editor of the *Union Land Register*. Perhaps somewhat boldly he defended one of his friends in another company suffering disciplinary sanctions. For this instance—which was not normally the case—it seems Spunk's spine was fashioned from spaghetti not steel: Rather than sign the letter truthfully, Spunk resorted to using the *non de plume* Omelio Krousse. Conjecturally had he consulted Frank first the letter may have been burned in the campfire prior to a post office drop. Absolutely Lieutenant Lam Sieker was in no mood for benevolence. He was under no little pressure to offer an explanation—an excuse—to Adjutant General Wilburn H. King who was madder than a stirred-up hornet. Delicately, trying to offer a modicum of protection for Spunk, Lieutenant Sieker replied that "the communication is but the opinion of an individual and is not the sentiment of this company."[26] Lieutenant Sieker's dousing the embers of administrative outrage with his unruffled tactfulness, somewhat cooled the hot passion for booting Spunk Jones out of the Rangers on-the-spot.

A significant change for the enforcement activities of Company D took place during Frank Jones' absence. Heretofore the majority of scouts originated from the headquarters camp, and returned upon completion, whether it was just a day or days later. Due to an unceasing staking of railroad tracks and the attendant riffraff following those tracks Ranger tactics were tweaked. Though the company was yet based at Camp King near Uvalde, a six-man detachment was located further west in Pecos County during June 1882.[27]

That West Texas could stand a Ranger or two is evidenced by the Record of Scouts submitted by the Pecos detachment the following month. They arrested two supposed burglars, one alleged thief, and four six-shooting fellows charged with Attempt to Murder, who they turned over to the county sheriff, John Edgar, a lawman of long-standing. They also captured a U.S. Army deserter and turned him over to military authorities at Fort Clark.[28] Lieutenant Sieker tended to some July business at Uvalde too. He handed Corporal Ruff Jenkins his walking papers, dishonorably discharging him due to his "drunkenness."[29]

Company D troops working out of Camp King were likewise busy. Spunk Jones and another Ranger private, M. D. Davis, arrested suspected murderer and thief Mike Kelly at Eagle Pass (in Maverick County) and turned him over to the local sheriff. Others chased after horse thieves in Edwards County, recovering a stolen mule before a torrential downpour washed out the suspects' trail. For the detachment stationed at Pecos the month of August was a blurred string of activity making arrests and transporting prisoners, routine duty—almost. Of notable significance was the detachment's participation with the local sheriff in seizing the McCafferty Saloon for dispensing distilled spirits absent the required liquor license.[30] Sponsors of what could be characterized as traditional vice would hardly ever be favorably disposed toward Texas Rangers.

As the time-honored reorganization date rolled around, the first day of September, Frank Jones reenlisted in Company D, still headquartered on the outskirts of Uvalde, at Camp King.[31] Chances that he delivered Lam Sieker, since promoted to captain, an ultimatum are slim—and certainly have yet to surface, but when Frank reentered the Ranger service it was as Company D's 1st Sergeant.[32] The march to a captaincy was underway.

The march for Private Spunk Jones was underway, too. When the round-Robin automatic discharges took place, Spunk either voluntarily or involuntarily did not want to or was not customarily reenlisted in Company D. He was a six-shooter-wearing and Winchester toting Texas Ranger no more: Notation on the Monthly Return simply being, "Discharged by reason of expiration of term of service."[33] Spunk Jones' days as a Texas lawman were finished.[34]

Captain Sieker wasn't too concerned—apparently—about Spunk Jones separating from the Frontier Battalion. His attention was focused on the headwaters of the Devils River, particularly since there had been no Texas Ranger presence in the area for quite some time. The unit's commander had processed hearsay chatter that there was "considerable cattle crookedness" in that section of Company D's assigned territory.[35] The following month, October 1882, Captain Sieker personally oversaw five Rangers scouting the Devils River country in surveyed but yet to be organized Crockett County (Ozona). As so often is the case in law enforcement work, it was learned that the "cattle crookedness" was but rumored supposition—the report "being false."[36]

Many would be the critics of Texas Rangers carping about the outfit involving itself in local and/or statewide politics. Generalized statements are inappropriate in most instances but suggesting that the ugly head of partisan politics showed itself during the Frontier Battalion era—and later—is unquestionably truthful. And though it's more frequently than not overlooked, in several of those cases the rank and file Texas Rangers were but doing what damn good Rangers had taken an oath to do—follow orders! The November 1882 election had spurred upper echelon Texas Ranger brass, answering pleas of borderland county sheriffs, to disperse their legions—Company D was in the mix. Specifically in response to one such order Captain Sieker ambled into Uvalde and from the Western Union office on the first day of November sent a telegram to AG King: "Will do as ordered. Start men to Rio Grande City tomorrow."[37]

Two days later Captain Lam Sieker updated the adjutant general with his deployment strategy: "In compliance with your telegram I dispatched 3 men to Rio Grande City by forced marches. I will go to Eagle Pass, and will have detachments at Del Rio & Brackettville. I have given men on this service special instructions as to their duties in this matter & cautioned against interfering at the polls."[38] Sergeant Frank Jones was not exempt. For this election cycle he was in charge of a three-man detachment sent to Del Rio, in what was then Kinney County, but is now Val Verde County. The first half of the sergeant's orders were/are rather easily deciphered. Frank

Jones was to "assist civil authorities in keeping peace at the polls." Although there is no indication of any problematic behavior taking place on the November 7 election day, the latter portion of Sergeant Jones' instructions was "to prevent illegal voting." Captain Sieker and two privates took a station at Eagle Pass for the election, with much the same intent, but with a helping of ambiguity: "to aid the civil authorities in keeping the peace and to prevent the voting of nonresident Mexicans during the election. . . ."[39]

Determining with concrete validity exactly who was legally entitled to vote may have been tricky, but assuredly Barney McCafferty had a nasty trick or two up his sleeve. The thoroughly disgruntled saloon man shot a scorching missive to a journalist and when readers unfolded pages of the *San Antonio Daily Express* there was an accusation that Texas Rangers had been behaving badly—bullying and bragging and popping caps on both whiskey bottles and the cartridges in wheels of their Colt's six-shooters.[40] The outrageous shenanigans, if true, were to have taken place aboard a train. Faced with the very public accusations, there was little Adjutant General King could do—except send Captain Sieker to investigate purported misconduct of his men.

Subsequent to conducting several interviews in West Texas—even the train conductor on duty at the time of alleged tomfoolery—Captain Lam Sieker, at length, met the angry Barney McCafferty head-on. To say the fellow was peeved would be an understatement. He owned a litany of grievances. The Company D commander heard an earful: "Yes, I reported the matter to the Express and I told them I would. I have been broken up nearly by Sheriffs & Rangers and I don't intend to let up on them until I get through with my suits. They closed up my saloon and sold me out and Kept my brother a prisoner for 7 days when I was taking in 70$ per day, sold me out for some 200$, sold my whiskey that cost 250 for .50 cts. per gallon. I have brought suit against the sheriff of Pecos Co for damages."[41]

When questioned by Captain Sieker, the disgruntled McCafferty sheepishly admitted that the only Texas Ranger on the train, Corporal B. D. Lindsey, was not drunk, but that a deputy sheriff that he just supposed was a Ranger may have been drinking. Yes, the Ranger and the deputy had disarmed three Mexicans who had been drunkenly shooting out a passenger coach's window. Holding a political hot potato is not much fun and Adjutant General King was dexterously maneuvering while waiting for word from his ace investigator, Lam Sieker. The Company D captain didn't miss a beat nor mince words:

> He [McCafferty] stated that there were several drunken men aboard which is not only a daily but hourly sight in that section, since the advent of the Rail Road. . . . And from what he had to say in general he is a sworn enemy to Rangers, Sheriffs and everybody else nearly. So to recapitulate the result of my investigation I find there was but one Ranger aboard the train and he was not drunk. There was no shooting at telegraph poles. There were no insulators shot off. The loads were shot out of the pistols taken from the Mexicans. Shooting off the train is almost a daily thing from San Antonio west. . . . So the charges as they appear to me are a glaring prevarication prompted by a dislike to Sheriffs & Rangers for a real or imaginary wrong done him in closing up his Saloon and selling it out according to law for taxes. . . . I don't want to be drawn into a newspaper controversy with such a man as nothing I could say would damage him much.[42]

There's little doubt that while Captain Sieker was off tending to matters—hoping he could put a lid on specious publicity about his detachment stationed in Pecos County, Sergeant Frank Jones was busy at Camp King. Designation of their headquarters as a "camp" is important, for a camp is exactly what it was—home for Company D, a canvas home, thanks to the arrival of two more "splendid tents." As the company's 1st sergeant it was part of Frank's responsibility to ensure their quarters were adequate for the upcoming winter. Company stores had to be amply stocked. Firewood had to be laid by. Enough hay and grain held in reserve. For a thoroughly committed and competent 1st Sergeant the work was never done. These Rangers, no matter how idyllic or romantic it may sound, were living in real time and an unforeseen Blue Norther can be real cold. Thanks to Frank's due diligence and developing managerial skills, he had—with the men's help—whipped the camp into shape. Proudly, Captain Sieker reported to Battalion Quartermaster Neal Coldwell: "I have gone into winter quarters and have everything fixed up very snug—stalls built for every horse and a good mule corral. Grass is good and I think stock will do well here all winter. Men are in good health and spirit, and horses & mules in good fix. . . . I was very sorry you and the General [AG King] did not pay me the promised visit, I wanted to show you a model Ranger camp."[43]

For Sergeant Frank Jones the last manhunt of 1882 was on the seventh day of December when he led three privates during an unsuccessful chase "down the Rail Road" after three U.S. Army deserters. By Ranger standards it had been a rather anemic scout of twenty-five miles, and one half-day.[44] There is little doubt the Company D boys were sticking close to camp, polishing their six-shooters and filling their cartridge-belts. Captain Sieker—almost with glee—reported that he and the men were "waiting for the usual Christmas rows to make some work."[45]

Unromantically for the testosterone-charged boys of Company D and contrary to Captain Lam Sieker's earlier prediction, December 25 came and went, serenely fading into the night: "Christmas passed off quietly and very dull for Rangers." The thermometer's mercury had plunged, not good news for chaps basically living outside twenty-four and seven. In fact, in two separate communications to Ranger headquarters the captain regrettably reported: "Some 3 or 4 men sick in camp with chills & fever and bad colds caused by bad weather" and "Some sickness in camp, chills & fever and bad colds, caused by bad weather."[46]

Sergeant Frank Jones wasn't answering to "sick-call" during January of 1883, a busy month. Aside from his routine administrative duties as the company's top noncom, he was tasked with hunting down a horse thief. Jones successfully carried out the assignment, recovering three stolen horses and arresting the alleged thief, identified only in the Recapitulation of Arrests as a "Mexican." Forthrightly Sergeant Jones turned his prisoner over to Uvalde County Sheriff J. B. Boatright, who was just shy of holding an indictment with a familiar name—his.[47]

While his 1st Sergeant was holding down the fort at Camp King, Captain Sieker rushed to the vicinity of Del Rio to probe the shooting and killing of an Indian—yet a newsmaker for 1883. From the best information he could develop a "Mexican" was afoot returning to his home near the Rio Grande. Drawing close he heard his wife's horrified screams and rushed to her rescue. Then, before his very eyes, he beheld an Indian—a Lipan Apache—in possession of one of his children, caught in the act. When the would-be kidnapper saw the homeowner he quickly let go of the child and started shooting at the father with a six-shooter. Daddy was in no mood for such. He raised his carbine and killed the Indian with a single shot. Other Indians in the nearby brush hotfooted toward the river and the safety it might provide. Upon examination of the corpse it was found that the Indian was wearing "four shirts, two pair of pants, coat, Hat, two pr socks and a pair of Mexican moccasins. His clothes were of American make." Captain Sieker was a day late and a bullet short but he vowed to the state's adjutant general: "I shall be on the alert, and should they show themselves again will pursue."[48]

Sergeant Jones was in pursuit, too! There was an officer's commission to be had, why not him? Successful had been the political try of Company F's recently commissioned commander, Charles Brown "C. B." McKinney. With aplomb during a hotly contested race he had reeled in the top law enforcing job in La Salle County (seat Cotulla). There was no longer an opening for the position of La Salle County Sheriff, but there was now a blank spot at the top of the Company F roster.[49] Several aspirants were vying for the job, Frank Jones in the lineup.

Frank Jones would be no shrinking violet: He damn sure wanted to land the job and would campaign for it vigorously. Taking pen in hand, Sergeant Jones scratched out a letter to Adjutant General King making his feelings known and pledging that he already had the support of Captains Sieker and Coldwell. Furthermore—and it's striking—Frank Jones apprised King that a judge and several members of the bar were visiting in Eagle Pass and unfortunately they had already willingly signed a petition of support for another eager applicant, Josephus "Joe" Shely. Had they known better, which they didn't, one and all "have since voluntarily expressed their regret that they had not Known that I would be an applicant as they would have much preferred endorsing me." [50] Perhaps Jones' aver is spot on. Or, were the gentlemen advocating for his opponent's backfilling the Company F vacancy taking the trouble-free route, telling Jones that they would have supported him but had they known? Thus far the record seems silent about anyone of those guys' publicly throwing support Frank's way.

Pulling out the stops, Frank Jones tried to double down. His brother Pinckney, now practicing law at Eagle Pass, was partnered with A. M. Oliphant for their private practice. On the public front Pinckney Jones was District Attorney for the 25th Judicial District of Texas.[51] Using letterhead stationery Pinckney fierce touted his brother Frank to no less a personality than the Honorable John Ireland, Governor of Texas: "My bother has been in the Front Batt three or four years, has the confidence of the Capt of his Company, and would be warmly recommended by Capt Neal Coldwell, Quartermaster, as in every way well qualified to command and especially fitted for the nature of the service required in the section where the Company is now stationed. . . ." Dipping into the well of barefaced partisan politics, attorney Pinckney Jones further elaborated, trying to cajole the chief executive: "and last but by no means least, like myself, he [Frank] has been an <u>Ireland</u> <u>Man</u> ever since the Schleicher canvass. Believing that his appointment would give universal satisfaction, I would most respectfully ask that you use your influence with General King in securing him the position. Noting with pleasure, the almost universal satisfaction which your administration, so far, has given. . . ."[52] Frank might have offered "universal satisfaction," but Joe Shely got the job!

Someone that didn't have a job was Private E. P. Flagg. Captain Lam Sieker was not happy. Private Flagg—unbelievably it seems—sold his horse without permission. A Ranger with no horse was no Ranger—and certainly not a good Ranger. Flagg earned a Dishonorable Discharge. Aside from an insight into Sieker's mindset, which was unquestionably serving as an example for up and coming Rangers with career advancement on their agendas, like

Frank Jones, the report of Private Flagg's firing contained a genuine clue about the Frontier Battalion's try at professionalizing. Captain Sieker advised AG King to put Flagg "on the list of weighed and found wanting."[53] Clearly, though it was not fodder for public consumption, the Ranger front office was keeping a covert roster—fellows that couldn't or wouldn't cut it.

Snooping into Sergeant Jones' frame of mind about being passed over for the Company F officer's job is not feasible if guesswork is disallowed. Likewise, though it will register as supposition, Sergeant Frank Jones could not have been pleased with the next promotion affecting Company D. Hardly anyone else was either.

Immodestly and vociferously Georg Heinrich "George" Schmitt, a former multi-term sheriff of Comal County, made it known he was bound and determined—dead set—on becoming a Frontier Battalion captain. Such an ambitious game plan for an outsider was no problem. Schmitt was an insider. At least he was in the eyes of a powerhouse political player, Governor Ireland. The fellows were personal friends. Therefore it should not be a shocker since no captain's slots were vacant Schmitt could be and would be commissioned a lieutenant until such time as a company commander's job became available. There was not a Company D lieutenant and had not been since the day Lam Sieker had promoted to captain.[54] By nature George Schmitt was aggressive.[55] By strength of personality he owned a colossal ego and outsized work ethic.[56] Lieutenant Schmitt's hardnosed and pigheaded line of attack may have put the fear of God in the minds of criminals he had promised to capture, but such style for camp life was not tolerable. Not for the rank and file of Company D: They despised him.[57]

Lieutenant Schmitt's arrival at Camp King highlights a Ranger truism in play at the time. Unmistakably the outfit was functioning—at least loosely—on a military model of organization. As such there was a well-defined chain-of-command and an equivalently distinct pecking order. Sergeant Frank Jones was both victim and recipient, as evidenced in a letter to headquarters. Undoubtedly the captain was badly in need of wall-tents to suitably house his men based on their pay grade. Captain Sieker's appeal makes such undeniably plain: "When I ordered tents I was not aware that I would have a Lieut, so I will be one short now that Lieut Schmitt is here. I will now require 8 tents in all, one for myself, one for Lt. Schmitt, one for supplies, One for the first Sergt [Frank Jones] and 1 man, and four for the Sixteen remaining men or 4 men to the tent. Hope you will comply with my request."[58] Later events will unmistakably reveal Frank Jones was not hostile to advantaging himself with the perks of advancement.

Spring of 1883 would find Sergeant Jones riding at the head of a four-man detachment, blistering forth south from Uvalde County and into unorganized Zavalla County (Crystal City), a genuine tough piece of ground near but not touching the Texas/Mexico border. The Rangers' work—on paper—was simple: Search for stolen horses in the gargantuan Bowels Ranch's main pasture. Sergeant Jones and his relentless Rangers rounded up seven head, and turned the stolen steeds over to their rightful owners. Toward the end of the month, the twenty-third of April, Sergeant Jones and two privates scouted up the Nueces River and across to the Frio River looking for another band of horses allegedly stolen. As but seemingly par business for Frank Jones, the horses were located and temporarily seized. However, upon inspection it was "found the title to the horses to be good."[59] The whole affair had consumed three days.

When Sergeant Frank Jones returned to Camp King on April 26 there were new recruits to greet, one he already knew, Wood Saunders from Curry Creek, and another who would shortly become, plausibly, the most widely known noncom of the Frontier Battalion era, Austin Ira Aten, a twenty-year-old from the Travis/Williamson County line.[60] One of the first orders of business was to see that Ira Aten was properly outfitted with arms. He was at once issued a Winchester carbine and Colt's six-shooter, as well as a saddle scabbard for the .44-40 lever gun, and a "Pistol belt and Holster."[61] Wood Saunders was already well fixed with firepower, having seen previous Ranger service near ten years earlier in Company F, during the summer of 1874—when he was but a seventeen-year-old.[62]

Certainly the managerial skills of Sergeant Frank Jones were sharpening as each day passed. In the absence of both Captain Sieker and Lieutenant Schmitt, Frank was the noncom in charge of company matters at Camp King, even directly corresponding with the adjutant general at Austin regarding company business.[63] Without doubt Frank had covered a great deal of ground on the pathway to maturity since those earlier days, when as a sixteen-year-old lad he had been hard riding to the sound of a bugle with the Kendall County Minutemen. The Jones clan was a bloodline of intrepid fighters and patriots and public spirited stalwarts. Frank would courageously carry that banner of tradition.

That Captain Sieker was ever steadfast with separating the wheat from the chaff, the weeds of disgruntlement from the flowering promise of boys turning into good men and good men turning into good Rangers may be drawn from another of his personnel actions. In but a heartbeat he sent a Texas Ranger private packing, because he "was dissatisfied and did not think he could faithfully discharge his duty and a whole string of complaints about his mistreatment." Furthermore the young man must have been suffering from "some abnormity of mind" even questioning the decision-making processes of his supervisor—not superior—but his boss.[64] Captain Sieker had another move on his mind, too. Taking advantage of the better condition of grass and fresh water the Company D headquarters camp was relocated, yet with mail picked up at town, but now on the banks of the Leona River about five miles southeast of Uvalde. Fittingly the new encampment was christened Camp Leona.[65]

Working the historic trail behind Sergeant Jones is doable but at this juncture a shortsighted methodology for taking a full measure of the man. During this period Jones exercised sound judgment and judicious supervisory tact, gradually building and earning his subordinates' admiration and trust and willingness—as will later be seen—to metaphorically follow him straight through the gates of Hell for duels with the Devil. Company D Monthly Returns and general correspondence files are not barren, but pregnant with reports of scouts, sometimes with good results and sometimes returning to camp tired, hungry, and empty handed.[66] This is a timeframe, where for the most part, Sergeant Jones was a conduit for orders filtering down from above. Every day he walked the tightrope between energetic privates and corporals who, at any given moment could slip off of the half-cock notch, and the upper management team concerned with finances and procurement and forging Texas Ranger policy. The top sergeant's life and day by day workload was/is never easy. On the other hand, those with gumption and grit and guts enough to stick with it develop technical and procedural skills irreplaceable. Sergeant Jones was not on vacation: He'd come to stay!

Sadly, pitiable news flashed from Eagle Pass. Pinckney Jones had unexpectedly died on the fifteenth day of July 1883, survived by his three-year-old son, Alexander Paul, and his pregnant wife Elizabeth (Barr) Jones who six months later birthed a beautiful baby girl, Lizzie Pinckney.[67] Though the documentable record is silent—at least up till now—whether or not a distraught Sergeant Frank Jones was able to make an appearance at his brother's memorial service is but speculative: Eagle Pass was spotted not too terribly far southwest of field headquarters for Company D, Camp Leona.

The intrigues and machinations of Lieutenant Schmitt had not abated. He yet yearned for a captaincy. Enlisting Texas State Senator George Pfeuffer to impertinently push his cause, Schmitt was unrelenting with efforts to elbow his way to fulfilling the dream. Pfeuffer hurriedly pitched in, writing to AG King: "Can you give Geo. H. Schmitt the Captaincy or put him in charge of a detachment himself? Del Rio would be a suitable place for him with a small force. Of this you know best. If you do not think him worthy of a more responsible position that he has occupied up to the present—I should advise him to resign—hence ask you to give the matter your earliest attention."[68] It seemed nothing would quench Schmitt's thirst for advancement, but there was a downside. For the boys of Company D nothing would slake their appetite better than the right fast departure of Lieutenant George Schmitt—straight out of the company and real quick, to boot!

A petition circulated around camp requesting that Schmitt find a home elsewhere. Whether the noise found its way into pages of the *San Antonio Daily Light* due to a blunder or on purpose is immaterial. The headline was gossipy: **Want Him Out**. The editor's comment that there may have been underlying motivation for

Schmitt's removal, such as, "Some other fellow most likely wants to step into his shoes" is a newspaperman's hypothesis but may have had a ring of truth.

Certainly, career wise, Lieutenant Schmitt's moving on, one way or the other, presented a possibility of benefit to Sergeant Jones. There is no quantifiable proof Frank Jones stirred the pot of discontent, none whatsoever. There are two hard truths, however. To assuage the incessant whining and backroom plots it was much easier to promote Schmitt than deny his ambition. Adjutant General W. H. King knew who buttered the Rangers' bread and who owned the churn; those state legislators approving or rejecting budgets, like State Senator Pfeuffer. In the end both the fellows of Company D and Schmitt were happy. Company C in the faraway Texas Panhandle had a new leader and Captain Sieker's boys at Uvalde were short a lieutenant.[69]

Pinckney "Pink" Jones, one of Frank's older brothers, and a powerhouse lawyer at Eagle Pass, Maverick County. Unfortunately Pink Jones died of natural causes at age twenty-nine. FROM *TEXAS RANGER SKETCHES*, COURTESY THE AUTHOR ROBERT W. STEPHENS.

Company D: General Camp photo illustrating that the rank and file Texas Rangers were living in tents, enjoying pleasantries and cleanness and aromas of an outdoor atmosphere—twenty-four, and seven. *Courtesy Armstrong Ranger Research Center, Texas Ranger Hall of Fame & Museum.*

Lamartine Pemberton "Lam" Sieker was truly one of the great Texas Ranger Captains, racking up more Frontier Battalion seniority than anyone. Though pictured here in his military uniform, Frontier Battalion-era Rangers were not required to don such attire. Texas Rangers as civilian Indian fighters and peace keepers wore clothes to suit their needs. Captain Sieker and Frank Jones were particularly close personal friends. *Courtesy Armstrong Ranger Research Center, Texas Ranger Hall of Fame & Museum.*

A delightful photo of a young Austin Ira Aten, about the time he became a Texas Ranger in Company D. Arguably Aten would become the most widely known noncom Texas Ranger throughout the Lone Star State. Much of the law-enforcing craft was incorporated into Ira's résumé by his service under the supervisory leadership of Frank Jones. *Courtesy Jeri and Gary Boyce Radder.*

Emmett "Spunk" Jones. Although a fine fellow at heart and a good Texas Ranger, young Spunk Jones erred when he took a ghost name of Omelio Krousse and penned a letter to the Union Land Register, interjecting himself into the disciplinary affairs of another Ranger. *Courtesy Lexie Van Tassel.*

CHAPTER 6

"Sixty Thousand Dollars to Spend"

Sergeant Frank Jones was as unyielding as Captain Sieker with bringing Company D Rangers up to snuff in regards to professionalizing and transitioning into crackerjack law enforcers. Frequently, during Captain Lam Sieker's absences from camp, Sergeant Frank Jones was left in command of company operations.[1] Such hard work and dedication was not lost on Captain Sieker but, perhaps more notably, the Frontier Battalion's front office was attuned to the young top-sergeant's keenness for accomplishing those ends. On May 13, 1884, Adjutant General King agreeably signed off on the Frontier Battalion's General Order No. 15. Among other noteworthy personnel actions, 1st Sergeant Frank Jones was officially commissioned as Company D's lieutenant, the promotion backdated to the first day of the month for payroll purposes.[2]

A new world had opened up for Frank Jones. Now he was fortunate enough not to have a roommate; lieutenants were afforded the privilege of privacy in their very own tent. Overnight he had transitioned into an elite status, more pay and more prestige. Promotions were not cost free. Now, as a member of the Frontier Battalion officer's corps, added weight was piled onto his shoulders. Intra-company squabbles were not unheard of and sometimes those messes imploded. Disciplinary matters were part of his purview, as was deftly fending off citizen complaints that Rangers were doing too much—or not enough. Even if the atmosphere was clear—not a cloud in the sky—it rained paperwork: invoices, receipts, inventories, reimbursements, and allotments guaranteeing proper rations for men and their mounts and the company's teams of mules. Strict accountability was now part of Lieutenant Frank Jones' new portfolio.[3]

Pocketing his newly earned officer's commission, Lieutenant Jones, perhaps having taken cues from his mentors, Major Jones and Captain Sieker, was not about to saddle himself purely with administrative duties, filling out paperwork beneath shade provided by a wall-tent's fly. During the same month of his promotion Lieutenant Frank Jones tracked down an alleged mule thief, Dave Ferguson. While on this scout Jones and one man also tried to find Charles Gatliff, charged with Murder, but were unsuccessful. Before returning to camp, Lieutenant Jones turned prisoner Ferguson over to the first appointed and then many times reelected Mason County Sheriff, John Calvin Butler, grocery store owner turned lawman, who had soon morphed into holy terror for would-be bad men. Before month's end Lieutenant Jones had returned to Mason County with intent to arrest Nick Ferguson (brother of Dave Ferguson?) but failed to find him.[4]

Due to unremitting lawlessness in Llano County, the Frontier Battalion management team had deduced that a detachment of Company D Rangers should take up residence at Bluffton, northeast of the county seat. The head man for the detachment was Benjamin Dennis "B. D." Lindsey, a Louisianan by birth, but now Company D's 1st Sergeant thanks to Frank Jones climbing rungs on the battalion's career-ladder.[5] Lindsey, Company D's former top corporal, was by any man's gauging a gentleman's gentlemen. Then again, when and if circumstances turned Western, Sergeant Lindsey was a fire-breathing lawman not shaking hands with trepidation—or fear.[6] For time spent scouting from his camp three miles west of Bluffton, Sergeant Lindsey's Reports of Scouts are jam-packed with perambulations throughout the countryside and an impressive trotline of arrests.[7] There was plenty of work.

Early on Ranger Lindsey noted that the section was home turf to at least "six or eight young men who are suspected as being thieves, robbers, and most anything else that is mean."[8] Additionally there were "old parties" that were keeping past feuds alive and were "continually waging war between each other." In the end, according to Lindsey's fact-finding tour and his informants' tips, "quite a bad element infests this section."[9] Rather disturbingly he also made note of surely not a subtle reality: "I learn from a reliable source that the local authorities in this [Llano County] and Burnett [*sic*] Co. are very inefficient in their duties and from my same observation of the men am not surprised."[10]

Assuring that the citizens, who were complaining loudly—in writing—would know that battalion headquarters and the Company D field commander were taking their concerns seriously by furnishing a Ranger from the officer's corps, Captain Sieker notified Adjutant General King: "I will send Lt. Jones to relieve Sergt. Lindsey in Llano Co. at once."[11] Lieutenant Jones, upon arrival at Llano, settled on incredibly prompt action, so notifying the battalion's brass at Austin: "I went to Bluffton on the 3rd inst. to take charge of the detachment there to ascertain if our services would be required in Llano during the present term of District Court. I saw Mr. Shaw (the Sheriff) and he said that he would write to you at once and that Rangers would be needed, and on that I moved the detachment here as Capt. Sieker had instructed me to do so if we were wanted. . . ." Lieutenant Jones, himself, concluded that his detachment was desperately needed at Llano and he didn't think "Court could hardly be held without the presence of Rangers." Once again, and somewhat sorry to say, he made the same observation as had Sergeant B. D. Lindsey: "The Sheriff is an utter failure as a peace officer."[12]

Augmenting Jones' less than favorable assessment of local law enforcers may be drawn from the fact that during the District Court's session he was "compelled to keep men in Town every night until 12 or one o'clock to keep the peace" and it was only the Texas Ranger presence at Llano that "prevented a serious outbreak."[13] Lieutenant Jones was anxiously anticipating the winding-down of cases on the District Court's docket. He had plans, personal plans, and he made them known to the adjutant general—an appeal:

> Sir: Can you give me ten days leave of absence to date from July 2nd. I have just heard from home and I am wanted there for a settlement of my father's estate. I have been home for only two days since Sept. 1882. Hoping to hear from you at once, I am Respectfully Frank Jones, Lieut. Co. D.[14]

Understandably and compassionately Adjutant General King approved Lieutenant Jones' entreaty for personal vacation time. With brothers as practicing attorneys the actual necessity of Frank Jones' presence at probating a Last Will & Testament or other matters of estate resolution will not be questioned. Also unchallenged will be realization that just because Lieutenant Jones took a holiday, the criminals didn't.

And some of that illegal handiwork was normally done under the cover of darkness and on the quiet: the clandestine snipping of barbed-wire. Contrary to popular belief, fence-cutting was not universally or even regionally or even locally condemned by everyone. In fact, during the introduction and initial stretching period of the prickly wire, most Texas neighborhoods were about equally divided regarding the product's worthwhile utility and actual economic value. Many folks—a majority—in San Saba County were not favorably disposed about the newfangled creation. Successfully banding together, those opposed to barbed-wire had made certain their elected officials were on record:

> Be it resolved by the Commissioners' Court of San Saba County that our members of the Legislature be required to use their endeavors to prevent the passage of any law making such fences legal, and to secure the passage of a law making it a penal offense for any one to use or own any such fence.[15]

Finally bending to reality, many of the big-time cattlemen—ex-Open Range cattlemen—were planting cedar post and tacking wire—miles and miles and miles of barbed-wire. Unfortunately in many instances their greedy approach to encircling as much land as they could grab—with good title or no title—was negatively impacting small-time ranchers, hardscrabble farmers, and sometimes even mail-carriers trying to get from point A to point B. There were demonstrable cases where someone living adjacent to or near a county's outer borderline, because of new four-wire fences, was unable to even navigate a necessary business trip to their very own courthouse. The metaphoric anchor more-or-less holding cattle to a given rangeland was water. Fences encompassing precious waterholes and live creeks could be a stockman's lifeblood—for cattle inside the wire. Outside the wire, cow creatures could dehydrate and die. The severe Texas drought of 1883 had not come at a good time relative to the reasonably recent introduction of barbed wire. During that year alone, 171 of the organized counties in the Lone Star State reported fence-cutting episodes, and in certain sections it was near pandemic. And here it's but important to note—most of the time—fence cutters were not simply clipping a gap to gain ingress or egress. No, their objective was to destroy the fence, snipping wire between posts, and then moving down the line and snipping wire between the next posts, and so on—mile after mile. The havoc they were purposefully fostering was to make it financially devastating to continually rebuild fences. Though exacting numbers are somewhat elusive, most estimates place the monetary loss incurred by fence cutting at about twenty million dollars. Too, the wire war that would revolutionize Texas was not bloodless: Barbs could be injurious, bullets could prove fatal. Otherwise honest men resorted to cutting a fence: Dishonest men gave it not a second thought. Texas Governor Ireland did, however![16]

He called a Special Session of the state legislature. Less than thirty days later, January 1884, the State of Texas had new laws on the books: Cutting someone's fence or burning someone's grassland pasture was upgraded to a felony—five years hard time at Huntsville, site of the state's penitentiary. The fresh statutes also required those putting up a fence to provide for an eight-foot gate every third mile—not locked—and made it a misdemeanor to open someone's gate and not close it after passing through. Oh yes, in light of lackluster performance in certain jurisdictions by local lawmen, Texas Rangers were specifically and lawfully handed the workload of catching Knights of Knippers, as fence cutters were sometimes called.[17]

Lieutenant Frank Jones and the Rangers of Company D were not idle or clueless about their newfound enforcement pursuit, catching wire cutters. Hardly having time to catch his breath after returning from his leave of absence, Lieutenant Jones was able to enthusiastically advise headquarters that the Llano detachment, which had recently repositioned from Bluffton, had "succeeded in capturing two fence cutters."[18] Credited with the arrest of George Stevens for Fence Cutting, Lieutenant Jones' old pal from Curry Creek, Corporal Wood Saunders, had turned his prisoner over to the no doubt taken aback sheriff of Llano County. Later during the month of July, Corporal Saunders and an unnamed private meandered into adjoining Mason County and arrested Will Putman for Fence Cutting. Thunderstruck may have been the sheriff after Rangers delivered Putman back to where the crime had been committed, Llano County.[19] Another Company D Ranger had a date with errant fence cutters.

In Edwards County the Greer brothers, Green B. and William Joseph, had in their minds acted with but a sense of self-survival. The previously alluded to drought was yet quenched, so the sheep raising brothers assured what precious water was still standing in deteriorating Green Lake—their lake—was for their use and their use only. A barbed-wire fence went up. A barbed-wire fence came down, at night. Loathing to just reconstruct the fence only to suffer its immediate destruction, again, Green Greer tuned to Governor Ireland—he wanted some Rangers to attend to business, his business: "Sir as I am almost certain that my fence is going to be cut as Soon as I close it I will wait one week longer before Closing it & would respectfully request you to Telegraph Capt. Sieker to Send Some men & let them come at Knight & Secret themselves So when I close it we can Ketch the fellows. They are going to be very Sly. . . ."[20]

Citizens' complaints to the governor's office, then or now, are handled deftly and speedily. Passing the buck is near effortless and customary for upper-level politicos dancing paths of least resistance. Green B. Greer's letter—the content—washed downhill from the governor's office to the adjutant general's office, then to Captain Sieker's Camp Leona and came to a stop just long enough for Company D's Corporal Philip C. Baird, and Privates Oscar D. Baker, W. W. Baker (no relation) and W. A. Mitchell to saddle their picketed horses and point noses northeast towards Edwards County and the Greer brothers' sheep rancho at Green Lake. Though it was scorching summertime, metaphorically, the boys weren't letting coattails bump their ass—get there quick and on the QT.[21]

Subsequent to the sun setting 28 July 1884, under the cover of darkness, the four Rangers pulled into the Greer Ranch making contact with the owners and were told where to best secret their horses. From that point they hoofed it about two miles, taking up a hidden position near Green Lake about 150 yards from the spitefully damaged and yet gaped open fence. The long night passed slowly.[22]

The next morning, right on schedule, the Greer's foreman John Landigan made an appearance with tools and materials to repair the downed fence. Also making a show were about 150 thirsty and bellowing beeves driven by four cowboys, M. D. "Mark" Hemphill, Henry Burton, John Brunson, and John Bailey, a courtroom convicted murderer and escaped convict using the alias John Mason.[23] Landigan's instructions had been plain spoken: Fix the fence and deny entry to anybody for any reason. There was good reason for John Landigan to demur from following his employers' orders: the ugly-looking muzzle of Mark Hemphill's Colt's .45 staring him straight between the eyes. The gaunt cattle drank. Landigan did naught. The Texas Rangers did naught. No fence had been cut!

Corporal Baird's orders had been plain spoken, too. Catch those damn wily fence cutters. Baird explained: "I witnessed the above fact from where I was concealed about 150 yds. from where it occurred but thought it best to remain silent until I had a sure case against them as I was confident they would cut the fence down again as soon as it was closed."[24] Corporal Baird had more to say:

> At this juncture it took quite an effort on my part to hold the boys down, as they "were raring to go" and anxious to open the ball, but in my judgment the time was not ripe for such action, owning to our position being at a disadvantage at this particular state of the game. I could see the "plum was ripening fast" and when the opportune time came to be plucked, business would pick up and get much warmer than it was on this already hot day.[25]

Time to pick the fruit would soon come. Several hours after watering the thirsting cattle, the four cowboys returned with a remuda of fifty saddle horses, clearly with intent to let them sip from Green Lake. This time, however, there was a problem—a big problem. The downed fence had been made upright—mended flawlessly by the thoroughly tired and sweaty John Landigan. Somewhat surprisingly in light of the early morning ugliness, Mark Hemphill did not whip out a scary looking Colt's .45 but did make a reach for something in his pocket—a pencil and paper. Instead of sending spiraling bullets Green Greer's way, Hemphill sent a handwritten message: The meaning was clear. Either make a gap in the fence so he could water the whinnying horses, or he and his boys would cut their way through, the law and the good boys Greer be goddamned! Shortly an answer from Green Greer was at hand, he had "refused to accede to their demands."[26]

Stepping from saddles, cowboys cut the fence. For Corporal Baird the plum had ripened. Remounting, the determined fellows drove the cavvyard of horses through the maliciously manufactured gateway and on to Green Lake. At this point in time Corporal Baird noted that he and his squad of Rangers had, indeed, witnessed "a bold and unlawful act." If they were ever going to, now was the time to "discharge their duty." Certainly not decked out in identifiable uniforms—Rangers didn't wear them—nor wearing shiny badges, Baird and his Winchester carrying troopers made tracks for the fence cutters—afoot. Not unexpectedly their clamoring movements did not pass undetected. Mark Hemphill and his pals beat a hasty retreat—for a second or two, then jumped from their horses and took cover behind the yet intact portion of a crumbling waist high rock fence. Then it turned Western.

Racing toward the barricade Corporal Baird could easily detect the muzzles of Winchesters pointed his way. He also could discern this would be no picnic, especially after one of cutters hollered: "Come on & take us in you damned sons-of-bitches." The Rangers continued to advance, Baird continually challenging a warning that the guys should surrender, voluntarily. The Ranger's fourth plea was answered in no uncertain terms: "Go to hell you son of a bitch." Mark Hemphill fired the first shot—and the battle was on![27]

From a nearby hillside—but well protected—Green Greer watched the asinine warfare below. From his perspective he estimated near 150 shots were exchanged, most missing but several struck with telling results. Texas Ranger W. W. Baker suffered a painful bullet wound to his left side, knocking him out of action. Ranger O. D. Baker was temporarily out of the game—for a few seconds—while trying to extract the pistol cartridge he had mistakenly tried to feed into his Winchester carbine. From his safe perch Greer was particularly—and favorably—impressed with the coolness of Corporal Baird, who was "ever ready with words of encouragement to cheer on the brave boys under his command." Green Greer also looked on as the Rangers drew blood. "Mason stepped from behind his bush and raised his gun to shoot Mitchell. Baker's gun cracked and Mason staggered back with a bullet in his breast. Quick as lightening Mitchell planted another one in his bosom. Mason moved back behind the brush, but is doing so he exposed himself to Baird's fire and soon the smoke boiled from that gentlemen's gun and down went Mason with a bullet in his brain."[28]

Fast realizing their untenable situation, the three remaining cutters stepped into stirrups and skedaddled, making a more-or-less clean getaway. Corporal Baird had consciously opted to just let them scoot: "the rustlers were soon rustling for cooler and safer quarters, making a dash for their horses near by. . . . Had I been supplied with ammunition I would have killed their horses, placing them on an equal with us as to mounts, but as I thought it best to save what I had for men in case of continued trouble, instead of killing horses."[29]

Even with desperate and dangerous fence cutters on the loose and an injured Ranger needing medical attention—which had been sent for—Corporal Baird knew full well the necessity of keeping the captain informed, and he rushed to Mason where he worded a message to be transmitted over the wires of the Erie Telegraph and Telephone Co. to the Company D chief:

> Send men to Green Lake Edwards County[.] had fight with fence cutters[.] Baker wounded bring wagon to move him[.] my wagon at Wrights please bring it[.] one cutter Killed.[30]

Captain Sieker right away dispatched a wagon to Green Lake, provisioned with supplies enough for ten days, and then following protocol made sure Adjutant General King was in the loop.[31]

By a genuine stroke of good luck and dandy policing, Corporal Baird and the uninjured Private Baker sleuthed about the county, locating John Brunson at Barksdale. The prisoner was tuned over to Sheriff Wheat to be held until the justice of the peace could be summoned. As would be expected Brunson was turned out, allowed to post bail bonds in amounts of $500 for Fence Cutting and $1000 for Assault to Murder.[32]

The brothers Greer, now that the fireworks were over and it was plain to everyone in Edwards County that they had cooperated with Texas Rangers, were afraid, understandably so. Private Baker wasn't making any judgments about retributive actions aimed at the Greer boys, other than he thought "the fence is safe now. Don't think there is a man on the creek that is 'game' enough to cut the fence."[33] On the other hand such an opinion had absolutely no validity to Green B. Greer: "I have been advised by several persons to leave the country as Mason's & Hemphill's friends hold me responsible for the death of Mason and say that I tried to run a blazer over them."[34] Fearing the worst and knowing that their not so alleged antagonists "violate the law with impunity in regard to carrying pistols" both Green B. and William Joseph Greer pled to Adjutant General King that they be made Special Rangers—allowed to carry six-shooters—but not drawing any pay from the state. Truthfully the Greer brothers were standing on shaky ground, according to their calculation the "nearest peace officer is forty miles distant and when the Rangers are withdrawn will leave us entirely in their power. . . ."[35]

By this time Lieutenant Frank Jones had returned to duty from tending to his father's estate and visiting with mama. Frank was, as he would soon discover, in for a very rude awakening. Heavy-weight thinkers at Ranger headquarters were not taking any chances. Lieutenant Jones was instructed to relocate the Llano detachment to Edwards County, "at once."[36] Within the week Lieutenant Jones was scouting Edwards County, hunting for a suitable spot to locate his camp.[37] Possibly somewhat politically reasoned, perhaps not, nevertheless for a 12 September 1884 update Frank Jones acquainted Adjutant General King: "I have located my camp near the Ranch of the Messer's Greer as this is the only grass there is anywhere on the South Llano."[38]

Astutely Lieutenant Jones didn't have his head buried under mushrooms. He knew for certain that Adjutant General King had taken a personal interest in the shootout at Green Lake and, correspondingly, the worry haunting the Greer brothers. Shortly after establishing his camp, Lieutenant Jones and "one man" set to work. Exactly how hard the manhunt was to manage is indeterminate, but rather quickly the pair snared Henry Burton, one of the Green Lake fence cutters. Unsmilingly they delivered their prisoner to an Edwards County JP at Barksdale.[39] Isolating his exact motive would require the talents of a peripatetic palm reader, but following arrests of his two fence cutting buddies, Burton and Brunson, Mark Hemphill jumped—straight into police custody. He voluntarily surrendered to Ranger Searce Baylor, brother of a first-term sheriff of Uvalde County, Henry W. Baylor.[40]

For Lieutenant Frank Jones some very disturbing reality began to set in: Not everyone was enamored with the Rangers. "Old Man [Joe] Burton" father of cutter Henry Burton, was furiously haranguing that in his penny-pinched coffers he had "sixty thousand dollars to spend in the prosecution of the Rangers who participated in the fight here [Green Lake]." Unsophisticatedly green vis-à-vis dealing with these type irrational hotheads, Frank Jones sloughed off the elder Burton's threat: "I do not believe he will have the audacity to even attempt to have them indicted."[41] On this Lieutenant Jones was outside the learning curve. Aside from friends and relatives of the fence cutters, Frank was at first aghast, then reflective, about part of the population's outlook: "I find the people up in the section of Green Lake very bitter against Rangers and say that they had no right to come into the country in the night. They say, and I guess truly, that if Hemphill had known Rangers were in the country he would not have cut Greer's fence."[42] Not just a few Edwards County folks thought Corporal Baird—seeing trouble about to erupt—should have stepped in and defused the volatile situation before allowing the lid to blow off—that was their complaint. Specifically there was a Complaint filed—a legal action initiated by Henry Burton charging the Rangers with Attempt to Murder.

Captain Lam Sieker right fast—and smartly—made his orders to Corporal P. C. Baird known: "I instructed them to go by Bull Head and wave [*sic:* waive] examination and give bond to appear before the Edwards Co. Grand Jury."[43] Prudently the captain didn't want Company D Rangers listed as fugitives. Acting as his right hand in the matter, Captain Sieker reported to the adjutant general with regards to Lieutenant Jones' investigatory positioning: "He is attending Justice Court there where Corporal Baird & squad are being tried before the Justice for assault with intent to Killing young Burton at Green Lake."[44]

Legal entanglements for Corporal Baird and his troops ultimately played out into nothingness. Prosecutorial zeal for punishing the Green Lake fence cutters waned and faded into an abyss.[45] The Greer brothers—for awhile—were carried on the Company D books as six-shooter carrying Special Rangers with no pay, but with appreciative sighs of relief.[46] The shootout at Green Lake had profound meaning to the brand-new Company D lieutenant: As a commissioned officer Frank Jones would not only have to stay hitched tight during the heat of gunfights, but amid the paperwork and invoices and receipts, he would also have to stand tall in the eyes of subordinates when they were right—and sometimes when they were wrong. Captain Lam Sieker knew the ropes, advising AG King: "Corporal Baird and squad deserve great credit for courage displayed in fighting four desperate men and they behind a rock fence. . . ."[47]

The sheriff at Fredericksburg (Gillespie County), the previously mentioned John Walter, wasn't ducking down behind a rock fence, but he was behind the eight-ball. While fence cutting events had been dramatically unfolding in Edwards County, a cold-blooded murder had shocked nearly everyone in the pretty Texas Hill Country. During a robbery gone awry John Wolfgang Braeutigam had been gunned down at his place of business on the outskirts of Fredericksburg. The murdered man was not only exceptionally popular with townsmen but Braeutigam's Beer Garten and entertainment complex was extraordinarily popular too. For joyful locals it was the chosen site for happily celebrating birthdays and weddings and reunions and picnics beneath the grapevine arbor—and horse races, too, on the nearby dirt track. The fifty-five year old victim, father of eleven and husband of thirty-four years, was an iconic village personality.[48] The awful crime—at least in the earliest stages—was a genuine whodunit? The busy sheriff needed help. Fredericksburg—in the main—was outraged, the uproar stupendous and a few nitwits were demanding summary justice for the lowlife perpetrators when, not if, they were apprehended. Captain Sieker's response was timely, but matter-of-fact: "Corpl Baird and 3 men made scout to Gillespie Co. to report to sheriff for duty."[49] Two of those three privates riding with P. C. Baird were Ira Aten and James V. "Jim" Latham, both fellows measuring to the mark in annals of Texas Ranger history.

Skillfully weaving bits and pieces of seemingly unrelated scraps together Baird and his squad were ultimately able to put names on their prime suspects—then it became a job of finding them. Ably conducting interviews and pledging confidentiality when necessary, the Texas Rangers cold-trailed the alleged murderers south from Gillespie County, down the Colorado River to the vicinity of Travis Peak, situated northwest of Austin, just shy of the Burnet County line.

With three of their targets' locations penned down reasonably tight the Rangers geared back to the standby mode—waiting for the shadows of darkness. The homicidal hooligans by the very act of murdering John W. Braeutigam had proven they were dangerous, and now they were desperate. Prudent tactics were called for. With stars overhead and not a hint of Rangers anywhere near, Jackson "Jack" Beam, William "Bill" Allison and C. Wesley "Wes" Collier in two separate residences laid heads on pillows, closed their eyes, drifting into dreamland. The Texas Rangers' entry was dynamic and disheartening for snoozing desperadoes: Nudged wide-awake with Colt's six-shooters pressing tips of their noses. Or, in blasé lexis of an onsite Ranger: "We rounded up their houses at night at two different places and caught them in bed."[50]

The outlaws' next beds weren't any too comfy: cold steel bunks in the Gillespie County Jail. Perhaps astutely surveying weakness of the local jail and flimsiness of any protective corridor capable of stopping enraged citizens imbued with lynch mentality, the Rangers and the sheriff made a decision. After a gala celebration at Fredericksburg honoring the Rangers' stellar work, the suspected murderers of Braeutigam would be hauled to San Antonio and imprisoned in the Bexar County Jail, a relatively new two story—1879—facility, at the time thought to be utterly "escape proof."[51]

Lieutenant Jones painstakingly committed to excellence and perfectly attuned to the fact that Rangers' good work was also a reflection on him personally and professionally, had kept two of his topnotch bloodhounds, Ira Aten and Jim Latham, on the trail of one of Braeutigam's alleged killers not yet "rounded up." Outlaw Ede Janes had earlier given Sergeant Lindsey and "3 men" the slip.[52] Rangers Aten and Latham had much better luck. They found Ede Janes lying low in the hidden recesses of Kimble County. Smoothly and safely the two determined Rangers arrested Ede on the eighth day of November without incident—which by implication suggests that they owned "the drop." He, too, was booked through the jail at Fredericksburg only to later join his depressed "fall partners" in the Bexar County hoosegow.[53] The 1884 holiday season's outlook for the Fredericksburg businessman's slayers was gloomy.

Those mean boys, however, weren't the only guys with sullen faces. As if taking a page from modern-era politicians' playbook, legislators were idly dithering about financial appropriations, the lifeblood for any bureaucracy—including the Texas Rangers. Captain Sieker's fix was real. As a result of Frontier Battalion General Order No. 20 he had been ordered to adjust the staffing level of Company D downward. On January 20, 1885, he reluctantly discharged five Rangers; O. D. Baker, A. P. Barry, W. W. Collier, C. D. Grant, and Jackson Herrage. Clearly the captain was troubled. These fellows were good Rangers. In a letter to the battalion quartermaster, John O. Johnson, Lam Sieker groused that he had complied with orders, but the fellows glumly cut loose "had very long faces on them and [were] praying for another appropriation so they can reenlist." Correspondingly, with the forced cutback, Captain Sieker could no longer justify operating the company as two separate detachments, shrewdly deploying his existing manpower to advantage: "I have ordered Lt. Jones to this camp [Camp Leona] and authorized him to sell to the best advantage any hay & corn he can't haul here." And, if discharging Rangers wasn't dismal enough, Mother Nature added to Captain Sieker's misery: "It is raining in torrents here and camp is a sea of mud, and stock is suffering." Uncharacteristically, and surely it chafed him, Captain Sieker was forced to acknowledge, "I have done but little on account of the bad weather. . . ."[54]

Hardly had Lieutenant Frank Jones put in his appearance at Camp Leona before he was ordered to draw rations for ten days, draft a half-dozen toughened Rangers, and make fast tracks for Carrizo Springs, Dimmit County. Big trouble was brewing along the Texas/Mexico border. Arriving after dark the Texas Rangers arranged an overnight residence at the county courthouse. According to Private Ira Aten who was along on this scout, when the February 1885 sun peeked over the eastern horizon casting her radiance he could see that the town did not exactly appear deserted as it had the night before. Now, in daytime, anxious men were "walking around with Winchesters." Not just a few of the Anglo citizens had surmised the scruffy looking gang of shadowy forms taking command of Carrizo Springs, "were the Mexicans who had come during the night and captured the courthouse."[55] Following a series of interviews with locals and making personal observations after scouting the Rio Grande, Lieutenant Frank Jones determined "everything in a violent state of excitement with the citizens of Dimmitt [*sic*] Co. in arms expecting an invasion from Mexico."[56]

The fear was not misplaced, though no doubt it was somewhat exaggerated. For advancing Lieutenant Frank Jones' narrative stopping and trying to cast blame as to who shot whose dog first is time wasted. The hammer of truth—rather than a feather of political correctness—forges a hard but not pretty product. Mexicans and Americans were literally at each others' throats. Generally the heartburn could be boiled down to whether one supplemented his diet with tortillas or sourdough. Perspective and prejudice underpinned the chaos then underway. Mexican bandits and Anglo desperadoes were splashing back and forth across the river, seemingly with impunity:

> Before the Carrizo Springs people had got into some trouble with the Mexicans across the Rio Grande. Mexicans were coming across, stealing cattle and horses, and there was a lot of feeling up. It go so bad that white men were killing every Mexican they caught over the line, and Mexicans were killing some of the white men.[57]

Clearly the situation was out of hand. An old-time cowhand recorded his take on reality: "It started out this way, you see, that whole thing started with stealing. . . . That used to be all open country in there clear up to the Eagle Pass road. Three or four of our boys would go out there and camp and the damn Mexicans would run them clean to town. They would just round up what they wanted [cattle/horses] and drive them through."[58] The first and many times reelected sheriff of Dimmit County, Joseph "Joe" Tumlinson, absent help from the governor's office, opted for a little corrective work on his own. He captained a hard-riding and hard-charging posse across the Rio Grande. It was short work. Sheriff Tumlinson, in the face of overwhelming and unyielding odds ordered a turnabout—right fast. One of the possemen scampering for his ever lovin' life nostalgically recalled that a near breathless comrade had shouted advice: "When you come up this hill you kind of zigzag." The cowboy was in no mood to entertain wittiness or advice: "Zigzag hell, if I ever get up that hill I will be lucky."[59]

That same cowboy, with the characteristic hardness of a Southwest borderlander, insensitively painted Sheriff Tumlinson's utter frustration egged on by—until then—an unresponsive governor. The Mexican bandits were hardhearted and hardcore: "But they knew Joe Tumlinson too. He was the same way. He would pull the trigger, and there would be a dead Mexican."[60]

Two "dead Mexicans" were sons of Rafael Reyes, a reasonably prominent border country cowman ranching in Mexico. Local lawmen scouting after cow thieves collided with the two brothers and four others driving a herd of suspected stolen cattle. There was no duty to retreat, and neither side skedaddled. During the blistering exchange of gunfire both Reyes boys were killed outright, subsequent to one of them wounding Deputy Sheriff William Negley.[61]

Once awakened to the turmoil and fearing the worst, Governor John Ireland stepped in with both feet, kicking orders downhill to the adjutant general. There was not a smidgen of ambiguity: "I wish you [AG King] to proceed at once to Dimmit Co. and restore order." Furthermore, the adjutant general was authorized to call upon any and all forces necessary to achieve that mission. And, more particularly for Captain Sieker and Lieutenant Jones, Company D was to at once be relocated from the vicinity of Uvalde to a camp "on or near the Mexican border. . . ."[62]

Before the middle of February 1885 Captain Lam Sieker and the remaining manpower of Company D had redeployed to Maverick County, southeast of Eagle Pass, making camp alongside San Ambrosia Creek just four miles from the Rio Grande but only one mile from where Dimmit County and Webb County (county seat Laredo) joined Maverick County.[63] Positioning of the Company D camp was thoughtfully strategic. Captain Sieker quickly notified headquarters about his thought processes: "I think Eagle Pass would be the best to get our mail as the man I would send every other day after the mail could look for trails of stolen stock going both ways to and from the river and would patrol 40 miles of river, it would also be a good and convenient place to get my supplies from."[64] For a subsequent update to Texas Ranger headquarters, Captain Sieker reiterated his reasoning for establishing Camp San Ambrosia. Among other reasons, he now rightly emphasized the weight of a communications network—the lifeblood for effective law enforcement applications. Not only is the 1885 letter delightfully informative of everyday logic, maybe it's also enlightening—for it illustrates the role advancing technology was having on policing, even in the southwestern frontier of nineteenth-century Texas: "I wrote you some days back that I thought Eagle Pass would be the best P.O. for the following reasons, they have a daily mail, telegraph & telephone. . . . In case you want to telegraph me for quick action send it in care of Capt. [Tom] Oglesby [Maverick County sheriff] and he will send it to <u>me</u> at once."[65]

The bane of relocation was that lawbreaking yahoos took up the slack in the absence of Rangers. No sooner had the Company D Rangers vacated the Uvalde County neighborhood than P. H. Wentworth Jr. was rightly complaining to Captain Sieker, in writing, that "the water had almost given out" to the west of his ranch and his foreman was advising the absentee owner that by the best information at hand, when that happened—the waterholes drying up—the "squatters say they intend cutting or destroying the fence around the ranch." Furthermore, in no uncertain terms Wentworth was assuring Captain Sieker that he was owner of all the land the fence was on or enclosed, and the waterholes therein. He wanted protection for his property and ranch personnel: Ranger protection.[66] Unfortunately Captain Sieker was pained to address drab reality: "I with the men I have can render him no assistance and watch the country I am stationed in."[67] It was a lightweight shielding blanket the Lone Star State was throwing taxpaying citizens: threadbare—patchwork protection. Legislators at the statehouse held dear the purse strings, especially when it wasn't their ox being gored or stolen or dehydrated.

Now, with no nonsense Texas Ranger presence sited to interdict or inform the front office about any invasions from Mexicans south of the border, an intelligence gathering mission was undertaken. Captain Sieker, after his scouting along the Rio Grande, reported to the battalion quartermaster: "I apprehend no trouble at present as the Mexicans will be afraid to come over the river in any force for sometime."[68] In a follow up letter to the adjutant general, Captain Sieker repeated a similar message: "find everything comparatively quiet, although there is an uneasiness among the Ranchmen who fear the Mexicans will Kill some Americans to avenge the 'Reyes boys' death."[69] Likewise, Lieutenant Frank Jones was dispatched on a fact-finding scout. The summation of Jones' observations was succinct: "Everything quiet."[70]

Ranger Captain Frank Jones as he appeared upon taking command of Company D, Frontier Battalion. *COURTESY CANDICE DUCOIN.*

A much published—iconic—photograph of Texas Ranger Austin Ira Aten. He would eventually run to ground the murderers of Mr. Braeutigam. *Courtesy Nita Stewart Haley Memorial Library & J. Evetts Haley History Center in Midland, Texas.*

Johann Wolfgang Braeutigam the very well liked and very well respected Fredericksburg, Texas, Beer Garden and Entertainment Center proprietor was foully murdered. He is pictured here with his beloved wife of thirty-three years, Christine. Texas Rangers working under the leadership of Captain Frank Jones successfully tracked down the murderers and, in the case of Wesley Collier, killed him when he opted to resist arrest by reaching for a brace of six-shooters. *Courtesy David Braeutigam.*

Christine Braeutigam. After the senseless murder of her husband, with true pioneering spirit she held the family together—through thick and thin, good times and bad. *Courtesy David Braeutigam.*

Texas Ranger Corporal Philip Cuney "P. C." Baird, veteran of the ghastly shoot-out with fence cutting fellows at Green Lake, and a future sheriff of Mason County, Texas. *Courtesy James Baird.*

Governor John Ireland. A former law officer, lawyer, Civil War veteran, local and state politico, Ireland was particularly concerned with criminal justice issues. He would, in due time, call a special session of the Texas State Legislature to deal with the pandemic fence cutting and its grave economic devastation. FROM *INDIAN WARS AND PIONEERS OF TEXAS* BY JOHN HENRY BROWN.

Ranger Private Oscar D. Baker, he too commendably participated in the sizzling gunplay at Green Lake. *COURTESY ARMSTRONG RANGER RESEARCH CENTER, TEXAS RANGER HALL OF FAME & MUSEUM.*

CHAPTER 7

"Most Bold, High-Handed Murder"

FOR THE MOMENT—and it would not hold—the Texas/Mexican border was reasonably tranquil. Pinpointing with exactness—from outside the tent—words exchanged in private between Captain Sieker and Lieutenant Jones is excusably not doable. Real big doings, though, were astir. The Company D commander was actively hunting advancement and that, in and of itself, was no deep dark secret. There was not any under-the-table inter or intra agency machinations. True to form Captain Sieker was upfront and aboveboard. Though it cannot measure past speculation, it's a reasonably safe bet that a young lieutenant from Kendall County was spring-loaded, ready to jump at the chance to backfill behind the company captain being promoted to headquarters. That Frank Jones was biding his time is but a safe call.

Taking pen in hand Captain Lam Sieker made his thoughts and aspirations a matter of Frontier Battalion record. Within the framework of political gossip Sieker had learned that the battalion's quartermaster, Captain John O. Johnson, was a likely candidate to receive the patronage position as postmaster for the city of Austin, a lucrative and laudable political plum. Should that be the case, and should the rank of battalion quartermaster be vacant, Captain Sieker wanted his name in the hat. Not only did he deem it appropriate to make mention of it to the governor and the adjutant general, but the ever honorable Lam Sieker also apprised Captain Johnson of his desire, candidly seeking his support.[1] In the interim, there was work to be done—plenty of it, too!

Two *vasierros* (salaried sheepherders), Jesús Sanches and Simon Prez, had been mercilessly killed: Cut down only because they were wage-working Mexicans. The Dimmit County murders were whodunits but for a short time. As the lucky recipients of a smidgen of actionable intelligence two gritty lawmen took up the case and the chase. Captain Joe Shely, Company F, Frontier Battalion, and C. B. McKinney, the La Salle County sheriff and ex-Ranger, were not bowled over by the speedy success of their investigative efforts, but after making arrests were shocked at the owlhoots' foul motives. One of the coconspirators proffered the not so rhetorical question of a vicious accomplice: "Suppose we kill a Mexican today, the first one we strike this morning?" And they did, two times over! Perhaps somewhat surprising and disillusioning to carping critics of virtually all Ranger exploits, Captain Joe Shely was truly aghast: "From the evidence attained it is one of the most bold, high-handed murders ever perpetrated in this section."[2] In fact, Captain Shely was more than a little concerned that the Anglo suspects could never be convicted of "killing Mexican herders in Dimmit County as it [has] been so common and no convictions ever resulting." He was, as best he could absent the legal authority, pushing for a change of venue to another county.[3]

Recognizing potential for volatility brought on by racial and cultural animas, and knowing delicacy and diplomacy were the order of the day, Captain Sieker assigned Lieutenant Jones a touchy assignment. Frank Jones, supervising a trio of Ranger privates, was to act as an escort to Rafael Reyes, father of the slain brothers, while he gathered cattle along the Rio Grande. It was an eight-day excursion—absent incident—covering more than 100 miles.[4]

Returning from his protective assignment Lieutenant Jones conferred with Captain Sieker regarding the possibility of taking leave. The captain had authority to grant the request, but only if the proposed absence was to be seven days or less. A furlough of more than one week required approval of the adjutant general. Dutifully, Frank Jones sought and was granted permission to forward his written request to Adjutant General King asking for an eight day extension, declaring "it will be almost impossible for me to transact my business in seven days." One way or the other Frank was going to make a trip home, as he clearly—respectfully—asked the adjutant general to notify him of the approval or disapproval in writing, addressed to Curry's Creek (common spelling at the time), Kendall County. AG King granted the extension.[5]

The nature of Frank's personal business in Kendall County has thus far escaped exactness. Speculatively there may be a hint. At the county seat, Boerne, John G. O'Grady, an Irishman with U.S. Army experience under his belt, was owner and operator of a "boarding house and inn on the south side of Cibolo Creek."[6] Mr. O'Grady was the father of Grace, in April 1885, an unattached twenty-seven-year-old. Somewhere along the way, either at Fort McKavett after John O'Grady discharged from the military and opened a store near the post, or at Boerne, Frank Jones made the acquaintance of Miss Grace O'Grady.[7] Wherever the introduction took place, the sparks of romance ignited. Now, besides family business and Ranger business, Lieutenant Frank Jones had Cupid's business on his mind.

Though given permission for an extended visit to Kendall County, Lieutenant Jones did not take full advantage of the time, but instead returned for duty with Company D, although he did forward a gracious "Thank You" to the adjutant general for his courtesy.[8] Captain Lam Sieker was also thankful. Funds had been okayed for beefing up the company. Quickly he reenlisted as privates A. P. Barry, W. W. Collier, C. D. Grant and O. D. Baker.[9] The apparent ease with which Captain Sieker, at Camp San Ambrosia, located the rehires might suggest—just maybe—that the boys had not shied too far away from Company D's camp. Hanging around a Ranger camp, conversing with buddies and sharing in hospitality of a state-paid commissary, all the while waiting for some silly politicians or persnickety bureaucrats to act, cut loose with some money that wasn't theirs in the first place, well, that wasn't crazy. Was it?

Captain Sieker had big plans for Lieutenant Jones: Sending him upriver on an extensive scout with a wagon to haul supplies.[10] Sometimes the best laid plans of mice and men—and Ranger captains—go astray. Bad news was breaking not from upriver, but from up country and an influential voice was not silent. John R. Baylor was in a tither. From his base at Montell on the Nueces River northwest of Uvalde, Baylor alerted Adjutant General King that his part of the country was flooded—not by overflowing creeks—but by "a swarm of lawless characters." Robbery and theft were commonplace. Stealing of cattle, horses, and goats was out of hand, as was burglarizing and burning homes. Within a six-month period Mr. Hedges who had purchased 1000 goats was tallying "6 Bucks (out of 30) and 100 nannies out of the 1000, all stolen from him." According to Baylor there were but two foreseeable outcomes: "Either peaceful citizens will leave the country or there will be war between those who steal for a living and those who work for it. . . ." John Baylor wanted Texas Rangers. The signal fact that he was not happy is easy even now to decipher from a distance, but at the time Adjutant General King got the message, too! Baylor ended his tirade by avowing he didn't want to be drawn into "a war with my own people but it looks as if there is no other alternative." And besides that, "The state is too poverty Stricken to afford protection to those who live on the frontier and in fact the only power it Seems to have is impose and collect Taxes. . . ."[11]

John R. Baylor was not the only bigwig player piping out a complaint. J. W. Jennings, a heavily invested Angora goat raiser in Edwards County—the county's leading taxpayer—made sure Governor Ireland was in on the know. Jennings was not reticent. According to him, Edwards County was a refuge for desperadoes under indictment elsewhere, declaring "No honest man has any Chance for life or property. . . . Renegades from every section rendezvous in the mountains and threaten every good citizen." Wanting the presence of ten Rangers for a period of at least six months would, in Jennings' opinion, alleviate much of the lawlessness, notwithstanding the fact that there may be other bad places in the state, "but this beats the Rio Grande frontier and should be looked after:

Edwards Co. and the Northern part of Uvalde Co. is now a field of operation for these desperadoes."[12]

Not surprisingly Lieutenant Frank Jones, a proven leader with an unruffled demeanor, got the call. He was to draw rations and ammunition, then take five men and reconnoiter throughout Edwards County, checking into the "general lawlessness."[13] Lieutenant Jones established his camp in Edwards County three miles from Barksdale, not too far north of the Uvalde County line. For the month of May 1885 Lieutenant Jones and his detachment were caught up in a whirlwind of scouting activity throughout the county; often as not they were accompanied by Sheriff Ira Wheat. Their perambulations covered ground, "up Bullhead fork of the Nueces" and days later to Robbs Run on the West Nueces, then even later, to the South Llano River.[14] Although investigating crimes and catching violators were important, the primary goal for Lieutenant Jones' Edwards County detachment was to figuratively show the flag: Let good men and bad men see Rangers were ever present in the mountains and canyons and secreted lairs. The Rangers were, indeed, trespassing on the heretofore hideaways of robbers and rustlers and reprobates, but none tested their steadfastness of purpose or their six-shooter resolve. Other Company D Rangers were not so lucky. They were riding Lucifer's Line—the Rio Grande—that last day of the month when a calm spring day turned Western, real Western.

Southeast of camp San Ambrosia, Sergeant B. D. Lindsey was in charge of a seven-man scout. They were riding with purpose: Hunting for escaped convicts and/or the culprits who had lent a helping hand to jailbirds flying the coop.[15] The manhunt was wide-ranging. Lieutenant Jones, yet scouting Edwards County, was particularly notified "to be on the lookout for them on the head of the Nueces river. . . ."[16] Captain Sieker was optimistically inclined to think his dragnet would prove productive: "I don't believe they can cross without being caught—we have every crossing on the Rio Grande up and down from Eagle Pass for 40 miles watched."[17]

Paring ensuing events to the nub is—for Frank Jones' story—all that's necessary. To be sure it's a whopping good tale, one spiked with high drama and scorching gunplay, but it is a narrative oft repeated. A recap, however, is obligatory. Even though Lieutenant Jones would not be an on-the-ground participant in the spilling or leaking of blood, the exciting episode would significantly impact his Texas Ranger career.

Besides Lindsey, the sergeant's scout was made up of Privates Austin Ira Aten, Oscar D. Baker, C. D. Grant, Ben C. Riely, C. W. Giffin (not Griffin) and Captain Sieker's youngest brother Frank L. Sieker, who measured his Texas Ranger service in months, not years. Privates Aten and Riely, because they were dawdling and leading a plodding pack mule, had somewhat strayed off course and though they could see their comrades were now geographically separated, riding the other side of a boggy arroyo swollen by recent and torrential rains.[18] In fact the isolated San Ambrosia Ranger camp had nearly been washed away during a downpour when the creek "rose twenty-five feet in about four hours time—fortunately we [they] were camped on a high point and escaped."[19]

The Rangers were always primed for action. Sergeant Lindsey and his boys were not riding with heads buried underneath the desert's floor. They were mindful—fully aware—of the adjutant general's and their company captain's passionate interest in bringing the fugitives to bay. The attention top brass was giving the matter was not lost on those Rangers cutting for sign southeast of Eagle Pass between San Ambrosia Creek and the Rio Grande. So, when they espied two horseback fellows in the distance, leading a third horse, there was but one right course to follow: Stop and identify the "Mexicans" and learn what business they were about. Were they up to no good? Had they broken out of jail—or aided someone in a sneaky jailbreak? Conversely, were one peacefully ambling along, eyeing seven heavily armed men in the distance it would be but reasonable to think that desperadoes might have been forking those saddles, fellows prowling for plunder and profit. Who knew? The perfect storm was in sight. Apolonio Gonzales and his teenage son, Pedro, could ill afford to sit still and possibly be overhauled by bandits. Duty called for Texas Rangers not to lazily look the other way, possibly letting two escapees and/or their accomplices escape. Father and son promptly put iron to their horses, racing for the Rio Grande. The Rangers followed suit.

By happenstance Privates Aten and Riely, due to their geographical positioning, were nearer the quarry, the other Rangers having yet to cross the swampy ground between them. What happened next? There are two competing versions and, ironically, both come from Rangers. Weighing each with due diligence, in the end, will not untangle the knotty question of who fired the first shot. Ira Aten, at a point in time—during an interview—quite candidly it seems said: "When about a hundred yards from them, we opened fire and they returned it, all of us shooting with Winchesters. . . ."[20] In his official written report to Captain Sieker, Sergeant Lindsey asserted that the Gonzales duo opened the ball by shooting first.[21] Despite the unanswerable, well, not provable, resolution of this issue there is a hard bottom line.

Private Frank Sieker was the first to catch up with Rangers Aten and Riely. Unfortunately he arrived shortly after Riely had been wounded, a bullet punching through his shoulder, another tearing a gaping hole into his thigh. Though Private Aten was doing admirable work with his Winchester the wounds he inflicted were not disabling his adversaries. Therefore, identifying with specificity which "Mexican" fired a particular shot is problematic, but the bullet ripped into Frank Sieker's heart "killing him while yet sitting upright in the saddle."[22] Though each were slightly injured, one shot through the hand, the other through the shoulder, Apolonio and Pedro Gonzales continued their unnerved—and understandably so—flight, finding safe haven at the Loyas' Rancho at the Rio Grande's edge.

The dead Sieker and the wounded Riley were not the Rangers' only casualties. While crossing the muddy arroyo C. W. Giffin's gelding bogged down—went berserk—and threw its rider, breaking the private's collarbone. Sergeant Lindsey and Privates Baker and Grant fared better, but only after some wild horseback gymnastics as their mounts gyrated beneath their knees trying to extricate themselves from mud high to their hocks. The rodeo was humorless and, thankfully, of short duration. The Rangers caught up with Aten who was in a dither, really pondering what to do next.

Sergeant Lindsey had no quandary: He was a Ranger, a good Ranger, and good Rangers got their man—or died trying to. So says the legend. Telling it straight, Lindsey was a good Ranger. The non-com's stoic remark to Aten was short, simple, and sharp: "We will go down." Boldly the Rangers rode into the Loyas Ranch stronghold and were greeted by Pendincia Herrera, a gutsy part-time Webb County deputy sheriff, who by this time was surrounded by fifteen steely-eyed and unsmiling *vaqueros*—all heavily armed. The expression Mexican Standoff is applicable. Lindsey wanted to take Apolonio and Pedro, as his prisoners, to Carrizo Springs. Herrera demanded that they be taken to Laredo, roughly eighty miles to the southeast, and turned over to his boss Dario Gonzales, the county sheriff. Sanity won the day. Sergeant Sieker agreed that the prisoners could be taken to Laredo, conditionally:

> Our force was too small to take them to Carrizo Springs, so I told him we would go to Laredo with them. It was agreed that three Mexicans & three Rangers should carry them. I detailed Baker, Aten & Grant as an Escort & the Party started at once to Laredo. . . . [23]

Sergeant Lindsey's attention then and, rightly so, focused on obtaining medical attention for the wounded Riley and the injured Giffin, while at the same time making arrangements for the respectful removal of Frank Sieker's remains. Too, the unpleasant task of informing Captain Sieker that his brother had been killed was obligatory. In turn Captain Sieker was duty-bound to keep Ranger headquarters at Austin updated. He messaged AG King on the first day of June 1885:

> Recd. telegram from Eagle Pass stating that my men had fight with mexicans [*sic*] fifty miles below Eagle Pass. F. E. Sieker Killed. griffin [*sic*] and Riely badly wounded. don't Know the particulars. will go there tonight.[24]

Indeed, the "particulars" are more than a little interesting. The escorting posse of Deputy Pendincia Herrera and his three *vaqueros*, along with Rangers Aten, Baker, and Grant, did manage the overnight trip to Laredo with their prisoners. There, they turned Apolonio and Pedro Gonzales over to the Webb County sheriff, Dario Gonzales.

For the Rangers it was the culmination of their assignment, but the story is far from over. Within thirty minutes the father and son were turned loose, high-stepping across the Rio Grande's bridge into Mexico. There, securely out of the clutches of Texas lawman, they were reasonably safe from extradition.[25]

Suddenly, much to their surprise, the Rangers were surrounded and arrested. Sheriff Gonzales had hastily impressed a meanly disposed posse after the Gonzaleses had sworn to and signed a written Complaint and arrest warrants had issued. The flabbergasted Texas Rangers were charged with Assault to Murder and ensconced in Webb County's two-story lockup at 1100 Farragut Street in Laredo. And there they languished—for twenty-six days. Though formally indicted by a Webb County Grand Jury—with no shortage of Anglos impaneled—the Rangers were suffering the explicit possibility of hard time at Huntsville, site of the Lone Star State's penitentiary. After much behind-the-scenes wrangling and political machinations it may be reported that the Indictment was quashed and the Rangers were, at last, free to go.[26] But, there was an ugly upshot.

Now examples of hardened racial animas were rooted even deeper in the mindsets of many Anglos and Texas Rangers, and not just a few Hispanics, as well. Though it's not particularly becoming for the twenty-first century marketplace of political correctness, Ranger Private Austin Ira Aten cut deep to the bone: "our feelings was too great after that against Mexicans for them to leave us there, as they knew we would be killing Mexicans whenever we got a chance."[27] Likewise, Captain Lam Sieker could and did forecast the real predicament of maintaining the San Ambrosia Creek camp: "All I could do at my present camp [San Ambrosia] would be in a negative way. . . ."[28] Too, a full dozen Webb County Grand Jurymen formally petitioned the governor, imploring that the Rangers be removed from San Ambrosia—forthwith: "Harm may occur at any moment, if the company remains. The citizens are excited and much opposed to the company remaining among them."[29] Newspapers across the state, such as the *San Antonio Daily Express*, the *Galveston Daily News*, *El Paso Times*, *Corpus Christi Caller*, and *Dallas Daily Herald* were not favorably reporting on the Texas Rangers' tactics for this installment of border country gunplay.[30] Did Apolonio and Pedro Gonzales really know they were running from Texas Rangers or was there any legitimacy in their assertion that the scruffy looking strangers shooting Winchesters and chasing after them were desperadoes with evil plans of plunder and piracy on the program? Lieutenant Frank Jones with an ingrained brand of his own personal prejudices—reflective of the place and times—propounded that it was myopic for anyone to mistakenly misidentify Rangers as possibly being borderland bandits. The Rangers, as lawmen, were readily identifiable because of "their general appearance" supplemented by the fact that a squadron of resolute Texas Rangers "rode big shod horses, and had pack mules."[31] Frank Jones' accountability for lawmen automatically presenting a clear-cut identification of themselves seems somewhat misplaced, backwards: A bitter and foreseeable recipe for absolute catastrophe. Clearly the onus should be on the policemen not the perpetrators—or alleged perpetrators. Nevertheless Texas Ranger front-office bigwigs bent to political expediency, commanding Captain Lam Sieker to move camp, without delay.

Lieutenant Frank Jones was, by order of Captain Sieker, to remain at Camp San Ambrosia overseeing the relocation from that end, while the company commander scouted for a suitable spot somewhat actually removed from the border per se.[32] In but reasonably short order the Company D commander had repositioned his headquarters. Captain Lam Sieker posted Ranger headquarters: "I have established the above camp [Camp Nueces] ten miles from Uvalde and have a splendid camp, plenty of wood, water, shade, and grass will soon be good, as it is coming out nice since the late rains."[33] Unfortunately it was a blistering Texas summer causing Captain Sieker to proffer a workable theory to Battalion Quartermaster John O. Johnson: "Everything quiet throughout this whole section. I think the thieves are laying up in this miserable <u>hot</u> weather." Not only was scorching temperature having an affect on thieving miscreants, at least half of the Company D Rangers' horses were for the time being sidelined, having "scalded backs on acct. of the excessive heat."[34]

Though actually incapacitated from taking part in any law-enforcing duties due to his broken collar bone, Private C. W. Giffin was not booted out of the Rangers nor was he allowed to malinger in camp. With his good hand he became responsible for completing Company D's Monthly Returns and other bureaucratic correspondence for the unit. Certainly Private Giffin was fortunate, though it seems that the gunshot Private Ben C. Riely was in a pickle. AG King was not too sympathetic about Riely's plight: "Replying to your [Lieutenant Jones] letter of 4th inst. I would inform you that I will not grant a two months leave of absence to B. C. Riely . . . I consider the doctor's certificate as too vague, and his prognostication of a period of two months [too lengthy] . . . unless he has some other reason for asking as long a leave. . . ."[35] Armchair leadership is—or can be—sometimes downright irksome. Again, in writing, Dr. Fred Herff certified Private Riely was at the time "entirely unfit for any kind of active service" and moreover he can "neither ride on horseback nor walk for any length of time and has to syringe out his wound twice a day through the drainage tube."[36] Once more Lieutenant Jones had "endorsed" the doctor's certification and forwarded it to the adjutant general.[37] Not to be left in leftfield Private Riely guaranteed to AG King "that as soon as Dr. Herff thinks advisable I will report to my Co. for duty."[38]

There was no time for Lieutenant Frank Jones to take any leave. He was busy. Jones, accompanied by two Rangers, made a scout through Dimmit County and arrested Juan, Clevis, and Augustin Reies (Reyes ?) charged with Resisting Arrest. The surprised but unlucky prisoners were at once turned over to the county sheriff at Carrizo Springs, Joseph "Joe" Tumlinson.[39] Finally, on the ninth day of August Lieutenant Jones and his two privates arrived at the new Company D headquarters in Uvalde County. Camp San Ambrosia was no more.[40]

Standing as a member of the Frontier Battalion's officer corps carried no exemption from performing nitty-gritty police work. Lieutenant Jones was expected to—and did—personally superintend horseback scouts and make arrests, in addition to fulfilling a mountain of routine administrative duties. Frank Jones was more than willing to bend to bureaucracy's burdens. The trade was equitable in his mind, social status for the niggling responsibilities of leadership.

There can be little doubt Lieutenant Frank Jones looked on the next big news for Company D with more than a little interest—personal interest. The Frontier Battalion's Special Order No. 85, dated October 12, 1885, portended the possibility of promotion. Ranger Quartermaster Johnson's resignation was accepted, feeing him to assume the position of postmaster for the city of Austin. In turn, on the backfill Captain Lam Sieker was named battalion quartermaster and assigned to the Capitol City. The company was now shy a captain's slot on the Muster & Payroll.[41]

For the interim Lieutenant Jones would command Company D. Captain Sieker passing the baton of company leadership to Frank Jones necessitated accountability. Lieutenant Jones quickly inventoried company stores and company property, issuing a receipt of acceptance to Quartermaster Sieker. Jones also took charge of Captain Sieker's horse, Old Prince, during the October transition noting that by December the hot-blooded animal would be "hog fat."[42]

Particularly updating Quartermaster Sieker that the Company D Rangers had been "quite busy" and were really doing "some good work" was not hyperventilated prattle on the part of Lieutenant Jones. Monthly Returns enumerate numerous arrests. Of particular note, Sergeant B. D. Lindsey arrested Pendencia and Tomas Herrera, charging them with Resisting Officer. Though the details are scant, could this enforcement action have been an offshoot of the earlier dispute with Deputy Herrera regarding the custodial arrests of Apolonio and Pedro Gonzales?[43] *¿Quién sabe?* Could the modern-era slogan "Don't mess with Texas" have had its nineteenth-century genesis corrupted from "Don't mess with Texas Rangers?" With most of his Rangers away from Camp Leona (the camp had been repositioned and renamed) on scouts, Lieutenant Jones received workable intelligence that a warrant had issued for M. M. Parkerson, charged with Theft of Cattle. Hurriedly drafting his camp guard, Lieutenant Jones rushed to the depot at Uvalde and just in the nick of time arrested Parkerson, taking him off the train and turning the surprised man over to the sheriff.[44] On another occasion Lieutenant Jones made a scout to the South Llano investigating reports of "the dead body of a Mexican." Fortunately the body was located. Unfortunately the murderer or murderers left no viable trail or other meaningful clues. Scratch one up for the bad guys.[45]

Though reading Frank Jones' mind is impossible, the hint that he was rather skilled at "buttering the bread" is more than evident. Subsequent to Captain Sieker being upgraded to the position of battalion quartermaster Lieutenant Jones penned this to the big boss: "You can rest assured that I am grateful to you for keeping me in this Country. I almost feel that you are in command of old Co. 'D' yet and know that she is safe in your hands."[46] Although at this time the relevance of Lieutenant Jones' P.S. on the letter is not apparent, it will prove significant: "George [Henderson, the Ranger's civilian teamster] says for me to ask you how many puppies you think old Blanche will bring. Says that 19 men have told him that you had promised them puppies and each one claims that you promised a dog [male] pup."[47]

Hardly had Lieutenant Jones been in the company's command saddle before he was ordered into the saddle—literally. The adjutant general had transmitted instructions that Lieutenant Jones and six men were to meet up with other Texas Rangers under the command of Captain George Schmitt at Pearsall, Frio County, southeast of Camp Leona. After joining forces the two Ranger squads were to move into the gigantic Butler pasture in Karnes County even farther east. Should their numbers be insufficient AG King's remedy was plainspoken: "You should also be able to get assistance from good citizens & from sheriff & their deputies as a posse and I do not doubt that by these means you can get together a force Sufficiently large to accomplish the breaking up of this gang of outlaws."[48] With his original spelling intact, Ranger J. Walter Durbin would later write: "wee had something of a little armey."[49] Their task was twofold: Hunt for two escaped convicts and a gang of cow thieves. After a grueling search the Rangers could not report making any arrests, but during the investigative sweep—with the assistance of area ranchmen—they could tally the recovery of eighty head of stolen cattle and two stolen horses.[50] All and all Captain Schmitt graded the Ranger performance A+ saying, "this trip done a heap of good."[51] Although he had considerable difficulty in getting along with most folks—lawmen and citizens—Captain Schmitt, after the Karnes County operation, complimented Frank and his Company D Rangers, notifying Captain Sieker that he "was well pleased with Lieutenant Jones and his men."[52] Shortly thereafter Lieutenant Jones was tasked with leading and temporarily locating a detachment camp on Sycamore Creek in Kinney County, northeast of the county seat, Brackettville. The assignment, in the supplemental Monthly Return, was straightforward: "Keep peace in that section."[53]

Shaping a touch of real time reality into everyday Texas Ranger camp life is doable. While Lieutenant Jones had been away on his special assignment, a misfortune took place at Camp Leona. With punctuation as is, Sergeant Lindsey explains:

> On the 8th inst. my horse broke his neck. he was tied near the Leona's bank, one wire between him & river. during the night sometime he was rubbing against the wire when it gave way & he fell off the bank & broke his neck. Would it be possible to obtain pay for him from the State. it was purely a providential occurrence no carelessness on my part whatsoever.[54]

Aside from Hancock the camp's dog siring expectant Blanche's puppies, and Sergeant Lindsey's horse snapping its neck, some of the Company D boys weren't ship-shape health wise, conditions that would continually pester Lieutenant Jones as he dutifully responded to an ever penny-pinching headquarters at Austin. While on a routine trip to see the dentist at San Antonio, Private W. W. Collier came down sick and was bedridden, under a doctor's care for four days. According to an attending physician the young Ranger's ailment was picked up in camp, prior to his trip to the Alamo City—and therefore the state was obliged to settle with the doctor for care and medicine. Another Ranger, Henry Pifer, "came near dying with something similar to Cholera Morbus and I [Jones] was compelled to call in [Dr.] Appleton."[55] Private Ben C. Riely was "yet and may for some time remain unfit for duty" but Lieutenant Frank Jones was respectfully forceful with his entreaty that he did not desire to have the Ranger "discharged" and was hoping the adjutant general would bend to his personal wishes, allowing the injured private to still be carried on the company rolls.[56]

Creatures that would not be carried on the company's roll were five of Blanche's offspring and, at this point, making mention of a fact is not for dramatic or shocking titillation but as time unfolds such will prove more than a little pertinent. In the short term, however, Lieutenant Frank Jones brought Captain Sieker up to speed: "Blanche had 13 puppies on the 7th of this month [December]. Six of them are dogs. George killed 4 of the females and Blanche has accidently killed one since herself."[57] Seemingly the Company D Rangers took a special pride in their camp dogs, viciousness aside. Some folks in Uvalde County were not—and would not be—of the same mind.

On the seventh day of December 1885 Lieutenant Jones made a direct appeal to AG King for a two-day leave of absence, stating that "More than likely I [he] will only be away the 14th and 15th and will return 16th at the latest. Hoping you will see fit to grant said leave."[58] Without hesitation AG King endorsed the request: "Send him leave."[59] Not only was the lieutenant happy, so too was Miss Grace O'Grady, Frank's sweetheart. At Boerne on December 15, 1885, the couple were wed, the stricture about Rangers being single applying only to the enlisted and noncom ranks—battalion officers could be married.[60] The blissful honeymoon was short.

Whatever may be said of Mr. Frank Jones, and shortcomings he owned, there would be no legitimacy in even mildly suggesting he avoided hard work and hazard, or whined about having to spend days or nights in camp or in the saddle. At this point in his life, by no man's measure could Lieutenant Jones be classed a homebody. His heart and hormones may have been directed toward his new bride, but his body and soul and Colt's .45 were anchored in the Ranger camp. Frank Jones was now a career lawman, one on the pathway to a captaincy and roadblocks could be damned.

Two days after his matrimonially uniting with Grace, workaholic Jones was back on duty at Camp Leona, evidenced by his official written correspondence. First, he informatively posted the adjutant general about Private Ben Riely: "I saw Riely in San Antonio the other day and he thinks he may be able for duty in two months unless he has to undergo an operation. In that event it will be six months before he can report for duty." Clearly Jones was concerned about the wellbeing of Ranger Riely, but he also was worried about the company being short staffed: "I need an extra man or two very much and could enlist two good men right away."[61] In a second letter that same day, again posted at Uvalde but two days after the wedding ceremony, Lieutenant Jones graciously acknowledged receipt of congratulations and warm salutations from Captain Sieker: "Many thanks for your Kind wishes for myself and wife & hope soon to hear of you following my example."[62]

Someone Lieutenant Jones did hear from was the governor—though indirectly. Passing orders down from above AG King instructed Jones to pick a trustworthy and competent Ranger, put him in charge of two or three men, and send them west to Concho County (Paint Rock).[63] A prominent rancher's fence had been cut—four miles' worth. Quite naturally the cowman squawked. And just as predictably the politico jumped into action, ordering Texas Rangers to respond. Due to his proven courage and strict attention to detail and skillful report writing, Private C. W. Giffin caught the tough assignment, leaving Camp Leona five days before Christmas 1885.[64] Five days after the holiday, as ordered to do, Private Giffin penned a preliminary report to AG King, which in part explained many frontier folks' hard spot:

> I found the fence cut as reported and that he had rebuilt the same but says he expects it will be recut. They have no suspicion of any party or parties in particular, but think it must be some of the outside Stockmen whose cattle were in the habit of watering at his water which is now enclosed. They can give me no clue at present to work on. The adjoining ranch will fence in a few days; they will enclose a water front of Eight miles in a straight line joining the line. . . . which was cut on the west and another ranch on the east: This will cut off all the water in this part of the country. There will be no water nearer than the Concho river which is Twenty miles distant. This will force the people to move their stock or cut fences and as near as I can learn the general opinion is that they

> will cut. The building of these fences will cut off about 15,000 or 20,000 head of stock that have been watering on this creek.[65]

Clearly not everyone had been lured by the sales pitch that barbed-wire was "Light as air, Stronger than whiskey," and "Cheaper than dirt" or that it was "Pig tight, Horse high, and Bull strong." As previously mentioned, at the time, Texans were about equally divided: 50 percent favoring the stringing of barbed-wire, while the other half thought, nay knew, that the newfangled invention was the Devil's work, pure and simple, no argument. In fact one wrought-up Texas cattleman was emphatic. Had he his way, "the man who invented barbed-wire would have it all wound around him in a ball and the ball rolled into Hell."[66]

As 1885 was fast coming to a close Lieutenant Jones was in a frenzy finishing up paperwork and inventorying Company D's state-owned property and ammunition. In the middle of it all—as it seems to always happen—Lieutenant Frank Jones had to set aside the ink pen for the pistol. One Mr. A. P. Spence either had too much eggnog or just slipped off the half-cock notch mentally. At any rate, he was on the festive streets of Uvalde shooting his six-gun, firing at the moon—or something. Sergeant B. D. Lindsey, who was uncharacteristically in camp, rather than in the field, and Lieutenant Jones rushed to the hubbub and arrested Spence. The doughty Rangers then delivered him to the Uvalde County Jail, before returning to camp to begin their holiday celebration that Christmas Eve.[67]

Grace O'Grady, the daughter of John G. O'Grady, a Boerne, Texas, Inn and Boarding House owner, and the first wife of Frank Jones. *COURTESY CANDICE DUCOIN.*

Benjamin Dennis "B. D." Lindsey, a genuine fire-breathing Texas borderland lawman: Ranger, U.S. Mounted Customs Inspector, and Sheriff of Bexar County, Texas—and a partner in the Tariff Saloons of Eagle Pass and Uvalde. FROM *TEXAS RANGER SKETCHES* COURTESY THE AUTHOR ROBERT W. STEPHENS.

From L to R: J. Walter Durbin, William Treadwell, and George W. Clark don a striking pose in the Thomas R. Hamilton Photographic Studio at Laredo, Texas. *Courtesy Suzanne Giffin-Garcia.*

CHAPTER 8

"Damnable Act of Savagery"

THE YEAR 1886 DIDN'T OPEN WITH the sound of gunfire for the Texas Rangers of Company D but there was an explosion—of paperwork. From his base in Concho County, though he picked up mail at Brady, McCulloch County, Ranger C. W. Giffin was caught up in a whirlwind of communication—all relating to expense accounts and vouchers and IOUs detailing the purchase of food for his men and fodder for the horses—and "two large mules."[1] Though he wished Captain Lam Sieker a "happy and prosperous New Year" the real purpose of Lieutenant Frank Jones' letter to the battalion quartermaster was final submission of "monthly and ration reports for Dec. 1885."[2] As the first month of 1886 waned the actual policing work of Company D was less than inspiring. Only two misdemeanor arrests were made and one of those was A. J. Spence, for a second time, Disturbing the Peace inside the cooperate limits of Uvalde. A pair of John Wolfgang Braeutigam's alleged murderers Wes Collier and Jack Beam had managed another jailbreak. As the month drew to a close Ranger Ira Aten and Edwards County Sheriff Ira Wheat were still in the broken Nueces River and Devils River Country hunting hard for the dangerous and no doubt heavily armed fugitives.[3]

For Lieutenant Frank Jones a smidgen of good news was ushered in with January 1886: AG King had authorized him to enlist "one good man. If however, you think one would not be Sufficient for your work, you can enlist two but not unless absolutely necessary."[4] Frank Jones had a good man in mind. On the twelfth day of February the Company D lieutenant enlisted one of his older brothers, Dood Jones.[5] Nepotism was not frowned on or thought unethical. Within ranks of the Frontier Battalion, at the time, such a practice was customary.

The first quarter of 1886 found Company D Rangers responding to first one supposed crisis, then another—virtually always following written complaints to the governor or adjutant general. The overall Frontier Battalion manpower model was skimpy, requests for Ranger presence great. AG King explained the situation to J. A. and H. P. Maurice of Kinney County:

> Your letter of the 1st inst. to Governor Ireland has been referred to this office. Lt. Frank Jones, Co. D Frontier Battalion at Uvalde has been instructed to send you three men as soon he can practically do so. The force is so small that it is difficult to send detachments where wanted immediately on call. To provide some detachments of troops they must be called from other points when their presence is not so much needed.[6]

Tallying the duration and number of scouts, miles traveled, and names of persons arrested for criminal offenses and by whom is workable in excruciating detail. The enumerations, though, are not necessary for advancing Frank Jones' biography. Simply said, he was busy![7] And so were the Rangers of Company D, especially Ira Aten. He had been summoned to the governor's office covertly, ostensibly delivering Captain Sieker's horse Old Prince to Austin.

That Braeutigam's suspected killers, who by this time had escaped from jail twice, were outfoxing the best efforts of the Texas Rangers was a thorn in the side of Governor Ireland, painful and politically embarrassing. Aten was, by authority of the governor, to use all means at his disposal and any resources of the great State of Texas to see that justice was meted out to two of the fugitives, Jack Beam and Wes Collier: bring them in shackled in chains or leave them horizontal on a mortician's stone-cold slab.[8] Ira Aten was to stay on the hunt till Hell froze over, then he was to buy an overcoat and carry on: No excuses, no stopping. Ira was a thoroughly committed Company D Ranger. Lieutenant Jones knew in this instance to let the game play out and not interject any supervisory nonsense or nitpicking into the equation. Any time the state's chief executive was personally dabbling in the battalion's on-the-ground affairs, a savvy lieutenant looking for career advancement best march in lockstep harmony. Frank Jones was sharp.

Private C. W. Giffin's enforcing accomplishments in Concho County were negligible at best. Nonexistent at worst—he and his detachment had not caught any fence cutters. He had, however, familiarized himself with the problem, banking understandings of the incompatible viewpoints. Therefore he was ripe for another special assignment subsequent to his and fellow privates Henry Piper and E. R. Goff returning to Camp Leona.[9]

No sooner had Giffin made his appearance at Company D headquarters before he was handed another out-of-the-ordinary mission. He was to proceed to Brown County and investigate the killing of a rancher's sheep. Giffin, however, was to assume the role of a "detective" and not conduct his affairs in an open and aboveboard manner. Although today the terms "detective work" and "investigative work" wash out as being one and the same, for nineteenth-century Texas Rangers use of the word "detective" equated to assuming an undercover persona and worming one's way into a suspect's confidence. Unfortunately such type work was seldom looked upon with favor. Many—most—Texas Rangers thought, and rightly so, that they were on the road to professionalism as crime fighters and peace keepers and could accomplish those ends overtly. There was something distasteful about sneaking around and lying and betraying someone's trust—even if the cause be just. For some Rangers it was actually interpreted as an "insult" to ask them to perform detective work.[10] Private Giffin was a real trooper though, and off to Brown County he went.[11]

Scarcely two weeks later no-nonsense reality landed in Private Giffin's lap. He had made an unintentional tactical error—in this particular case one of significant weight. AG King's letter to

Lieutenant Jones is self-explanatory for the time—and enlightening for the historic overview:

> Pvt. C. W. Giffin of your Compy. has been ordered back to your headquarters for having imprudently given away his business in Brown County to the Sheriff of Said County. You will detail one other man to replace Giffin on return of Giffin to camp and the man so detailed will receive from Giffin all the information he has attained in connection with the killing of sheep. . . . This information received from Giffin will be used in the further protection of the case. Caution the newly detailed man to keep his own counsel & and to act strictly as a detective, not telling any one about his business, except those that Giffin says have been giving him information or other reliable persons who can do the same.[12]

Assuredly Lieutenant Jones was not overly concerned regarding any cat jumping out of the bag in Brown County. Private Giffin was a good man, a good Ranger. On the other hand he had something else on his mind—a trip home. Jones applied to the adjutant general for a leave of fifteen days, which was approved commencing on the fourth of May 1886. Sergeant Lindsey was to take command of Company D in Frank Jones' absence.[13]

Although defining the exacting purpose of Frank's vacation at home is vague—from a health standpoint Grace was frail—but surely he wanted to spend time with his wife and extended family. And, he would have big news to share. On the May 1 he had been commissioned as a Frontier Battalion captain, Commander of Company D.[14] In a personal communication the adjutant general congratulated Frank on the promotion, particularly noting his past performance and anticipating that degree of competency would be maintained into the future.[15] Captain Frank Jones had arrived, working his way up from the very bottom of the chain-of-command structure. Was he now on the road to fame, Texas Ranger fame? Greatness?

Someone else had been working hard, too. Successfully Ranger Ira Aten had tracked down one of John Wolfgang Braeutigam's killers, Jack Beam. At the suspect's brother-in-law's place on prettily situated Pedernales Creek in Travis County—after a two-day watch—Aten jumped out of the brush and poked his Colt's six-shooter in Jack's face, warning him that resisting arrest would be wrongheaded—dead wrong! Ira Aten turned his hapless prisoner over to authorities at Fredericksburg, subsequent to their solemn pledge not to lynch him.[16]

Just prior to Frank Jones' promotion to captain, Aten had had the good fortune to escape unscathed during a gunfight with the other fellow he was hunting, Wes Collier. During this exchange of gunfire the fugitive made good his escape.[17] Shortly thereafter—and consequent to Jones' elevation to the captaincy—Ira Aten again found his man. Wes Collier was hanging out at the residence of Nicolas Dayton east of Liberty Hill in Williamson County, paying especially close attention to the landowner's teenage daughter. Accompanied by civilian John Reynolds Hughes, who himself would later become a Texas Ranger captain, Ira Aten placed the Dayton homestead under surveillance. Charging Hughes with the responsibility of maintaining an outside position to cut off any escape, Aten burst into the house—.45 in hand, catching a bleary-eyed Wes Collier yet in bed. Aten reported: "He fell back across the bed towards his pillows as soon as he saw me and jerked his six-shooter with both hands, and as he was bringing it up from the pillows over to line it up on me, I shot him through the heart. He dropped his gun, fell over on his back upon the bed and mumbled something. He was quick as a flash and in another instant would have killed me."[18]

There's little doubt that Ranger Aten's assessment was spot on, logically taking into account Wes Collier's armament. According to a newspaperman covering the story, outlaw Collier was well fixed: "Under his vest, on each side, was concealed a pistol, and another was found in an inside pocket. The pistols on his sides were arranged in a very ingenious manner, being connected together by a strap which passed over his shoulders, terminating at each end in a scabbard, and in each of these scabbards was a six-shooter, one of them being a Smith & Wesson, .45 caliber; the other a Colt's of the same caliber. The smaller pistol which was found in his pocket, was an Invincible, .38 caliber. The whole of them were loaded all around and in prime condition."[19]

Ranger Aten was receiving much favorable press and public adulation for ending the criminal career of desperado Wes Collier. AG King penned a letter to A. P. Patton of Fredericksburg praising the Ranger's work:

> Wesley Collier was killed by Aten, at great expense both to the State & himself and at great risk, for which he certainly deserves a part of the reward offered. Aten is a good & courageous officer, & the killing of Collier has saved infinite trouble to the citizens & authorities of your county.[20]

A supplement to the Company D Monthly Return was concise, simply indicating that Ira Aten "met and killed Collier who resisted arrest."[21] Captain Frank Jones was incapable of leaving it at just that, jumping on the roaring bandwagon of public exaltation, particularly remarking in correspondence to headquarters that "Aten is deserving of both credit and reward for the work after those murderers."[22]

From the evidence at hand it would seem, that at least to some extent, Captain Jones' planned furlough at home had been somewhat delayed. Nevertheless, it may be reported he made the trip. And just as certainly it may be said that all of the time he spent at home was not enjoyable. From Boerne he updated AG King: "Since coming here I have contracted a severe cold which as settled on my chest and as the weather is very cold <u>and</u> disagreeable I am afraid to venture out. I thought it best to notify you of this fact. Just as soon however as the weather is <u>at all</u> favorable I will return to my station."[23]

Clearly Captain Jones had returned to field duty by month's end. In fact he was fit enough to personally command a hurried scout into Val Verde County in response to a rather ambiguous "Mexican scare" during late June 1886.[24] The trip would prove somewhat insightful about an apparent streak of pretentiousness coursing through Mr. Frank Jones' system. The front office questioned part of his expense voucher. Captain Frank Jones' answer to the inquiry is revealing: "The $14 is for my board and lodging while out on the Rio Grande [Del Rio] and while I could have lain out with the men I did not for a single instant think that the Genl. [AG King] would require a Commissioned Officer to lie around Camp yards with the men. . . . I had rather pay my own expense than to lie around in the dirt in towns. Since taking command of the Co. my personal expenses have not amounted to $10 and I have honestly tried to conduct the Co. on as economical a basis as I could and perform good service. I would not ask for a single dollar to be paid me that I do not consider just and honorable."[25] As common with near any organizational structuring, particular benefits accompany upper level positions, the Frontier Battalion was no different. Clearly Jones felt entitled to capitalize on the perks paralleling the promotion. Frank Jones was now a captain of Texas Rangers and with the job went the rewards. Lest there be any misunderstanding, he was no martinet—not even close—and as will become apparent the rank and file of Company D adored him, the headquarters staff respected him, and the general public by and large gave him high marks.

Someone not receiving high marks was a Company D fellow, George A. Dalzell. Though at the time of several off and on again appointments with the unit his personal problems are not particularized, there is a hard and disturbing bottom-line bubbling to the surface. Regrettably Captain Jones wanted to make sure Captain Sieker was updated regarding the ex-Company D campmate: "I guess you saw an acct. of old George Dalzell dying in Uvalde last Sunday of whiskey and morphine."[26] Personnel problems were always the bugaboo of an upper level management team, including Captain Frank Jones.

Private Wood Saunders was in the doghouse but not now in the Texas Rangers. He had been involuntarily discharged, subsequent to an alleged incident of drunken misbehavior. According to a distraught mother, Saunders was accused of insulting a young lady by going to her room at night and by attempting "to force an entrance in spite of her daughter's protests." AG King stridently graded the conduct, "if true," as outrageous and had ordered the young Ranger fired, but was leaving not just a little wiggle room in case the accusation was overblown and Saunders was innocent of any wrongdoing. Saunders' plea to Ranger hierarchy for reinstatement was not out-of-hand dismissed. The AG would allow Captain Jones to make an impartial investigation and determine whether or not Wood

Saunders had the potential for making "a good, law-abiding, sober Ranger." Should Captain Jones give the okay Saunders' employment with the battalion could be restored.[27] Subsequently Captain Jones either overlooked or unfounded the allegations lodged against his boyhood friend from the Curry Creek neighborhood and reenlisted Wood Saunders as a Ranger, effective August 22, 1886.[28]

Hardly had Captain Jones returned to Camp Leona than orders from the adjutant general's office propelled him back to the border, expressly to Eagle Pass, Maverick County. The governor had snappily decreed that Captain Jones "go there yourself with all your Company."[29] After covering the seventy-five miles and burning up three days Captain Jones established his company headquarters at Eagle Pass.[30]

Working east from camp and into Zavalla County, Private Giffin leading a three-man detail was in search of a suspected or not-so suspected murderer, Bill Ware. Fortunately the Rangers' hunting skills had been honed to razor-sharp exactness. Their marksmanship was wobbly, however. The good—or bad—Ware had no intention of surrendering to lawmen and he didn't! When his "arrest was demanded he ran and Giffin and J. W. Saunders fired two shots each at him, but failed to stop him."[31] The boys dejectedly returned to camp empty handed. Several days later Captain Jones saddled up and led a five-man detachment into Zavalla County looking for Ware but was quickly apprised that the fugitive had quit the country.[32]

Something that was not in short supply was Captain Jones' inclination to contentiously do a good job, but also to take advantage of every opportunity to polish an apple. At the tail-end of one report to headquarters Captain Jones had a distinctive and, perhaps partly self-serving, message for Quartermaster Sieker: "Do not be surprised if you get a small boom for next Adg. Genl. but charge it to me."[33] Likewise, the previous month in a letter's Post Script, Frank Jones had matter-of-factly complimented Sieker: "I was delighted to get your photo and think it a splendid one—Just like you." [34]

Unquestionably Captain Frank Jones was a man's man, and a commander wrapped hard and fast with the notion of leading from the front. That he did not shy away from field duty is more than adequately exhibited by his taking four Rangers with him and embarking on a horseback scout into Crockett County (Ozona) checking into the general "lawlessness."[35] He would not return to Company D's Eagle Pass campground for nineteen days, after scouting through the counties of Val Verde, Kinney, Edwards, and Crockett, covering some 475 miles.[36]

Sometimes seeming capricious, battalion headquarters ordered Captain Jones to move camp again, this time establishing winter quarters "in the vicinity of Camp Wood or Barksdale, taking wood, water & grass in consideration." He was to obtain necessary supplies from vendors at Uvalde.[37] By the nineteenth day of October 1886 Captain Jones had anchored his new nerve center a mile and a half west of Camp Wood, and somewhat in keeping in character, boldly named the new spot Camp Sieker.[38] In this regard any touch of bashfulness on the part of Captain Jones was wholly nonexistent. After staking out his new campground Frank Jones notified Austin, specifically Captain Lam Sieker: "I have an excellent Camp for protecting from cold weather and have christened it in honor of our efficient Quarter Master."[39]

Permanently repositioning or temporarily moving Ranger companies on wall-maps in the big office is a snap. In the field it's more problematic: saddling horses, packing mules, loading wagons, harnessing teams, and then navigating across swollen streams or atop muddy roadways or stretches of ground absent a hint of water. On the very same day that Captain Frank Jones set up Company D's spanking new Camp Sieker in Edwards County (now Real County) AG King at Austin penned him orders, not necessarily strict orders but guidance nevertheless. The worried sheriff of Kinney County, Frank S. Fritter, was desirous of having Rangers make appearances throughout his county at polling places located in the various precincts for the November elections.[40] Wisely, Captain Jones complied with the adjutant general's wishes the best he could with the available manpower; stationing two-man teams at selected election sites. Not to be tagged a fellow too good to work, Captain Jones and two privates took up their peacekeeping position at the McWeaver Ranch on the day ballots were cast.[41]

After returning to the Company D headquarters Captain Jones took pen in hand for a routine report to Captain Sieker on the sixteenth of November 1886, making sure to wind it up with honey: "Come out to 'Camp Sieker' and pay us a visit. A good many people out here still remember 'them Siekers boys.'"[42] A week later Frank was yet touting the fun to be had if Captain Sieker but would pay the Company D men a personal visit: "The boys have noticed considerable bear sign (not Ranger) and this evening one of the boys saw about 25 turkeys. Four deer have been killed since we came here right near Camp. I am satisfied you would have a good time. I can get a good pack of hounds and will do all I can to insure yourself and friends a lively time."[43]

Someone that had had a lively time was Ira Aten. He had been away from camp on another special assignment, this one lasting a total of 144 days and tallying, all told, 2,660 miles.[44] Aten had been working undercover since late summer, primarily in Brown County (county seat Brownwood) trying to nab some troublesome fence cutters. In the end, after getting the help of Captain William Scott and other Texas Rangers and a few trusted local citizens it boiled down to a blistering nighttime shootout, best explained by Ranger Aten:

> . . . . Captain Scott arranged his men accordingly. . . . about 11 o'clock the night of Nov. 9th 1886 four men came along cutting Mr. Baugh's fence & the night being bright moonlight we could see them coming plainly. When opposite the Rangers Captain Scott demanded their surrender which was answered by a shot from one of the parties cutting the fence. The shooting then became general & the fence cutters tried to run. After the shooting was over two men who were cutting fence were found lying on the ground in a dying condition from wounds received from Winchesters & since have died. There [*sic*] names were Jim Lovell, Constable. . . . The other Amos Roberts. The two that got away was John Mathews & Charley Johnson. There are several other parties. We have evidence left in charge of Capt. Scott in Brown Co. after night of the 9th 1886.[45]

While Aten had been busily sneaking and snooping and shooting in Brown County, Ranger Private Wood Saunders was detailed to make an investigation into reports of fence cutting in Kendall County, his home county. Though Captain Jones had initiated the request, AG King unmistakably was not ready to just willy-nilly give Private Saunders a carte blanche. The uneasy adjutant general still owned some reservations about Wood Saunders, and had explicit orders for Captain Jones. "Let him [Saunders] however, act with tact and judgment. Keep his operation Secret & if successful Keep clear of newspapers or newspaper correspondents. Caution him also as to incidental expenses."[46]

Santa Claus may have been making his preparations at the frozen North Pole, but before Captain Jones could take any holiday, leadership responsibility demanded attention. Not just a few folks were clamoring for Ranger help, and one, Uvalde County Sheriff Henry W. Baylor, had an inside track with the frontier battalion's front office. Covering his bases, Sheriff Baylor went straight to AG King with his request: "I would like to have a detachment of State troops Stationed here for a few weeks. There is some trouble in pasture [fence] being cut or rather torn down and stock driven into the pastures. Grass is very scarce and I fear there will be trouble unless a close watch is kept."[47] Clearly, at least some cow owners were contemplating allowing their livestock to munch grass not theirs. Three days after Baylor updated King, Captain Jones was told, in writing with explicit wording: "Sheriff H. W. Baylor of Uvalde County applies to this office for a detachment to prevent fence cutting or destruction of fences in his county. You will therefore send a detachment of three men to report to Sheriff Baylor for duty as above."[48] Captain Frank Jones, already in receipt of his own letter from Sheriff Baylor about cattle stolen from "Gage's pasture on the Nueces" was formulating his own law enforcing plans. He had promptly assured Captain Sieker: "In the morning I will start out two scouts. I am going to worry some of these cow stealers awfully this Winter."[49]

On the calendar Winter equates to several months, and Captain Jones could worry those cow thieves for most of the Winter, but for two weeks—starting three days before Christmas—he was going to vacation at Boerne with Grace, and visit with his family.[50] He would, however, before taking off, track down and arrest suspected thief

Henry Thompson on the Upper Nueces and haul him back to Camp Sieker. Then, the next day, he would send two steely-eyed Texas Rangers to meet up with a deputy sheriff from Mason County and turn the prisoner over to authorities holding the warrant.[51] That done Frank Jones left for home.

Captain Jones had placed 1st Sergeant B. D. Lindsey in charge of Camp Sieker, a logical and wise choice in light of the fellow's no nonsense deportment and proven pluck. Sergeant Lindsey was a confirmed man of action and dutifully assuming the role of acting company commander was, well, boring. In an unavoidably mandated administrative report to Captain Sieker, Sergeant Lindsey opined: "Christmas is quite dull with us here in Camp. Capt. Jones being absent—of course necessitates my being in Camp. . . ."[52]

Unmistakably, as the first part of 1887 opened up, Captain Frank Jones was back in harness at Camp Sieker, overseeing enforcement activities of Company D. Assuredly there was plenty of work to be done—livestock thieves were about as reflected by arrest enumerations in the company's Monthly Return: Theft of Cattle, Theft of Horse, Theft of Goats, Theft of Cattle, and Robbery. A couple of fellows, one charged with Murder, and the other charged with Assault to Murder had managed to give Rangers the slip that January of 1887. Apparently the alleged or not so alleged fence cutters in Kendall County had given Private Wood Saunders the slip too, not discounting the fact that he had expended more than a month on the case. Captain Frank Jones' pleasure or displeasure with regards to such undercover assignments will be left as it stands. For an entry in the monthly report his remarks were decidedly terse: "Jan. 4—J. W. Saunders returned from Kendall County, accomplished nothing, out 34 days, mchd 500 miles."[53]

Perhaps after cognitive reflection Frank Jones had readjusted his thinking regarding the suspected fence cutters in nearby Kendall County, the nippers who had eluded Wood Saunders. The captain's rationale is not necessarily wrongheaded from a practical standpoint at the time, but binding his thought processes with today's political correctness should be intentionally and neutrally sidestepped. What Frank Jones said is what he said. In regards to that particular case the Company D captain appraised the Texas Ranger front office: "Saunders failed to accomplish anything in Kendall County in the way working up the fence cutting Case in that County. The cutting was done by Germans who speak no English and it will be almost an impossibility for an American to do anything in that Case."[54]

Someone who was trying to accomplish something was former Ranger Corporal P. C. Baird, Winchester-shooting veteran of the horrific gunfight at Green Lake. Now, advantaging himself of a better paying employment opportunity, he was serving as chief deputy for Mason County Sheriff John Calvin Butler. But, just like so very many other local lawmen of the day he needed help—Texas Ranger help. Taking pen in hand Baird messaged AG King.

> There is a party in My County charged with Murder and other offenses elsewhere, who, I Would like very much to effect his Capture. If seems almost impossible for Me to do the Work Myself owing to my being Known so well and the locality and situation of things. If you could favor Me with Ira Aten's services a short time I could do the Work Without any trouble, as he is Not Known in this Section. . . . I have a hard set to deal with and will very probably be compelled to make a Killing is why I want Aten to help Me. . . . [55]

AG King had no problem with sending Ranger Aten to Mason County. Within three days of receiving the letter of request he had answered Deputy Baird affirmatively and forwarded a like message to Captain Jones. The adjutant general, in this instance it seems, was much more worried about finances than fireworks. To both Baird and Jones he cautioned that when Ira Aten made the trip to Mason—from wherever he was—the Ranger would have to make the trip by "horseback" and not by stagecoach or rail.[56] Persnickety—but necessary—inquiries were also being directed toward another of Frank Jones' Company D Rangers, the young man undergoing treatment by a physician and having the doctor submit his bill straight to Austin for the patient's "medicine and vapor baths."[57] Many of Captain Jones' daily battles were fought with pencils not pistols. Bureaucracy!

Predictably if one were considering grazing cattle on another's pasture—enclosed or not—the presence of Texas Rangers in the county would not be agreeable. Were one blotching brands and/or killing cattle for beef or hides, having Texas Rangers in the section would be downright troubling and risky. So, Captain Jones clearly supposed that he had better let the front office in on the rumblings wafting his way, covering his fanny so to speak: "I am informed that there is a petition gotten up by the thieves of this County to have me moved out from here, but it is being kept pretty close and none of the good citizens have seen it."[58] Indubitably, forewarned is forearmed—politically and professionally, as well as physically.

Though there's an arguable tinge of irony, Sheriff N. O. Reynolds of Lampasas County, one of the Rangers who had earlier resigned rather than arrest his friend Scott Cooley, was now squawking about someone else purportedly not doing their job. Perhaps an old-time Ranger might have thought the sheriff's current request bizarre in light of such earlier lackluster performance. The nub is this, according to Sheriff Reynolds. There were some murder suspects wanted in Lampasas County but residing or lying low in Kerr County. For whatever the reason Sheriff Reynolds made inquiry of Captain Sieker regarding the then Kerr County sheriff, Frank M. Moore, an ex-Ranger company commander from bygone days. To Reynolds' way of thinking he was "afraid to trust" the matter to Sheriff Moore and, therefore, wanted Rangers to make the arrests in his stead.[59] Not surprisingly Captain Frank Jones jumped, advising the adjutant general he would send a Texas Ranger to Kerr County at once, one tasked with spotting Reynolds' murder suspects, Lorenzo and Isaac Clawson. Jones himself would follow later.[60] There was another big investigation on tap, too: A monster.

Mrs. E. E. Johnson had written newly installed Governor S. L. Ross about what she was decrying as a deplorable reign of lawlessness in Kerr County, one directly touching her household. She had previously penned her concerns to Governor Ireland, who may or may not have essentially discounted them, but he surely hadn't alleviated her agony. According to the widow Johnson, wealthy enemies coveting her ranchland, which she had refused to sell, had hired outsiders to run her and her brood out of the county—by fair means or foul. The actual depths of any conspiracy may be up for grabs, but the hard bottom line is not. One dark night outriders had made an appearance at the Johnson place, set fire to the house—and fatally shot one of her boys. Despite the fact one of the murder suspects, George Payne, had been taken into custody and was then securely ensconced in the Kerr County Jail, Mrs. Johnson wanted—was demanding—a fuller investigation and that the state furnish around-the-clock protection for her other son as he rambled about the county on the family's routine but necessary day to day business.[61] Needless to say Mrs. Johnson was a little more than critical of Kerr County officialdom. Mrs. Johnson in her seeming blanket indictment of county administrators touted that County/District Clerk McFarland would back her assertions.

Forthrightly McFarland messaged AG King at Austin, but there's little doubt Mrs. Johnson might have been somewhat disappointed, maybe mad. In part the less agitated McFarland said: "Mrs. Johnson is mistaken in that the officers of this county are afraid of the vigilants [*sic*] as she calls the murderers of her son because they are rich and strong. No braver, truer, or finer man holds office in Texas than is our Sheriff Capt. Frank Moore, late of the State Ranger Service. Our jail is one of the most secure in the State and Mr. Payne in my view of the situation is in no danger of a rescue by either friend or foe." Be not misled, the Kerr County Clerk was not making light of the crime, declaring the Johnson boy's death the "most damnable act of savagery" that he had seen in the region. He did not, however, cast the net of nefariousness as wide as the grief stricken Mrs. Johnson.[62]

Clearly the distraught mother was justified in her sorrow and maybe even her suspicions, but the criminal justice system spins on an axis of admissible evidence, and therein is the sometimes irksome rub for lawmen—they are sworn to uphold the law not become laws unto themselves. By sheer magnitude of the crime and weight of suppositional allegations a Ranger investigation was fitting. So thought the adjutant general, but it called for tact and diplomacy and sound reasoning—it was no head-thumping job. A commissioned officer had best look into the matter. AG King directed an explicit letter to Captain Jones, which in part said that while he didn't personally "place any great credit" in Mrs. Johnson's "vague statements," nevertheless he wanted Frank—as soon as practicable—to include Kerr County in one of his upcoming scouts, "making special inquiries about the alleged outrages of which Mrs. Johnson complains."[63]

Polishing off some more or less routine duties Captain Jones hotfooted to Kerr County, not only to look into the Johnson boy's murder, but also to try and nab the Clawson boys. Though he did not find the Lampasas County fugitives, Captain Frank Jones made what he deemed an appropriate—and telling—investigation regarding the Johnson homicide.[64] Straightforwardly Captain Jones deduced and reported: "In compliance with orders contained in your [AG King] letter of the 21st ult. I went to Kerr County and made as thorough an investigation as possible concerning the murder of young Johnson and the supposed existence of a vigilance committee in that County. There can be no doubt but that an organization was formed there for the purpose of intimidating the Johnson family into leaving the County, but I am satisfied there are not more than five who were really concerned in the murder. I interviewed the County officials and think that they will do all in their power to have the matter sifted to the bottom and they think that when the grand jury meets that some indictments will be found implicating others besides this man Payne who is now in jail. I saw Mrs. Johnson, and while she is full of conjecture and surmises, [she] knows nothing tangible. She gave me a list of the members of this vigilance committee which I enclose."[65]

Furthermore Captain Jones was in no position to furnish twenty-four-and-seven security for Mrs. Johnson's other son, which the lady was "imploring" him to do. She was advised that the sheriff would gladly give the boy protection, but he would have to remain in Kerrville, not be flitting around the county hoping officers could—or would—keep up with him. Captain Jones reiterated the hard and uncompromising fact that he "could not send men there to follow him around over the county."[66] With a big swathe of territory to cover, Captain Jones and the Rangers of Company D had headaches elsewhere, too.

Jones had just received a dispatch that trouble was brewing on the border. S. G. Ragland, manager of the huge A. B. Frank & Company cattle ranch along the Rio Grande, was in dire straits. Due to drought conditions all of the water had dried up within the ranch's interior pastures, even though they were gargantuan. To water cattle the fences had to be taken down along the river—all thirty-two miles of their Rio Grande frontage. Not unexpectedly, with near unhampered access, all so very soon "the Mexicans are [were] raiding from the Mexican side of the river" driving off the cattle to a place where they could not be legitimately recovered absent chancing an international incident. Ragland was in need of help—Ranger help.[67] Seemingly always in a reactive rather than proactive status there can be little surprise that a prominent landowner and big-time cattleman's bellyache brought direct Texas Ranger action, as reflected in Company D's Monthly Return for March 1887 highlighting the enforcement action of Sergeant B. D. Lindsey's three-man detachment: "then went to Eagle Pass to protect A. B. Frank's ranch from Mexicans stealing cattle and crossing them. . . ."[68]

Should the heartburn associated with trying to make heads or tails out of the Kerr County mess, siphoning manpower to guard a cattlemen's interest in Maverick County, and putting two Rangers on the trail of fugitive Bill Mitchell aka Baldy Russell wanted for a killing in Hood County (Granbury) not be enough to contend with, Captain Jones had other nitwits drawing his attention: namely the Odle boys, John, Will, and Alvin—first-rate outlaws all. Pitch in trailing and tripping up the hodgepodge of lesser lights with outstanding warrants and/or prices on their heads, and Frank Jones' law-enforcing duties appear overwhelming—staggering—not even factoring in supervising a whole company of independently minded free spirits carrying Colt's .45 six-shooters, as well as jumping to the what-for with paper and pencil responding to bureaucracy's bulldozings.

Unlike some speciously puffed Hollywood types, hawking their stories to scriptwriters during twilight years, as a gunfighter Texas Ranger Ira Aten, though he might not appear so, was the Real McCoy—no brag, just fact. *Courtesy Jeri and Gary Boyce Radder.*

Captain Bill Scott's Company F Texas Rangers. The first four standing Rangers from L to R: Jim (Frank) Carmichael, John Rogers, Captain Scott, and J. A. Brooks. Assisted by Company D's Ira Aten, after being tipped off these four were onsite shootists the night two fence cutters were killed in Brown County snipping wire. *Courtesy Armstrong Ranger Research Center, Texas Ranger Hall of Fame & Museum.*

As a committed civilian John R. Hughes guarded the front door at the Nicholas Dayton residence in Williamson County while Texas Ranger Ira Aten dashed through the backdoor, engaging Wolfgang Braeutigam's accused murderer Wes Collier in a deadly gunplay. *Courtesy Jeri and Gary Boyce Radder.*

Elijah Robert "E. R." Ashcraft was a member of Brown County's Farmers Alliance, an organization by and large opposed to cattlemen's stringing barbedwire, and not just a few on the outfit's roster were known fence cutters. E. R. Ashcraft was one, an assertion not denied by more than one straight-line blood relative. Seated from L to R: E. R. Ashcraft and his son Simon Franklin Ashcraft. Standing from L to R: Amanda [Arnold] Ashcraft and Annie Ashcraft. *Courtesy Jan Devereaux.*

John Calvin Butler, Mason County Sheriff. As a grocer turned lawman Butler recruited Corporal P. C. Baird to the position as his chief deputy. The duo often worked with Texas Rangers. Courtesy Mason *County Historical Commission.*

Brown County Courthouse. The up-and-coming town of Brownwood was the site of negotiations later characterized in history books as the Fence Cutters' Convention. The summit forestalled fence-line Winchester justice for awhile—a little while. *Courtesy Brown County Public Library—Local History & Genealogy Branch*

A hallmark of the success of Texas Rangers—then or now—is adaptability. Advantaging themselves of the latest in advancing technology the men of the Frontier Battalion discarded their single-shot Sharps and Springfield shoulder guns, replacing them with improved Winchester repeaters. The weapon pictured here was Ira Aten's personal Winchester rifle. *Courtesy Jeri and Gary Boyce Radder.*

CHAPTER 9

"He Caught for a Pistol"

WITHIN REASONABLY SHORT ORDER Sergeant Lindsey and his detachment had their assigned section of the Rio Grande under control. Enough so that he could report to Captain Sieker that even though some thieving "Mexicans had been depredating" along the river, since his arrival and commencement of the overt and random scouts everything—relatively speaking—was "quiet."[1] All was not serene for Frank's older brother William Kenner Jones, however, now the elected county judge of Val Verde County (county seat Del Rio). Judge Jones was miffed that more than one of his inquiries to the governor's office concerning the posting of a reward for the apprehension of suspected killer Ricardo Esparza, "a Mexican who was indicted in this Co. last Fall for the murder of one James Woods" had been ignored: Or in the judge's words, his letters had "simply been pigeonholed."[2] Collectively the Jones brothers were not the Lone Star State's most influential powerbrokers but by any standard they spoke with authority, antedated by the fond and positive memory of their patriarch, William Early Jones. Casually sloughing off their concerns was maybe not suicide politically but it was not real smart politics. The Jones name was good, especially in the Texas Hill Country.

Captain Jones had an item or two causing him no little worry, too. First and foremost would he even have a job? There was talk in legislative hallways of cutting costs, and a frontier battalion captain here or there was not off the parsimonious lawmakers' budgetary table. Frank made it known that he appreciated any consideration, and "would like very much" to remain in the Rangers and retain his position, but if there must be reductions he would graciously "bow to the inevitable and hunt some other occupation."[3] In the meantime, though, he would hunt for outlaws—three in particular.

During the middle of April 1887 Captain Jones, accompanied by Private Ira Aten, embarked on a dicey apprehension mission, capturing the crooked and cunning Odle boys, sure enough hard characters. The owlhoots, despite their ages, were making quite a name for themselves in the Texas Hill Country and down towards the Rio Grande and all the territory in between—and it was not one mamma would be proud of. In the upper stretches of Edwards County and with a stroke of good luck—or a damn good tip from a spy—Jones and Aten caught the bad boys napping in a secluded cabin, their saddled horses tied outside. Wisely choosing to wait until good daylight, the two Rangers placed the cabin under surveillance. The next morning, as luck would have it, a young boy came out of the house, bucket in hand, heading for the spring where Jones and Aten were hiding. Was their plan about to collapse on the utterance of an innocent but excitable boy? Though but a youngster the lad was made a momentary prisoner, so he could not sound an alarm. With the startled child either locked in a shed or in tow until the very last second (versions vary) Captain Jones and Private Aten rushed the house, one to the front door, one to the backdoor. Their actions had been gutsy, but more importantly, successful.[4] Without firing an irretrievable shot they had—absent fanfare—arrested Henry Cavius aka Henry Wilson, as well as the highly prized Will and Alvin Odle, in due course handing them off to the authorities in Burnet County where they were being sought for Horse Theft.[5] Time and time again, even though he was a part of the Frontier Battalion's management team, Frank Jones could and would stand his ground in the field. His backbone was ramrod straight.

With summer fast approaching Captain Frank Jones had to make a geographical readjustment. Grass around Camp Sieker had about played out. Jones, sticking with customary protocols and/or political good sense named his new headquarters Camp Ross, in honor of the sitting governor. He acknowledged that it would have been nice to be situated on a railroad, but in this instance he thought he could accomplish more real good working out of the "camp he had fixed up for the Summer" in the huge Edwards County pasture: More so than any other point that he knew of.[6]

The Frontier Battalion was and always had been a merry-go-round of personnel shuffling and reshuffling, comings and goings. Sergeant Ben Lindsey, although far from finally bidding law enforcement adieu, wanted to don the clothes of a respectable barkeep, becoming a saloon owner in partnership with another ex-Ranger, W. W. Collier.[7] The vacancy created by the top-sergeant's April 30 resignation opened the doorway for Captain Jones to name his replacement. Not surprisingly Austin Ira Aten got the nod and the job.[8]

No sooner had Aten been promoted than news broke just outside of Austin. At McNeil Station—a tiny depot fourteen miles north of the capitol—wicked train robbers did what train robbers do. These boys, though, were poured from a different mold: They were mean to the core. Highjackers taking part in the May 17, 1887, robbery were captained by two genuine misfits, escaped convict Brackston E. "Brack" Cornett, who was "as quick and strong in his movements as a panther" and William Henry "Bill" Whitley, a career-minded horse and cattle thief—or anything else that paid without working, save laboring at a real job. Outlaw Whitley was a compassionless and expressionless man who "could look into the muzzle of a double-barreled shotgun in the hands of an enemy and never flinch." These boys were legitimately illegitimate. Recklessly and remorselessly as the outlaws scooped up their $4000 haul they also gunned down two innocent folks—thankfully not fatally. Then the whole gang, which numbered seven, hightailed it for parts unknown. Austin area newspaper editors howled. Such audacity: Attacking a train almost in the State Capitol's shadows.[9]

Not content to idly pass time while trains were running up and down the tracks, crisscrossing the Lone Star State carrying strongboxes of cash, the energetic but loathsome Cornett/Whitley gang struck again. This time the big score was near Flatonia, Fayette County, about the midpoint between Houston and San Antonio. There, on the eighteenth of June, the gangsters attacked the Galveston, Harrisburg & San Antonio No. 19. During this robbery the guttersnipes again put on display their propensity for viciousness. Express messenger Frank Folger stashed the keys rather than submit to the indignity of surrendering the contents of his safe. Folger's motivation may have been just, but his actions were ill-advised. The coldhearted bandits pistol-whipped him unmercifully and tortured him by pulling out their pocket-knives and slitting his ears until they recovered the keys. Though the robbers may have been behaving foully, they knocked a homerun. Their take, after emptying the express car and the pockets of passengers, tallied near $14,000. The crooks didn't leave a dime behind, but they forfeited something much more costly: Their identities. A traveling Texas sheriff had been riding the rails and it was he who fingered Brack Cornett—the dominos of guilt by association fell from there.[10]

Governor Ross was more than a little embarrassed by the brazenness and brutality of the Cornett/Whitley gang. Their tearing into the progressive image he was promoting for Texas would not stand. He would—he decried—commission 400 Rangers just for the purpose of guarding the railway lines and railroad yards, guaranteeing that there would be at least five to ten well-armed fighting men on each and every train. In no uncertain terms Governor Ross avowed: "Train robbery is to be a fighting business and attended with almost certainty of failure and destruction."[11] The bombast was rich!

The reality was far less dramatic. Instead of beefing up the Frontier Battalion with hundreds of new hires, the fulltime job of catching the headlining robbers was assigned to two guys, and one of them was—at the outset—only enlisted provisionally, explicitly for that task. Although there is a paucity of documentable paper trails, there's little doubt that in one combination or another there were meaningful consultations between the governor and/or the adjutant general and/or Quartermaster Lam Sieker and/or Captain Frank Jones. The Company D commander had just the man for the job, his 1st Sergeant Ira Aten, already proven a tiger on a manhunt and a terror during a gunfight. In due time—a couple of months—Aten would seek and receive the h[illegible] John Reynolds Hughes, the civilian backing Ira's play fr[illegible]t porch when the Ranger burst through the rear [illegible]Wes Collier. Hughes, with Aten standin[illegible] his oat[illegible] of office at Georgetown, Willi[illegible] in the Rangers.[12] On special assign-[illegible] Private Hughes hunted train robbers.

[illegible]eanwhile, at the height of summer, Captain Jones was not [illegible] holiday; there was other police work to do. [illegible]887, he was going take a detachment and [illegible] scouting the West Nueces in search of "cattle that have had the brands burnt out." He was, if everything went as planned, to be joined by cowmen from the surrounding "two or three counties." Particularly to AG King, Captain Jones emphasized the significance of the task at hand: "This is an important move and I have had a great deal of trouble to get stock owners to go with me. The West Nueces is the head center of most of the cattle and horse stealing in this section."[13] On the same day Captain Jones also notified Captain Sieker that he was going to initiate a campaign to "work the burnt cattle" and he thought the stolen cow critters would tally somewhere—if he was figuring right—in the neighborhood of 300 head.[14]

Realistically, Captain Jones missed the mark. He and his crew of Rangers did, however, manage to round up 100 head of "burnt branded cattle" and turned them over to Animal & Hide Inspector Basham for rightful disposition. Just to make sure the beeves were not "forcibly taken" by cow thieves, Captain Jones assigned two Rangers to remain with Inspector Basham, while he and the rest of the detachment returned to Camp Ross.[15]

Knowing Jones had his head around livestock doings, the adjutant general forwarded a hot July message to the captain at Montell, northwestern Uvalde County. The content is interesting in that it's illustrative of just how skimpy much of the criminal intelligence was that the Rangers were actually working with. AG King was tipping Captain Jones off about a quartet of horse stealers—though they had stolen but the one horse—who the adjutant general perfectly described as follows:

> The description of the thieves is as follows. The one having the horse is about 27 years of age, 5ft. 10 inches high, Sandy chin whiskers, short mustache & grey eyes. Another is dark complicated, black mustache & heavy dark hair. Another [is] very dark, black mustache & unshaven for two or three weeks. The fourth, youthful, light complexion & smooth faced. Horses, two bay and two sorrels.[16]

AG King cautioned Captain Jones that the fellows he described, though they may have been reasonably young were armed all around with "Winchesters & Six shooters." Then as today the bullet plowing into a lawman's chest is not greased with remorse and good sense, nor is it totally reliant upon an aged and mature trigger-finger. Young men can kill. Old men can kill. Lawmen can die absent due caution. As Captain Jones' biography uncorks, the billowing blue smoke of Colt's six-shooters and Winchesters will continue to play into the story. He was living a Wild West drama and every now and again it turned Western!

That Captain Jones owned not just a little pluck is evidenced in his August 23, 1887, letter to the adjutant general. Although his reasoning may have been sound—personally justifiable—due deference was not apparent. Captain Jones requested and then hinted that one way or the other he would get his own way, regardless:

> I write for the purpose of asking your permission to remain away from my station for part of the month of September. My wife is in delicate health and expects to become a mother soon and is nervous and afraid when I am away and I feel that it is impossible for me not to be with her. I could have gone and the chances are that you would have never heard of it but disliking any underhand proceedings and relying on your generosity I make this application. I shall not be away a day longer than I deem absolutely necessary. Hoping to hear from you and favorably. Respectfully. [signed Frank Jones][17]

Adjutant General King, thoroughly committed to his subordinates' well-being physically and psychologically, understood Jones' predicament. He did not, however, appreciate or accept the childish logic exhibited by Frank, a full-grown and full-fledged Texas Ranger captain. Reading between the lines is not necessary. AG King replied to Captain Jones' letter on August 26, not letting too much time burn between imprudence and response:

> Your application for leave of Absence from your Company for some portion of September is somewhat indefinite as to the length of time you desire to be away, but as the circumstances are peculiar and the matter of great importance to you, personally, your application is granted. It will be better for you to remain with your Company however until its reorganization, unless you feel your presence at home to be necessary without delay. As to an officer absenting himself from his Command without permission, it would be a clear violation of positive orders and the circumstances would have to be unworkable that could cause such a breach of discipline to be excused. Put your Company in safe hands while away, and return to it as soon as possible. Respectfully [signed W. H. King][18]

Not taking a chance for any retractions, Frank Jones rushed home to be at Grace's bedside. Cutting it rather close, as it turns out, on September 1, 1887, an adorable baby girl was born to Frank and Grace at Boerne. Frank was overjoyed with the birth of Grace Kathleen, but though it's not documentable, there's little doubt that he—living in a tough man's world—internalized some very real misgivings about Grace's overall health and well being—she was frail and childbirth was hard.[19]

Maternity Leave was years into the future, and before the month was out Captain Frank Jones was back with the Rangers of Company D, tending to his administrative duties and conducting proactive scouts from Camp Ross.[20] Examining the Monthly Returns and Correspondence Files for Company D during the months of September and October 1887 is informative—and amusing.

In the first instance the enumerations of scouts and arrests are rather extensive, covering a wide-ranging geographical swath and accounting for a multitude of sins—criminal infractions with fixed penal code punishments.[21] Likewise, those same periodic documents reveal the nightmarish bookkeeping expected of the Frontier

Battalion officers' corps. How much it did or did not rankle him is not a matter of written record, but in one particular instance Captain Jones was forced into admonishing his Kerr County detachment: They had "an overdraw of potatoes and pickles." Therefore, no matter how much the boys craved them, since those items had been overdrawn they "could not have more until the time had expired for which these articles would do."[22] Pickles weren't his only problem.

Captain Frank Jones got caught flatfooted. Through miscommunications or subconscious denial the captain missed the proverbial boat—the company had caught a transfer to the Texas/Mexico border. In writings to Captain Sieker, the flabbergasted Captain Jones either feigned ignorance or was truly in the dark: "Your Letter of the 26th inst is at hand. I have rece'd no letter from Genl. King. I am starting a man to Uvalde tonight to telegraph that I have not rece'd any instructions from Headquarters and of course do not know what is meant in your letter."[23] Make no mistake, by the end of the month Captain Jones had got the message—loud and clear. On the thirty-first day of October he acknowledged same to AG King: "Your letter of the 25th was rece'd only yesterday morning and I at once broke camp. . . . Your letter was at the Uvalde Post Office and the man I sent down to telegraph you found it here [Uvalde]. The two men I have in Kerr County I will write and instruct to follow me. They have a pack mule. It will hardly take me seven days to reach Laredo unless I have some accident on the route."[24] Rhetorically a question pops up, although a hard and fast answer is elusive. Could Captain Jones' earlier insinuation to AG King about taking a secretive Leave of Absence have pushed his name to the forefront when selecting a Frontier Battalion company for service along the Rio Grande?

In any event the boys of Company D were on the march. Their new duty station was to be in Starr County (seat Rio Grande City) downriver from Laredo and upriver from Brownsville.[25] The best laid plans of mice and men sometimes suffer readjustment, and so it was with relocating the headquarters camp for Company D. The march to the river was relatively easy, though time consuming. From where they struck the Rio Grande at Laredo to Rio Grande City was dreadful travel due to sand and lack of grass for the horses. Besides the natural impediments of nature and geography Captain Jones was more than a little concerned about two internal deficiencies within the company. First—perhaps foremost—he was now working a territory predominately populated by speakers of the Spanish language and no one in Company D spoke "Mexican." Not too fluently anyway. He wanted permission to enlist a bilingual Ranger, even though it was ratcheting his staffing model up a notch.[26] Secondly, Captain Jones noted that his 1st Sergeant Ira Aten was constantly away from camp on lengthy special assignments which he did not object to—in fact he recommended them—but the regular absence of a noncommissioned officer to help with administrative and supervisory duties was noticeable. Particularly Jones pointed out to AG King that "A private put in charge is not near as efficient as a regularly appointed officer."[27] Therefore he sought the go-ahead to have a corporal assigned to the company and he particularly asked that J. Walter Durbin be transferred from Company F.[28]

Assuredly Captain Jones—despite his other concerns—had not lost sight of management's objective for beefing up the Texas Ranger presence on the border. Even while repositioning the Company D camp he noted—based on data furnished by an area deputy sheriff—"that here are about ten in the party who have been raiding in Starr Co. and that four of them reside in Guerrero, a small town about 4 miles from here in Mexico and are wanted in this State for crimes committed here."[29] Too, Captain Jones noted that he had been overtaken by the two Rangers who had been on detached service in Kerr County, his brother Dood Jones and Ernest Rogers. The pair had come by way of Cotulla due to the Nueces not being fordable as several crossings. Their temporary inconvenience was another fellow's misfortune. Before reaching Company D's stopover camp, while in Zapata County, the two Rangers arrested a "Mexican" wanted for the theft of thirty-seven horses. The prisoner was turned over to the sheriff.[30]

While still in the drawn-out process of properly positioning his borderland camp, Captain Jones and five Rangers scouted with Starr County Sheriff W. W. "Wash" Shely, brother of former Ranger captain Joe Shely, and one of his deputies, a "Mexican." The posse was in search of persons responsible for the earlier kidnapping of Juan García Barrera, a prominent borderland stockman ranching in Starr County. Somewhere near the Hidalgo/Starr County line the lawmen latched onto two of the suspects, Viviano Díaz and Cicilio Ybarro.[31] Others were yet on the run, so Captain Jones and his Rangers took another road in search of them, while Sheriff Shely and deputy struck out for Rio Grande City with their prisoners. The hapless fellows never became inmates in the Starr County Jail. They were, according to a *Galveston Daily News* account, taken from the sheriff by a heavily armed band of about fifteen "Mexicans" (vigilantes) and summarily lynched.[32] Soon, Mexican officials on the south side of the river applied the hardcore policy of *la ley de fuga* and executed two others.[33] Frank Jones' account is revealing and somewhat regrettable. Factually, Jones updated battalion headquarters: "Shely only had one man with him and a party of men took the prisoners from him and hung them."[34] Rather crass and inexcusable for a professional lawman was the captain's follow-up remarks to Quartermaster Sieker and to Adjutant General King. To Captain Sieker: "They were notorious scoundrels and the good people are jubilant over the matter."[35] And for AG King's edification: "They were very bad characters and the good citizens here, American and Mexican are greatly rejoiced at their taking off." In conjunction with that train of then widespread thought there's little reason to be taken aback at the last sentence in Jones' missive to the adjutant general: "There is no clue as to who did the hanging."[36] And there would not be! Shely became journalistic cannon fodder for a subset of the Starr County populace. Extralegal justice may be explicable, but it's not defensible.

Conversely, Captain Jones saw to it two other alleged kidnappers of Juan Barrera, Gregorio and Edward Ramos, were tracked down, arrested, and delivered into the clutches of Sheriff Shely. Privates Henry Pifer and A. "Tooney" Dillard, formerly of Company F, were credited with the arrests and safe delivery of the prisoners to Rio Grande City. "Mexican" vigilantes did not choose to test their pluckiness. Assuring Juan Barrera's safety, Ranger Ernest Rogers was assigned to act as his personal "bodyguard" on the man's intended trip to Roma.[37]

At long last, subsequent to several indecisive fits and starts, the border region campsite for Company D was set: In a pasture belonging to a ranchman named Bob Savage about five miles from Realitos, southern Duval County, county seat San Diego, Texas. Camp Savage, though not situated right on the border, was spotted strategically for interdicting the nefarious criminal activities of banditos and desperadoes and cow stealers and smugglers launching forth from both banks of the meandering Rio Grande.[38] The Realitos Station was an important depot on the Mexican National Railway-Texas Division, a line running between Laredo and Corpus Christi. But just to make sure the border per se was not neglected Captain Jones positioned a five-Ranger detachment at Rio Grande City. The relocation had been a logistical nightmare fighting sand and wind and wet weather, but the boys of Company D were now well fixed—for war: They had 2,520 pistol and Winchester cartridges on hand.[39]

Captain Jones now turned his personal attention to another matter, visiting home for the Christmas Season. This time around he was not hinting or implying that he could slip away undetected if need be—he'd apparently learned a lesson. His wording to AG King was not presumptive: "Can I leave my station on the 22nd instant and spend the holidays with my family? I can leave a good man in charge until my return and can safely promise that everything will be all right during my absence."[40] The adjutant general signed off on Frank Jones' vacation.

While home at Boerne, enjoying his time with Grace and baby Grace Kathleen, Frank was not too busy to take pen in hand on Christmas Eve and wish Captain and Mrs. Sieker a "Merry Xmas and happy New Year."[41] Then, unexpectedly, once again while on a trip home Frank Jones came down sick, "very sick with a cold and fever."[42]

By mid-January 1888, Captain Jones was back on duty at Camp Savage, even managing a trip to the seat of Duval County for a two-day jaunt classified as "official business."[43] Upon his return to Realitos the captain was greeted with unwelcome news, which he reported to AG King: "I have just heard that my wife is very sick and I am going to start for Boerne this evening. . . . I will remain away not an hour longer than I deem imperatively necessary."[44] During

Jones' January absences the Company D Rangers—especially the detachment at Rio Grande City—was busy, racking up multiple arrests for Disturbing the Peace, as well as arresting the two aforementioned Ramos fellows charged with Kidnapping, along with Juan Juarez charged with Theft of Horse, and Andres Coto for Assault With Intent to Murder.[45] Down-time for lawmen, if it comes at all, doesn't last too long.

Although exacting details of Grace Jones' health maladies are indefinable it's not outlandish to postulate that Mrs. Jones was a person in a delicate spot, constantly teetering between vitality and virus, perkiness and puniness. Assuredly Frank Jones loved his wife and was dedicated to her well being, but once her condition improved and/or stabilized he returned to Camp Savage. He too was caught betwixt and between, fidelity to wedding vows and faithfulness to an oath of office. Frank Jones, after all, besides husband and father was a captain of Texas Rangers.

Upon his return to Realitos it wasn't dodging bullets that caused Captain Jones to duck for cover, but he was caught in a kerfuffle with S. H. Bass, Esq., Mexican National Railway-Texas Division. Confusion and arguments over the issuance of Railroad Passes for Rangers was and would be a never ending headache for Frontier Battalion managers. In this instance the adjutant general had to step in, writing Mr. Bass that he had forwarded Captain Frank Jones instructions (read: orders) that in the future would "remedy the evil complained of."[46] Smartly, Captain Jones made explicitly clear to AG King: "Your instructions will be obeyed."[47]

Any immediate abrasiveness about railway transportation for Rangers from Company D was smoothed, evidenced by Captain Frank Jones' trip from Realitos to Corpus Christi on February 6, 1888, and the return trip two days later.[48] Also during that February the Company D's 1st Sergeant made his initial appearance at Camp Savage. Ira Aten had been on detached service since June 28 the preceding year, and though he had traveled 5,000 miles testifying in various courts regarding fence cutting and smuggling and horse stealing cases, his manhunt for those violent train robbers had not met with success.[49]

What was meeting with success was Captain Frank Jones' leadership style. Perhaps not all, but by any measure the vast majority of the Rangers under his direct supervision thought highly of him—exceptionally highly. In a world where men wear pistols to work everyday mutual admiration and respect is earned, not bestowed. Captain Frank Jones could hand out disciplinary penalties and guarantee the compliance of battalion orders, but always face to face, man to man. He too, when those situations turned Western and life and death danger was at hand, would lead from the front—by example.[50] Adjutant General King would and did epitomize Frank Jones: "An excellent man, and a most efficient, energetic, and fearless officer and Ranger. . . ."[51] The men's and the captain's reciprocal feelings may be laid bare by mentioning two happenings within the same month—March 1888—at the same place—Realitos.

On the first day of March in a letter to Captain Sieker, Captain Jones, though he didn't have to, bragged on the men of Company D: "I have the best and most honest lot of men that I have ever known." There were to his way of thinking not a deadbeat among them.[52]

Twelve days later—and though they probably knew not of the captain's praise for them to the front office—Frank Jones' subordinates had a surprise for him—they'd all chipped in. They not only bought him an A. W. Waltham & Co. pocket watch and chain but they had secured the services of a jeweler and had the exquisite timepiece engraved: "For Captain Frank Jones From The Men of Co. 'D' Rangers, Realitos/March 12, 1888."

Interagency or intercompany celebrations were quickly squelched. Hell was popping near Wharton, Wharton County—and it wasn't pretty. Half a dozen black men had been viciously murdered near Spanish Camp, west of Wharton. The county sheriff, J. Wade Jones, the 23rd Judicial District Judge, the Honorable W. H. Burkhart, and the district attorney were hollering for help, insisting that state troops be sent to "assist the civil authorities."[53] The governor was not happy and the adjutant general was not happy—rightly so, the wheels had come off at Wharton. Turning to his crackerjack company of Rangers, AG King ordered that Captain Jones handpick the detachment of Rangers and by the most practical and fastest route hasten them to Wharton. Oh yes, Captain Jones could now—as he had wanted to—have a corporal's slot on the Muster & Payroll, a promotion he would have the managerial liberty of filling. J. Walter Durbin, who had earlier transferred into Company D, was selected as the corporal, a man characterized by Captain Jones as "an old Ranger and has been an officer before and is a good man."[54]

Realizing the significance of the case at hand and the importance of coordinating the exigency of transportation issues, Captain Jones opted to accompany the detachment headed to Wharton, at least as far as Corpus Christi so that he could make arrangements for railway passage for men and horses.[55] In this instance the Mexican National Railway-Texas Division came through in splendid fashion, granting transportation to Corporal Durbin and "3 men with 1 mule and 4 horses from Realitos to Corpus Christi."[56] Subsequent to working out travel arrangements for the next leg of the trip from Corpus Christi, which in the end would yet prove convoluted and confusing, Corporal Durbin and his detachment headed for Wharton, while Captain Jones returned to Camp Savage.[57]

Upon arrival at Wharton it took but a jiffy for Corporal Durbin to be brought up to speed. There had been a series of murders. The one hanging the most notoriety was the aforementioned instance where a tenant farmer's house had been set afire, and the group of black men shot down as they fled the inferno.[58] By at least one account the victims "had been somewhat overbearing and had experienced trouble with white renters" but that's not a free pass for murder in any good man's book. Corporal Durbin was a good man and good Ranger.[59] Not unexpectedly, as nearly always was the case, not everyone in the county was extending the hand of welcome to Rangers. Corporal Durbin had it pegged tight: "the Sheriff and a few Officials are highly pleased with us while others are doing all they can to get us away as they think we are likely to make the shoe pinch too close."[60] That Durbin and his boys were kicking ass and taking names is confirmable: They made nine arrests for Murder in as many days.[61] Shortly thereafter they, the Rangers, even made more arrests in the horrific homicide.[62] In correspondence to Captain Sieker, Corporal Durbin placed the number of murders in the county at fourteen within the last six months. He, too, was anticipating "getting more of the gang" and he was downplaying the apprehension creeping into J. Wade Jones' mind: "The Sheriff fears trouble During Court but I hardly think any of them be so boaled [*sic*] to try any thing of the Kind."[63] Durbin would later be able to report that the Wharton County Grand Jury was successful in "finding bills [Indictments] against all the men we arrested here Some time a go charged with murder. . . . We are guarding the jail at present."[64]

Meanwhile back at the Rangers' Camp Savage there was a new face reporting for duty on April 1, 1888. One of Sergeant Aten's younger brothers, Calvin Grant, had arrived at Realitos to be sworn in as a Company D Ranger.[65] After payment of the $.25 fee to an official empowered to administer official oaths, Cal Aten was no longer a civilian.[66] He was a Ranger, a real Ranger. Young Aten was, despite customary hype, weaponless. It was an embarrassing shortfall his top-sergeant brother would fix. Cal fondly remembered:

> Just think of my joy that first evening when my brother Ira handed me (A Belt Four Inches Wide). . . . full of cartridges with a scabbard and a .45 six-shooter in it. He told me to put it on and on it went. I wasn't afraid Ira would joke me. I looked around and saw that every man there, ten or more had their guns strapped on. It seemed to be a tradition that rangers must go armed and stay armed and about the only time we took off those guns were when we were asleep.[67]

Scarcely had young Aten been at camp long enough for an orientation period into Ranger business, before he was approached by Captain Jones and told to make preparations for a scout. The captain and his brother Dood Jones, accompanied by Cal Aten, would travel southwest by horseback to the border, visiting the little community of Carrizo (now Zapata) in Zapata County, on the Rio Grande between Laredo and Roma.[68]

At the first night's campground, before they broke out from their ration pack "a piece of salt bacon, a few pounds of flour, baking powder, salt, sugar, and coffee" Private Cal Aten erred. After unsaddling he had placed his Winchester, still in the scabbard, muzzle down against a mesquite bush. All so quickly Captain Jones imparted a few words of wisdom. Cal had no trouble recalling: "I remember how mortified I was when the Capt. said 'Cal you didn't do that right. You should stand your gun stock down as if it rains the scabbard will keep your gun dry.' Then I noted my mistake." Cal also noted, though he held his own counsel, that Dood Jones "was grouchy and a little wrong in the head. Fell out of a tree when he was born," Cal guessed.[69]

Upon arriving at Carrizo the Rangers were given a quick tour of the Zapata County Jail by Deputy Thatcher, Sheriff Robert A. "Bob" Haynes' right-hand man. Although he would visit many county lockups during the days ahead, this one made a lasting impression on rookie Ranger Aten. It was as Cal remembered "a great stone dungeon with iron rings set in the concrete floor to chain the prisoners' legs to at night. In the daytime the prisoners would be loose with chains dragging. They looked like wild animals."[70]

The next morning, just after sunup, Cal Aten was immersed in real world reality—some of those "wild animals" had grabbed Thatcher's six-shooter, wounded him in the hand, and were scampering for the Río Bravo, intent on leaving Texas as but an unpleasant memory. Naturally Captain Jones and his two companions gave chase. Luckily, the sheriff was Johnny-on-the-spot and caught the escapee who had grabbed Thatcher's pistol. Indeed, this was heady stuff for a brand-new Ranger, one on the job less than a week. Interestingly, Cal's naivete shines through, a dynamic he unreservedly admitted after realizing that the only man with a gun had been caught: "That was disappointing to me, there couldn't be much fun hunting men I know were unarmed."[71] Cal wanted to shoot his gun—at somebody.

The three other escaping prisoners had made the river, which was up and was a quarter mile wide with considerable driftwood floating in the middle. Cal Aten, squinting, spied a fellow's head way out in the river, trying to hide amongst the debris. With eagerness he turned to Captain Jones and blurted out his question: "Capt. Can I shoot him?" After studying the situation, Captain Jones gave the okay: "Cal, shoot his head off." Frank Jones turned his horse's head back toward the jail and rode away. Cal began blasting away with his Winchester, lobbing bullets downriver. Finally, Captain Jones' nonchalant attitude dawned on Private Aten: "The Capt. knew I had no chance of hitting the head in the water at least five hundred yards away with the guns we carried in those days, but he wanted me to have the fun of trying."[72] Jones made note.[73] Needless to say the novice Texas Ranger didn't draw blood.

Corporal Durbin did! After winding up the Ranger involvement in the Wharton County murder investigations—prosecutors dealt the cases away—Durbin was sent on a peace-keeping mission to Six-Shooter Junction, on the record incorporated as Hempstead, Waller County. While there, on patrol, he rightly or wrongly stopped a black man. For dead sure the fellow did wrong. Ranger Corporal Durbin, in his own words, justifies: "He jumped the horse from me and pulled the pistol[.] I fired Killing him instantly[.] He fell from the Horse and never Spoke a word[.] A .45 cal butt [bullet] had gone clear through his body near the Hart [*sic*].[74]

After returning from his scout to the border, within days, Captain Jones made the decision to relocate the Company D camp, moving it to a point four miles farther from Realitos Station, but having access to several stone buildings negating the use of tents, which were continually being whipped to shreds due to the gusty winds and sharp sandstorms. Camp Savage was no more. Now the Company D headquarters was Camp Collins.[75] In addition to repositioning camp, Captain Jones wanted another trip home to Kendall County, so that he could "attend the next sitting of District Court. . . . I am involved in a law suit to try title to a piece of land, and although I am not a witness, would rather be present when the case is tried."[76] In due time, Frank Jones would make it home to Kendall County for tending to family business—and tendering a bullet. But first, there were serious doings in South Texas. A Company D Ranger had touched the trigger, letting the hammer drop on finality. Captain Jones notified the Ranger brass at Austin:

> Private Dillard shot and killed a Mexican, name not known to me, at Rio Grande City on the 16th inst. The man killed was implicated

> in the kidnapping of Manuel Guerrera. Dillard was compelled to kill him to prevent his escape. District Court is in session in Starr County and the matter will be fully investigated. I am confident that Dillard will be exonerated.[77]

The deceased prisoner was Abraham Recéndez. The unfortunate or mindless Recéndez's ticket had been punched while he was making a frantic break for liberty—so goes one side of the story. By most accounts he had been in the custody of Sheriff Wash Shely, though Texas Ranger reports—the Monthly Return—clearly indicate he was their prisoner, charged with Kidnapping, not Theft or Robbery as sometimes is mentioned.[78] Logically it would seem that the sheriff, the Ranger, and U.S. Customs Inspector Victor Sebree, a former Texas Ranger, were working cooperatively on the investigation and mutually backing each other at the time of the arrest. Whether the detention was just or unjust is indefinable. Although Inspector Sebree is normally attributed with this killing—for reasons that become apparent—Frontier Battalion reports clearly cut the mark on Ranger Private Tooney Dillard's notchstick. Conceivably both could have fired shots. Maybe there was a tendency to capture false credit. Perhaps inflammatory newsmen from one or both banks of the river were caught unawares muddling through misinformation and/or mischievous innuendo and/or muckraking with zeal. That would really be no great revelation? Then or now, impassioned newspapermen—and ladies—time and again sacrifice truth for titillation. Sometimes, well, the truth is just inconvenient for pushing a good storyline or driving an agenda. The Monthly Return—May 1888—for Company D is not fuzzy: "Abraham Recendez [Charge] Kidnapping [Where] Starr County [By Whom] Private Dillard [Result] Killed when attempting to Escape."[79]

For whatever the reason—and it may come as a shocker to those bent toward suspending logic and ignoring facts while blindly crucifying Texas Rangers for every wrongful act under the South Texas sun, even Rangers weren't exempt exposure to the Texas and/or federal criminal justice system and its punishments. Captain Frank Jones would discharge Private Dillard, scratching him off the Company D roster, at least subsequent to the Starr County grand jury's returning an indictment and pending a petit jury's verdict at trial. Or, on the other hand a defendant entering a guilty plea, throwing himself at the court's mercy taking his chances in the blind or even advantaging himself of a prosecutor's plea bargain.[80] Drawing Ranger pay—then or now—was not/is not a guarantee of immunity.

There's little doubt Frank Jones was home at Boerne; there is some confusion as to whether or not he satisfactorily addressed the lawsuit revolving around land titles. There was another, even more imperative reason for taking leave and rushing home: "I came here a day or two ago to see my child who is very sick, intending to go on to Austin on the 1st of June."[81] While home at Boerne it turned Western!

Somehow, someway, a Kendall County deputy sheriff had developed or just luckily happened onto a piece of gossipy news. A fellow was lurking about in the county, one wanted for several felonies, in several counties, one case being below San Antonio in Wilson County. The deputy needed a hand and turned to the Ranger captain. Dereliction of duty was not in Frank Jones' repertoire. Dutifully Frank Jones saddled his horse and checked the loads in his Colt's .45 and Winchester. Accompanying the deputy, the pair of lawmen set off in search of their quarry—a jailbird to be. At length, about three miles from Boerne, the cock-of-the-walk was flushed and just about penned. Authoritatively a thunderous call to surrender was barked. Stupidly desperado G. C. Neeley figuratively stretched his wings but couldn't fly—not very far. Captain Jones would officially report their speedy action to the adjutant general "when we demanded his surrender he caught for a pistol he had in his pants and wheeled his horse and ran. We killed the horse and it is thought fatally wounded him. He is now in jail."[82]

Ranger Private Calvin Grant "Cal" Aten, one of Sergeant Ira Aten's younger brothers. Captain Frank Jones authorized Cal to take pot shots at an escaping prisoner swimming the Rio Grande—but was well aware of the impossibility of the young Texas Ranger inflicting any harm. Later, Private Aten would endure the anguish of participating in a deadly gunplay at the foot of Bullhead Mountain. *Courtesy Sally Walker.*

Governor Lawrence Sullivan "Sul" Ross, himself a former Indian fighter, ex-Ranger and Civil War veteran. The Lone Star State's Chief Executive was favorably inclined towards the Frontier Battalion and Captain Frank Jones. From *The Indian Wars and Pioneers of Texas* by John Henry Brown.

It's obvious these Company D Rangers at Camp Savage were not camera shy: From L to R: J. Walter Durbin, Ernest Rogers, John Hughes, Dood Jones, Tink Durbin, Charley Fusselman, Wood Saunders, Baz Outlaw, Sergeant Ira Aten, Captain Frank Jones, and an unidentified civilian teamster. *Courtesy Nita Stewart Haley Memorial Library & J. Evetts Haley History Center in Midland, Texas.*

Grace Kathleen Jones, the first-born child of Frank and Grace Jones. *Courtesy Candice DuCoin.*

A. W. Waltham & Co. pocket-watch presented to their esteemed captain by the Rangers of *Company D. Courtesy Donald M. and Louise Yena. Watch currently owned by noted collector Kurt House.*

CHAPTER 10

"A Strong Undercurrent of Excitement"

THOUGH IT WOULD TAKE SEVERAL months to unravel, an assertion that it was Ranger Private Dillard that had actually popped the cap—or was thought to have popped the cap—killing Abraham Recéndez is further buttressed by another missive. Captain Jones posted AG King: "The Jury in the Dillard case could not agree, some for conviction and some for acquittal."[1]

What could be agreed on by most everyone was that things were a mess in South Texas. Rightly or wrongly the killing of Abraham Recéndez fanned the flames of cultural, racial, and economic discontent. Perhaps true character is best defined by actions. Depending on perspective, Catarino Erasmo Garza Rodriguez was either a firebrand or patriot. Or both! Highly educated and articulate, Catarino Garza over the years had cleaved unto himself a burning—raging—purpose in life. Maintaining residence on the Texas side of the Rio Grande, though a Mexican by birth, Catarino harangued and agitated for political and philosophical and pecuniary and personal causes dear to his heart and/or self-interest.[2] As with most men of the place and time, Catarino Garza carried his own baggage of interpretative nationalism and racial insensitivity.[3] More popular with "working class" *Tejanos* rather than the more prosperous, with much to lose, Garza demanded notice.[4] Shrillness of his voice secured amplification—not necessarily credibility—through the openly partisan pages of his newspapers, *El Libre Pensador* and *El Comerico Mexicano* and elsewhere, too: Anywhere anyone would sit still long enough to listen if vats of folklore may be distilled to demijohns of unpolluted truth. Idolizing biographers sometime proffer maudlin excuses for some of Catarino's actions, but when pulled objectively tight the chain of substantiation is historically unbreakable: Garza, despite dreamscape *corridos* to the contrary, continually overestimated his own political popularity, demographic influence, and organizational talents, while repeatedly underestimating the martial ability, willpower, and logistical strengths of his adversaries. Garza's spurting and sputtering revolutionary insurrections and planned invasions of Mexico were indelibly marked with military mismanagement and failure.[5] Garza's ranting was rousing but his impotence at blueprinting an uprising with bullets would—in the end—crumble in disarray.[6] He could bite from the hard plug, but couldn't chew.

Although the actual strength of his popular support is often overblown and unmistakably belied by solid facts, he did have a long list of perceived grievances and no doubt some were not out-of-hand unfounded. Catarino Garza was anything but bashful or quiet about airing them. History records he had his following—men of unblemished integrity and purposeful democratic intent. That same fidelity to truth also exposes that part of his crowd were heavily armed border bravos—ruthless ruffians, fellows plundering ranches and guiltlessly maintaining an image of the "stereotypical Mexican bandits."[7] Aside from a white-hot hatred of Lone Star law enforcers, Catarino Garza "had enjoined a small but tempestuous revolutionary cell that stood twenty years ahead of their time—in open opposition to the dictatorial Porfirio Diaz regime in Mexico."[8]

In the long term Catarino's plots and subplots and intrigues and duplicities would ignite what was popularly tagged the "Garza War" by newspaper correspondents, but later it would in fact deteriorate into wholesale banditry, resulting in more than half a thousand federal indictments on the American side of the river.[9] In the short term, however, at Rio Grande City, the rhetoric between Victor Sebree and Catarino Garza about many things, the killing of Recéndez among them—heated. Indeed, if it's a fact—as indicated in official Texas Ranger documents—that it was Private Dillard primarily involved in the killing of Abraham Recéndez, at least a portion of the ambiguity about Inspector Sebree being publicly lambasted in the papers by Catarino Garza as a murderer, "assassin" and "coward" washes away. From Inspector Sebree's viewpoint, it would and did seem, as a bare minimum what Catarino Garza was saying in print was insulting, inaccurate, inflammatory, and criminally libelous.[10]

It was ex-Ranger Dillard who had faced the July 1888 legal music—in Starr County's courtroom—apparently not Sebree. Possibly an esteemed professor's remark that Recéndez had been "gunned down while trying to escape from Shely's companion Victor Sebree, who was the U.S. Customs Inspector" could be particularly relevant—insightful—dead straight on the mark. In fact was Texas Ranger Dillard actually the gunner? Somebody thought so! Ultimately, at least one somebody was not convinced Beyond a Reasonable Doubt that the killing had been criminal. At the time—in Texas—firing at fleeing felons was lawful.

Purportedly and there's not reason to doubt it, Augustine and Silurio de la Peña standing strong against Starr County's sheriff, had persuaded or bought Garza's services to use his newspapers as bludgeoning clubs crossways against Shely's and Sebree's and seemingly all other Anglo and Hispanic and Mexican lawmen's foreheads, as well as any native vigilantes.[11] Weighting inflammatory allegations with the cold hard truths of actuality would always be the wiser course. At the time not just a few thought the Peñas were surely stirring up a war between the races, pitting "Mexicans against Americans."[12] Catarino with abandon began swinging the journalistic bat, laying into thumping out knots of dissension and discord, while excoriating the U.S. Customs Inspector, though he had not been held criminally accountable for anything whatsoever, at least to this point by most reports.[13]

At any rate Inspector Sebree filed a sworn Complaint before a legally constituted magistrate and an arrest warrant issued for Catarino Garza, charging him with an alleged violation of the Criminal Libel laws as promulgated in the state's Penal Code—the laws applicable to everyone on the Texas side of the Rio Grande—like it or not, agree with it or not. Ethnicity shaped no exception. Somewhat imprecisely it's been innocently or slyly suggested—that apparently with some evil motivation—the arrest warrant had been placed in the hands of Texas Rangers rather than Sheriff Wash Shely, a calculated—and ostensibly conspiratorial—contravention of normal legal procedures.[14] Such incorrectness is not unusual: Agenda driven borderland histories and wistful fantasies purport that Rangers can hardly do right. The facts, based on a demonstrable paper trail, are these.

The formal criminal charges lodged against Catarino Garza had initiated in Starr County. Either purposefully or by happenstance fugitive Catarino Garza was nowhere to be found within Sheriff Shely's lawful bailiwick. Garza was, however, across the county line not too far from Company D's Camp Collins outside Realitos. So, the warrant—by hand or telegraphically—was placed for service with the Rangers. There was, plainly speaking, not a damn thing unusual or sordid about that. Rangers were Texas peace officers and Texas peace officers served warrants! Particularly noted throughout this text—and all Ranger narratives—are many examples wherein these state troops executed arrest warrants on fugitives that had skipped across county lines. Again, relying on archived documents, the record is not unclear. On the nineteenth day of August 1888, a reasonably inexperienced Ranger, Private John R. Hughes, and another unnamed Ranger placed Mr. Catarino Erasmo Garza under arrest at Realitos, Duval County.[15] The fiery talking insurrectionist had surrendered absent incident. Sometimes barroom blather dissipates, especially when opting whether to yield to sanity or yank a gun. Rather than turn him over to Duval County Sheriff Linton Lafayette "Lon" Wright, an ex-Ranger and gunfighting dynamo having no pending charges against Garza and who didn't want to hold him, guard him, or feed him in the first place, Private Hughes and his partner just took the lucklessly beleaguered and cowed prisoner back to Camp Collins for safekeeping.[16] The next day, Captain Jones fashioned a four-man Company D escort detail under the nominal leadership of Private James R. "Jim" Robinson, a genuine fire-breathing Texas

Ranger of no little experience with making arrests and securely moving prisoners from point A to point Z. Following proper protocol for safely transporting prisoners, Catarino Garza was shackled, then delivered to Rio Grande City and nondescriptly turned over to the "proper authorities."[17] Shortly thereafter Catarino Garza posted a $500 bond and was allowed his liberty pending resolution of the charges.[18]

From across the river Mexican language newspapers, well, newspaper, *El Mundo*, picked up the banner of hot rhetoric, accusing the Rangers of handcuffing Catarino Garza like a common murderer or livestock thief. Too, it was alleged in the racially partisan and emotionally charged newspaper that prisoner Garza had been turned loose ten miles from town and forced to hoof-it into Rio Grande City.[19] Why Captain Jones would assign four Rangers to move Garza from Realitos to Rio Grande City—under arrest—and then for them to just turn their charge loose ten miles from town—presuming the prisoner would indifferently march to town and surrender on his own volition—and then the Rangers would intentionally and knowingly falsify their official Monthly Return, would have defied logical explanation then, even if the abject silliness of such an assertion did help propel prejudice and sell newspapers.

With the atmosphere already roiling thick with animosity and bleeding undercurrents of cross-cultural antipathies, coupled with the very real economic disparities between classes within ethnic subsets and the incessant editorial agitations underway, the next turn of tragic events at Rio Grande City should come as no bombshell. Not unexpectedly, however, depending on station and/or ethnicity, two versions emerge. The distinction between competing renderings is not how the dance ended, but who opened the ball, and open it did. On the twenty-first day of September 1888 a gunfight erupted between Inspector Victor Sebree, on the one side, and Catarino Garza and Federico López on the other. During the noisy and blistering exchange of gunfire Mr. Garza and Mr. López finished in second place, both wounded but not mortally, though early newspaper editions were at first reporting Catarino's demise. Inspector Victor Sebree came through the mêlée unscathed, which in light of the fact he was a veteran working lawman and an ex-Ranger is not particularly amazing, although partisans sometimes naively postulate, that, in and of itself indicates just who let the first round fly. Such suppositional reasoning is lame, naively so. Regardless, for pushing Captain Jones' saga such argument—no matter how well intentioned—is pointless. There is a close-at-hand outcome, and it remains unchanged. Federico López and Catarino Garza lay bent and bleeding, while Inspector Victor Sebree jumped on his horse and burnt the wind.[20]

Barely ahead of an enraged mob of Catarino's infuriated sympathizers and supporters, Inspector Sebree had sought and was granted refuge behind a scary looking .45-70 Gatling Gun protecting the U.S. Army's Fort Ringgold on the outskirts of town.[21] An armed horde of several hundred "Mexicans" converged on the fort with one thought in mind: laying hands on Sebree. The installation's steadfast commander, Colonel David R. Clendenin, could hardly allow that. And, quite bluntly the insolent crowd was told that Inspector Victor Sebree would not—under any circumstances—be surrendered for the administration of summary or any other strain of extralegal justice, end of story. They could put that in their pipe and smoke it—or lock and load. Storming the fort would not be wholly cost free! Fortunately, wiser heads or timidity prevailed. The would-be righters of wrongs wandered back to the streets of Rio Grande City where they collectively blundered big-time. In an act of asininity someone among them cut the telegraph wire to Fort Ringgold. Hotly converging on a U.S. Army fort while carrying arms and making demands of its commander had not been smart, but maliciously isolating the military by severing its communications was more than a dimwitted move. Especially in light of a crucial but little known fact, the telegraph wire had been snipped behind rather than in front of any outgoing messages to the rest of the world. The governor and adjutant general of Texas were already in the loop—and the Rangers of Company D soon would be.

The next day, September 22, 1888, the adjutant general telegraphed Captain Jones, ordering him to "Call in all near detachments to join you at Rio Grande City and proceed without delay to that point with such men as you have with you. Take your entire camp."[22] Captain Jones' reply was not unexpectedly prompt, but also reflective of just how thin the Company D Rangers were spread: "Men are all out will try and call them in but it may take several days."[23] The following day Captain Jones, yet at Camp Collins, took the time to sit down and offer AG King a broader clarification, explaining that he had four men scouting somewhere in Cameron County (county seat Brownsville) and two men looking for horse thieves in Nueces County (Corpus Christi). Corporal Durbin and detachment were yet on duty at Hempstead. Captain Jones had already been advised that "The wires have been cut and there is no telegraphic communication with Starr Co. Sebree is in the U.S. post under protection of the Commander. I am informed that 60 armed Mexicans demanded that Sebree be delivered to them, and had to be threatened with Gatling guns to induce them to leave." Captain Jones' plans, as he advised the adjutant general, were to prepare camp equipment for movement so that it could follow under management of his teamster, and just as soon as the two Rangers from Nueces County could join him, he would report to Rio Grande City "without delay."[24] The delay was short lived. On September 26 the captain and three men started for Rio Grande City, where upon his arrival Captain Jones pledged to the adjutant general that he would "report the situation fully to you by letter when I reach there and investigate."[25] Though traveling separately from Captain Jones, Corporal J. Walter Durbin and the two Ranger privates in his detachment were ordered to immediately leave Waller County on the back trail and report to Rio Grande City.[26]

Also charged with getting to Rio Grande City as quickly as possible working under instructions from the governor were Sheriff Santiago Brito of Cameron County with eighty men, another posse of forty-five rescuers from Hidalgo County (county seat Edinburg) under the leadership of a deputy sheriff, and the top law enforcement official from San Patricio County (Sinton), Sheriff James M. McGloin and thirty men. Moreover ordered to the area with haste were Rangers of Company F commanded by Lieutenant James Abijah Brooks. Not infrequently partisans with a preprogrammed format portray the marshalling of state troops and local reinforcements for deployment to Rio Grande City as an overreaction on the one hand and/or sensationalism on the other. Certainly far removed by distance and time such putrefying assessments might seem plausible, but for awhile—on the ground—those folks actually living in real time and possibly facing jeopardy knew not what the future would hold.

Perception is reality, and with a mob of several hundred outside the fort's perimeter marching and milling throughout the tiny town, not just a few carrying weapons, many citizens and elected leaders throughout the state believed a full-scale riot was under way—and maybe in many respects they were right. Certainly normalcy and peacefulness had jumped the track.

Starr County Sheriff Wash Shely—whether by his own doing or not—was in a political pickle. The upcoming county elections were just around the corner and the sheriff's constituency was predominately numbered by native Spanish speakers, some not very sympathetic to Shely and not just a few openly hostile to his candidacy. If truth be told Wash Shely was hustling and scuffling for votes, more interested in politics than policing.

Captain Frank Jones and three men had hurried by horseback to Rio Grande City, arriving there on September 29.[27] On the last day of the month he reported by letter to the adjutant general. His letter is illuminating:

> I reached this place yesterday just as the Sheriffs from other Counties were leaving. The County Judge and Sheriff Shely signed an agreement with the ring leaders of the riot that they would not prosecute them. This morning County Atty. Hoad wrote out a Complaint against Garza and Lopez, the men who were engaged in the street fight with Sebree, charging them with intent to murder and cannot get a man here to make the affiant [swear to the Complaint]. There is still a strong under current of excitement and Americans do not feel safe, that is those who have families. Shely is no good at all as he is working for re-election. Judge Kelsey plainly says that he has acted with a view to re-election. The only chance to bring any of the parties who were engaged in the riot to justice

> is for me to make the Complaint. I thought it best to communicate the situation to you and ask your advice as to whether I shall make the Complaint. Please let me hear from you at once and by telegraph.[28]

Frank Jones' willingness to put his name on the dotted line speaks volumes about the man. Discounting any debate about the rightness or wrongness of any of the players, Captain Jones' readiness to take on adversaries and underwrite their arrests in the face of overwhelming odds, with the potential for serious retribution on the part of an emotionally charged majority population is telling. Even though he was without doubt carrying his own brand of ingrained racial biases, Frank Jones had sand—grit! He was hardly afraid to step to the mark.

Adjutant General King answered at once, reining in his stalwart captain ahead of six-shooter disaster: Texas Rangers were doers, maybe not at all times right, but men of action nevertheless. His message to the Company D captain was plainspoken and practical. Captain Jones was to concern himself only with keeping the peace and "not to interfere with the administration of the law, as this must be left to the local officials & citizens." Furthermore the adjutant general was of the unwavering mindset that if the citizens would "do nothing to vindicate the law, they are the sufferers as it is not the provenance nor duty of the Rangers to step forward in this [that] capacity." Captain Jones was specifically ordered to confine himself and men "strictly to keeping the peace." Additionally, Jones was to make affable contact with Colonel Clendenin and work out "a mutual plan of action in the event of any outbreak." He was also to "report conditions of affairs as often as necessary in order that such Modifications of instructions may be made as the circumstances demand."[29]

On the same day Captain Jones penned his initial report to the adjutant general, Corporal Durbin and his detachment made their appearance in Rio Grande City, followed merely days thereafter by Lieutenant Brooks and his boys from Company F.[30] Possibly—and it's only conjecture—Frank Jones now felt more at ease surrounded by fellow Texas Rangers. With Captain Jones in the lead, and Lieutenant Brooks serving as second-in-command, backed up by a complement of proven hard-core no-nonsense law enforcers, the Ranger team at Rio Grande City was formidable—by any man's measure.

Early on with the odds equaling more of a one to one ratio the rioters or insurrectionists or demonstrators or spectators had lost any ardor for settling real or imagined grievances with belligerence or brutality or bullets. In fact, Colonel Clendenin posted officialdom with reality: Aside from the cutting of telegraph wires and the adamant demand for Inspector Victor Sebree "no property had been destroyed or depredations committed in Rio Grande City and that affairs were not so bad as reported." Furthermore, had things materially progressed to the danger zone he would have employed his "troops to prevent bloodshed."[31] When Sheriff Santiago Brito and his posse left for Brownsville they had taken Victor Sebree, who had posted a $2,500 bond for shooting and wounding Garza and López, with them for his own bodily protection. The other contingents of local officers, likewise, after discovering the volatile situation had been somewhat defused, returned to their home counties.[32] The Rangers remained at Rio Grande City.

They would not, however, remain inactive: They were Rangers. Before the Rangers of Company D and Company F could get to policing, Captain Frank Jones had to tend to unpleasant business, disciplinary business. On the sixteenth day of October he issued Private John Woodard Saunders his walking papers, again. The extent of Ranger Wood Saunders' inebriation is not particularized, but common sense would suggest he was more than a little tipsy: the reason for discharge being characterized as "drunkenness." The following day he enlisted Riley Barton to take Saunders's spot as the newest private on the muster roll.[33]

And assuredly Captain Frank Jones wanted a full-strength staffing level; arrests were imminent. What could best be described as a dragnet, reminiscent of Major John B. Jones' investigative sweep through Kimble County more than a decade earlier, was to kick off in Starr County.[34] Perhaps AG King had undergone a change of heart. During the roundup in Rio Grande City and upriver at the

Río Bravo village of Roma, Captain Jones oversaw the arrests of as many as three dozen individuals charged with Conspiracy to Murder and Assault to Murder.[35] Purportedly it was during this stringing of arrests that the ever indomitable Corporal Durbin iced the cake about his coworkers' headstrong doctrinaire: "The Rangers will attend to all the killing to be done in this county for a while."[36] There was no killing, thankfully. How solid the legal footing Rangers were standing on might rightly suffer debate. A percentage of those swept up during the policing action were some of Starr County's "prominent ranchers and local businessmen." Tellingly, even though a handful of indictments were returned by a Starr County grand jury, no courtroom convictions followed. Probable Cause, the U.S. Constitutional standard for an arrest, is not tricky but it's a necessary benchmark for prosecutors to hurdle. Whether it was due to an electioneering deal made with the devil or an insufficiency of admissible evidence is moot. The criminal cases mysteriously fell off the docket book—deep into decomposition of a judicial abyss.[37]

November is election time in Texas as elsewhere. In South Texas, particularly in those counties bordering the Rio Grande, chicanery at the polls and the potential for trouble was always a possibility. Most borderland sheriffs—no matter ethnicity—relied on the assistance of Texas Rangers to maintain order while ballots were being cast. Captain Frank Jones disbursed his legions, men from both Company D and Company F. He assigned Lieutenant Brooks and Ranger Privates Cal Aten, Ernest Rogers, and Charley Fusselman to patrolling the polling place at Rio Grande City. At Saliñeno, right on the river and just south of the Zapata County line, he assigned Sergeant John Harris Rogers, Company F, and Company D new-hire Riley Barton. Captain Jones with seven men performed like duty at Roma, an expected hot spot for disruption. Private Jim Robinson, one of Jones' regulars, and Company F's Private J. B. Harry pitched in with their share of poll-watching duty.[38] Although there must have been but minimal difficulty with maintaining the public peace during the electoral process, Captain Jones' managerial finesse shines through. Purposefully he was pairing men from different companies for this assignment, making a wide-awake effort to preserve and instill battalion cohesion. For Captain Frank Jones *esprit de corps* was just as meaningful and important as it was for his mentor, Captain Sieker.

And though it's but a sidebar within the biographical narrative, it is not inappropriate to point out that during the joint-company Rio Grande City deployment it was Captain Jones in command as ranking officer. Aside from simple chain-of-command structure, the fact that Captain Jones was the senior and responsible officer may also be drawn from AG King requesting that Frank, because he had "probably formed an opinion as to existing troubles," make suggestions and proposals to the Austin command center about "looking to the preservation of peace in the future" for that section of country.[39] Frank Jones' ideas were worth something—at headquarters. The Frontier Battalion was organized on a military model and, as previously highlighted, title mattered: How else could order and discipline and unit effectiveness be maintained? With diplomacy and forethought Captain Frank Jones was overseeing the enforcement activities of Lieutenant James Abijah Brooks and Sergeant John Harris Rogers, both future Texas Ranger captains with publicly acclaimed law enforcing records and, later, prominent career positions outside state service. Captain Jones too, though little could they have appreciated it then, was also managing the workaday career of Private John Reynolds Hughes, in due time another fêted Texas Ranger captain to be.[40]

And speaking of Private Hughes: He and Company F Ranger Marcellus R. Daniels had not been assigned duty protecting voters and maintaining the peace as ballots were being cast. Captain Jones, keeping with his ideology of coupling Rangers from differing companies together for specific assignments, had tasked these two with a major felony investigation—out of town.

By chance Marcellus Daniels might have needed a break from Starr County. According to Colonel Clendenin at Fort Ringgold the spring-loaded Texas Ranger had "roughed up" U.S. Army private Isaac Terrell during some type of unspecified dustup at Rio Grande City. Shortly thereafter, a concerned local citizen would lodge a similar complaint, alleging Ranger Private Daniels during an arrest or unofficial brouhaha issued a vinegary dose of rough mean street therapy to a whining—maybe justifiably so—sore headed civilian. Not in the least surprising—maybe rightly or maybe wrongly—Company F Lieutenant J. A. Brooks stood by his man, guaranteeing that the Ranger was doing his "duties and that any rough treatment was likely deserved."[41] Perhaps Captain Jones was right. A trip out of town would be therapeutic.

Though much travel throughout Texas was now accomplished comfortably seated in speeding trains' coaches, stagecoaches yet ran between many towns. A horse-drawn coach traveling the roadway below Peña in southern Duval County had been highjacked. On October 28, 1888, Privates Hughes and Daniels were sent to look into it.[42] Unfortunately the Rangers came up empty-handed and returned to camp after an absence of nine days, but apparently the fruitless manhunt bothered Private Hughes. Just the previous summer he had been working undercover on a fence-cutting case in Central Texas and the investigation soured subsequent to someone making "a confident of the rong [*sic*] man and gave the whole thing away."[43] Coming up short is never enjoyable. Shortly, a determined Private Hughes, believing he had a workable lead and a viable suspect for the stagecoach robbery struck out again, leaving camp on the thirteenth of November.[44] From Peña he trailed his man into San Antonio and from there northward to San Marcus where, apparently, he confronted the target—a person of interest—only to discover that after nearly a month he had been tailing and trailing "the wrong man."[45] In the hard game of enforcing the law, there are winners and losers.

In the meantime Captain Jones had promptly notified Captain Sieker regarding the election results, posting a letter from Rio Grande City on November 5, 1888: "Shely is defeated by only 20 votes." Frank, in that same communiqué had another message—a desperate plea—for Captain Sieker: "Hope you will move me out of this section."[46] This letter closed with "Very Respectfully" rather than Frank's typical "Respectfully." South Texas politics, perhaps, was taking its toll on Frank Jones.

Two weeks later Captain Jones had clearly not had a change of heart, but the election had been upended. Jones notified headquarters: "The County Commissioners of this County [Starr] threw out one Precinct and that elects all the Shely party except surveyor. The Peña-Garza party have entered suit for the office and the matter will doubtless be in the Courts for several months." Doubling down on his earlier message—this time for AG King's eyes—Frank tried again: "I am now confident that one Co. of Rangers will be amply sufficient to keep the peace in this section."[47] There would be unfortunate news—in the long analysis—for the Peña-Garza faction, most especially regarding their antipathy for Sheriff Wash Shely. Despite any barbs hurled by political enemies then or partisan historians later, the real world fact is that Shely would hold onto the office of Starr County sheriff through a dozen election cycles, stretching into the twentieth-century.[48] It would seem, based on outcome, that political rivals consistently underestimated Wash Shely's power and popularity, while overvaluing their own standings as unifying voices of the people.

Too, since his biographer candidly acknowledges that in the end Catarino Garza entered a guilty plea to the libel charges, is it tactless to suggest that he may have had second thoughts about whoring himself to political factionalism and fractiousness that was overblown?[49] Could Inspector Sebree's ire at what was being maliciously said about him in Garza's newspaper articles, that part about being an assassin and coward, have had merit as being libelous? As unsettling as it may be for culpable Rangers, despicable desperadoes, misguided insurrectionists, and/or full-of-themselves political activists, guilty pleas usually equate to guilt.

Regardless political power games playing out in Starr County, Captain Jones received the news he was hoping for: Company D was to be removed from the border, transferred to the vicinity of Uvalde or Edwards Counties—Frank's choice. Lieutenant Brooks and a detachment of Company F Rangers would remain on duty in Starr County at Rio Grande City.[50] Within two weeks Captain Jones, the men, and Company D's commissary and camping gear were packed and on the road, leaving Rio Grande City on November 29, 1888, with an anticipated unloading date in Uvalde County by about the middle of December.[51] While Company D was making tracks, Quartermaster

Sieker had been busy in the outfit's behalf. He contracted with F. A. Piper of the city of Uvalde, "A Wholesaler and Retailer of Everything You Want," to furnish necessary supplies for Captain Jones and the men of Company D.[52]

Sergeant Ira Aten, after an extended and unproductive assignment in Navarro County (county seat Corsicana) trying to catch fence-cutters who were really reluctant to do any cutting, was cleaning up court appearances regarding other cases and was ready to return to duty with the company.[53] Learning that Company D had been repositioned from a newspaper report and that they were already on the road headed for Uvalde County, the top-sergeant jumped into action. Making contact with a local rancher Aten received permission for "camping in the pasture" which was just "about fifty yards below" where their previous camp had been located. Sergeant Aten particularly noted that the "grass was good back next to the hills" but they would require hay for the remaining winter months. Too, and it's indicative of deference and respect paid to upper echelon officers, Sergeant Aten made particularly certain that upon his arrival Captain Frank Jones' personal tent would be positioned perfectly for privacy "in case he should bring his wife to camp."[54]

After easy marches from Rio Grande City via Laredo and Carrizo Springs and the expenditure of twelve days the Company D boys had covered the ground to Uvalde County, establishing their headquarters about six miles from Uvalde on the Leona River—reactivating old Camp Leona.[55] Rank and file Rangers were ecstatic with being back in the picturesque Texas Hill Country and, according to Ira Aten, "all the boys seemed pleased" with the new/old campsite.[56]

The adjutant general was not particularly pleased with the legislature's funding allotment. He was worried—and he put Captain Jones on notice—that due to budgetary realities one or two men might have to be discharged from Company D by the end of the year. Therefore, the captain should be mentally identifying his "most undesirable men."[57] Captain Frank Jones didn't keep undesirable men on the Muster & Payroll. Although he didn't respond to AG King in writing regarding this personnel matter, any news he would have had about forced reductions of manpower would have been negative.

As the end of the year was closing in Captain Jones was in receipt of some pleasing news too. Frank really wasn't gloating, though he was noticeably satisfied with the outcome—as most career lawmen would be. He notified AG King: "I got Neeley, the man I shot last summer sent to Huntsville [penitentiary] for 5 years."[58]

Whether or not Frank Jones spent any of the Christmas Holidays at Boerne is indistinct, but on the last day of 1888 he was at Camp Leona making plans for the upcoming year, predicting that Company D would "have considerable work to do in the section north of here and some in Maverick County [Eagle Pass]."[59] The frustrated sheriff of Uvalde County, Henry W. Baylor, had for several months been clamoring for placement of a company of Rangers back in his area, "as there is plenty of work for them" and that it seemed to him that the horse and cattle thieves riding from Edwards and Zavala Counties and raiding into his area had "broken loose afresh."[60] Clearly Frank Jones didn't have a crystal ball: But he was right, 1889 would be a busy year!

Although later, after earning promotion to captain, James Abijah Brooks would be characterized as one of the Texas Ranger "greats," it's not unimportant to reflect: During a time on the Texas/Mexico border Lieutenant Brooks was deployed for an enforcement action commanded by Captain Frank Jones. Here Brooks is standing at far left, flanked by his Company F Texas Rangers. *Courtesy Armstrong Research Center, Texas Ranger Hall of Fame & Museum.*

In the same vein as the preceding photograph, John Harris Rogers would earn his place as one of the subjectively awarded "greats" but during time of the aforesaid assignment on the Texas/Mexico border Sergeant Rogers answered up the chain-of-command to Lieutenant Brooks, then to Captain Frank Jones. *Courtesy Armstrong Research Center, Texas Ranger Hall of Fame & Museum.*

Texas Ranger Captain Frank Jones, Company D, strikes a handsome and dashing pose for this portrait snap at Rio Grande City, likely at the Joe R. Lewis photography studio. *Courtesy Suzanne Giffin-Garcia.*

Two of Captain Jones' intrepid Texas Rangers. From L to R: Wood Saunders and J. Walter Durbin. As the Company D corporal Durbin would remark and admit that he supervised some pretty good men, but they could be "a little fussy and dangerous when drinking." *Courtesy the Nita Stewart Haley Memorial Library & J. Evetts Haley History Center in Midland, Texas.*

Starr County Sheriff Washington W. "Wash" Shely is seated at far left. His brother, Texas Ranger Captain Josephus "Joe" Shely, Company F is standing center, watch-chain draped across his holstered Colt's six-shooter. *Courtesy Armstrong Ranger Research Center, Texas Ranger Hall of Fame & Museum.*

Perhaps one of the most widely distributed and most often published Texas Ranger photographs. Standing, from L to R: Jim King, Baz Outlaw, Riley Boston, Charley Fusselman, Tink Durbin, Ernest Rogers, Charles Barton, and Walter Jones. Seated, L to R: Bob Bell, Cal Aten, Captain Frank Jones, J. Walter Durbin, Jim Robinson, and Frank Schmid. *Courtesy Armstrong Ranger Research Center, Texas Ranger Hall of Fame & Museum.*

CHAPTER 11

"By God, They Will Never Come Back"

FOR THE MOST PART—and facts seem to confirm—the year's first couple of months for spirited Company D Rangers were rocking along at a reasonable pace. There were scouts and arrests. During one investigative assignment, Captain Jones and Sheriff Baylor working in tandem ten miles below Uvalde tracked down an alleged embezzler, Sebe Elliott, wanted by authorities in Travis County. In the vicinity of Wilderness Lake, Privates Riley Barton and Cal Aten latched onto two suspected burglars, Bud Saunders and Blake Rowland. After his pilfering from a Uvalde business house had been discovered, R. L. Rauge was trying to lie low in neighboring Kinney County, but Sergeant Aten cold-trailed him and cuffed him.[1] As the year continued to unwind the Company D Rangers—all fifteen of them—were inordinately busy, primarily hunting for and occasionally catching cow thieves.[2]

Captain Jones was dutifully spending most of his time in camp coordinating investigative activities, dealing with matters of expenditures and market value prices for corn and hay for horses and six mules and foodstuffs and camping necessities for the men. Paperwork, well, there was plenty of that: Bureaucracy is demanding, red-tape unremitting. There's little doubt that thirty-four-year-old Frank Jones had found his niche. Law enforcement was to his liking, and the upper-level brass liked what they saw in Captain Jones. What Frank Jones was not seeing—at least too much of—was wife Grace. The Frontier Battalion's figurative guidebook made little allowance for an overabundance of downtime at home, though officers were more privileged in that regard than enlisted personnel. And though surviving personal letters seem not to exist—they have yet to surface—there's absolutely no reason to doubt that Frank's daydreams and mental digressions were carrying him back to Boerne, where life was good. Every now and then he'd made it home: Grace was expecting their second child. Toddler Grace Kathleen, now walking, was a joyous delight, laughing and running and jumping and gingerly dabbing her toes in Kendall County's sparkling and inviting Cibolo Creek.

Further south, however, in Maverick County along the river, four family members were not gleefully dabbing their toes or wading or swimming in the murky Rio Grande—they were underwater, weights tied around their lifeless waists. It was a sensational crime, a quadruple murder, the whodunit of whodunits!

And even though the murders were horrific newsmakers in one sense, seemingly local law enforcement authorities were taking a somewhat lackadaisical approach to making a meaningful criminal investigation: At least so thought a genuinely concerned ex-Ranger. As previously cited B. D. Lindsey, Company D's former 1st Sergeant and past Ranger Private W. W. Collier had quit the Frontier Battalion and gone into business for themselves. Under the business name of Lindsey & Collier they were proprietors of The Tariff Saloons, with B. D. Lindsey operating their establishment at Eagle Pass, while W. W. Collier managed their setup at Uvalde.[3] The troubled Ben Lindsey took pen in hand, writing to Captain Jones: "There has been within the last 4 days four dead bodies taken out of the Rio Grande river Six Miles above Eagle Pass—all white, three women and one man. Up to this writing No clues to the murder & above all No attempt whatever has been made by authorities on this side to feret [*sic*] it out. If you have a good man you could put to work on it you would be doing the county at large a good deed."[4]

The day after receiving Lindsey's letter, Captain Jones initiated correspondence with the adjutant general, a letter which is reflective of mutual tribal mentality along the Rio Grande borderlands, but also spotlights contentiousness sometimes glossed over: Not everyone—even Anglo lawmen—were star-struck fans of the Texas Rangers. Captain Jones' automatically jumping to an openly biased conclusion is evident: "I have a half breed Mexican in the Company and if he is sent to Maverick County he may be enabled to ferret out the murderers. . . . by staying around awhile among the Mexicans." At this point in time—victims or suspected perpetrators had not been positively or negatively identified as "Mexicans." Captain Frank Jones' premature supposition, though understandable due to geographic positioning, was not a fitting tactic for conducting an open-minded and impartial homicide investigation. Regardless, should he adopt this approach for gathering evidence of the crime, Jones was imploring AG King to keep the investigative strategy under his hat: "I do not consider the Sheriff of that Co. at all reliable and is moreover an enemy to the Ranger force and I do not want him to know anything about this matter." After posting the adjutant general that if the matter be left solely in his hands, Captain Jones thought the smart move was to "send a man down there." Perceptibly Jones knew money would be tight for any open-ended investigation. The logical question as to exactly why Sheriff William N. Cooke was "enemy to the Ranger force," at least in Captain Frank Jones' estimation, remains unanswered.[5]

What does not remain a mystery is AG King's first and foremost worry—Jones was astute. There was that constant bugaboo of Frontier Battalion funding and some legislative detractors, at this time, were wondering—out loud and vocally—about strangling the outfit out of existence by cutting its financial appropriations. The adjutant general did have a solution—of sorts—advising his Company D captain: "If the citizens wish for the Services of a ranger, and will guarantee his pay for Service & all expenses in just such a way that there will be no possible doubt of it being forthcoming when wanted, you may detail a man Suitable for the purpose."[6]

A few days later AG King again messaged Captain Jones at Uvalde County's Camp Leona. Although the correspondence is wholly unrelated to bodies submerged in the Rio Grande and then buoyantly popping to the surface, the letter is relevant on another front. The Rangers were ever taking advantage of advancing technology, be it with transportation or communications or improved armament. Clearly Rangers were on the road to professionalism—as crime fighters. The adjutant general updated Captain Jones: "I enclose herewith the photo of Mack Brown who with his brother Joe Abe Brown murdered Col. Griffith in Kimble County. Large rewards are offered for their arrests."[7] Utilizing photography as a newfangled crime fighting tool was a fitting application. Rangers were ever adaptable innovators. Forensics would break wide-open the Maverick County murder cases—and Texas Rangers would crack the nut.

The long and the short of Captain Jones' decision making process is easily captured, though how or if he obtained any specialized funding to conduct the murder investigation is nonexistent, at least as of yet. Maintaining executive control, Captain Frank Jones tasked Sergeant Ira Aten, now a seasoned investigator, with making the trip to Eagle Pass and looking into the horrible crime. Employees have differing areas of competency, their varied talents particularly suited for certain assignments. The captain's mission—of the many on his plate—was to match the right man to the right job. At that Captain Frank Jones was masterful. As a helpmate for the homicide investigation either Sergeant Aten or Captain Jones selected Private John Hughes, who by now was a Ranger veteran of eighteen months. Such an assignment was noteworthy for a lawman shedding his rookie status.

Upon their arrival at Eagle Pass the two Rangers were updated as to known facts about recovery of the four decomposing bodies—and those facts were not encouraging from an investigative perspective. Over a period of several days beginning on February 27, 1889, the remains of three women and a young man had been fished from the Rio Grande. One and all had suffered blunt-force head trauma and one and all had been weighted with heavy rocks, obviously intended to anchor them to the river's floor until turtles and Alligator-gar nibbled the evidence to nothingness. As best determined at the time, the four victims because of their apparent difference of ages did not suggest free spirited companions on a lark, celebrating at the river's edge before being overtaken by evil: It was more familial. The oldest lady was well past middle age. The next in line stair stepped downward, an adult female with a twisted apron string around her neck in addition to the knotted plow-line around her waist fastened to a hefty—30 pound—rock. Aging the third female revealed she was a late teenager or young adult, dreadfully decomposed. The male victim was about five feet seven inches, slimly built, not yet grown to full manhood.[8]

Initially the real dilemma facing area lawmen was elementary but especially challenging. Who were these deceased people? Certainly there were not four folks from that part of the borderland country unaccounted for. Subsequent to intensively working toward having the corpses identified, but absent conclusiveness, Justice of the Peace G. B. Dunn had ruled the deaths homicides committed "by party or parties unknown" and justifiably ordered that the remains be respectfully buried at public expense.[9]

Captain Jones' choice of Sergeant Aten to head up the investigation for the Rangers was smart. Aten handpicking Hughes—if he did—as his understudy was discerning and foreseeable. These two Rangers were becoming fast friends and Ira, during twilight years, would warmheartedly reminisce, "whenever I had a tough case I always took Hughes with me."[10] Frank Jones' less than stellar assessment of the local sheriff was not—cannot be—sustained, not if a contemporary news report is anywhere close to precise. The *Dallas Morning News* article, although it failed to make any mention of Private Hughes, particularly touted the investigative efforts of Maverick County Sheriff Bill Cooke, Kinney County Sheriff J. W. Nolan and "State Ranger Ira Aten. . . ."[11]

Employing rudimentary forensic acumen Sergeant Aten made sure the ropes and rocks used to weight down the bodies were preserved for evidentiary purposes. Airtight cases are built with purpose. He, too, after consulting with local officers and civilian witnesses who had visually examined the remains prior to interment, made note of two key tidbits of information: The oldest of the two grown women, he was told, had worn a professionally made dental plate and the young male had a noticeable gap between his front teeth and "the canines were very pointed."[12] Otherwise, decisive clues were in short supply.

Opting to work the crime backwards, establishing the victims' last known movements is a competent analytical technique for homicide investigations. Aten and Hughes began scouting the Rio Grande's banks hoping to discover additional evidence and/or the scene of the murders. While ambling and eyeing the underbrush the two Rangers quite naturally engaged in general conversation. According to most accounts, Private Hughes made mention of the fact that days before the bodies were discovered, while on a routine scout along the West Fork of the Nueces he had chatted with Richard H. "Dick" Duncan and "Picnic" Jones, who were horseback and riding ahead of a wagon occupied by three women and a young man. According to what Hughes was told by Duncan, Jones was his brother-in-law, married to the young girl, and the older ladies were his mother and sister. The wagon was piled high with household goods and the object of their trip was relocating the family to Old Mexico where they had a parcel of land, a small scale rancho. There was, at that time, nothing at all suspicious about the backcountry encounter, and after the small talk the Texas Ranger went his way and the Duncan party theirs. Private Hughes did make mental note, however, that the carefree travelers were driving a brand-new Mitchell brand wagon, freshly painted green, and on the tailgate was a hammer-stamped advertisement, "Sold By J. S. Clark, San Saba, Texas."[13]

Sergeant Aten took especial notice. He too had had contact with Dick Duncan. On the first day of March 1889 he had arrested Dick and George Taplin "Tap" Duncan, Dick's brother, along with another fellow named H. W. Landers in Edwards County charging them with Unlawfully Carrying Arms. At the time Aten supposed the fellows to be horse thieves but surmised he had stumbled onto them ahead of their sneakily rounding up any horses, and since they were carrying six-shooters hauled them in for an appearance before Justice of the Peace Steiber who allowed them to post a bail bond before granting their walk-around freedom.[14] Something was rotten in Denmark, so Sergeant Ira Aten mused. Leaving Private Hughes with instructions to continue scouting the Rio Grande the best he could, looking for a possible blood spattered crime scene and/or an outcropping of rocks similar to those used as anchors—Sergeant Ira Aten eagerly struck the road for San Saba.[15]

There, he conferred with the San Saba County Sheriff, S. B. Howard, a tough lawman serving his second two-year term.[16] Sergeant Aten was now in receipt of shocking and newsworthy investigative intelligence. The Williamson family, consisting of the widow, Mrs. Mary Ann Williamson, her widowed daughter Lavonia Holmes, her teenage daughter Beulah and twenty-year-old son Benjamin "Ben" Williamson were no longer hardscrabble residents of San Saba County. They had sold out to Dick Duncan who, in addition to the $400 cash payment for title to their farm, had bought the more-or-less impoverished family a brand-new wagon from the Joe S. Clark Farm Machinery & Hardware Store, a wagon painted green. Adding to the buzzing din of tittle-tattle and gossip was the fact that Dick Duncan and Walter Landers, aka Picnic Jones, had promised to escort the Williamson clan to Old Mexico and had even been seen helping them—in the middle of the night—loading furniture into the wagon prior to taking the road south out of San Saba.[17] All of the Williamson family were riding in the Mitchell wagon, while Duncan and Jones were horseback, Dick atop an eye-catching and "handsome sorrel pacing horse with a striking appearance."[18]

What was even more surprising to Sergeant Aten was the fact that Dick and Tap Duncan were already in jail, having voluntarily surrendered to Sheriff Howard. Chatter regarding the gruesome murders had been the hot boiling point, the spillover for statewide stories. The San Saba rumor mill was grinding—overtime. Though no positive identification of the deceased victims had been officially made, the general public—at San Saba—had already jumped to its conclusions despite lack of any valid conformation. Accusatory talk had been so widespread and invective that the Duncan boys had decided to turn themselves in and let the state make its case—if it had one.[19] Sergeant Aten didn't claim false credit, alerting Captain Sieker: "Sheriff Howard of San Saba co. arrested two of the Duncan boys yesterday morning. . . ."[20]

Walter Landers, so it seemed, had simply vanished; fallen off the face of God's green earth. Dick Duncan was gambling: Betting that the water-logged and decomposing bodies could not have been definitely identified and, even if so, there were no eyewitnesses able to pin the nasty rap on him. If any damn sheriffs had the goods—let them prove it!

It was just such an attitude a twenty-something-year old might host. Born just above the Caprock in Lynn County before it was even officially organized and raised in San Saba County, Dick Duncan was "a man of considerable natural ability but little cultivated and raised a cowboy upon the frontier of Texas."[21] Colorfully, Duncan was further characterized as a "red-headed, dancing, idling, singing cowboy, who had been known all his life as belonging to the class that would as soon go to a fight as a frolic, and a little rather."[22] Sergeant Aten interviewed Dick inside the San Saba County Jail, understandably trying to elicit a confession, an admission of guilt. Dick Duncan would have none of it—he wouldn't let his milk down (police lingo for talk). He told Sergeant Aten he had last seen the Williamson folks alive and well after accompanying them to the border, and if, indeed, they were the persons pulled from the Rio Grande there shouldn't be any doubt that "Mexicans" killed them for their money—cut and dried—the widow Williamson had been irresponsibly flashing that $400 roll as if she were a new-rich $2.00 whore. As far as Picnic Jones, well, Duncan didn't give a hoot-in-hell where he was—maybe Brazil. Sergeant Aten didn't buy into the story.[23]

Well aware, thus far, there was no viable case against Dick or Tap Duncan, Sergeant Aten knew he would have to unravel bits and pieces and weave them into a plausible scenario—even if it be a circumstantial blanket smothering the defendants. But, even though the bodies had yet to be positively identified—a must for homicide cases—Sergeant Aten had a starting point. From there he would march, wherever the evidence and testimony took him. At San Saba he first talked with blacksmith Tom Hawkins. From him Aten learned that during a conversation between Hawkins and Duncan, Dick told Tom, "Yes, I'm taking your neighbors away, taking them down to Mexico to locate them on some land down there." Hawkins, who didn't like the Williamsons in the first place, informed Aten that he told Duncan: "I hope you will never let them come back." Dick Duncan assured the blacksmith: "By God they will never come back."[24] Powerful words spoken from the mouth of a murder suspect, an incriminating utterance for the ears of a crime-buster.

Taking up the most likely trail south from San Saba to Eagle Pass, Sergeant Aten began the methodical process of tracking the movement of the Williamsons, Dick Duncan and Picnic Jones. Rather quickly and rightly Aten eliminated Tap Duncan as a viable murder suspect—he had not been traveling with the others and his whereabouts could be logically established. Without resorting to a step by step recounting, it may be reported that Sergeant Aten through skillful interviews and deductive reasoning followed his target's movements south through the communities of Brackettville and Spofford Junction, Kinney County, then into the neighborhood above Eagle Pass. During the course of talking with witnesses and learning that Dick Duncan had bought a lengthy section of plow-line at George Hobbs' general store at Spofford, the noose was tightening. Too, the sleuthing Aten learned that on the trip south Dick Duncan had been carrying a Winchester lever-gun in first-class working order, but on his return trip to San Saba a witness recalled that the carbine's barrel was bent—fearfully so.[25]

That a statewide agency—the Frontier Battalion—was a touch more capable of marshalling scarce resources than were most local sheriffs is evidenced by Sergeant Ira Aten's next move. While at San Saba the intuitive Ranger had learned that on occasion the Williamson family had been seen by Dr. A. E. Brown, a dentist. Although he had relocated from San Saba, Sergeant Aten tracked the tooth doctor down, making needed arrangements for him to come to Eagle Pass. There, after touching the necessary legal bases, the bodies were exhumed. Whether it had been done elsewhere in the United States is indistinct, but for the first time in Texas there would be an attempt to make identification of a deceased person by the layout of their teeth and/or any corrective dental work. In this case it was a snap. Sergeant Aten had been as sharp as a leather-stropped straight razor. Dr. Brown conclusively identified the dental plate he had made for Mary

Ann Williamson. And, he could also testify that the young man was Benjamin Williamson because he was specifically familiar with those very pointed canine teeth. Yes, it was the Williamsons who had been bludgeoned to death and fed to the fishes, no doubt about it.[26]

During Aten's absence, according to secondary sources, Private Hughes had been busy, too. Purportedly riding the river he eventually located a "drag." A distinct trail—a rut—made by pulling some heavy object across the ground. And, nearby, just by sheer coincidence, was an outcropping of rocks very similar to those used to ineffectually affix four lifeless bodies to the Rio Grande's mysterious floor. The find was of rather iffy evidentiary value lacking a way to tie any prospective defendants to the site—maybe a crime scene—but Private Hughes' hard work should not be underplayed.[27] Texas Rangers could not always find every piece of evidence, every clue, or every alleged perpetrator. They surely couldn't find Mr. Walter "Picnic Jones" Landers, nor could anyone else. Area lawmen and Company D Rangers had a theory though. Sergeant Aten expounded, asserting that Dick Duncan was

> laying it off on Landers & says he is the one that done the murder. . . . never heard of Landers any more. The supposition is that Dink [*sic*] Duncan had Landers killed. I don't know whether that will hitch up with it or not. That was Landers' home [San Saba]. He had never gotten there from Mexico after the trip. The supposition is that Dink Duncan killed him on the way back.[28]

Though the Williamson murders were basically dependent on circumstantial evidence, it would be good enough for the jury, who would eventually convict Dick Duncan of Murder and sentence him to die draped with the black hood while suspended beneath Sheriff Bill Cooke's Maverick County jail yard scaffold.[29]

All told Ira had been away from Company D for thirty days, but Captain Frank Jones could be—like supervisors should be—extraordinarily proud of his decision to put 1st Sergeant Aten on the case, measuring the hard work by its end result—a murder conviction.[30]

On the personal level, though there's no record of him whining or grousing about it, there should be no doubt Frank was unpleasantly entertaining mixed emotions about the morrow. Grace Jones' due date was drawing near: AG King's orders were explicit.

Acting at the bequest of two sheriffs, both former Rangers, the adjutant general ordered Captain Jones to send a five-man detachment to far West Texas. The men, upon their arrival were to specifically make contact with Sheriff Pat Dolan, Fort Davis County, and at Alpine, meet with Sheriff J. T. Gillespie of Brewster County. The Ranger in charge of the detachment was to make an on-the-ground assessment and report whether or not a larger manpower deployment was necessary. If he should think more men were needed, the kicker was this: "If he should do so, you [Captain Jones] will proceed to that Section in person and determine the advisability of moving your Head quarters & Company to some point in those Counties & remain there for Some time."[31] There is a lot of real-estate between Boerne and Alpine.

Captain Jones was a dutiful and obedient Ranger and ready to comply with orders, however, in this instance knowing battalion purse-strings were tight, wondered whether he should ship the men, horses, mules, and supply wagon by rail or overland.[32] The adjutant general's response provides an insight into progressive and proactive law enforcement thinking steadily enveloping the Rangers: "I would suggest to Send the men to Brewster & Jeff Davis Counties mounted & with wagon in preference to shipping by rail. By Scouting the country as they go along, they may render assistance to the civil authorities on the route and being seen by everyone, their presence may have a good moral effect."[33]

The Company D commander, aside from his other worries and responsibilities had a problem of immediacy. On the same day as AG King penned the above cited instructions, April 18, 1889, Corporal J. Walter Durbin arrested a fellow named Kinney for cow theft in Zavalla County, hauling the fellow back to Uvalde County where a Complaint had been lodged against him. At Uvalde the prisoner was turned over to Sheriff Baylor. Whatever the reason, justifiable or not, the fellow was never actually placed in jail, but the maddened Kinney made a formal Complaint of his own, charging Durbin with False Imprisonment. Complying with the letter of law the Ranger was required to post bond and await the prosecutorial outcome—would or would not the district attorney press the matter. Captain Jones, knowing not to keep the top brass in the dark regarding such matters, stepped to the plate and hit a homerun for his man: "He [Kinney] was never in jail and was only held one day without papers. I am informed that a complaint will be laid before Gov. Ross about the matter. If it is I can fully exonerate Durbin in the matter as having acted as Rangers have always done [arrest without a warrant in hand, but knowing one issued]."[34] Shortly Corporal Durbin would be able to report—gleefully or not—"I come out all OK. . . . in the arrest I made a Short time back. . . ."[35]

What was okay by Frank Jones was the big doing at Boerne. On the ninth day of May 1889 little Grace Kathleen welcomed her baby sister, Frances Marguerite, into the Kendall Country world. Naturally, Frank was overjoyed with the healthful arrival of the newborn, his "heart's delight." Other sentiments were attendant to the birth. Grace Jones, already in delicate health, had had a hard go with this delivery. Her energy sapped, the recovery period for Grace was inordinately slow—her days of recuperation lengthy—in fact, Mrs. Jones was "quite ill."[36] Understandably Frank was more than a little worried, caught between duty and devotion.

Just as a new arrival came into Frank Jones' family, others were saying *adios* to Company D. During the middle of May three pretty damn good Rangers voluntarily sought their discharge. Corporal J. Walter Durbin and Privates John R. Hughes and Bazzell Lamar "Baz" Outlaw had made a career-minded decision. Captain Jones' behind-the-scenes advocacy, though not a matter of record, is justifiably suspect. The three Rangers, advantaging themselves of more lucrative financial prospects, had quit Company D to undertake employment as gun-carrying guards for the Fronteriza Mines at Sierra del Carmen, State of Coahuila, Mexico. By mere chance, or not by mere chance, the mining operations were under the direction of John G. O'Grady, Grace Jones' brother and Captain Frank Jones' brother-in-law. What the Ranger front office did or did not know is unclear, but when notifying Austin of the resignations Captain Jones only reported: "Three of my best men have quit, Durbin, Hughes, and Outlaw."[37]

The loss of Corporal Durbin, the Ranger in charge of the detachment at Alpine, opened the doorway for a promotion. Although he had only been a Texas Ranger for a year and was "somewhat lacking in experience" but since he was truly a "good man" Captain Frank Jones awarded the position of corporal to Charley Fusselman, so notifying headquarters.[38]

All so soon Captain Frank Jones would alert the Austin command staff about the hardcore and hell-in-a-hand-basket enforcement action of his newly promoted corporal in distant West Texas. Corporal Fusselman had run square up against a *mal hombre*, one dead set about making dead meat out of a Texas Ranger. The first hint of the confrontation is when Captain Jones put the adjutant general on notice: "C. H. Fusselman killed a Mexican in Brewster Co. yesterday while resisting arrest. I will give particulars as I hear from Fusselman."[39] What the gutsy corporal said—wrote—makes for exhilarating reading today, well removed from any chance of jeopardy. That Charley's first-hand exploit was real thrilling is secure. Thankfully, it offers much more: windows into his utter unpretentiousness, bulldog tenaciousness, and the depth of his courage. Or, as a dyed-in-the-wool Southwesterner would favorably say: "Ranger Fusselman had sand!" This is what the young corporal told Texas Adjutant General W. H. King—in full, with but minimal correction for clarity:

> Yesterday morning [June 4, 1889] while in discharge of my duty as Ranger I killed one Mexican name Donaciano Beslanga. I will explain. Sunday eve as I road in to Alpine I met Capt Gillespie who had a telegram from Haymond station stating that the man deceased had the town terrorized, he had shot one man a flesh wound & was riding through town shooting & all was endanger of their lives. Capt. Gillespie asked me to go with his Deputy & make the arrest. We took the 8:52 train & when we arrived at Haymond the now deceased had gone to Maxom Springs. We got a hand car & went down but did not find him & was informed over the wire that he was at Haymond. We returned on 3:20 train & the Deputy gave up & returned to Alpine. I stayed to try & find some other trace

> of him & found that he was at Maxom Springs & we had missed him if we had seen him we did not know him by the description. I borrowed a mule & went again to Maxom Srings & found he had left at sunrise. I lay & watched his wife until 10 at night when a heavy storm blew up which drove now deceased in to his home for shelter. I run on him but he slipped me as it was so dark. I followed his course to water tank & as I was looking under the tank for him lightening flashed & he shot at me at about 100 yds. I did not see where he was until he fired second shot, then I run toward him & returned the shot. Lightening flashed & he was down on the track & fired several shots & run & I lost him as it was so dark & raining so hard. Next morning I got a rifle & took his trail at daylight. When about ¾ mile from Station, I heard him cough. I went toward him & the instant I saw him he saw me & sprang to his knees & I could see there was no chance of his giving up as he had a bad expression on his face, so I fired as he did, both at the same time. Witnesses said that the two shots were so near together that they could just be distinguished. Then about 15 shots were exchanged. All this happened in about 20 seconds. I emptied my gun & run in on him & grabbed his gun & shot him once with my pistol before he would give up. He was hit 8 times, 5 shots were fatal. He would of fought 10 minutes longer if I had not grabbed his gun & took it away from him. I then wired Gillespie who came at night with Justice & held inquest & we returned to Alpine. The officers all say I am justifiable in the killing as it was self defense in the Discharge of my Duty. Please excuse this long explanation. Very Respectfully, C. H. Fusselman, Corpl. Co. D, F.B.[40]

Were Captain Jones to have thought Corporal Fusselman's gunplay would have been the last time bullets were sent flying Company D Rangers' way during 1889 he would have been mistaken. The calendar had a great deal in store for Frank Jones to contend with, both on the battlefront and the homefront. And the year was but half gone.

What Captain Jones did or did not know is hazy, but the adjutant general knew plenty and it wasn't real good. The lid was about to blow off in Fort Bend County, just southwest of Houston. A local feud was underway and had been brewing for several years—since Reconstruction—and, yes, there had been sporadic acts of violence and occasional shootings, but now the whole community, especially at Richmond, the county seat, was about to ignite. The undisguised urgency of AG King's orders to Captain Jones is evident. The Company D commander was to proceed to Richmond at once—taking his entire company with him except for the detachment assigned to far West Texas. Punctuating the adjutant general's order with the speed he demanded is reflected in the fact Captain Jones and his men were to proceed by rail, leaving their horses in camp guarded by one man. Furthermore, and in King's mind it was damn important, especially worth noting, Captain Jones was to be particularly conscientious about his "conduct and management while in that county [and it] will have to be exceedingly careful and prudent in order to preserve the peace between the opposing factions. . . ." Doubling down the adjutant general emphasized to his Company D captain that "some if not most of the county officers are on one Side of the local feud, while many if not Most of the white democratic citizens are on the other. The sheriff is directly concerned in the local feud, and this increases the necessity for careful and capable Management on the part of Yourself and Men while in that County as your duty will be to Keep the peace and preserve order" irrespective of either factions' ill-advised or outright criminal conduct.[41]

That Frank Jones hopped to is patently clear! He immediately responded, notifying AG King that he had dispatched a rider to locate Sergeant Aten and his detachment in Edwards County, ordering them to immediately report to Camp Leona.[42] As soon as he could marshal manpower, and after sending a telegram to the adjutant general about his departure, Captain Jones was aboard the train with seven Rangers bound for Richmond.[43]

The hubbub Captain Jones and the Rangers of Company D were responding to would go down in history books as the Jaybird/Woodpecker feud, a bloodletting spate of partisan insanity. Though a brief stage setting is obligatory for pushing Frank Jones' narrative, a detailed recap and an exhaustive analysis must give way to expediency. The crux of the matter is this. Fort Bend County was Plantation

Country, a farming and pastoral countryside wholly based on an agrarian economy. That may have been the nub, but there was a rub. The majority population was lopsided, heavily in favor of freedmen or the descendants of freedmen or other folks not trapped by an upbringing festooned with blind racial prejudice. With the preponderance of ballots being cast, quite naturally, many of the countywide political offices were in the hands of black men. Behind the scenes, according to many accounts, the political strings of power and tax-collecting authority were actually being pulled by whites, the Woodpeckers. Standing in opposition to the Woodpeckers were the landed gentry and their heirs apparent, the Jaybirds: ladies and gentlemen and some agitators thoroughly permeated with Old South heritage, tradition, culture, and a firm and uncompromising sense of personal honor—The Code of the Duello. Were one a hotheaded Jaybird an affront—real or likely—meant stylish gloves came off and loaded pistols came out. Even in neighboring Harris County a sagacious correspondent for the *Houston Post* noted that if a fellow was big-dogging and thinking he was the "Bad Medicine from Bitter Creek" a quick trip into Fort Bend County was guaranteed to call his bluff, because if "somebody don't call him, it won't be in this time or generation."[44]

That they were really playing for keeps is evinced by the fact that J. Kyle Terry, on the twenty-first day of June 1889, shotgunned to death Ned Gibson on the main street of Wharton, a town across the San Bernard River and just down the road from Richmond in neighboring Wharton County. The coldblooded murder—and that's what it was apart from poisonous politics and/or pigheaded partisanship—had been the last damn straw for Adjutant General W. H. King: He'd ordered the Company D Rangers to Richmond.

Fearing violent retribution from Gibson's friends and relatives, particularly Volney Gibson, Ned's loose-cannon and quarrelsome brother, Wharton County Sheriff J. W. Jones was not shy about accepting supplemental security from Captain Frank Jones and four Rangers during the Preliminary Hearing for J. Kyle Terry. In fact, Jones and his men spent ten days at Wharton.[45] Upon his return to Richmond, Captain Jones took the community's temperature but mistakenly thought that because he and his men seemed to be on "friendly terms" with both Jaybirds and Woodpeckers that the mere presence of Rangers had a "soothing effect." Perhaps his assessment or judgment was somewhat clouded by his personal desire to go home—no doubt with good reason. He didn't ask permission, simply informing AG King: "I am going to Boerne tomorrow [July 13, 1889] to see my wife who is very ill. Everything is very quiet here."[46]

Exactly how much time he spent at Boerne is fuzzy, but for certain Captain Jones was all so soon back at thorny Richmond. No doubt in large part based on the captain's appraisal, AG King ordered that Jones and Company D return to their base of operations in Uvalde County. With due respect Captain Jones suggested that Sergeant Aten and three picked men "be left in this section until after District Court in this County [Fort Bend] and Wharton, which will be in September and October. . . . I am under the impression it would not be a prudent idea to remove the entire force for some time. The men are on excellent terms with both factions and all the citizens are well pleased with their work and conduct."[47] Within the first week of August citizens of Uvalde County could find Captain Jones and a crew of Texas Rangers at Camp Leona.[48]

Sending Captain Jones back to Uvalde County was a sly tactical move on the part of the governor: that's where the Rangers' horses were pastured. Under a letter marked "Confidential" the Company D commander was instructed to personally prepare to lead a scout with four or five privates to San Saba County. There were special instructions: "Make quietly your arrangements to have your horses at Uvalde prepared for a move & do not mention this in case you should not be called on."[49] Speeding events beyond Frontier Battalion control overtook and redirected any clandestine march to San Saba for Company D.

The overworked slogan "One Riot, One Ranger" could be put into the ash heap of hyperbole. At Richmond on the sixteenth day of August 1889 there was more than one Texas Ranger on duty and there was a full scale, take-no-prisoners riot. A shooting war had broken out between Jaybirds and Woodpeckers. Sergeant Ira Aten, along with privates Jim Robinson, Seth Roberson, and Frank

Schmid had not made the move back to Uvalde but had been detailed to keep the peace in Fort Bend County. Obviously in this instance they were overmatched and outgunned, relegated to the sidelines as Richmond's cobblestone streets ran red with blood. Sergeant Aten had tried to intercede, but the Fort Bend County sheriff, J. T. "Jim" Garvey had a message for Company D's top-noncom: "Aten, I am sheriff of this county and am going to handle this situation myself. You keep out of this." Turning to the other camp—the Jaybirds—a like message was proffered from Volney Gibson: "I don't want to hurt you, Aten, but you can't take my gun or stop this crowd. We are going to clean them all out of the courthouse this time."[50] Though it blows a hole in some generally accepted Texas Ranger hoopla, Ira Aten's next move—as repeated through his own voice—was a plain spoken command to two of his subordinate Rangers: "When the shooting commenced I said, Boys this is not our fight, save yourselves!"[51] And they nearly did. Private Frank Schmid caught a bullet to the thigh, a life-threatening wound. Jones wasn't at the street-fight but he would battle bureaucracy about the Ranger's medical expenses.

Others, on or about August 16, 1889, gave up the ghost while a few more nursed gunshot wounds. An innocent girl, a black teenager had been needlessly killed during the madness. Of particular interest for this storyline is the death of Sheriff Jim Garvey. Fort Bend County, if it ever had any, was now without law—formally. Exclusive of droning details, suffice to say the governor rushed to Richmond, and under the threat of martial law cajoled the Jaybirds and Woodpeckers into accepting his recommendation for provisionally backfilling the sheriff's office vacancy until the regularly scheduled election could take place: Governor Ross pushed Texas Ranger Sergeant Austin Ira Aten into the spot created by Garvey's untimely death. Right fast Fort Bend County had a brand new sheriff, and Company D was, effective August 20, 1889, lacking a top-sergeant.[52] The following day, filling the opening created by Sergeant Aten's resignation, the ever hardworking Corporal Fusselman, who was tearing 'em up throughout the Rio Grande country of what later became known as the breathtaking Big Bend area, was promoted, becoming Company D's 1st Sergeant.[53] Not unexpectedly Captain Frank

Jones, who was then attending business at Del Rio, was instructed to "Proceed at once by first train to Richmond, Texas and take command of rangers as there is no commissioned officer with them."[54] In the interim, before Captain Jones could reach Richmond, Captain Lam Sieker recommended that Captain Samuel A. "Sam" McMurray, Company B, and three privates be hurried to Fort Bend County to supplement the then wholly understaffed detachment being supervised by Corporal Jim Robinson.[55]

Sheriff Aten was and always had been a go-getter. Within a week of assuming office as the sheriff of Fort Bend County, with the assistance of Company D and Company B Rangers, he oversaw the arrest of twenty-three of the so-called "rioters." Not having sufficient room in the jailhouse Sheriff Aten "had them at the courthouse very promptly every day & they were guarded loosely every night. . . . I put fifteen under bond & the balance was turned loose by the court."[56] The filing of charges and counter-charges would be ubiquitous as Jaybirds sought to roast Woodpeckers and during the topsy-turvy lunacy Woodpeckers sought to skewer Jaybirds. The very real tragedy had turned comedic.

Obediently the Company D captain had returned to Richmond to take command, and dutifully complied with orders to relieve the Company B Rangers so they could return to their designated stations.[57] The assignment back to Richmond couldn't have come at a worse time for Captain Frank Jones. There were dark clouds on the horizon.

The inner turmoil Frank Jones was suffering is intelligible. He was a man in the middle, being torn and tortured. The letter to AG King is self-explanatory:

> General I am placed in a peculiarly distressing condition. It is plainly evident that my duty demands that I should remain here and my wife is surely dying. Can I leave with Robinson in charge, under the supervision of Sheriff Aten? He would see that they are kept straight. If you deem it necessary to have a Commissioned officer in charge can't Capt. McMurry take charge in my place for awhile. If I were in a condition to quit the service I would tender

> my resignation instead of troubling you about my personal matters. Please let me hear from you at your earliest convenience.[58]

Clearly recognizing the tormenting stress Frank Jones was undergoing, the newly inaugurated sheriff of Fort Bend County piped in. Sheriff Aten backed Captain Jones, telling Captain Sieker: "Captain Jones is here now. He wants to go home to his wife very badly. Robinson can manage his men in his absence."[59] Compassionately the adjutant general acceded to Frank's request for authorization to go home, particularly instructing Jones to "advise this office of the Situation & of your P.O. address. . . . Hoping that your wife is not as ill as represented. . . ."[60]

Notwithstanding his personal anguish, even before rushing home to his wife's bedside, there was unpleasant Company D business to address: Captain Jones was not a shirker. He'd take action expected of him. Maintaining Company D discipline was imperative to good order. Private J. W. "Jim" King may have been a pretty fair Ranger when in control of his faculties, but alas, he earned an involuntary discharge due to his inability or unwillingness to put the bottle aside. Captain Jones reported letting King go for "drunkenness" and lamented: "He has not been disorderly but is now too drunk to be efficient and it is impossible to Keep him sober. . . . I will furnish him transportation back to Uvalde where his outfit is."[61] With that unpleasantness taken care of Jones rushed to Boerne.

Less than a week later, from Boerne, Captain Frank Jones, among other matters addressed in a letter to the adjutant general, updated King about the physical wellbeing of his darling Grace: "I am sorry to say that my wife is in a very low state."[62] And she was! Sadly, the lengthy illness had whipped her into submission; she was never able to recover and attain a healthful condition. She passed away at Boerne and was peacefully laid to rest in the city cemetery.[63] Frank was heartbroken. He, too, was a widower and father. Frank was at one of the untenable crossroads of life: Making the hard choice of voluntarily giving up his career as a Texas Ranger and picking up the plow to make a living as a single father raising two daughters, one yet an infant in arms, or choosing to remain a lawman drawing a wage-working salary from the State of Texas. Were he to choose the latter, mobility expected of Rangers would demand that the occasional trips—furloughs—to Boerne would be of fleeting duration. Thankfully, Grace's relatives stepped in, offering care and comfort and home to the two motherless daughters.[64]

The appropriate length of a mourning period is best decided by the mourner. Captain Frank Jones had Ranger business to attend to, and on the twentieth day of September was back on duty at Richmond, finding "everything very quiet and orderly."[65]

The following month, upon Captain Jones' personal assessment and concurrence by AG King, Company D was officially transferred back to the Texas Hill Country, reactivating Camp Leona where the Rangers' horses and camp equipment were yet to be found. Very shortly these Rangers would find that everything was not very quiet and certainly not very orderly.[66]

Subsequent to his debilitating gunshot wound during the Jaybird/Woodpecker madness, Private Frank Schmid would make short visits to Company D's Camp Leona. Here the injured Ranger is pictured third from left—propped up by crutches. Though not everyone in the image has been identified, reading from L to R from Private Schmid would be John O'Grady, Baz Outlaw, Captain Frank Jones, Walter W. Jones, and Solon Costley. *Courtesy Armstrong Ranger Research Center, Texas Ranger Hall of Fame & Museum.*

San Saba County Courthouse, San Saba, Texas. Big doings at the courthouse always attracted a crowd. *Courtesy San Saba Historical Commission.*

Brewster County Sheriff J. T. Gillespie was an ex-Ranger captain and formidable frontier-era lawman known favorably throughout the state. He would frequently work with Rangers stationed in West Texas on matters of mutual interest. *Courtesy Archives of the Big Bend, Bryan Wildenthal Memorial Library, Sul Ross State University.*

J. S. Clark Wagon Yard. Dick Duncan's purchase and trading of a wagon from Joe Clark was but one of several clues leading to his undoing: A Maverick County execution after conviction for a brutal homicide. *COURTESY SAN SABA HISTORICAL COMMISSION.*

As Captain Jones' top Company D noncom—which he would become—Charles Henry Vanvalkenburg "Charley" Fusselman proved to be a holy terror during one gunfight. As the saying goes, "He'd fight a Grizzly with a willow switch." The word "fear" was not in his vocabulary. *Courtesy Armstrong Ranger Research Center, Texas Ranger Hall of Fame & Museum.*

Chapter 12

"Just Plain Legal Assassination"

WHETHER OR NOT CAPTAIN JONES was riding and hiding his pain is, of course, but speculation. Men raised on the wild and woolly Texas frontier, as had been Frank, were well attuned to the fragility of life. Perhaps as a career lawman he was even more aware that the Grim Reaper was always lurking nearby. For good guys and bad guys heartbreaks and heartbeats were but hanging by a thread; a split-second could change all, every plan, every dream. However, the record is clear. Captain Frank Jones was not content to sit around Camp Leona in a blue funk. During the first part of November 1889 he personally supervised a horseback scout through Zavala and Dimmit Counties hunting for cow and horse thieves.[1]

Exposure to the chilly November elements coldly robbed Captain Jones of vigor and vivacity. He took sick. Somehow, even though feverish and weak, he had managed to make it to Del Rio, where he could be cared for by his older brother William K. Jones, the powerhouse Val Verde County lawyer and public official. Surrendering to illness was grating on Frank Jones' nerves: "In nearly nine years service I was never before compelled to give up and go under the treatment of a physician and it has been a pretty expensive case."[2] Under the care of a doctor the prognosis was realistically good, but being bedridden was as tough to swallow as Doctor Nicholson's prescriptive pills. Noting that he had done so with the charitable assistance of his brother, from the sickbed Frank completed the required pay certificates, so notifying the adjutant general. A few days later, on December 4, Frank advised Ranger headquarters at Austin that one of his Company D men had resigned to take a better-paying position and was now seeking appointment as a nonpaid Special Ranger. Through the coughing and wheezing, Captain Jones toed the mark for his man, writing that W. W. Jones had "made a good Ranger while in my Company and I can cheerfully endorse the application." Less than a week later, December 7, 1889 the Company D commander submitted the mandatory expense accounts, optimistically advising: "I am still in bed most of the time but improving rapidly and hope to be in camp in a few days." Though it goes unspoken, the captain must have been at least somewhat peeved about having to defend his actions concerning expenditures for the treatment of the seriously wounded Frank Schmid. The front office was questioning the funds spent on the "brace and splint" as well as his hiring of a "negro boy at $3.00 per week" to look after the "absolutely helpless" and bedridden Texas Ranger while at Richmond. Even with the glass thermometer under his tongue Frank Jones was scratching out memorandums. Captain Jones may have been nearly flat on his back or racing for the outhouse, but his devotion to duty was not ailing.[3]

At length Captain Jones was well enough to travel, returning to Camp Leona during the evening of December 15, 1889. Slowly recuperating, Jones was yet administratively skirmishing with Ranger headquarters, having to justify money spent caring for Private Schmid. Dissecting that correspondence is revealing about Frank's overall character, his upbeat feelings toward the Rangers of Company D, and why—nearly unanimously—they revered him.

Two examples stand out. Perhaps the state was justified in seeking an explanation, but the rank and file already knew. Upon recommendations at Richmond, Captain Jones had personally overseen the removal of Private Schmid to Houston. There, at the St. Joseph Infirmary he intended to have the Ranger admitted, seeking high-quality care and therapy for Private Schmid. At the hospital's front door admission was provisionally denied—that is unless Captain

Jones would personally stand good for Schmid's board and medical bills while there. Frank didn't hesitate a second: "His condition requiring first class nursing and attention I left him at the said Infirmary and of course became responsible for his bill. This I have already paid out of my own private funds."[4] To the man Company D Rangers knew, had it been one of them instead of Schmid, the captain would have dipped into his pocket for them too. Frank was a stand-up guy. He'd do to tie to!

Second of the reasons that illustrate why everyday working Texas Rangers respected Captain Jones so much is clear after perusing but two sentences of his rationalization for hiring the altogether debilitated Schmid a personal aide while in Fort Bend County: "In regard to the hire of the negro boy in Richmond will say that Schmid was at the most public place in the town and no Ranger would want to carry out and clean bed pans and people passing in and out all the time. If he had been wounded where no one could be procured to do such work I would cheerfully do everything that was needed myself, but in this instance I thought it best to get the boy."[5] Again, the Company D Rangers took notice. Rangers were armed with six-shooters and Winchesters—not smelly and stained slop-jars.

If one were an on-the-ground Texas Ranger at Richmond it's not inordinately difficult to appreciate Captain Jones' concern about public perception, but the adjutant general wasn't at Richmond and his laundry list of probing questions was lengthy—extending well into months yet on nineteenth-century's calendar.[6] Suggesting that disgruntlement between Captain Jones and AG King played a hand during any part of their next disagreement is inconclusive, but butt heads they did.

Aside from routine Ranger business and justifying expenditures Jones had another matter on his mind. Due to his geographical positioning in the isolated and humongous Big Bend Country, Sergeant Charley Fusselman in addition to his Texas Ranger commission was also commissioned a Deputy United States Marshal. Though a great deal of vagueness attaches to his reasoning, Captain Jones had deemed the dual appointment "hurtful to the interests of the State" and was "firmly of that opinion yet." He had instructed—ordered—Sergeant Fusselman to resign his commission as a Deputy

U.S. Marshal.[7] Captain Jones had kicked the wrong dog, U.S. Marshal for the Western District of Texas, Paul Fricke.

Marshal Fricke took pen in hand, addressing AG King. The multi-page letter was polite but pointed. He had, in fact, actually refused to accept the written resignation of Fusselman, who with deference had followed Captain Jones' explicit order. Fricke would accept the resignation, but only subsequent to the adjutant general being made fully aware of what was happening under his watch. Furthermore, according to Fricke, Fusselman's

> duties as a ranger Kept him on a portion of the frontier, infested with Smugglers and 'mescaleros' and his services, since he received the appointment, have been valuable in the suppression of that class of violators of the law. . . . Fusselman is an active and valuable peace officer and I am informed that since he has been a Deputy Marshal, there is decided less Smuggling and mescal, reducing horse stealing from Mexico, etc. than there was some months ago. It is not unlikely that he may have incurred the ill will of some persons who are interested in Keeping up a Contraband trade with Mexico and Complaint has been made (of which I Know nothing) it will probably be found to have originated in that quarter. . . . I make the request of you that you will permit him to retain his Commission and assist the Civil authorities of the U.S. where he can do so without detriment to the State Service.[8]

How bad it troubled AG King to countermand Captain Jones' order to Sergeant Fusselman is unrecorded, but countermand it, he did! "At the solicitation of Mr. Paul Fricke, U.S. Marshal, I have authorized him to retain Sergt. C. H. Fusselman as one of his deputies, believing that the interest of the State will not suffer while Sergt. Fusselman acts both as a Ranger and Deputy Marshal."[9] In this instance, right or wrong, cross-deputation had been a long-standing practice in the frontier Southwest.[10] There's no doubt Captain Jones sincerely had the best interest of the Rangers in mind, but this time he was sparring with a windmill, fighting a battle he couldn't win. Some of his Company D Rangers, that very same month, made a six-shooting play they could win, first-place finishers at a holiday gunfest.

Whatever the reasons, and excuses are many, by opening day of the last month of 1889 Baz Outlaw and John Hughes were, once again, Company D Texas Rangers.[11] The grass and greenbacks may have only appeared greener south of the border. J. Walter Durbin had opted not to reenlist with the Texas Rangers, having decided to give the saloon business a try, but the law enforcing call was too strong and he ultimately pinned on a South Texas sheriff's star. Ever witty and never prone to timidity, Durbin characterized Baz Outlaw, the man he had parted company with: "This man was with me two years in a Ranger company and went to Mexico with me and I must say of all the bad men I have knew [*sic*] he was one of the worst and most dangerous. He never knew what fear was."[12]

Some folks in Edwards County knew what fear was: A crime-wave was sweeping across their neighborhood, drowning their chances at sustaining economic stability or upholding any semblance of peaceful security. Edwards County was Company D territory, Captain Jones' territory. He was positively not a man—or a lawman—that was bent toward inoperativeness. Though there's a possibility—and good reason to believe—that had Captain Jones been granted a do-over he might have rethought his choice, life's second chances are seldom very handy. He put Private John Hughes as the lead Ranger in a three-man Company D detachment assigned to Edwards County with a specific agenda scribbled in the playbook. Riding with Private Hughes were Baz Outlaw and Cal Aten, also privates. Their job was to apprehend the Odle brothers.

Captain Jones and Sergeant Aten had already "rounded them up" once before, but the siblings were slippery and had slithered out of jailhouses absent permission. They were by any man's measure pretty tough customers. Will and Alvin Odle, besides stealing what wasn't tied down or closely guarded inside a picket corral, were boys of hair-trigger temperament. Their propensity for six-shooter settlement was a matter of record at several Texas Hill Country courthouses. The Odles were more than capable and more than willing to sidestep surrender behind fire-belching Colt's .45s or nastily barking Winchesters. In lawmen's jargon they "were bought and paid for" which translates ever so easily: If they made a false move or wiggled the wrong way—shoot! Red ribbons are valueless prizes for gunfights.[13]

Of late the Odle boys had been stealing with abandon. Cattle or horses stolen in Texas were pushed south and crossed into Mexico where brands and earmarks were not a matter of record. Cattle or horses stolen in Mexico were pushed north and crossed into Texas where rightful owners had no say-so and little hope of recovery. The Odle brothers were first-rate racketeers.[14]

They were, too, thoroughly adept at advantaging themselves of the winding canyons and near inaccessible hiding spots in that mountainous country drained by the Nueces and Llano Rivers, real estate dotted with secret caves and underground caverns. Game trails there were many. Though there's surely a romantic tinge many biographers fall for—that part about trailing guys based on squashed grass, bent twigs, overturned rocks, and doodle-bug tracks inside dints laid down by horseshoes—the truth is usually less glamorous, far less quixotic. Blindly bumbling around in tight and foreign places hunting for mean guys that will kill you is not too smart. Spiders have cobwebs. Rattlesnakes have patience. Good lawmen, well, they have snitches.

The high-sheriff of Edwards County, Ira L. Wheat, had an informant—a damn good one too. A somewhat prominent area cattleman had suffered the formality of an Indictment for knowingly buying stolen livestock from Will and Alvin Odle. Sheriff Wheat had a take it or leave it offer: Ride the pony around the hillsides of Edwards County or ride the bucking horse to Huntsville. The prospective defendant opted for the less dramatic trip. The Odle boys would be delivering horses to the vicinity—the east side—of Bullhead Mountain sometime after dark Christmas Day. Sheriff Wheat updated his chief deputy, Will Terry, who in turn assembled a posse of trusted Edwards County citizens. Will Terry also cut Rangers Hughes, Outlaw, and Aten in on the plan: All would be well in place—hidden—when outlaws Will and Alvin Odle made their show.

Skirting around the little community of Vance, avoiding raising an alarm, and picketing their horses at a safe distance so as not to inadvertently put their prey on notice, the man-hunters settled into their frigid nighttime surveillance. The wait was short. At around eight o'clock the unsuspecting desperadoes crossed the threshold—riding into the lawmen's open field of fire. Niceness and legalities would customarily dictate a verbal challenge be hurled at the bad boys. In this instance actually apprehending Will and Alvin Odle took a back seat to self-preservation. Private Cal Aten, who was an on-the-ground player that crisp Christmas night didn't mince or mumble his words: "but you will understand that it pertains to the time when the Odle boys were assassinated. That is all it was, just plain legal assassination. However, there would have been someone else assassinated if we hadn't got the first shots."[15]

Purportedly and, there's really no sufficient cause to dispute it, one of the posse members, Jim Rhodes, was individually distressed about what had just taken place. To right fast demonstrate that he had personally taken no part in the actual shooting, Rhodes "ejected every cartridge from his Winchester to prove that it had not been fired."[16]

Will Odle and his horse were killed outright. Alvin Odle took a bullet or bullets during the opening volley but was yet clinging—barely—to life. No one at the scene doubted he would die. No one at the scene wanted to put him out of his misery with a *coup de grâce* or by coldheartedly stepping on his neck; they weren't murderers. Lucifer could have his man. Texas Ranger Aten, subconsciously allowing compassion to override any adrenalin rush, knelt to comfort Alvin who was clearly struggling, sinking fast, gurgling and gasping for air as blood leaked from his body. Unmistakably troubled, Cal Aten would later write:

> I have held a dying outlaw [Alvin] in my arms. One of the worst ever-known in the Southwest. Took his pistol out of his dying hand. The same pistol I keep under my mattress now. It was a wonderfully beautiful gun then without a blemish on it, beautiful engraving. I was sorry for that boy. Just a few years older than I and I have often wondered what he would have done had our positions been reversed. Just rode off and left me like a dog, I think. . . . [17]

Private John Hughes, within two hours of the killing, was understandably concerned with setting down an official version of the episode. Notifying the adjutant general of the two outlaws' demise he covered the necessary bases: "They resisted arrest and made a hard fight and we had to kill them in self defense. Also killed one horse and shot an other through the neck. It took place about 8 o'clock tonight."[18]

Captain Jones' initial response was, perhaps, a touch insensitive as he updated Captain Sieker: "I guess you have seen in the paper where some of my men celebrated Xmas day by Killing the two Odles in Edwards County."[19] Two days later he again messaged Captain Sieker and clearly Captain Jones' rehashing of the ferocious episode had undergone a crucial tweaking: "I have no particulars of the killing of the Odles except that they drew their pistols when commanded to surrender and then the firing began. Hughes who is in charge of the Edwards County detachment simply stated that they made a hard fight and they (the Rangers) were compelled to Kill them."[20] Officially for the Company D preprinted Monthly Return of December the entry is succinct: Will and Alvin Odle were "Killed while resisting arrest."[21] There was, conceivably, some compulsion on the part of Captain Jones to elaborate further, for in a Supplement to the Monthly Return he penned: "Private Hughes and two men with Deputy Sheriff and posse in attempting the arrest of Will and Alvin Odle wanted for murder were fired on by them. The shots were returned resulting in the death almost instantly of both."[22] Subsequent to the celebratory mood about offing the Odle brothers washing away, Captain Jones may have been justifiably worried about the legal fate of his men, as he had within the month put Captain Sieker on notice that the Edwards County sheriff "will not work with Rangers," which in light of events does seem particularly weird.[23] Evidently the newly installed sheriff of Fort Bend County, Ira Aten, was concerned about the possibility of his younger brother paying some sort of heavy legal penalty, notifying Cal: "I will write to Ira Wheat about not having you boys indicted in Edwards co. I wish I had time I would go up there & could tell in a short time which would be best, to have you indicted now or not. I expect Wheat would like to make some fees in the matter. . . ."[24] In the end, the Rangers came clear—legally.

Three days after Christmas some more of Captain Frank Jones' Company D Rangers drew their six-shooters but didn't draw blood. As head of a three-man detachment sent to keep the peace at Sonora in Sutton County, Corporal Jim Robinson filed his report. That he was a good and gutsy Ranger will not stand challenge, nor will the fact that any time he spent in classrooms was short: "They Schoat the little town up often. I and one man tried to Stope two men the other night, they Schot at us and we Schot two Schots apeace. They run out of the place So I will arrest thim when I finde thim. . . . this is a Wilde place."[25] For the Monthly Return, Captain Jones dressed up his corporal's report: "[Dec] 28. . . . Corpl Robinson and one man in attempting the arrest of Jeff Taylor and Bob Williams while firing off their pistols on the streets of Sonora exchanged two shots with them but they ran out of town horseback and escaped."[26] But there was more for Corporal Robinson to recount: "Last night the Deputy Sheriff of Kimble Co. got on a Drunk and I unarmed him. I cante tell what will turn up yet. He will have his trile to day."[27] Without doubt Captain Jones concurred that Sonora was a "Wilde place," notifying headquarters of an opinion that Sonora was in a pretty bad state of affairs, "Something like Kimble Co. was some years ago. . . . John Gorman, ex-Sheriff of Kimble Co. is there in the whiskey business."[28]

Clearly the three partners operating The Sonora Supply Company, a general merchandising establishment specializing in ranching supplies, were appreciative of having Rangers in their town and so notified AG King: "Corporal Robinson & 3 men have been sent us by Capt. Frank Jones, Co. D. who have done good service here in quieting the lawless element. They have made two arrests and are a general terror to the rowdy element. There are several hard cases, whose track they are on who have been depredating on & terrifying good citizens & we believe they will be either soon arrested or driven out of the country. We hope you will allow these boys to remain here, at least until our county is organized."[29]

From the foregoing tribute one might be lulled into supposing Company D Rangers were universally welcomed. Captain Frank Jones learned otherwise. Some folks in the neighborhood of Camp Leona were desirous of seeing the Rangers removed from Uvalde

County altogether, and they made those feeling known to the adjutant general. The Rangers' campground was unfenced and therefore the feed and forage for their horses and mules was an attraction to the cattle and hogs roaming the nearby Open Range. As noted elsewhere within this text, the Company D Rangers were right proud of their dogs—even though their pets were viciously inclined toward any outsiders, be they two-legged or four-legged. According to aggrieved petitioners, the Company D dogs had torn and maimed their livestock. Multiplying their utter frustration and adding to financial losses, in other instances their animals had "been found dead near Said camp of State Rangers caused by gun Shot wounds." The stockmen's complaint was not mush-mouthed: They wanted the "State Rangers to be removed from our midst and the vicinity of their present encampment" and of that request the petitioners "will ever pray."[30]

Quite naturally a high-level public official like the adjutant general couldn't be bulldozed into action by a bunch of Uvalde County stockmen, but for the short term Captain Jones and the Rangers not on detached service elsewhere were—at least temporarily—redeployed under orders of the adjutant general. Though it's but mere coincidence coming but four days after the concerned citizens south of Camp Leona corresponded with Ranger headquarters, AG King had a particular message for Captain Jones, after advising him the redeployment would be of at least several weeks, maybe months: "Uvalde and vicinity can apparently Spare your Company at this time and if So it may be well for you to go in person with all the Company except the Sutton County detachment. . . ."[31] Understandably Sergeant Charley Fusselman's small detachment in far West Texas was unaffected.

Trouble was brewing in the ranching country north of San Angelo in a section that had been recently lopped off from Tom Green County and fashioned into the barely organized Coke County. Until readjusted to the settlement of Robert Lee, the first county seat was Hayrick, about dead center of the survey at the base of Hayrick Mountain, a rise in elevation to a magnificently towering 1401 feet. The county sheriff, W. T. Buchanan, had been officially in office less than a year and the county was filling up fast with some unsavory characters—and nice folks, too! Following orders was but what good Rangers did, and Captain Jones made ready for the move, dutifully advising the adjutant general: "I expect to leave on the 16th for Coke County. Will leave the Teamster who is a faithful old negro to look after camp."[32]

Within but a few days Captain Jones and Company D Rangers were camped in the pasture of L. B. Harris, "an extensive ranchman" with his Coke County headquarters on the Colorado River between San Angelo and Hayrick. Frank Jones' personal assessment of the potential for six-gun turmoil was level-headed, and not overly hyped: "The trouble, if there is ever any, will be caused by a conflict between ranch men and squatters and the latter are in a great majority. If a pasture man should chance to Kill a squatter then this whole section would be in a State of anarchy." Diplomatically, Frank Jones counseled with Mr. Harris about the wisdom of settling disputes over land in court through civil lawsuits and not through the muzzle of a Winchester.[33]

Although everything seemed comparatively quiet in Coke County, Captain Jones did notice "an undercurrent of bitter feeling existing between the ranch men and squatters." Taking it upon his own initiative to leave the area and return to Camp Leona, Jones opted to put a safety-valve in place, leaving Private Hughes and two men behind, though he didn't think they would have too much to do, but he thought "their presence will do much to Keep down any trouble."[34]

While deployed west of Camp Leona and scouting in Coke and Tom Green Counties, a heartrending telegram finally caught up with Captain Jones. Rushing home to Boerne was first and foremost in his mind. Secondarily, upon arrival, he took pen in hand to update the adjutant general about his hasty and unplanned trip: "I came here from San Angelo in response to a telegram announcing the dangerous illness of my baby. The crisis is now at hand and she will either recover or I will lose her."[35] Thankfully—in a way—Frank made it home in time to tenderly kiss nine-month-old Frances Marguerite's feverish forehead. Sadly, though the malady is not specified, it claimed the baby girl's life. Frank's wife Grace had just passed four months earlier, the loose earth around her grave not yet packed tightly by Mother Nature's weathering. After taking a lock of hair from Frances to put with the lock earlier taken from Grace to be placed with a soothing book of poetry Frank carried in his saddlebags, the baby was lovingly interred with her mother.[36]

While tending to funeral arrangements and consoling his daughter Grace Kathleen—the best he could—Frank learned of another death, a murder. The captain updated Ranger headquarters:

> The man J. W. King who I discharged at Richmond for drunkenness was foully assassinated in Zavalla County on the 11th of this month [February] by parties who I am thoroughly convinced thought King was yet a Ranger and on detective work. Sometime before I went to Fort Bend County I sent King into that section as a dishonorably discharged man, to try and work up some cattle stealing. He said at the time that if he was suspicioned that he would undoubtedly be murdered. Since then it was known that he was in the Company and they evidently thought he was trying to play the same game again. I shall do my best to ferret out the murderers and see that they are punished.[37]

Naturally there's no way of knowing for sure, but it's interesting to note that shortly after learning of Jim King's death Captain Jones made a special request to his pal Captain Sieker, asking him to go to an Austin gun store and have a specifically cataloged six-shooter shipped to him at Uvalde: "A short Colt's nickled plated rubber handle .45 pistol."[38]

Shortly, that same month, AG King notified Captain Jones of the Governor's Proclamation offering a reward of $250 for the "apprehension and conviction of Murderers of J. W. King. Said reward to stand good for Six months."[39] Although it necessitates an ever niggling chronological skip, it may be herein reported that the Zavalla County sheriff, C. C. Akers, did in due course make arrests with regards to two of ex-Ranger King's alleged murderers. Unfortunately from a law-enforcing perspective "the defendants would ultimately skate around legalities."[40] Neither man was ever convicted for any involvement in Jim King's homicide.[41]

With little to no enforcement activity being reported out of Coke County, Captain Jones, sailing his own boat, ordered Private Hughes to report to Sergeant Fusselman in Presidio County, where there was plenty of wild geography to scout and plenty of wild *mal hombres* to corral.[42] But if Frank Jones thought he had enduringly scratched out some home-turf in Uvalde County at Camp Leona he was mistaken. The governor had other ideas. And the governor had the stick. Headquarters for Company D was shifted from the Texas Hill Country to South Texas. Captain Jones and his Rangers, those not on detached duty, could now call their camp outside of Cotulla, La Salle County, home.[43]

Texas could rightfully lay claim to a few extremely tough—not necessarily rugged—pieces of real estate: Cotulla qualified. Although La Salle County's line on the map did not actually touch the Rio Grande, its proximity to Webb County (county seat Laredo) presented its eligibility for being categorically classed as a perilous section of the Texas/Mexico borderlands. Doctor J. W. Hargus, who had practiced medicine in the area, unflappably remarked: "more than once I was led blindfolded into a thicket to doctor a wounded outlaw. I have treated gunshot wounds of 259 men and have seen 108 men with bullet holes in them that did not need treating."[44] Just four years prior to Company D relocating to La Salle County, the county sheriff and former Texas Ranger, C. B. McKinney, had been murdered. According to a January 3, 1890, petition from some concerned citizens, the then-sheriff and precinct constable were in wholehearted sympathy with and active "abettors of the liquor element." Subsequent to a probing trip to the border, Governor Ross had personally verified that "a terrible State of affairs exist in La Salle County." Those citizens petitioning Austin for relief had specifically asked that "a Squad of rangers be sent here at the earliest moment possible. . . ." Captain Jones being ordered to "take all the force you can & proceed to that Section" should come as no surprise. Rightly or wrongly politicos abhor dealing with petitioners or protestors.[45]

And Texas Ranger company commanders cannot tolerate insubordination or ineptness. Whatever the reason—and there seems to be no record—the no doubt self-assured Corporal Jim Robinson was reduced in rank because of "incompetency." Rather than suffer the indignity of disciplinary action—rightly or wrongly—Robinson tendered his resignation. Although Private Hughes had actually been the Ranger in charge of the Edwards County detachment that had ended the Odle brothers' crime spree, along with Outlaw and Aten, Jones skipped over him and gave the now vacant corporal's position to Baz Outlaw.[46] Could the fact Jones had earlier arrested both—absent any gunplay—been part of his decision? *¿Quien sabe?*

Personnel matters aside and dutifully following repositioning orders, Captain Frank Jones established the Company D headquarters camp on a high point approximately one mile east of Cotulla. There he had plenty of water for their livestock but would be forced to haul their drinking water and, despite that inconvenience, the captain reported to Austin that the camp was in "a good healthy location." Two days later he filed another report declaring the unhealthful state of La Salle County: The untamed province was in a "lawless condition" and it would indisputably "take time to restore peace and quiet and a strong force of Rangers will have to be retained in this section almost permanently." Furthermore, according to Jones, good men were in the minority and the county sheriff was "a perfect nonentity." Fully realizing that a certain element would be opposed to anyone enforcing the law and/or keeping the peace, the intrepid Frank Jones wasn't buffaloed: "and if they want a fight you can rest assured they will get it and in good shape too. It is pretty hard for good men to have their lives threatened for simply doing their plain duty."[47]

From Private Frank Schmid's viewpoint not everyone responsible for sailing the Ranger ship was doing his duty. Practically speaking, the gunshot wound he had received at Richmond on August 16, 1889, was an absolute medical mess. Whether it may be rightly charged to therapeutic incompetence and ineffectiveness or plain stupidity, would have been wholly irrelevant for the suffering Frank Schmid's mindset. Subsequent to treatment at the Houston infirmary, he was given the okay by doctors to return to Uvalde. Unfortunately he was advised to seek lodging at a local hotel, and was at the time more-or-less prohibited from spending too much time at the admittedly unsterile Camp Leona. Regrettably, his wound was not healing suitably. Now it was April of the following year and the distraught patient was—at the instructions of physicians—in San Antonio at the Santa Rosa Infirmary, an institution under the charge of Sisters of the Incarnate Word. Private Schmid had already undergone one operation, which according to him "was mostly scraping" but he was understandably worried. The next course of action would be "to burn all the sore places with a red hot iron." In the interim the festering and oozing wound was being kept open through application of a "drainage tube." Even then Private Schmid was keeping his chin up: He was a Company D Ranger, one of Captain Frank Jones' Rangers.

But realistically he could not have been any too happy—as was the captain—with continually having to defend expense vouchers submitted to Austin—expenditures he had no control over. Even more distressing, however, was the apparent front office disinterest—other than money—in his plight. Extracts from his correspondence back up such a claim, but on another front also help shed light on roles evolving technology was playing, even during days Rangers were scouting horseback: "The General came to San Antonio yesterday and wishing to see him I telephoned to hotel yesterday asking him to call, as yet I have not met him but hope to." Private Schmid was, dejectedly, desperate: "Would have liked very much to have seen Genl. King while he was here, as he then could have investigated matter himself. I telephoned to him three different times asking him to call to see me, and he failed to comply with my wishes."[48]

Meanwhile, back at Cotulla, Captain Frank Jones had not had a change of heart, but was even more appalled at the unsavory situation in La Salle County. He was learning more everyday. Obviously Frank thought the adjutant general and the governor, who had sent him and Company D there in the first place, should be cut in on the know:

> There is a great deal of work to be done in this and adjoining Counties. Affairs are in worse condition in this section than I have ever Known in nine years service in different Counties of the State. Men are afraid to be seen talking to me and want to skulk off in a

> dark corner and then swear me to secrecy. It seems hard to infuse any self reliance, or confidence in any legal redress. I shall use the utmost means in my power to right matters while I am here.[49]

Assuredly committed to doing his duty and not distressed due to any man's or men's badness, soon after setting up camp Captain Jones personally led a scout north of Cotulla into the vicinity of Millett in search of a gang of suspected murderers. The manhunt was unproductive through no fault of Captain Jones or the Company D Rangers.[50]

Upon returning to Cotulla the frazzled Rangers may have thought—hoped—the next few days would be worriless. They were wrong. One of their Company D comrades had fallen—killed in the line of duty. Sergeant Charley Fusselman's five-man West Texas detachment had been working throughout the Big Bend Country but more-or-less headquartered at modestly populated Marfa, the county seat of Presidio County. Soon, according to plans, they were to shift their base camp to the mining settlement of Shafter, giving them closer access to the Rio Grande and the borderland villages up and down the river, like Presidio, where most of the criminal activity was taking place. Private Hughes, therefore, was at Marfa when he received a telegram from El Paso where his sergeant was attending court.

Exactly who authored the telegram to Private Hughes is indeterminate, but in turn he immediately telegraphed Captain Jones at Cotulla and AG King at Austin: "Sergeant C. H. Fusselman has been killed by horse thieves near El Paso."[51] Upon receipt of the distressing telegram Captain Jones wired Private Hughes:

> Have fusselman nicely buried and write his father.[52]

Understandably, Captain Jones in turn notified Frontier Battalion headquarters pledging to give "full particulars" of the April 17, 1890, murder as soon as he was made aware of them, which with ever improving communications technology and a continually upgrading U.S. Postal network, wouldn't take long. Too, and it but speaks to Frank Jones' aggressiveness and attention to duty, he matter-of-factly mentioned to AG King: "I have been in the saddle almost every day since coming to this place."[53]

The particulars of the murder of Sergeant Charley H. Fusselman, in a thin nutshell, are these. He had been summoned to testify in legal proceedings at El Paso and during a normal period of downtime had ambled into the office of the county sheriff, James H. White. The sheriff was elsewhere but Fusselman, Chief Deputy Frank B. Simmons, and city policeman George Herold, the ex-Texas Ranger usually credited with the 1878 killing of outlaw Sam Bass at Round Rock, were engaged in a genial chat. Unexpectedly area ranchman John H. Barnes made an appearance and reported that Mexican bandits had raided his place in the Franklin Mountains just north of town, butchering a calf and stealing several of his prized horses. With most of the local officers tied up with duties attending to or testifying in court or catering to District Court Judges' whims, Fusselman without any hesitation volunteered to try and apprehend the thieves. Having traveled to El Paso on the train, Sergeant Fusselman was horseless and his Winchester was at the hotel. Accessibly he was promptly handed the reins of Sheriff Jim White's horse, which was tied at the nearby hitch-rack, and he borrowed a lever-action carbine from Deputy U.S. Marshal Bob Ross, who was tending to the federal court's docket. George Herold was not particularly occupied with pressing city or court business, so he, along with John Barnes, nodded their support and set out with Sergeant Fusselman to try and overall the outlaws.[54]

Snubbing the story to the post, in the high-country outside of town the lawmen calamitously overran the outlaw's noonday campground and the reverberations of gunfire echoed through the mountains. Sergeant Fusselman being a gritty fellow, screamed to his two trailing companions: "Boys we are in for it, and let's stay with it!"[55] Hardly had he spoken those words of encouragement when his head wrenched sideways, a bullet tearing through his right temple and "carrying away nearly the whole of the right lobe of the brain." The next bullet punched its way under his chin, exiting through his left ear. Fusselman was dead in the saddle. Unable to dislodge the assassins, and wholly unsure of their numbers, Herold and Barnes beat a hasty retreat for El Paso and reinforcements. Promptly a heavily armed posse took to the field while an overwrought newspaper correspondent safe from harm prophesized: "If the thieves are captured and it proves true that they have killed Fusselman it will go hard with his murderers."[56] And it probably would have.

There is an interesting backburner story revolving around Ranger Charley Fusselman's death, one meriting mention when appropriate. In the short term, however, suffice to say the young Texas Ranger's killers made good their getaway to Mexico, despite the gallant efforts of the posse riding hard to overtake them.

Not unexpectedly the gloomy news was emotionally sensed all through the Ranger outfit, from top to bottom. The adjutant general messaged Captain Jones about "the Sad intelligence of the Killing of Sergt. C. H. Fusselman." Captain Jones was deeply saddened as were the rank and file who had ridden with Company D's top-sergeant. On the other hand, Frank Jones had a host of imperative administrative issues to deal with, and one of immediacy was naming Fusselman's replacement. At the time, for Frank Jones the choice was not particularly difficult. Once again he would choose Baz Outlaw over John Hughes, promoting the former to 1st Sergeant and the latter to corporal. Frank Jones' confident estimation of Baz Outlaw—though it would change—was for the moment splendid. The captain's words were not veiled: "He was a man of unusual courage and coolness and in a close place is worth two or three ordinary men."[57] And, if lurid assertions coming out of the far-flung Big Bend Country were even but half true, men of courage and coolness were in demand.

A Presidio County attorney, S. J. Hensley, took it upon himself to pen a three-page handwritten letter to AG King, which in part summed up the situation in the Big Bend, and in part shored up how area citizens felt about the killing of the Ranger: "As regards Fusselman's death I will say that the people of this county feel it deeply. . . . his demise is a great loss to the state of Texas and there are many men in this county who would go to Kansas to hang the villains who murdered him if they thought they could succeed in doing so."[58]

Less than a month after Texas Ranger Fusselman's murder, some irate ranchmen, elected and appointed public officials, merchants, settlers, mining superintendents, and publisher of the *Marfa New Era* had banded together, making their feelings and concerns and worries known to the state's chief executive, Governor L. S. Ross. Strikingly their plea was not handwritten, as most petitions of the day, but accenting the importance they attached to their cry for help is the fact a typesetter was pressed into service—it was a formal request in a formal format and is worthy of repeating herein—in full:

> We, the undersigned citizens of Presidio county, most respectfully represent to your excellency: First, That this county borders on the Rio Grande, opposite the mountainous districts of Chihuahua, Mexico, the same being the hot bed of bandits, whose only occupation is smuggling, thieving and the cold blooded butchery of any and all who may be suspected of possessing a few dollars, and who may for an instant be caught off their guard. Second, That numerous murders of the most violent and blood-curdling nature that have been recorded in the history of Texas, have been committed in this county within the last year; that the country is continuously being devastated by raids of the hoards of horse and cattle thieves from the Mexican side; that our best citizens are being butchered and robbed on all sides, and that the best interests of this county are thus paralyzed; that although we have an honest and efficient sheriff, he is unable to render us the required assistance. Third, That the ranger force lately stationed in this county is insufficient in strength, and have their headquarters so far removed from the point of danger as to be of little or no use; that owing to the foregoing the progress of this county is being retarded, and the lives of the honest and law abiding citizens are at the mercy of the red-handed villains from Chihuahua.
>
> Now, therefore, we humbly and confidently pray to your excellency that you will cause to be placed at the town of Presidio, in this county, a force of rangers of not less than ten men, with orders to continually scout the river front of this county, for at least one year; that you will use your influence to have troops removed from interior posts, and placed on the river where they may be of service to the settlers, who are so honestly and

> energetically trying to build up and fortify the border, and make west Texas what it should be, the garden, and not the slaughter house of the United States.[59]

At this juncture in Captain Frank Jones' riveting story it should come as no remarkable surprise. Written orders emanating from the adjutant general's office and directed straight away to Cotulla and the Company D commander were childishly easy to grasp: "Further demands for rangers coming from Presidio County and it has been decided to send your Company to that Section." Shortly thereafter, as the good trooper that he was, Captain Jones replied: "I have torn down and am anxious to get off."[60]

Elaborately engraved Colt's .45 six-shooter Ranger Private Cal Aten took from the bloody hand of a "dying outlaw," Alvin Odle, following the desperate and deadly gunplay near Bullhead Mountain in Edwards County. *Courtesy Joseph Trobaugh II.*

Though he would later become Company D's 1st Sergeant, Baz Outlaw was one of the Ranger shooters that Christmas night the notorious Odle brothers bit the dust. Captain Frank Jones characterized Outlaw as "a man of unusual courage and coolness and in a close place is worth two or three ordinary men." *Courtesy Armstrong Ranger Research Center, Texas Ranger Hall of Fame & Museum.*

Rangers posing for the photographer at Company D's Camp Leona near Uvalde, Texas. Not infrequently the standing Ranger, coffee cup in hand, is incorrectly identified as Captain Frank Jones, when in fact the Ranger is Sergeant Austin Ira Aten, a photo taken prior to his resignation to become sheriff of Fort Bend County. The Rangers are, from L to R: Jim King, Frank Schmid (before being wounded), Ernest Rogers, Cal Aten, Walter Jones, Charley Fusselman, J. Walter Durbin, Jim Robinson, John R. Hughes, and Baz Outlaw. *Courtesy Jeri and Gary Boyce Radder.*

Subsequent to fortifying themselves by sipping hot coffee and wolfing down cathead biscuits these intrepid Company D Texas Rangers—while Captain Frank Jones is away—continue their play acting, supposedly mounting up to chase desperadoes. *Courtesy Jeri and Gary Boyce Radder.*

CHAPTER 13

"The Shooting Was Promiscuous and Lively"

COGNIZANT OF THE NECESSITY FOR maintaining a Ranger presence in La Salle County the adjutant general ordered J. A. Brooks, since promoted to captain, to move his Company F to Cotulla, replacing Company D. Following an exchange of letters between Captain Jones and Ranger headquarters regarding the pros and cons, principally economic issues, it was determined to move Company D to Marfa by rail rather than the time consuming overland route. Although they arrived in Presidio County on June 4, 1890, a permanent camp for Company D two miles outside Marfa was not officially sited until the twenty-sixth day of the month.[1]

While in transit, other forces that would impact Company D were in the works. In the end, years later, a great deal of heroic blathering would attach to the running down of at least one of Charley Fusselman's killers, primarily from secondary sources. Closer in, time-wise and closer to consciousness of the contemporary Company D Rangers, another revealing chapter was unfolding—long before any overly pumped mythology overrode the hard truths of Texas Ranger history were corrupted for a twentieth-century marketplace. But halfway through 1890, however, the indisputable—irrefutable—identity of the murderers was yet a mystery.

At Austin the adjutant general had received mail very relevant to the bushwhacking of Sergeant Fusselman. According to the information at hand, after killing the young Texas Ranger the yahoos scampered west, straight across southern New Mexico Territory or northern Chihuahua, alighting voluntarily or involuntarily in or near the Mexican border town of Palomas, thirty-odd miles due south of Deming. Real fast putting a great deal of ground between oneself and the bloody crime scene wherein a well-liked Ranger had been assassinated was not dumb. According to AG King's source: "If you Know a good man that Speaks Spanish it would be better for the Mex Graels [Rurales] has Fusselman's pistol, gun, & Saddle at Palomas in State of Senora [*sic*]." That the story given to the adjutant general could be ringing true was the valid and documentable claim to the State of Texas for reimbursement submitted by Sheriff Jim White for the theft of his horse and saddle, and by Deputy U.S. Marshal Bob Ross for the loss of his Winchester: "The gun and horse were both carried off."[2]

Avoiding speculation, thus far it remains uncertain how much Captain Jones did or did not know regarding the foregoing message to the adjutant general. That Frank was determined to correctly identify and apprehend Fusselman's killers is manifest. True, within two days of the murder the *El Paso Times* was naming possible suspects with the predicate "it is believed" but that is woefully inadequate drivel and not sustainable evidence. Inside the courtroom proof Beyond Reasonable Doubt is the necessary standard for conviction. Competent lawmen, like Captain Jones, may in their mind know who did a dirty deed, but that counts for naught—and of that they are well aware. Getting the goods on the right guy is key. Little more than a week after AG King became aware of the intelligence, Captain Jones reported:

> I am going to make an extended scout above El Paso to try and Capture the murderers of Sergt. Fusselman and will be absent from my station about 30 days. Will take my wagon and a pack mule. Corpl. Hughes and 5 men are at Presidio on the Rio Grande and that section is very quiet. Six or eight fugitives are in the town just across from where Hughes is in Camp. He has been

trying all this month to decoy them over but so far has failed, but may succeed yet.[3]

Clearly John Hughes had not been assigned on an extended basis to hunt down Fusselman's slayers. The industrious Corporal Hughes had been stationed on the Rio Grande at Presidio with his small detachment consisting of Privates Walter W. Jones, who had re-upped with Company D, John R. Gravis, Charles Barton, John C. Mayfield, and Cal Aten since the fifth day of May 1890 when he had permanently moved his camp from Marfa. Private Aten, working out of the Company D's detachment camp at Marfa—at the time of Fusselman's death—had apprised Captain Lam Sieker of the wholly miserable condition of a hard country victimized through the "Deviltry of a lot of cowardly thieves and murderers." Likewise is the fact Corporal Hughes, after attending to Fusselman's funeral arrangements and conducting a dutiful but short-time search for the killers, was due back in the Big Bend Country on April 23, less than a week after the fallen Ranger's memorial services and first burial at El Paso.[4] Declaring that Corporal Hughes and his detachment were more-or-less tied up at Presidio trying to entice fugitives hiding at Ojinaga, State of Chihuahua, Mexico, but wanted on the Texas side of the Rio Grande is amplified in the Company D Monthly Return of June 1890: "Corpl. Hughes did not scout any this month." Certainly the notation does not mean—nor imply—that this detachment wasn't working—but that they were stationary at or near Presidio trying to keep the peace, protect honest hardworking folks, and nab any owlhoots wanted by various judicial officeholders of the Lone Star State. In fact, Corporal Hughes had written from Presidio on May 6, 1890, that because there was "so much lawlessness at & near Presidio" that he thought it would be best to camp there "about a month." He too shrewdly theorized, "I don't think it best to stay long in one place, especially in Presidio as the mexicans can watch us pass out & in the town."[5]

Unfortunately Captain Jones had to scuttle his enthusiastic campaign for hunting down and capturing Sergeant Fusselman's killers. It was summertime in Texas—hot and dry—forcing Frank Jones, subsequent to a quick exploratory train trip to El Paso, to seriously rethink and reset his arrest blueprint because "the country was so very dry that I deemed the trip impracticable." Rangers working horseback are wholly dependant on good grass and water. Perhaps, in the end, cancelling this scout was accidently advantageous. The worried captain had to catch a train bound for San Antonio and then rush to Boerne: "My little girl was quite sick and I was compelled to stay with her."[6] Shortly the child regained her health and Captain Jones was back on duty doing Ranger business at Marfa by early August. And it was a good thing, too! There were more big doings on tap for the Rangers of Company D.

Spotted only eighteen miles north of Presidio on Cibola Creek was the rough and tumble mining town of Shafter, not too far southeast of the area's rugged and rocky Chinati Mountains. The dominate employer at Shafter was The Presidio & Cibola Mining Company, a silver mining outfit with some 300 employees on the payroll: Mostly hard-scrabble miners of Mexican ancestry. As might be imagined the majority population was heavily weighted with single males. While big-time mining moguls were extracting riches from the earth and sweat and sore backs from poorly paid laborers, other business interests were bleeding them—rather their pockets dry. There was no shortage of whores, whiskey peddlers, and worthless wayfarers set to make a buck. There were, however, not just a few hardworking and upstanding folks, and they were and had been clamoring for a Ranger presence "on the river or at Shafter." And that, in part, was why Corporal Hughes and his Company D detachment had taken residence at Presidio.[7]

Representing Company D at Shafter was Texas Ranger John F. Gravis, a twenty-two-year-old ex-cowboy from Webb County, a young man familiar with the boisterous border town of Laredo. Private Gravis nominally worked with his partner W. W. Jones and with a Presidio County deputy sheriff and ex-Texas Ranger, Isaac "Ike" Lee, who was also cross-deputized as a Deputy U.S. Marshal. These lawmen were sometimes backed up by a local precinct constable, Ben Bowers.[8] On the night of August 4, 1890, W. W. Jones was elsewhere, while Private Gravis and Deputy Lee pulled the duty as protectors of Shafter.

Generally, depending on whether one is pro- or anti-Texas Ranger, there are two divergent scenarios as to what happened that night at Shafter, though neither version substantially amends the role Captain Jones would play. The pro-Ranger account is straightforward: The lawmen were on duty, doing their job trying to make an arrest. But, due to anti-Anglo sentiments they were gratuitously gunned down by a run amok mob of Mexicans and *Tejanos* who had morphed into a drunken throng of recklessly shooting and rioting revelers. Were one's outlook tilted the other way, lawmen Gravis and Lee brought the gruesome wrath upon themselves by fraternizing with locals at a dancehall and consuming way too much tarantula juice and acting way too hateful. How much stock to put in a newsy story carried in the *Brooklyn Daily Eagle* quite naturally grinds across the fulcrum of partisanship and prejudice:

> News was brought in yesterday morning by J. E. Ontbes, foreman of the mines at Shafter, of a killing which took place at 2 o'clock that morning. It seems a crowd of Mexicans had got on a spree and were firing off their weapons when several of the white miners, rangers and deputy sheriff went down to see what was the matter. Suddenly they were fired upon from ambush and State Ranger J. F. Graves [*sic*] was instantly killed and J. Lee, deputy sheriff and deputy United States marshal, was seriously wounded in the arm. The fire was returned and it is believed one Mexican was killed and several wounded. A physician, Captain Jones, several rangers and deputy sheriffs have left for the scene. Trouble has been brewing with the Mexicans at Shafter for some time, and it is believed that the intention was to rob and burn the mine. Graves, the dead ranger, belonged to company D. and was very highly thought of by his fellow rangers.[9]

The newspaperman writing for *The Luling Signal*, too, had everything figured down to the nub: "A row occurred at Shafter mines near Marfa, last Monday between a lot of drunken Mexicans on one side & State Rangers and miners on the other, in which a number of Shots were fired."[10]

What can be reported as truthful is that Captain Frank Jones, at company headquarters near Marfa, was notified of Private

Gravis' death at 10:00 a.m. and was at once on the way to Shafter at the gallop. The captain and his Company D Rangers pulled into Shafter at 4:00 p.m. primed; ready to fight bears, bad men, Mexicans, *Tejanos*—or the goddamned devil if he spit sideways. Captain Frank Jones took especial pride—and rightly so—in the fast trip from Marfa to Shafter: "It is 50 long miles. My Company is splendidly mounted and there is hardly an animal that could not cover a hundred miles in one day."[11]

That Ranger Gravis had been murdered is not up for argument. That there was a full-scale riot underway at Shafter might stand squabbling. Such silliness was not in the Rangers' game-plan. Extracts from the Monthly Return of August 1890 reveal: "Captain Jones and six men went to Shafter to investigate killing of Private Gravis during a riot at that place. Returned on the 7th with seven Mexicans charged with murder. . . . Privates Barton, Jones, [William] Kipling and Mayfield, assisted by citizens, arrested 12 Mexicans charged with riot and murder and assault to murder. . . . Private Kipling then came to Marfa with body of Private Gravis and shipped it to Laredo by request of his family. . . . Private Kipling assisted by Deputy Sheriff arrested near Marfa three Mexicans charged with the Shafter riot and murder. . . ."[12] The Ranger roundup—with no small amount of racial profiling—netted negligible results.[13]

Though the justification or motivation for Lieutenant T. R. Rivers, U.S. Army, submitting a report on the Shafter situation is unclear, nevertheless, he did. His after-the-fact findings based on hearsay were critical of the dead Ranger's behavior. When a copy of the report landed on AG King's polished maple desk he might not have gone ballistic, but he was to the core ready to challenge that whippersnapper Rivers, whoever he was. At Austin the thoroughly miffed and mindful adjutant general had findings of his own: "Lieutenant Rivers was evidently misled by partial reports of this transaction and being misled he did an unintentional injustice to the character and conduct of the Ranger who was killed, and indirectly to the others."[14]

That was for public consumption. Privately AG King was more circumspect, cautiously spinning an advisory warning to his smart captain of Rangers stationed in the Big Bend Country. The message was plain: "Whether these assertions are true or not, it becomes necessary to put you on guard, So that you may caution the members of your Company against the danger of promiscuous meddling or mixing, either for pleasure or otherwise, with an element over which & with which, you are likely at any moment to come in contact."[15]

Captain Jones was reading from the same page as the adjutant general. Energetically making plans for Company D to go into winter quarters at a location suitable and cost effective for acquiring feed and forage for the men's livestock and the state's mules, Frank Jones looked beyond the obvious with his campsite selection. He would relocate his company headquarters from Marfa, to a spot five miles from Alpine, Brewster County, where there was plenty of wood and water and good shelter. Too, there was an added advantage in moving camp. At Marfa the men "would be compelled to remain in town" due to supply issues, but at the new site five miles removed from temptation, the locality would be perfect. Captain Jones did not like "to have the men loafing around any town."[16]

By the time crisp October evenings were enveloping the Big Bend Country, Company D was comfortably positioned outside Alpine at Camp Hogg from where Captain Jones headquartered. At Shafter, still a hot spot, Sergeant Baz Outlaw tended to the activities of that four-man detachment. Before the month was out, there had been a "street fight between two Americans resulting in the serious, if not fatal wounding of one. . . ." And, shortly thereafter: "A Mexican woman prostitute killed an American at Shafter last night. He was no loss to the Country, but more killing may follow." Yes, at Shafter it was "absolutely necessary for Rangers to be right in town," so Captain Jones advised Captain Sieker.[17]

There's little doubt it troubled him to bother AG King with a personal matter that October, but Frank was, in his mind, desperate and unsure. He had gradually been losing his hearing, and felt that he should seek treatment and that the infirmity should "not longer be neglected." If the leave was approved Jones would try to obtain medical treatment at San Antonio, and was guessing he would be out of service for three or four weeks. Understandably, in light of the tough time the injured Private Frank Schmid was having with vouchers and explanations and counting pennies, Captain Jones was wondering if the "State would allow the necessary expenses?" Clearly—and he was making sure Frontier Battalion hierarchy knew—that the irritating partial deafness was a job-related affliction: "I have lost my hearing in the service from no fault of mine, caused possibly, from exposure in bad weather."[18]

Within the week Captain Jones received notice that his request for an extended leave had been granted and that there would be no resultant "loss of pay." As to the treatment of his hearing impairment, those expenses would be picked up by the State of Texas, as long as they were reasonable. Furthermore, the captain was to leave his 1st Sergeant in charge of the company with instructions to "open official mail & act as you would."[19]

As pages for November and December were removed from the 1890 calendar, were it necessary to follow Frank Jones' footsteps—loosely—the task could be accomplished but such an exercise would not add to measuring the man or reveal spine-tingling adventures for the Rangers of Company D. Eighteen-hundred and ninety-one, well, that's a different story!

Politically it was a different story, too! January 1891 would herald a changing of the guard in top-tier executive offices of Texas. Captain Frank Jones christening the relocated Company D headquarters near Alpine as Camp Hogg should not be seen as some unpredictable happenstance. The newly inaugurated state governor was James Stephen Hogg. Although he had held down the Frontier Battalion's fort as adjutant general for a tumultuous decade, Wilburn H. King's time to bid the state-paid job adieu had come. Of the Frontier Battalion's Captain Frank Jones, AG King would soon characterize him—in writing, for the record—as "an excellent man, and a most efficient, energetic, and fearless officer and Ranger." Not too shabby of an endorsement coming from a man who had supervised and rode herd over some rather illustrious and legendary Ranger captains. The out-going adjutant general's politically appointed—not elected—replacement was Woodford Haywood Mabry, an East Texan from Jefferson, Marion County; a thirty-five-year-old businessman and entrepreneur well versed in matters of finance and logistics.[20]

Pinpointing with exactness Captain Jones' therapy for the hearing deficiency is unworkable. Authenticating where he was in January is a snap: Head down, nose to the paperwork grindstone at Camp Hogg. Not unexpectedly—and really quite properly—AG Mabry wanted all company commanders to inventory state-owned property, its condition, identifying those items—animals or wagons or tents or pots and pans—that were no longer serviceable. Likewise he also was desirous of what the captains thought they needed in the "way of transportation & equipment to place the Company in good working order." Captain Jones jumped to, advising AG Mabry that Company D's three wagon mules were in good condition, but the two pack mules were "very old and slow. . . . these pack mules were brought into the service in 1874." Furthermore, according to the captain's assessment and in response to AG Mabry's request: "To place my Company in good working order I need one good wagon mule and three pack mules. I can manage about tents for the balance of this winter. One wagon and two sets harness and riggings for pack-saddles. I am very well supplied with mess outfits." In closing, after posting the new boss that he had been about to "freeze out" but that he "got some lumber to fix my quarters. . . . the weather has been fearfully cold," Jones also gave the previous two-year arrest tally for Company D: 169.[21]

One of those fellows not under arrest was Finus "Fine" Gilliland. Gilliland was wanted by legal authorities for killing Henry Harrison Powe, "an old one armed ex-confederate soldier" during a dispute about the ownership of a "brindle bull yearling." The not so alleged murderer was on the run, his whereabouts of great interest to Company D Rangers who had scattered out through the section's mountains in hopes of bringing their prey to bay. Captain Jones, himself, was in the field leading one detachment of salaried manhunters. For this chase the captain's luck was sour, as was the destiny of 1st Sergeant Baz Outlaw who had been scouting throughout three neighboring counties after Gilliland.[22]

Ranger Private James Mitchell "Jim" Putman hit the jackpot. Riding with the Ranger was Deputy Sheriff Thalis Tucker "T. T."

Cook, ex-Ranger but now working for the Brewster County sheriff, James Buchanan "Jim" Gillett, who was also a former Texas Ranger. Private Putman introduced himself to fugitive Fine Gilliland in the Glass Mountains north of Marathon, Texas. The meeting did not go well! Gilliland's first shot knocked Deputy Cook from the saddle, the bullet ripping into his kneecap while a follow-up shot killed his horse outright. Though his mount was gyrating between his knees, Ranger Putman managed to pull his Winchester from the saddle-scabbard, sending his greetings to Fine Gilliland. Putman's first bullet dropped the damn rascal's horse as if it had been pole-axed. Taking cover behind his dead steed, Gilliland returned the Ranger's salutation with a six-shooter welcome of his own. He had erred. Private Putman delivered a hot round to Fine Gilliland—square between the eyes, killing him instantly. The gunfight—as most always are—was fully cooked in a matter of seconds. The administrative gumbo stewed much longer. During the exchange of gunfire Putman's horse had caught a bullet, forcing Captain Jones to make a command decision: "I [Frank Jones], the undersigned certify that I saw the horse owned by Private Putman after he was shot and instructed him to Kill him as he was utterly ruined and it would be an act of mercy to finish him. Putman is justly entitled to pay for same."[23] In the end Private Putman came clear of paying any legal penalty for killing Fine Gilliland, plainly a case of self-defense, but the State of Texas finally paid its just debt: $75 for the loss of the Texas Ranger's horse.[24]

Assuredly the scorching clash between Private Putman and desperado Gilliland would not be the last 1891 gunplay for Company D Rangers and, in fact, Frank Jones would be a shooting participant in one, but for the interim the captain would be hogtied by bothersome issues dealing with paperwork and personnel. Old-time Texas Ranger correspondence between Captain Jones and Ranger headquarters at Austin is chockfull; disposing of state-owned property at auction after advertising, acquiring new items for the company, conferring with citizens regarding complaints and/or commendation—all the while trying to keep the front office happy.

Agonizingly it may be suggested, Captain Jones during that first month of 1891 dishonorably discharged Private Ernest St. Leon for "committing petty thefts from commissary." Or, as subsequent events will highlight, could that action have been a well-planned and secretive proactive law enforcement maneuver? Such had been the case with Jim King's first discharge. Did Captain Jones recognize the inherent value of undercover work? Hmmm![25]

He was sure of one thing, damn sure. And in the broadest and prudent overview it really does set him apart from other sometimes more celebrated badge wearers. Captain Frank Jones was a committed hardcore professional and he expected the men of Company D to be professionals. Specifically to pay their bills: "Occasionally complaints are made to me that in some instances individual Rangers are contracting or have contracted more debts than his pay amounts to. . . . When a few Rangers spend more money than they make it insures to the detriment of those who do, and can pay their indebtedness, and gives the Company a bad reputation." Undoubtedly the captain, knowing he was on firm ground, acknowledged the anticipated response from AG Mabry: "If a ranger of your Company persists in contracting debts which he knows he cannot meet, you will discharge him."[26]

Lest there be any confusion, though overburdened with the tedious, mundane, and less than glorious clerical duties required for keeping Company D afloat, Captain Frank Jones wasn't just a pencil-pushing Texas Ranger. Two times during March 1891 he notched his gunbelt tight. After learning the presumed whereabouts of T. B. Spencer, a fellow "who had made off with the city funds of Uvalde," the captain personally reacted. Because he anticipated that Spencer would be "with a hard crowd" Jones deemed it but smart to enlist the aid of Private Jim Putman—a proven shootist—and after making the arrest, remarked that "it was well I did." Make no mistake Captain Jones had used good judgment: The arrest was made in the isolated country fifteen miles north of Langtry and the infamous Jersey Lilly Saloon operated by the waggish Judge Roy Bean, a scandalous place iniquitously inhabited by "a hard crowd." However, once Spencer was in hand Private Putman returned to Camp Hogg, while Captain Jones, alone with the prisoner, went the opposite direction to Uvalde, making sure Spencer saw the jailhouse—from the inside.

Although alleged cow thief D. D. Baker had been a fugitive from justice for near ten years, Captain Jones found him lying low at Marfa, handcuffed and jailed him so legal authorities from Dimmit County would know where to find him.[27] From behind the folding camp-desk or from behind a Colt's .45, Frank Jones was—as the saying goes—the Real McCoy.

Simply resting across an axis of factuality and hard truths, the biography of Frank Jones is not underpinned with any predetermined myth-busting ideology. What it is, is what it is. Though it's seldom if ever mentioned, the fact that Sergeant Charley Fusselman's murderers were yet to be positively identified, much less brought to justice, was troubling not only to Texas Rangers, but the young Ranger's brother as well. Somewhat independently John H. Fusselman, from afar, had been corresponding with a hush-hush source that was passing on helpful criminal intelligence. That same confidential informant—whoever he/she was—also had clued in Thomas A. Falvey. A native Texan from Jasper County, the thirty-eight-year-old attorney was a legal-beagle not knowing fear—having survived numerous threats of harm after moving to El Paso and eventually becoming the district attorney. Now, 1891, however, he was respectfully titled District Judge Falvey, sitting on the bench for the 34th Judicial District of Texas and traveling widely throughout West Texas. Exactly how much secrecy or attorney/client privilege or plain professional courtesy was involved does not register as any too meaningful, but Judge Falvey had straightforwardly updated Texas AG Mabry, who wrote: "I have seen Judge Falvey who tells me that the same informant who has been writing to Fusselman has also been talking to him regarding the whereabouts and identity of these assassins."[28]

The overwrought adjutant general was adamant. If at all possible he wanted action "at once." Should the reprehensible killer or killers actually be "caught and convicted he thought the Governor will pay something as a reward for the assistance rendered you in their capture."[29] The "you" AG Mabry was referring to was Captain Frank Jones. While later another Ranger would ultimately be rightly awarded credit or unduly take credit, on April 23, 1891, the words of the adjutant general to the Company D captain were abundantly clear: "Therefore you will proceed to El Paso and see Judge Falvey and communicate with the party above [informant] mentioned. I think it best for you to go alone and work up the case on account of the Expenses, while your superior intelligence will give you the advantage over any other one man in your Company. Judge Falvey informs that when you are ready to act that you can then get all the help you will need." Not only were the adjutant general and district judge favorably inclined toward the Company D captain, but another jurist as well, Judge Winchester Kelso, who had even earlier written Governor Hogg about Frank Jones' service, and that it had been "meritorious and faithful to the state and the people. . . ." of Texas.[30]

There is, in fact, a little borderland truism which may be unsettling, but nevertheless it obligates a mention now, and was also noted by Captain Jones then. Plagued with more than its fair share of cruelty and criminality and corruption, the Rio Grande borderlands was also the land of *la mordida*—the bite—the bribe. Although Frank Jones was at the starting gate, ready to investigate, he wanted to make sure AG Mabry was up to speed on Texas/Mexico border reality:

> The case stands about like this. If you extradite, the fees of all Mexican officials are invariably outrageous. I do not think they have any regular scale of charges but just take all they can get. If you entice the party to this side, you are compelled to fee some Mexicans to do this. If you could induce Gov. Hogg to offer a reward I am satisfied the party who is at work on the case will redouble his exertions.[31]

Taking his cue from the adjutant general, Captain Jones made his fact-finding trip to El Paso. There seems not to be any written record of visiting with any confidential informant, which really is not an unwise protocol. That he met with Judge Falvey is probable, though an educated guess. On the one hand his but cursory report to AG Mabry was discouraging, though on the other, he maintained "some hope of yet being able to run in those assassins." Whatever the plan was, Captain Jones had "a scheme for entrapping these parties" but putting it into a written format would be "too lengthy" and contain an inordinate number of "tiresome details." The burden of establishing criminal culpability is on the state and it must be done—can only be done—through the introduction of admissible evidence. And, at this point, that worried Frank Jones. In the captain's judgment "testimony will [would] be harder to procure than it will [would] be to get the men who really murdered Fusselman."[32] Seemingly, and it's but conjecture, Captain Jones had a reasonably good idea of just who he wanted to lure across the Rio Grande and into the clutches of American lawmen, but was genuinely concerned the necessary evidence—enough for a guilty verdict—was in short supply.

What was not missing from Captain Frank Jones' workaday Texas Ranger life were those matters not requiring a six-shooter and handcuffs, but issues that continually demanded his thoughtful consideration and deliberative responses. That Captain Jones really was a cut above some of his Texas Ranger supervisory counterparts may be revealed modestly; Frank, too, was engrossed with policy, not just policing. But one sterling example would be his memorandum to AG Mabry regarding the reformatting of one of the preprinted Frontier Battalion's report forms. The recommendation, if adopted, "would be a great convenience to each Company Commander and we could send in our work cleaner and neater." Of course there were other more vexing problems. Such a case in point would be his decision not to reenlist a particular Ranger because, according to Jones, "he generally either has a sick headache or the rheumatism troubled him, and then he is disposed to be insubordinate to any non Commissioned officer or Private who may be placed in charge of him" although the captain did recognize the fellow had "sufficient courage and intelligence." Sometimes problem children need to find a new home. And sometimes good guys wanted to go home. On May 27, 1891, Frank Jones requested a two-week leave of absence so he could travel to Boerne and transact some "private business." Though he had not specified the nature of his personal affairs AG Mabry approved Captain Jones' request two days later.[33] Whatever the reason he had for going home, there's no doubt Frank wanted to also spend time with Grace Kathleen, now three and a half years old.

For Texas Rangers of Company D the summer of 1891 was more-or-less routine—though law enforcing is seldom routine: Trouble and/or tragedy are ever around the next corner or just over the next mountain's crest. Willingly living and working—putting oneself in the game—in that space between peacefulness and pandemonium, as peace officers do, defies rational explanation. Unfitting as it is, during that summer a window opens up showing Frank Jones was but a product of place and time, and it's not necessarily a pretty picture.

Due to a mean gang of active cow thieves, Colonel John F. Camp was paying Luciano Leal "to work in the interest of the stockmen in Val Verde County." Captain Jones readily agreed that Camp and "other stock raisers are losing a great many stock and they are of course more than anxious to have this gang broken up." Camp, understandably, was seeking a degree of financial relief, and that could be accomplished by placing his operative on the pay roll of Company D. Since the good J. F. Camp had assured Jones that should Leal's work net a hot workable lead and since Camp Hogg was quite a distance removed, once notified via telegraph he and three or four Rangers "could run down" being met at the depot with fresh "saddle horses" to pursue cattle or horse thieves. Frank Jones really had no objection to putting Leal's name on the books, but strictly as an "outside" man, and then only for three months. In other words, it was quite okay for Luciano Leal to draw state wages while living apart from the Texas Rangers, but as Captain Jones clearly informed the colonel: "I would not, under any circumstances, enlist any Mexican to remain in Camp among my men."[34]

There were yet "deep divides between Mexico and Texas. Two places became the flashpoints of hatred: the Alamo and Goliad. Approximately 200 men died at the Alamo, and approximately 400 were massacred at Goliad. . . . It is no wonder that a long legacy of dislike and mistrust came out of the Texas Revolution. . . . Also, in any calculus of hatred, one must not overlook the payback slaughter of Mexican troops by Sam Houston's army at the Battle of San Jacinto, where, after the eighteen-minute battle was over decisively in Texas's favor, the killing of 600 or more Mexican troops went on into the afternoon."[35] A decade later as byproduct of the Mexican War, America gained a whopping chunk of real estate at Mexico's expense, and many Mexicans were now citizens of the Lone Star State—like it or not! And many didn't. During Frank's day, there were yet living grandfathers and fathers who could speak with first-hand authority of those chilling and bloody events—men from both banks of the Rio Grande. Shedding learned and ingrained prejudice is not easy. No excuses. Bigotry is not exclusive, it can be jointly owned. Along the American/Mexican borderlands, regardless of ethnicity, there was not too much open-mindedness washing about, not in Texas, nor in her sister states in Mexico.

Although drunken idiots jerking six-shooters and killing each other, or wild-eyed cow thieves and horse stealers with red-hot running-irons, or the wanted *mal hombres* slinking across county, state, territorial, and international borders were keeping the state and local and federal lawmen busy, it was another class of thugs really catching America's imagination and handing Rangers a plateful of misery: Train Robbers.

For reasons yet not fully understood, during the Wild West era when Frank Jones captained Company D, at the top of the criminal pecking order, enjoying a special place, were the bandits with the "derring-do involved in overpowering a huge locomotive and its cars, trains then being a symbol of growth and commerce. . . ."[36] Daydreaming of molesting a gigantic train was sinfully enticing: "For cowhands who lived with the reality of earning a 'million dollars in a million days' the glitter of gold at the end of the railroad's rainbow continued to tantalize. . . . Most cow-herders never acted out, of course. They remained content to share vicariously the exhilaration, if not the dangers and potential rewards of those few who did."[37] Rangers hunted those that did!

Sometime near 4:00 a.m. on the second day of September 1891, four—maybe five—train robbers struck the westbound Galveston, Harrisburg & San Antonio Railroad's No. 20 about one mile east of Samuel's Siding (now Pumpville) near Horseshoe Bend in Val Verde County. Although the engineer had been forced to stop due to obstructions purposely placed on the tracks, Messenger J. Ernest

Smith, Wells, Fargo & Company, who had previously killed two would-be train robbers with a pistol bullet and buckshot from a shotgun's blast, refused to open the bolted door of the express-car. Prepared for such stubbornness, a heavy charge of dynamite solved the resourceful outlaws' but short-lived crisis. Such an explosive tactic was a first for train robbers. After gathering their booty, $3,600, the Winchester-toting and Winchester-shooting chameleons changed colors, one, wearing a charming smile, even extended a sociable proffer to share drinks with the train's terrified and terrorized crew: "We will treat you boys, the first time we catch you in San Antonio." Then they were gone.[38]

Local posses from Del Rio, the county seat, and from Judge Roy Bean's bailiwick, Langtry, took to the field, following intuition and indistinct trails west. Upon learning the news, Captain Jones immediately made arrangements with the railroad for transportation and from Alpine was rushed east on a special train with five Rangers, horses, pack mule, and gear. By late afternoon on the day of the robbery the posses had merged, then followed a pretty favorable trail toward the Rio Grande, one littered with "cigar stumps and peach peels" which were leavings of tobacco and fruit pilfered from a newspaper vendor's box of goodies kept for the passengers—plus $10. At the river's edge the real and the part-time lawmen stopped and made camp, though there was not a blade of grass for the horses to munch on. At first light Captain Jones and men crossed into Mexico hot on the outlaws' tracks, followed them back across into Texas, and continually seesawed, splashing through the wet boundary line time and again, as the cagey crooks did their dead-level best to elude any pursuit, even removing horseshoes and later re-shoeing jaded horses. It was a nightmare of twists and tangles.[39]

The hunt for train robbers was not a just-for-show effort; it lasted for days and days, though at this juncture was only successful by half. After grueling hours spent horseback, and subsequent to setting fire to cane standing taller than men in the saddle, the Rangers found an extraordinarily inaccessible, and now abandoned and burned-out campsite. Geographically the spot—a flood plain straddling both banks of the Rio Grande—was where the river makes its dramatic upswing coming out of the Big Bend, at a point where wandering Maravillas Creek empties onto the watery borderline. Southwestern history would soon name the section *Las Vegas de los Ladrones* (the Meadows of the Bandits). Although the forsaken hideout did not give up any outlaws, it did relinquish clues to their identity. Reasonably secure with their knowledge as to who had highjacked the train, Captain Jones and men, because their "horses were completely broken down" returned to Camp Hogg, noting that "the robber camp is about one hundred miles from here."[40]

In a somewhat puzzling and open-ended letter the adjutant general, after authorizing and imploring Captain Frank Jones to "organize for another scout" after the train robbers, remarked: "I have information that they desire to surrender but I do not give credence to said report. I think they desire to create this impression so as to stop pursuit—Thus enabling them to get out of the Country—They claim that they will surrender, but not to you now. I am anxious to have the Rangers to do the capturing. . . ."[41] So was Frank Jones.

With fresh horses Sergeant Outlaw and seven men picked up the pursuit—or daringly tried to. After an absence of nine torturous days and subsequently covering 275 miles of roundabout searching the Texas Rangers returned to camp empty-handed. It seemed that cowboy turned cow thief, turned suspected murderer, turned train robber, John Flynt and his pals Jack Wellington, Jim Lansford, and Tom Fields, aka Tom Strouts, had simply vanished. Despite the bad boys' whereabouts a federal grand jury at El Paso would not be foiled—they had meddled with the U.S. Mail—after Indictment warrants would last till the cows came home, forever!

Meanwhile, a Val Verde County deputy sheriff, Joseph Russell Sitter, investigated his way into good fortune. Learning where the desperadoes were and where they likely would be going, Deputy Sitter made sure Captain Frank Jones received the urgent telegram, and then began the dangerous job of slow-trailing until reinforcements arrived. After some daring surreptitious work, Joe Sitter was joined the next day by Captain Jones and Texas Rangers who had made the rushed train ride to the Comstock depot, a point where they had unloaded and saddled horses for the overland hounding.

Steadily working the ground sign—horseshoe dints and yet softly moist manure—and valuing the information supplied by a youthful 77 Ranch cowboy, the lawmen and the brigands had an unscheduled meeting about 1:00 p.m. on October 16, 1891, in the wild and broken and sparsely populated backcountry of Crockett County. It turned Western!

When the Rangers, purposefully paralleling the outlaws in the bed of a dry ravine, topped out they were within but a half-mile of their objectives—four fellows fast pulling Winchesters from their saddle scabbards. The first command from Captain Jones was to the guttersnipes: "Stop!" The next directive was to his racing Rangers: "Kill their horses and take them alive—if you can."

Jim Lansford understood the message, loud and clear, wheeling about and meekly surrendering. Once his fagged horse started blowing snot and blood and heaved, gasping for air, Tom Fields, stopped and waited his turn at arrest. John Flynt and Jack Wellington, well, they'd have none of such foolishness: For them it was do or die, and they were doing—and popping rounds at pursuing lawmen as they raced the wind. Deputy Joe Sitter, spurring madly, trying to close with the outlaws, characterized the shooting as "promiscuous and lively."

There was little chance of the yahoos making a clean getaway, and Jack Wellington was guaranteed a tight spot when his horse caught a bullet and lurched sideways, then slowed, then wobbled, then trembled while Wellington—in a panic—bailed out of the saddle, hurriedly making for a nearby outcropping of rocks. Since this is Captain Franks Jones' life story, perhaps hearing from him is best:

> When he dismounted I was sure that Flynt would too and that they would fight to the death. I dismounted and shot at Wellington 3 times but it was at a long distance and I undershot him. He had a much better gun than mine, it being a large long range rifle with cartridges as long as your finger. I knew that he was a famous shot and at long range had a decided advantage. . . . I remounted my horse and ran up to about 100 yards of him where I felt pretty sure I could kill him the first shot. I then called out to him that I

> was an officer and did not wish to hurt him and he surrendered. In the meantime, Flynt ran on and the two men who were next to me [Deputy Sitter, and civilian Bob Stockman] I sent on after him telling them to follow him until they ran him into some hole and that as soon as I captured or killed Wellington I would follow on. . . . There had been so much talk about Wellington that I was anxious to try conclusions with him and I guess we would have had a regular Winchester duel only he saw some of the men coming on up the flat and knew that in case he drilled me he could not get away with his life. He was not a particle unnerved.[42]

After a chase covering near seven miles, John Flynt finally went to ground. Taking cover in an arroyo it seemed he was making ready to do battle. The nearest peace officer was Joe Sitter, who was barely outside rifle range when Flynt popped out of the ditch, raced for his winded horse and retrieved something from the saddlebags. Reining to a stop and ducking behind screening underbrush, Joe Sitter "hallooed at him, trying to get a talk out of him in order to get him to surrender. He paid no attention. . . ." Stealthily and uneasily Joe Sitter began working his way through "lots of shin-oak bushes" when he heard a gunshot. Bob Stockman thought Joe Sitter had shot. Joe Sitter thought Bob Stockman had fired. John Flynt didn't hear the booming sound of gunfire—he had just "suicided." The unofficial and rudimentary postmortem revealed that sometime during the chase, apparently while Flynt was twisting in the saddle shooting at his pursuers, someone had succeeded in planting a bullet "in the right nipple of his breast, evidently done by one of our men." If not Sitter or Stockman—it would have been Texas Ranger Private Carl Kirchner or the ever salty Jim Putman. Shortly thereafter, prisoners in tow, those at the scene of outlaw Flynt's death-site were joined by Captain Jones and Privates, T. F. Tucker, J. A. Wolfe, Gus Jones, J. L. Faubion, and civilian teenager Joe Bendele, who had only been armed with a six-shooter. Aside from the $75 in gold stuck in his money-belt and the $4 Mexican in a shirt pocket the Rangers made another find. Tucked into the high-top of a boot was a note, one telling officers to turn over Flynt's personal property to his brother, Joe

M. Flynt. By then it had dawned on Deputy Joe Sitter what the dead man's last-minute dash to the panting and lathered saddle horse was all about; to grab a stubby pencil and scrap of paper. Even train robbers need a Last Will & Testament!

During their mopping up operation, inventorying the robbers' property, Captain Jones found that they were in possession of greenbacks, plus four bundles of gold and silver on their pack horse tying them to the crime, as well as a Colt's six-shooter with the serial numbers filed off, one taken from Express Messenger Smith during the train robbery. Evidentiary wise, prosecuting the case would be a slam-dunk.

In due time, after a light argument with the sheriff of Val Verde County, August H. Kieffer, regarding jurisdictional ownership of the prisoners, Captain Jones and Rangers deposited their charges in the jailhouse at El Paso. Federal prosecutors would take over.

Upon learning the news AG Mabry was ecstatic, writing to Captain Frank Jones that his leadership was not only of benefit to the State of Texas, but favorably added to the overall reputation of the Texas Rangers as being "efficient and worthy." Sometimes overlooked is the adulation to the captain coming straight out of the state Chief Executive's office. Governor James S. Hogg, personally, singled out Frank Jones for congratulations, and further predicted: "Such efficient work will prevent the repetition of such Crimes."[43] Editorializing, a journalist writing for the *San Antonio Daily Light* of October 24, 1891, added his two-cent commentary:

> Flint [*sic*], the suiciding express robber, was the right kind of a thief. If a man is going in for that kind of thing and proposes to defy law let him have the courage of his actions and not squeal when it comes to taking his gruel.

This quartet of Rangers, by any man's measure were the "Real Deal." Standing from L to R: J. Walter Durbin and Jim King. Seated from L to R: George Parker and Robert McNamar. FROM *TEXAS RANGER SKETCHES* COURTESY THE AUTHOR ROBERT W. STEPHENS.

Thalis Tucker "T.T." Cook was a career lawman, with Texas Ranger service in Companies F and D. However, at the time he was severely wounded while he and Texas Ranger Jim Putman were executing the arrest of murder fugitive Fine Gilland in the Glass Mountains, Cook was employed as one of Sheriff Jim Gillett's deputies. FROM *TEXAS RANGER SKETCHES* COURTESY THE AUTHOR ROBERT W. STEPHENS.

At the statehouse Woodford Heywood Mabry replaced Wilburn Hill King, becoming the Lone Star State's adjutant general, a strong supporter of the Frontier Battalion's Captain Frank Jones. *Courtesy the Texas State Library & Archives Commission.*

Texas Governor James S. Hogg, the very first native Texan to hold the state's governorship. He was an ardent law and order man. District Judge Winchester Kelso advised Governor Hogg that Ranger Captain Frank Jones' service to the people of Texas was "meritorious and faithful." Governor Hogg's adjutant general, W. H. Mabry, likewise was favorably impressed with Captain Jones, particularly noting that his "superior intelligence" was a decisive advantage over any other man Company D. From *Indian Wars and Pioneers of Texas* by John Henry Brown.

Joe Sitter, a seasoned man-hunter and lawman. While a Val Verde County deputy sheriff Joe Sitter helped Captain Frank Jones and Company D Rangers run train robbers to ground in Crockett County. Later he would serve as a Texas Ranger and U.S. Mounted Customs Inspector. *AUTHOR'S PHOTO.*

John Flynt, the cowboy turned train robber who—after some desperate gunplay—chose suicide over surrender. *COURTESY ARCHIVES OF THE BIG BEND, BRYAN WILDENTHAL MEMORIAL LIBRARY, SUL ROSS STATE UNIVERSITY.*

Seated from L to R: Captain Frank Jones and Sergeant Baz Outlaw. Standing from L to R: Unknown, Unknown, T. F. Sellers, unknown, Arthur Jones, and unknown. *Courtesy Armstrong Ranger Research Center, Texas Ranger Hall of Fame & Museum.*

James B. Gillett, Sheriff of Brewster County, Texas, and also an ex-Texas Ranger and most relevant for the story at hand, the ex-husband of Helen Baylor Gillett. *Courtesy Archives of the Big Bend, Bryan Wildenthal Memorial Library, Sul Ross State University.*

CHAPTER 14

"We Have Been Compelled to Do Some Killing"

NOVEMBER 1891 WOULD NOT BE A FUN month for Captain Jones. A type of traveling circus, Zamloch's Congress of Wonders, had made a stopover at Marfa. Promoters were promising a freaky and magical performance, guaranteeing attendees would be astounded but entertained. Naturally it was a big attraction for locals—plus several unnamed Rangers from Company D. Well, all but one of the Texas Rangers was unidentified. C. E. Van Horn, the show's manager, made sure Governor J. S. Hogg had the name of Sergeant Baz Outlaw. According to Van Horn, Outlaw in "a drunken condition" had tried to "force his way into the house without paying," even though the other Rangers had willingly forked over admission fees. The manager was asserting that quite a scene took place. Outlaw was making six-shooter threats and declaring that the only thing saving Van Horn's bacon was the "presence of ladies." Adding insult to psychological injury happened the next day in downtown Marfa. Still drunk and geared for a fight, Baz once more angrily confronted Van Horn and again "commenced his abuse and making threats." After more than one person advised that Sergeant Outlaw was "a bad man and has killed several men in the same way," Van Horn chose penmanship over marksmanship.[1]

Not only did Mr. Van Horn fire a scorcher to Governor Hogg, he sent one to Captain Jones. Dutifully the captain began his Internal

Affairs investigation, though there's little doubt he rated the concern more a nuisance than a big-time crime. Before heading out for Marfa he personally interviewed "the men who were with Outlaw" having each one make a statement, and seemingly all were in agreement, "the matter is very much exaggerated." However, he was committed to getting Van Horn's side of the story—as a good investigator would—but to his disappointment discovered the man with a grievance had already left for home in San Francisco. Not dissuaded, the captain contacted Presidio County Judge B. F. Adams, who, more-or-less sided with the circus manager's story. Taking it a step further Captain Jones, after learning that Sheriff Jim Gillett had been at the entertainment and was an actual witness to the first dustup, visited with him. Sheriff Gillett told Captain Jones that Mr. Van Horn had actually "seized Outlaw by the arm and pulled him backward in a very rude way" and to his no-nonsense way of thinking "Outlaw would have been justifiable in knocking him down on the spot." Despite the fashionable and sometimes convoluted derogatory rhetoric coming from the caste of opinionated modern-era armchair detractors, Captain Jones' thoroughness and the adjutant general's comments clearly put the Ranger service on the road to professionalism. AG Mabry, in part, said: "Every Ranger must so deport himself as to reflect credit upon the force—to compel that respect which is due from the people to every conservator of the peace. The position of a Ranger is one of trust and when any member of the force fails to appreciate this fact, and shows by his example his disregard of the importance of such trust he should be relieved of it." Since there wasn't clear-cut accord as to exactly what had happened and who said and did just what to who, Sergeant Outlaw, in this particular instance and for the time being, was given a tolerant benefit of the doubt. Baz was yet riding for the Rangers in West Texas, but the cinch binding him to the outfit was frayed—wearing thin.[2]

On another personnel matter Captain Jones was not benevolent—the Rangers in question not having too much history with the outfit. Measuring Frank Jones' temperament and devotion to the good of the service is an easy call. Due to a dispute between Rangers regarding whose time it was to sleep, and whose turn it was to stand watch, the captain unceremoniously cut two boys loose: "This young man Jones is a relative of mine and it is disagreeable to have to discharge him for such a dirty trick, but think they richly deserve a discharge."[3] And gone they were—kinship counting for zilch.

While the captain was checking into alleged rambunctiousness of Baz Outlaw, the company's top noncom had been busy in adjoining Jeff Davis County looking into murder and madness. During an argument gone terribly awry, Mexican freighters were letting their burros graze on William T. "Bill" McCutcheon's irrigated alfalfa patch at the Seven Springs Ranch—without permission, and after being forewarned to cease and desist. The long and short of the story is simple, quick, horrendous—and inexcusable. Bill McCutcheon began shooting the donkeys and Jose Ceniceros began shooting Bill. Jose scored the last hit, dumping the ranchman in a lifeless heap—an appetizer for buzzards circling overhead. Before the next morning's cock crowed, Sheriff J. R. Chadborn and Charlie Owens, while riding headlong for the crime-scene avowed that they had not found Ceniceros, but had discovered his two pals, dead in the road—weighted by more lead than they could comfortably carry. So went that story. *¿Quien sabe?* An extract from the Company D Monthly Return adds a nasty dimension: "Sergt. Outlaw went to Fort Davis to investigate the reported lynching of 2 Mexicans by a mob. Learned the Mexicans were killed but got no clue as to who did it."[4]

Captain Frank Jones, as commander of state law-enforcing troops in far West Texas, was sitting on the proverbial powder keg, and a careless spark would light up the Davis Mountains and run Limpia Creek red; so he told the adjutant general:

> At present everything is very quiet and I think will remain so unless the Mexicans attempt to retaliate for the death of the two who were killed. If they murder anyone there will be a number of them killed before any steps could be taken to prevent [it]. I do not think I exaggerate when I say there would be at least one hundred & fifty men from these three adjoining Counties, Brewster, Jeff Davis and Presidio who would rise as one man and take the law in their own hands in the event of any white man being hurt. If the

> Mexicans remain quiet there will be no further trouble. I am of the opinion that the Mexicans realize the fact that it is to their interest to remain quiet.[5]

The situation, although tense, did not erupt into unspeakable acts of vigilantism from either quarter, gradually petering out into but an unpleasant page in the Big Bend Country's history. There would be, however, many more pages in those succeeding chapters. But, for the moment all was quiet and Captain Jones took off to Boerne with purpose: "to visit my little girl whom I have not seen in several months. . . . Will be absent only a few days."[6]

And that, as it turned out, was quite true. The irascible and indefatigable Catarino Garza was, as alluded to earlier, trying his damndest to laboriously mold pirates and patriots, nationalists and ne'er-do-wells, loyalists and looters into an army capable of ousting Mexico's well-established dictator, Porfirio Díaz. South Texas was awash with troubles and being flooded with U.S. Army personnel, U.S. Marshals, and a ragtag assortment of newspapermen reporting on the Garza War and the criminality and catastrophes of the *Garzistas*. At the time it was no laughing matter, and the bigwigs in Washington and the wheel-horses at Austin were astir and not any too happy. Frank Jones wanted in on the action, cutting his Boerne holiday vacation short, writing from Camp Hogg and almost begging AG Mabry: "I only remained at home long enough to have dinner Christmas day and then returned, hoping you would order me to the scene of trouble on the lower Rio Grande. I know Garza well, having once had him chained up in my Camp when stationed in Duval County. This section is unusually quiet and I could be spared from here a month or two easily."[7]

Unfortunately Frank Jones—as 1892 opened up—could have sprinkled gunpowder on his morning cereal and choked on those words about everything being "unusually quiet" in his jurisdictional sphere of West Texas. Company D's six-shooter scorecard would be significantly readjusted upward.

Perplexed and financially devastated were executives at the Shafter mines. Substantial quantities of raw ore were continually coming up missing, without a doubt being stolen and then slyly shipped across the Rio Grande for refinement. Texas Rangers were alerted. The job of catching the crooks fell to Corporal Hughes, already working that section of country. Hughes was at a disadvantage. Though the corporal may have had a good idea as to just who the thieves were, they were just as well acquainted with his status as a Ranger.

Compounding Hughes' dilemma was the fact he had not a clue as to exactly when or precisely where they would strike next—but pilfer they would, he guessed. Following them around in the daytime was unworkable; surveillance at night was impossible. The need for a snitch or an undercover operative was a no-brainer. And John Hughes had the perfect man for that job in mind: Ernest St. Leon, the ex-Ranger with purported sticky fingers. Whether St. Leon was psychologically disposed toward recklessness doesn't matter. By any measure he was a crackerjack at infiltrating and running with low class *mal hombres* and he would, wearing a devilish smile, fight a bear with a pocketknife during a tornado. Always sporting a gift from his adoring mother, a stickpin, "one of the largest and prettiest diamonds seen on the border," Ernest was known as "Diamond Dick." Adding to his colorful persona and real handy for the job at hand, Ernest St. Leon was bilingual, having picked up Spanish from his rather young but stunningly attractive Mexican-born wife, María de Jesus Ornellas.[8]

Due to his know-how at laying down the right cover-story to the right folks, in but short order St. Leon had wormed his way into the gang of ore thieves, earning their complete confidence. His role-playing had been so believable, for the next midnight run Ernest would be a participant. This news, of course, was surreptitiously passed to Corporal Hughes, who then enlisted the help of Alonzo Van "Lon" Oden, a Company D veteran of but ten months. After dark on the night of January 12, 1892, the two Rangers were in place, shotguns in hands for some close quarter work. Unknowingly working their way toward the secreted Rangers, cajoling heavily burdened burros loaded with ore, were Matilde Carrasco, José Villeto, and Quinlino Chaves. Diamond Dick, now a part of the tough gang—by design—was lagging somewhat behind, acting as a rear guard. To the sneaky ore thieves St. Leon's positioning made perfect sense. For Rangers Hughes and Oden, knowing exactly where their helpmate was, well, that was critical.

Three fellows know whether the challenge to submit and surrender was hurled before or after the shotgun blasts. Villeto and Chaves weren't able to give details: buckshot cut off their version. Carrasco fared better—for a moment, not greeting death at the first volley. Though suffering wounds, Matilde managed to gain cover but by then had no viable option but to die or fight hard. At the exact instant he exposed his station, "St. Leon rose up and shot him between the eyes."[9] Naturally, Ranger headquarters would need an update, and Captain Frank Jones reported, making an official record: "Corporal Hughes reports in attempting the arrest of four Mexicans, caught in the act of stealing ore from Shafter. . . . he and his party were fired on by the Mexicans and they returned the fire, Killing three. . . . This ore stealing has been carried on for some time, the ore being taken to a smelter in Mexico and it has amounted to thousands of dollars."[10] The fourth "Mexican," the one that got away, of course, was Ernest St. Leon, a necessary deceptive ploy to insure the integrity of his undercover role in the eyes of other gang and family members well aware of just who was supposed to be hauling filched ore into Mexico that night. Suggesting that Ernest St. Leon wasn't in on the game because he wasn't expressly mentioned in any paperwork is understandable but only a case of naivete in the hard ways of real world cops and robbers. Ranger Lon Oden's name is also absent from the record. The Company D Monthly Return is, perchance, purposely vague: Only naming Hughes and then noting that the three Mexicans were "Killed while resisting arrest."[11] Even Captain Frank Jones, who was not necessarily favorably disposed towards Diamond Dick, notified the adjutant general that while at Shafter his services had "been very useful" to the Rangers. Six months later, writing for the *Chicago Daily Tribune*, an Illinois based reporter wasn't baffled: "Matilde Carrasco was killed by 'Diamond Dick' . . ."[12] Perhaps putting any ambiguity to bed may be extracted from a letter of recommendation Corporal John Hughes wrote to AG Mabry the very same day Captain Jones made his formal report to the adjutant general: "He [St. Leon] has assisted me in detecting a lot of Mexican ore thieves and is in danger of being killed at any time in this country and wishes to carry his pistol for self defence [*sic*]."[13]

Someone that was glad he was carrying his six-shooter was Captain Jones. During a scout into the rugged but somewhat picturesque Glass Mountains, hunting for suspects wanted for Robbery, Frank Jones and three Rangers triumphed, the snaky trio of bad guys lost, two stupidly earning another case: Conspiracy to Murder. Rather than submit wrists to be handcuffed, they jerked for Colt's handguns. Captain Jones and his boys had an answer for such pigheadedness. By time the shooting died down Mr. Eduardo, last name unknown, and José Blanco had forfeited any keenness for fireworks; they were in Ranger custody. But poor Pedro Eureto, well, he was just dead.[14] Captain Jones, with bodies piling up in the Big Bend Country, put on his apologetic clothes, writing to headquarters:

> As you will see by report we have been compelled to do some Killing which I regret. I have no desire whatever to get up a bloody record, as I have always considered it far more creditable to Capture than to Kill.[15]

On another front, quite sheepishly Frank Jones had to suck up and apologize to AG Mabry. Though there's little question his intentions were honorable—in the best interest of the Rangers—the captain had jumped the chain-of-command, a breach with capital Ns, a big time No-No! Frank had written to the governor, directly. He was seeking written permission to accompany a Special Agent of the U.S. Treasury Department in the seizure of stolen livestock being smuggled from Mexico. The captain's inquiry had been handed down to the adjutant general from the governor's office, rather than adherence to the normal protocol of allowing AG Mabry to learn of the matter first, and then render a decision as to whether to consult with or not consult with the governor. Rather quickly the error in judgment was brought to Jones' attention. Forthwith he responded, openly declaring that his letter to the governor "was not intended to slight or ignore your [AG Mabry's] official position. I never thought of it in that light until after I reced. your letter. Now I can very readily understand my mistake."[16]

Whatever may be said of AG Mabry, he held no grudges, at least regarding administrative matters, and Frank Jones' blunder was not taken as a personal affront. Blood and thunder narratives are engrossing; of that there's no quarrel. However, gauging Frank Jones' contributions to Texas Ranger history and to the Lone Star State must also take into account his utter fidelity at trying to suggest fixes and develop workable enforcement strategies. Search as one may, not every one of the "great" captains delved into the swamp of governmental bureaucracy looking for ways to improve the Texas Rangers. Whether it was an administrative tweaking or hardcore policing tactics, Captain Jones—it may be said with much frankness—was always deliberating. Learning through an edition of the *Texas Volunteer* that there was talk of putting Rangers in uniform, Frank Jones marked his letter to the adjutant general "Personal." Characterizing himself as "an old time Ranger" and never bashful about sharing his opinion, Frank Jones put forth his. Aside from budgetary concerns he thought the proposal would be good, chiefly for two reasons. First and foremost an unmistakable identification as peace officers would counteract any claims by persons shooting at or killing Rangers that they were under the wrong impression: thinking they were being attacked by ruffians or vigilantes. And that was exactly what had happened regarding the shootout with the father and son near San Ambrosia Creek—wherein the Rangers were jailed at Laredo—and also as aftermath of the episode at Green Lake.

Secondly, and more subjectively, Frank, rightly or wrongly, was of a belief that putting the Rangers in uniform "would add dignity to the force and not distract from its usefulness in a single particular." Recognizing human nature, Frank was perfectly aware: "There is almost always more or less opposition to any innovation on old established rules and for some, doubtless the idea of wearing uniforms will not be approved." In closing, whether it was with tongue in cheek or damn straight advice—the reader may choose—Captain Jones cautioned that should the decision be made to dress the boys out it would be okay with him, provided the uniform was not "Yankee blue."[17]

Though it does sound ludicrous in light of the Frontier Battalion's day-by-day law enforcing efforts throughout some wild and moderately populated slices of West Texas and border country, there was even talk—essentially a cost-cutting measure—of transforming at least a few Ranger companies into infantry units, primarily acting as city policemen, traveling by train from town to town as hotspots demanded attention. Captain Jones and Sheriff Baylor at Uvalde were analyzing positives and negatives. The sheriff told Frank: "I do not think infantry Rangers would be of any Service in our Section."[18] They were thinking!

Adding to Captain Frank Jones' continual headaches were the requests from different quarters wanting Company D Rangers sent to their area to solve this or that problem, some no doubt valid, other obviously overreactions and overreaches. From within the company, personnel matters demanded no little attention. And for those men like Private J. A. Wolfe who had "made a good and faithful Ranger," Captain Jones was never too busy to back them up with a letter of recommendation when they left the service for better paying prospects.[19] Although it is lifted from mail and not his speaking voice, the captain's pronounced frustration is clearly noticeable: "I am decidedly short when it comes to material for detectives. . . ." And, too, Company D was moreover soon shorter by a factor of one. Private Marcellus R. Daniels, when instructed by Sergeant Outlaw to "assist in sweeping out Camp" rather than—if he had had a legitimate gripe—confer with the captain, the tetchy Ranger had "put his pistol under his coat to conceal it" and thereafter was spending his days at Camp Hogg so heeled. Considering Daniels "a man of no discretion" and, although he was honest, that he had a "most ungovernable temper" and truly owned but "little intelligence" and deeming that good order could be shattered in a second by an act of six-shooter stupidity, Captain Jones hastily handed out the verbal discharge and declared: "I want no Ranger in my Company who carries concealed weapons around the Camp where men should feel toward each other almost as brothers."[20] End of story? Not quite!

Obviously with the aid of an attorney or someone quite familiar with wordy legalese, a thoroughly disgruntled Marcellus Daniels, wanting a certificate from the state reflecting an "honorable discharge" from the Texas Rangers, fired off a letter to AG Mabry with scattergun style. Working within a reverse chronology, going backwards in time, the typed three-page submission—on legal sized paper—was a litany of complaints lodged against his enemy, Sergeant Baz Outlaw. Although skipping over Captain Jones' rationale for dismissing him, Daniels asserted that on a previous occasion at Alpine the drunken sergeant had with the muzzle of his Winchester pointed at a fellow, and did "induce and compel" him to point out the place where a prostitute was residing; that the drunken Outlaw had, even before that, behaved badly at the entrance to the aforementioned circus and the next day on the streets of Marfa; and going two years further back, at Shafter, the thoroughly besotted Baz and another Ranger, E. S. Fisk, had "by force and displaying their pistols" vehemently compelled a pair of Presidio County deputy sheriffs, on the way to the county seat with a Mexican prisoner, to return their detainee to Shafter. Assistant Superintendent J. E. Outhouse from the nearby mines had witnessed it all, and in fact, later, reported same by letter to the Company D captain, though now the message to the adjutant general had been reworked by the hand of a red-mouthed lawyer:

> He, said Outhouse, requested Capt. Jones to remove said Outlaw from said town of Shafter; that upon on receipt of said Report and letter by said Capt. Jones from said Outhouse, he, Capt. Jones went at once to Shafter and upon the investigation of said affair by said Capt. Jones, he, Jones then and there proposed to discharge said Outlaw from the service; but did not do so because he, said Outhouse, and other good citizens of Shafter, fearing violence at the hands of said Outlaw, requested Capt. Jones not to discharge him, and leave him, said Outlaw, in their midst; whereupon said Capt. Jones removed said Outlaw from said town of Shafter to the headquarters Camp of said Company D at Alpine, Texas, and that he, said Outlaw has been kept at Alpine under the eye of Capt. Jones since the removal of him, Outlaw, from Shafter as aforesaid. . . . [21]

Whew! And it was while all this mumbo jumbo was waxing hot in the attorney general's office that Captain Frank Jones was in El Paso—under subpoena—regarding federal indictments lodged against the train robbers. At trial Frank "gave testimony as to the pursuit and capture of Wellington, Fields, and Lansford and the death of Flynt." Although the defendants had secured first-class legal talent by hiring prominent and high-powered lawyers Trevanion "T. T." Teel, W. M. Merchant, and Leigh Clark, a transplanted Mississippian with legislative experience and brother to Judge Edward D. Clark, their spirited cross-examination failed to rattle Captain Jones or the other prosecution witnesses. Evidence was as strong as dynamite used at the crime-scene. And even better than that, Jim Lansford who from the get-go had been characterized as "weak-kneed" and would be the "first to limber up" did just that, cutting a deal to testify against his cronies, snitching them straight into prison carrying a dime—ten years.[22]

Frank Jones' tending to consequential criminal doings was temporarily put on hold in lieu of family business. He asked for and was granted a twenty-day leave of absence to return to Kendall County and put in an appearance in Probate Court so as "to qualify as the legal guardian for my [his] child [and] to represent her interest in some land matters." Once that situation was correctly—legally—taken care of, Frank was planning a therapeutic visit to mineral hot springs about twenty miles above El Paso. He was seeking at least a modicum of relief from the reoccurring bouts of rheumatism in his hips and shoulders, which Frank earnestly believed had been contracted though inordinate exposure to inclement weather. Ever conscientious about his leadership role and primary responsibilities, Jones assured AG Mabry that he would remain "near a telegraph station" throughout his period of rejuvenation, and could be reached promptly "in the event my [his] services were needed."[23]

But even while home at Boerne, Captain Jones didn't take a holiday from Ranger business. He didn't want to miss the opportunity for latching onto a Company D sergeant from days past, the sure-enough salty Tom Carson, a man Jones thought "was worth any two ordinary Rangers." The services of Carson were to be particularly valuable to Captain Jones, he wrote AG Mabry, because he had "rather a boyish lot of men and would like to have Carson as he has had so much experience in the criminal business."[24]

Frank's dedication to duty was put to the test. During the time Frank was taking his Boerne vacation he received urgent word from Camp Hogg. Captain Jones immediately wired the adjutant general on the fifteenth day of June 1892: "I leave on the 4:35 train this evening and will reach Alpine tomorrow. Sergt. Outlaw telegraphed me there was an important letter there from yourself." AG Mabry was somewhat taken aback, and he assured Captain Jones that he "did not wish to cut short your leave of absence and I regret you did not get my telegram in time to prevent you leaving for your Company Hdqs."[25] The mix-up can be attributed to Baz Outlaw; his self-interest was at stake. AG Mabry's letter to Frank at Camp Hogg—which was not urgent—and apparently opened by Baz Outlaw, was the adjutant general's order for Captain Jones to conduct an internal investigation as to charges leveled against Outlaw as set forth in Private Daniels' typewritten tirade.

There is nothing in the record indicating Captain Jones was put off or put out about returning to camp and getting back to work. In fact according to his bookkeeping, after foregoing the trip to El Paso, he actually had not returned to Camp Hogg "until the expiration of his leave of absence." But once back in West Texas he tackled the assignment at hand with gusto, traveling about and conducting interviews. Jones talked with friend and foe of his top sergeant, trying to ascertain a true picture of his noncom's personal deportment during the episodes of alleged misconduct. He also got Baz's side of the story regarding each allegation. Clearly, because even he admitted that Outlaw, besides his fearlessness, had "some fine traits" and that he had "always felt a warm personal feeling for him," Jones' impartiality was pretty wobbly and an outsider might have been a better choice for conducting a detached review. In conclusion, though he conceded that Outlaw "at times drank to some excess," Jones' findings were that ex-Private Daniels had made the charges with no other motive than "spite" and in the end Captain Jones measured the discharged private wholly "unfit" for service with the Rangers. Sergeant Outlaw kept his job—this time.[26]

While Captain Jones had been listening to folks rattling their jaws in answer to his inquiries, down closer to the Rio Grande three of his Texas Rangers were creating another type of racket. Corporal Hughes along with Privates Lon Oden and Jim Putman were scouting some fifty miles upriver from Presidio near the State of Chihuahua village, San Antonio de Bravo—a former Mexican penal colony—opposite Candelaria on the Texas side of the river, desolately spotted underneath the Sierra Vieja and Candelaria Rims. They were hoping to track down and arrest Desidario Durán, a fugitive charged with raiding the section house at Chispa.[27] Somewhat luckily it may be suggested, the Rangers nabbed their man, but after stopping at a borderland trading post also got more than they bargained for: a desperate shootout with Florencio Carrasco, brother of the now very dead ore smuggler at Shafter, Matilde Carrasco. Florencio's brother Matilde may have no longer been a threat, but that was in the past, for now two of Florencio's *amigos* were very alive and were very actively thumbing hammers on six-shooters. Chalk one up for the Rangers. During the hot gunfight, one or all of the Rangers killed Florencio Carrasco, who Captain Jones thought was "one of the worst Mexicans on the border." The other two made good their getaway across the river, and then all was dead quiet. Frank Jones, in telling the adjutant general about the gunplay, though not taking any personal credit, would swank that the Mexican's "death is hailed with delight by all good citizens."[28]

While any murders or mischief attributable to Florencio Carrasco could be wiped off the slate of Ranger interest, Captain Jones still had the helm of Company D and its overall maintenance to contend with. As the baking summer sun shone down drying grass and scarce pools of potable water in Frank Jones' bailiwick, it too seemed to be dehydrating the mean spirited enthusiasm of *banditos* and bandits. Seemingly they were—at least temporarily—on hiatus partaking of a welcome *siesta* or a long-awaited nap. Though his Rangers were still statistically keeping their arrest numbers reasonably static, scouting horseback though the hottest months was somewhat curtailed.

As example, for the month of July 1892 the detachment at Shafter made no scouts, but did manage custodial arrests for Disturbing Religious Worship, Carrying a Pistol, Illicit Liquor Dealing, and Theft of Sheep. The following month five fellows went to jail.[29] The company's headman, however, was always busy.

As early as April 1892 Captain Jones had been pondering realigning his headquarters' camp. This he mentioned to the adjutant general, particularly noting that although it was absolutely necessary to maintain a Ranger presence at Shafter, he could probably make a better showing by relocating to El Paso or Eagle Pass.[30] Those locations, besides the opportunity for presenting more activity for Company D Rangers on the whole, also were of personal interests to Frank. However, as August was slowing surrendering, Captain Jones responsibly knew the importance of making ready for Old Man Winter blowing into West Texas, noting that "the winters are very severe in this Altitude and we require a great deal of wood. . . ." Captain Jones, taking it on with his brand of initiative, notified AG Mabry that he would be moving Company D's camp thirty miles east to Marathon, and "presumed" it wouldn't make any real difference to the adjutant general. He was right![31]

Frank Jones had been wrong about something else. During his last trip home to Boerne he had—inadvertently—found out that he had not complied with one of the Probate Court's persnickety rules, that being to "give 20 days notice." Therefore, he was compelled, in the best interests of Grace Kathleen's inheritance, to return to Kendall County, but the trip would be quick, as he would only remain there one day.[32] Continually juggling his personal affairs as a single father and attending supervisory duties required as a member of the Rangers' management team was doable, but never effortless and sometimes trying.

And at Alpine the company's first sergeant had tried Captain Jones' patience for the last time. Perhaps, in hindsight and in private, Frank Jones would have admitted to having seen it coming. Private Lon Oden, who truly valued Baz Outlaw's friendship, had not been blinded by reality. The young private, so it seems, may have even had an inkling, a premonition—not spiritual or mystical—just something predictable, as he recorded in his diary "all of us knew" that something bad would come to pass. Though it saddened him, Lon went on to write that his pal was incapable of putting down the bottle and when Baz was in his cups he was an absolute "maniac; none of us could handle him, none of us could reason with him, we just stayed with him until he sobered up."[33] Laura Carr Hay, who would become Mrs. Lon Oden, knew Baz Outlaw rather well but she was not sightless or speechless: "he was a true Southern gentleman, soft spoken, well educated and courteous. We loved to talk to him and to have him in our home but several drinks made a beast of him." But after learning that Baz had had those several pulls from the bottle, "doors were locked, children brought in off the street and all of us kept silence and hoped for the best."[34] Captain Jones couldn't afford to just hope for the best. During mid-September his top-sergeant "got on a spree and acted disorderly in town." Recognizing his long service to the State of Texas and to the Rangers, Captain Jones allowed Baz Outlaw the option of bowing out of Company D or being booted out—but out he must go. Granted, as Frank Jones acknowledged, Baz Outlaw was "as a fearless officer, he has no superior in the State service," but he "simply could not control himself" when away from Captain Jones' influence. Baz Outlaw chose voluntarily resignation over compulsory termination. This time, Corporal John R. Hughes wasn't passed over and was promoted to fill the vacancy created by his sergeant's discharge.[35] Not having a crystal ball, nobody knew so at that tick of time, but Outlaw's future would be measured by more days wearing a badge and more days bending an elbow.

Big news would spill forth from Company D's relocated headquarters, Camp Cleveland, during September of 1892's waning days. The good news, presumably, was that Frank Jones was going to take a bride. Posting Ranger headquarters, Captain Jones made them aware of his future plans, declaring: "I will be married on the 3rd proximo [the next month] at Ysleta to a daughter of Col. Baylor, and want to run down to San Antonio after my little girl." Frank's thoughts on this matter were more than straightforward, as he told one of his nieces: "It would indeed be an unnatural father who wouldn't want his child with him."[36]

Frank Jones' father-in-law to be was George Wythe Baylor, an Indian fighter, ex-Ranger, and future news contributor for the *El Paso Daily Herald*. Throughout Texas the Baylor name was prominent, most places favorably: And as his biographer somewhat amusingly but spot on right points out, "there were two kinds of Baylors in Texas—fiddlers and fighters." George Baylor was adept at drawing the violin's bow, or issuing his calling card with bullets.[37] Frank Jones was not marrying Mr. Baylor. His eye was set on twenty-seven-year-old Helen Baylor Gillett, a divorcee living at her father's home with her preadolescent son, James Harper.

Mentioning Helen's martial status as a single, but divorced lady is not gratuitous, but relevant. She was the ex-wife of former Texas Ranger, but now sheriff of Brewster County, Jim Gillett. The depth of or shallowness of their friendship is not—as a matter of public record—fathomable, but it's worthy of noting that Frank Jones and Jim Gillett, as brothers of the badge, were well acquainted with one another. The previous November, Captain Jones had interviewed Sheriff Gillett regarding Baz Outlaw's conduct. And later than that, during August of 1891, working together, Jones and Gillett jointly participated in a manhunt, remaining in the field together for seven days, covering some 240 miles.[38] Speculative assertions about what Jim Gillett may or may not have shared with Frank Jones about his ex-wife while sipping coffee at the campfire may well be inappropriate—certainly any naughtiness would be. Conversely, Helen Gillett had plenty to say when her ex-husband's name came up.

According to Helen, Jim had been wasting time hanging around the house—a whore house: Specifically, Madam Roland's parlor house.[39] Should reports be true, and there's no sound reasoning for dispute, Helen wasn't necessarily the epitome of an industrious and hardworking housewife and dutifully devoted mother. Helen was a butterfly. She had been, and had grown up "pampered."[40] So then, not surprisingly, she came across to most folks as "an 'uptown' kind of a girl, singing at church programs and musicals, and getting her name in the social column of the newspaper. She was known to read romantic love stories in bed until almost noon and leave the bed unmade most of the time."[41]

Regardless of any domestic deficiencies within the framework of mopping and scrubbing and mending and carrying out the laundry or making an early breakfast, Helen Baylor Gillett was Captain Frank Jones' choice, his new lease on life. And coming to her defense is relatively easy. Though she had changed the last name of her son from Gillett to Baylor, she had plenty of room in her heart and home for Frank's daughter, Grace Kathleen—James Harper would share his mother and front yard with a newly acquired stepsister.[42]

Frank and Helen were united in matrimony at the Ysleta home of the bride's prominent father on October 3, 1892.[43] On that very same day—as was fitting—prior to the ceremony Frank was messaged by the Texas adjutant general. AG Mabry gushed: "I heartily congratulate you on the approaching nuptials & wish you and Mrs. Jones well the happiness and long life deservable."[44]

What was not in the cards, however, was romanticized arm and arm wedded bliss—unlimited. Captain Jones had gained a wife and stepson, but hadn't forfeited his title or his command of a Ranger company, and Company D was headquartered at Marathon, not Ysleta. At least in the short term, the romance would be tempered—maybe made stronger—by absences.

Demonstrably Captain Jones was back at Camp Cleveland later in the month, meeting with the sheriff of Presidio County at Marfa on the twenty-second regarding the upcoming November elections. The sheriff wanted Texas Rangers stationed at the various precinct polling places because in his opinion there was a conspiracy underfoot to "have men at the different precincts in the Co. and intimidate the Mexican voters." According to Captain Frank Jones—though he wasn't free of prejudice—his remark that the sheriff had a Mexican family and, in fact, it was a fact that many of the Presidio County officials were "connected in some way with the Mexicans and of course have a great deal of influence with them," was a statement rendered with neutrality. The party standing in opposition to the sheriff, Frank believed, would "no longer submit to the imported vote" and intended to stop it at all "hazards." Through reliable sources it is presumed, Jones believed he had dissected the conspiratorial blueprint: The sheriff's political adversaries had secured the appointments of several "Dept. U.S. Marshals and will no doubt arrest a few Mexicans for illegal voting and that will frighten the balance." Astutely recognizing the grave potential for a clash between federal and state lawmen, Captain Jones made sure the adjutant general was on his page: "According to my idea of a Ranger's duty on such occasion he could only keep the peace, but not interfere with Deputy Marshals no matter how many men they arrested on trumped up charges." Jones accented his belief profoundly: Rangers deployed on election day would faithfully mind their "Ps and Qs" regarding politics, but their "their presence would do much towards Keeping the peace. . . ."[45]

The front office at Austin was reading from the same page: "You are ordered simply to preserve the peace and prevent any disturbances of same whenever you or your Rangers may see it, overtly committed, or prevent it whenever you may know disturbances may occur if in your power to do so."[46] Statewide elections took place during November 1892 and the Company D Rangers apparently did not see or learn of any dustups worthy of their presence. They would however be working with new sheriffs. In Presidio County voters had chosen Denton G. Knight, and for Brewster County the electorate had picked D. W. "Doc" Gourley, an ex-Company D Ranger tracing his roots to the Curry Creek section of Kendall County.[47] For the moment, and it was a bit out of character for that far-flung stretch of tempestuous but scenic Big Bend County, all was relatively quiet.

Real trouble was brewing elsewhere. Had Captain Jones been the least concerned about spending the fast approaching holiday season filling out paperwork in camp or scouting the backcountry of the Big Bend and missing the chance to snuggle with Helen or play Santa Claus for the kiddos, he would soon receive a letter relieving him of that worry.

Captain Frank Jones and the Texas Rangers of Company D worked closely with Deputy U.S. Marshal George A. Scarborough, the man who killed John Selman, who had killed John Wesley Hardin at El Paso. *Courtesy Nita Stewart Haley Memorial Library & J. Evetts Haley History Center in Midland, Texas.*

At Alpine, Brewster County, Company D Rangers assume the position—for a West Texas photographer, Standing from L to R: Unknown, T. F. Sellers, Unknown, Arthur Jones, Carl Kirchner (?), Unknown. Seated, from L to R: Unknown, Captain Frank Jones, Baz Outlaw, and (Bob Bell ?). *Courtesy Armstrong Ranger Research Center, Texas Ranger Hall of Fame & Museum.*

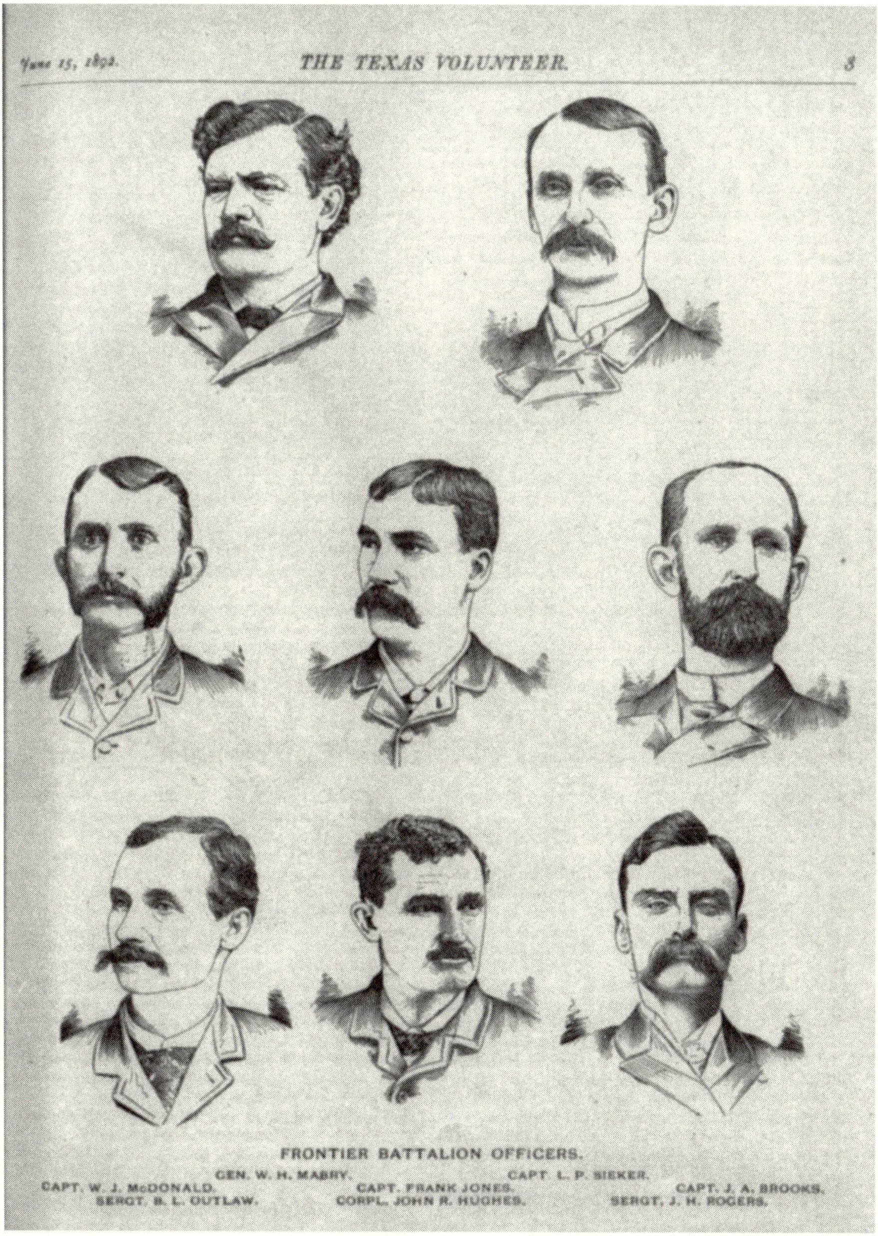

June 15, 1892. THE TEXAS VOLUNTEER. 3

FRONTIER BATTALION OFFICERS.

GEN. W. H. MABRY. CAPT. L. P. SIEKER.

CAPT. W. J. McDONALD. CAPT. FRANK JONES. CAPT. J. A. BROOKS.

SERGT. B. L. OUTLAW. CORPL. JOHN R. HUGHES. SERGT. J. H. ROGERS.

Attesting to the fact that Captain Jones was well and favorably known throughout the Lone Star State is evident by even a cursory look at *The Texas Volunteer* of 1892. The name captions and status of rank are straightforward. Interestingly, Captain Jones is on the same plane as two of the later catalogued "great" Ranger captains, McDonald and Brooks, who Frank outranked by seniority in battalion staffing models. The two others, Sergeant Rogers and Corporal Hughes, at the time have yet to climb the stairway to a fêted Ranger captaincy. *Courtesy Texas State Library & Archives Commission.*

No-nonsense Company D Frontier Battalion Rangers sit for a West Texas photographer. Standing, from L to R: Robert "Bob" Speaks and Jim Putman. Seated, from L to R: Alonzo "Lon" Van Oden and Corporal John R. Hughes. *Courtesy Armstrong Ranger Research Center, Texas Ranger Hall of Fame & Museum.*

Frank Jones and Helen Baylor, no doubt a wedding photograph. *COURTESY LEXIE VAN TASSEL.*

Slyly working undercover and infiltrating a hard gang of ore thieves in West Texas at Shafter, Presidio County, Ernest "Diamond Dick" St. Leon with a well-placed shot lastingly tapped out the running lights of felon Matilde Carrasco. As an undercover operative he was a crackerjack—admired and respected for his fearlessness. *COURTESY ARMSTRONG RANGER RESEARCH CENTER, TEXAS RANGER HALL OF FAME & MUSEUM.*

George Wythe Baylor, ex-Ranger captain, Indian fighter and West Texas journalist. And, too, the father of Frank Jones' second wife, Helen Baylor. *COURTESY DONALD M. AND LOUISE YENA.*

Chapter 15

"Boys, I Am Killed"

COUNTY JUDGE F. E. HUNTER, ACTING as spokesman for the El Paso County Commissioner's Court, signed off on a typewritten appeal to Governor J. S. Hogg. The gist of his message was up-front and clear-cut: the county was overrun by a "band of marauders." The desperadoes had developed into experts at stealing cattle at an alarming rate on the Texas side and selling them in Mexico. The wholesale thefts had become so outrageous that eighty-three signatories had signed the dotted line on a petition seeking relief. The good work of former chief deputy Frank B. Simmons, but now the new El Paso County sheriff, his deputies, and precinct constables was not questioned—they were simply overwhelmed. In their own minds and heart of hearts these wrought-up citizens were in dire need of help and that could best be accomplished by stationing a company of Texas Rangers on the Rio Grande about twenty miles below the city of El Paso. The petitioners would, respectfully, await word from the governor.[1]

Governor Hogg wasted no time in kicking the can down the hallway for the adjutant general's attention. Likewise AG Mabry, on 20 December, but four days after Judge Hunter's letter, issued orders for Captain Jones to at once proceed to El Paso, make an investigation, and then write a report of his findings with recommendations.[2] Even prior to departing Camp Cleveland, three days before Christmas, Captain Frank Jones' opinion was made known to his Austin based boss: "I have Known for some time a bad state of affairs existed in El Paso County."[3] Such an assignment—right out of Frontier Battalion Headquarters—coming when it did was great news for Frank, even if the underlying reason was disconcerting. Without having to ask for a leave of absence and able to travel on the state's dime, he could make a Christmas time visit with wife Helen—now pregnant—and also celebrate a couple of joyous days, or parts of days, with young Grace Kathleen and James Harper.

Illustrating that Frank Jones was no shirker in this instance is a no-brainer. Had he wanted to boondoggle the trip into an extended all-expense-paid vacation the opening had certainly presented itself. There can be little doubt he spent some time with family—but he worked too. Frank interviewed County Judge Hunter, Sheriff Simmons, and other El Paso residents. From there, after procuring a horse, he made an excursion downriver to Socorro, conferring with the county commissioner from that precinct. After returning to El Paso, had he chosen to stay a few days the Rangers' top brass would not have cared—they probably would have—but not Frank. Catching a train on Christmas Eve he returned to Camp Cleveland.[4]

Captain Jones' Christmas Day fare may have been grand or austere but after the meal he took pen in hand for the promised and obligatory letter to headquarters. Frank's findings were not encouraging. The captain noted that Sheriff Simmons was "a wide-awake vigilant officer" and was anxious to "rid the county of the lawless element" but it was simply impossible for him due to monetary and manpower restraints to keep a permanent posse in the field: "The Rio Grande is perfectly dry from El Paso for fifty or sixty miles and this fact, enables predatory bands to raid our side of the river and return before the Sheriff could possibly have time to organize a posse Comitatus with any chance of overtaking them." There was, according to Frank's interpretation, no doubt that the primary violators were "citizens of old Mexico" but he was not blind to the fact that they were working with accomplices from Texas. Subsequent to enumerating several specific raids, Captain Jones iced the cake: "I have never known of a section during all my experience as a criminal officer that needed assistance more from the State than El Paso County does." That said, his unambiguous recommendation was to relocate Company D headquarters to El Paso County but did not think simply deploying a detachment of four or five men to that section of Texas/Mexico borderlands would prove especially beneficial for the job at hand, nor would those Rangers "be able to protect themselves."[5]

Frank Jones was interested in protecting himself, too. Not from steely-eyed bad men from Bitter Creek—he'd handled plenty of that ilk—but from financial disaster should the ever fickle Texas State Legislature do away with a Ranger company or two, or the whole Frontier Battalion. Frank's name was in the hopper for consideration as a patronage appointment for the position of U.S. Marshal for the Western District of Texas. Captain Jones sought permission to travel to Austin while the state legislature was in session.[6] AG Mabry granted Frank's request, provided it did not interfere with his public duties.[7] Speaking well of Frank's character was the fact he was not seeking the position secretly under the table, but was upfront and aboveboard. Whether Frank withdrew his name by choice or was passed over for a lack of enough pure political horsepower goes unrecorded, but the job he thought he wanted—may have really wanted—was awarded to an ex-Ranger, another of those gunfighting veterans of the 1878 Round Rock shoot-out with Sam Bass and his gang, and later a remarkably popular six-term elected sheriff of Mitchell County (Colorado City), Richard Clayton "Dick" Ware.[8]

While at Austin, on at least one occasion Frank personally met with the adjutant general. All of what they discussed would be conjecture. An item they did not cover may be etched in stone. And, somewhat out of character for Frank, it was a slipup. Poor Frank Schmid, the young Ranger wounded during the 1889 Jaybird/Woodpecker riot in Fort Bend County was yet, in 1893, undergoing medical treatment and still submitting claims for reimbursement. Hardly meeting with any success he had contacted his elected state congressman Representative W. W. Turney, who was to introduce a bill in the legislature covering those job-related expenses the state seemed to be reneging on. Jones, either in person or by mail had assured Private

Schmid—who was still a Ranger at heart, though working as a clerk in the statehouse—that during his stay at Austin he would bring the matter to AG Mabry's attention—again. In view of his meticulous nature there's little doubt Schmid was dumbfounded when Captain Jones admitted that he had "forgotten to mention it."[9]

That blunder aside, Frank Jones, dissimilar to some other Ranger captains and subalterns, was a thinker—a practical philosopher. With him it was not all about simply jerking a Colt's six-shooter or snapping handcuffs tight or thumping an unruly belligerent's head with a pistol barrel. One aspect Jones and Mabry had discussed was how a change in scenery would possibly open up a whole new vista for rank and file Rangers, perhaps perking their interests and inspiring them to "work with renewed energy." Captain Jones knew well that the Rangers of Company D would be more than capable of doing "excellent service" were they ever moved to El Paso. Jones was not wishy-washy: "I sincerely hope you will move me to El Paso Co."[10]

Captain Jones' suggestion would not and did not fall on deaf administrator's ears, but while most time bureaucracy's wheels are grinding—sometimes it's ever so slowly. AG Mabry would take the matter under advisement and render a decision "in a short time."[11] Political factors would be at work, and that would not go unnoticed at Austin. Adding to the din already coming out of El Paso County hollering for—almost begging—for help from the state's first city was another petition to the governor, this from the sitting grand jury impaneled for the 34th Judicial District of Texas. Their written plea was for Rangers to protect the populace and property from "the depredations of criminal characters who flit across the frontier."[12]

Also flitting through the frontier mail service were the incessant letters to Austin, notably from a few high-profile folks. The one from Sheriff Simmons was not whiny but written in plain English: He, acting alone, could not put a stop to outrages taking place.[13] Captain Jones in writing to Quartermaster G. A. Wheatley, who had replaced Lam Sieker following his future promotion to Assistant Adjutant General, was working somewhat in a state of limbo: "I have not purchased any hay or corn, except as I consumed it as I have been expecting orders to remove my Camp to El Paso County. I presume you can learn from Genl. Mabry if my Camp will be kept here and then instruct me as to the purchase of forage."[14] George Wythe Baylor put his letter-writing ante into the pot. Excising a portion of his down-to-earth entreaty is relevant to the biographical story at hand: "It is with a feeling of embarrassment that I address you on the subject of sending a squad of Rangers to this point owing to the fact that Capt. Frank Jones is my son-in-law and therefore my feelings and not my judgment would seem to prompt me in the matter."[15] Baylor's logic, in his mind, was solid:

> The men who killed Fusselman were never caught and the posse only followed them across the El Paso Mts. & down to the Rio Grande & then returned to the city. A squad of Rangers with their pack mule & 20 days rations would have Kept on the trail without regards to State or national boundaries & captured or Killed the murderers and this that element Knows and the presence of the Rangers would soon give us peace & security.[16]

That Captain Jones and his father-in-law were cutting the matter up among themselves is apparent. At the time George Wythe chimed in, Frank was at Baylor's Ysleta residence where he had rushed to check on his wife's undisclosed illness. As with excising part of George Baylor's missive is germane, so, too is Frank Jones' response to AG Wheatley regarding State Senator John M. Dean's suggestion to station four Texas Rangers at San Elizario and call the matter done. The captain's reply reveals a great deal about law-enforcing realities and correspondingly probes Frank Jones' mindset about the use of deadly force:

> I do not consider that number sufficient. In almost every locality Rangers in an emergency can call on good citizens for assistance, but in this section, where the population is wholly Mexican, they are practically alone. Of course I think 4 good Rangers can do much good, but I consider that number of men too small to be really effective. A few men so often are compelled to make a fight to effect the capture of criminals when a good number will overawe and the arrest is made without the necessity of a shot being

> fired. Of late years the Rangers have been compelled to do Killing simply because there were so few in numbers it emboldened fugitives. During the first years of my Ranger service we never went out except there were 8 or 10 men and we never had to kill anyone. . . . I think I am in a position to Know more about the situation than Senator Dean.[17]

Captain Jones, no matter the need or the desire, could not just up and move Company D absent authority from Ranger headquarters. While waiting for dithering to gain functional traction, by no measure was the captain idle or indecisive. Particularly after capturing the train robbers, Frank's working relationship with railway supervisors was exceptionally favorable, perhaps eclipsing that of other company commanders: At least that's what he thought and so mentioned to AG Mabry: "I will be glad if my Headquarters are Kept on the Southern Pacific road as I have a 'stand in' with this road that I think no other Ranger officer can have. I can get trip passes for the men and have annuals for myself and Sergt. between El Paso and San Antonio."[18]

Of particular interest to railroad bigwigs was Frank's crack at forestalling another robbery. Spending due diligence, and it speaks well to his overall enforcement competency, Frank had developed a rather weighty piece of criminal intelligence. On the twenty-second day of March 1893 he traveled to Val Verde County.[19] There he met with Railroad Detective J. P. Long, representing the Southern Pacific line. The word was, according to Jones, that there was a plan underfoot by "some outlaws (Americans) on the Mexican side of the Rio Grande" to highjack a train in Texas. According to his best information, they would only cross the river for a "moonlight flitting." That is, to rob the train and hightail it back into Mexico where Rangers dared not go—so certain idiots thought! Using railroad company funds, the captain had a "man over there to watch them." If somehow an interdiction was foiled, and there actually was a train heist, Jones pledged that he "would certainly follow them anywhere they may go."[20]

Though it necessitates that niggling out-of-chronology sidebar and cannot be absolutely assured, there's hardly any doubt Captain

Jones was working a strategy to capture a train-robbing owlhoot from Bexar County named Charles Small. Lawmen from Arizona Territory and New Mexico Territory as well as Texas would know Mr. Charley Small well. He'd even done hard time in a Mexican prison for holding up a train. Hanging out on the south side of the snaky Rio Grande, primarily across from Langtry and Comstock, Val Verde County, purportedly Charley Small was a hired killer, too.[21] Though Frank Jones wasn't there when it happened, the notorious Small would meet his maker and a mortician at the hands of a Ranger. Charley's last day unfolded by the railway water tank outside Judge Bean's Jersey Lilly Saloon during a 1890s shoot-out. Ranger Sergeant D. L. Musgrave's handiwork with a Winchester was as quick and short as his report to Austin, a classic in Ranger brevity:

> This morning we were fired on by Chas Small a noted desperate character and he was killed by me.[22]

What wouldn't die, it seemed to Captain Jones, was the stubbornness and misguided mindset coming from some quarters that assigning but four Rangers to El Paso County would be ample. Although the clamor for a company of Rangers had started in earnest during December/January, it was by now mid-April 1893 and Frank Jones was still at Marathon, still defending the obvious: "If I am sent to El Paso County I hope you can allow me to take more than 4 men. Old 'residenters' below El Paso say that 4 men will simply be murdered and will do no good. From the best information I have on the subject, think there must be fully 50 in the gang that has caused so much trouble and they are well organized too. . . ."[23]

Regardless how much attention Captain Jones was devoting to philosophizing or daydreaming about establishing his Ranger camp in El Paso County, immediacy and the adjutant general focused his attention back to Val Verde County and that stretch of Rio Grande near Langtry, and upriver quite a distance on the Pecos.

AG Mabry ordered Captain Jones to the region post haste.[24] The fact that Captain Jones could read the urgency of the adjutant general's instructions is reflected by his telegram to that office: "Am on train with 2 men for Langtry. Will write you later."[25] The two

Rangers riding with the captain were Corporal Carl Kirchner and Private Richard Bascom "Dick" Chastain.

Reading tea leaves at Langtry was not necessary; some very concerned cattlemen and the Deputy Collector of Customs T. A. Cunningham were out of sorts regarding cow thieves and cow smugglers haunting their ranch country neighborhood.[26] There was reason to be. Captain Jones would later sum it up succinctly to Ranger headquarters, coldly declaring that Langtry was "one of the toughest places" on the Southern Pacific's tracks.[27] Area ranchers were seeking a go-ahead from the adjutant general's office to carry six-shooters, so they could guard against the "lawless element." They were not, in truth and fact, receiving any protection from the state, and their herds "were scattered from Fort Stockton to Langtry & up the Pecos on both sides for a hundred miles."[28] Because of feuding between cattlemen over ownership of wandering cattle up and down the Pecos and livestock being stolen in Mexico and smuggled across the river, U.S. Custom's Inspector Cunningham was—and probably rightly so—fearing that on any given day he might be "assassinated."[29]

Exhibiting initiative Captain Jones decided to return to camp alone, leaving Kirchner and Chastain at Langtry.[30] Even a cursory look at the Scout Report submitted by Corporal Kirchner for the month of May 1893 discloses Captain Jones' decision had been smart. The pair of Rangers, working closely with U.S. Deputy Marshal Lee Cochran and U.S. Mounted Customs Inspectors made numerous arrests—primarily for smuggling cattle into Texas.[31] And to Captain Jones way of thinking, it was a well known fact "that the very worst element we have along this border are smugglers. A professional Contrabandist is always a thief."[32]

That there were Rangers at Langtry and Rangers at Shafter and Rangers at Marathon did not lessen Captain Frank Jones' administrative and commissary and property inventory headaches. And, too, he had a headache—literally. A throbbing toothache had almost downed the captain. So much so, that he didn't seek permission to leave camp; he merely advised the front office that he would be away from his station a few days "to have some dental work done," adding that he had suffered long enough and "I must go."[33]

And he went. As might be supposed Captain Jones had sought treatment at or near El Paso. During this trip or a quick follow-up visit to the dentist Frank Jones made critical observations and conferred with Sheriff Simmons regarding the most logical place to headquarter Rangers when word of that move was approved—and surely it would be okayed. Adding insurance to that decision-making process the sheriff picked up the pen and wrote AG Mabry: "I wish you would send the Rangers as soon as possible as I am very much in need of them now. I asked Capt. Jones to make his headquarters at Ysleta if he was sent here. . . . Ysleta is the most central point and they could be of more assistance to me at Ysleta than any other point."[34]

Frank Jones, notwithstanding that his family was at Ysleta, was also prompting the adjutant general to settle on Ysleta rather than El Paso or San Elizario proper. From Ysleta the Rangers would be centrally located, able to scout upriver and downriver from El Paso/Ciudad Juárez. Another of his observations was more personal than professional—and prejudiced:

> some of the old Churches which were built in the 16th century. Talking among the common people here I am under the impression that they have not advanced a single step in civilization. They are as ignorant and superstitious and as much under the rule of their priests as when this county was first settled. . . . [35]

Subsequent to examinations and repairs by the good tooth doctor, Frank Jones returned to camp. There the captain would continue to faithfully oversee his responsibilities as a front-line lawman. And wait, and wait. There was, finally, word from the home office that Captain Jones and his chomping-at-the-bit Texas Rangers were to go. The move to El Paso County had come through. Specifically the headquarters for Company D would be Ysleta and Sergeant Hughes with "one or two" Rangers would move from Shafter to a point on the railroad line at or near Marathon or Alpine where they would be available to "scout and control the most disturbed Section of that part of the Country."[36] Not unexpectedly some folks at Shafter howled, including William M. "Bill" Noyes, head-honcho of the

Presidio Mining Company.[37] From El Paso came a letter penned by Representative Dean hoping that the "rumor" that had reached him about redeploying Texas Rangers from Shafter was "incorrect."[38] Though not just a few politicians find it hard to believe or accept, many upper-level governmental folks know full-well their appointed tenure is but temporary. AG Mabry it may be presumed had no internal hemorrhaging when he advised lawyer/politico J. M. Dean the rumor was no rumor and, moreover the decision—the Executive Branch's prerogative—would stand!

The news had long been awaited. Within but four days of notification Captain Jones and the Company D Rangers were marching for El Paso County. Ten days later they were at Ysleta.[39] Whether the men pitched tents or moved into adobe quarters is hazy, but the latter would be most likely had the choice been theirs.[40] Captain Jones had a place to sleep: At his father-in-law's house, with his wife Helen, now heavy with child. Absolutely there's no reason to doubt that Grace Kathleen, nearly six, was ecstatic now that her daddy was home. Conjecture that young James Harper was anything but pleased as punch that his stepfather, a captain of Texas Rangers, was in the house would be groundless.

While jockeying the ten days between Marathon and Ysleta there's not—especially now—a reliable method of knowing what lines of communication Captain Jones kept open or did not avail himself of. Mentioning the fact he may have been—or most likely was—out of touch for more than a week is of note. Odds are high he first heard the news after arriving at Ysleta.

The report from Austin was assuredly devastating. At twenty-six years of age former Ranger Private Frank Louis Schmid, Jr. was dead, passing to the other side on the seventeenth day of June 1893.[41] Earlier, John Robert Baylor, George Wythe Baylor's older brother, had publicly decried the undoubtedly shabby treatment that had been awarded Frank Schmid: "Surely Texas can afford to care for a man wounded in the discharge of his duty and not leave him in his condition to chance and charity."[42] Despite the operations and admittances to hospitals and infirmaries the gunshot wound had not healed and it had years later claimed its life. True, the state legislators had eventually enacted Senate Bill No. 255 and appropriated $584.50 for Schmid's reimbursement, but had the Lone Star State really paid its just debt of gratitude to a Texas Ranger killed in the line of duty?[43]

Life is for the living, and Frank Jones was living in real time. The two big troubles on the captain's enforcement calendar were geography and genealogy. Tackling problem number one was tricky. Due to a myriad of causative dynamics such as long spells of drought, deluging downpours, eroding overflows, injudicious irrigation techniques and, perhaps Mother Nature's sweet revenge, the real Rio Grande's earliest channel was ill-defined. In certain places the old river vanished underground; the topside was but a loose bed of ever treacherous shifting sands. As an international border—sovereignty's edge—it was diplomatically messy and problematical. For wheeling and dealing envoys negotiating treaties or surveyors drawing thin marks on maps, the Rio Grande was in a practical sense only an abstract concept: surely important, but innocuous. For borderland lawmen it was Lucifer's Line.[44]

In the eyes of Rangers and sheriffs and river guards the prolific Devil had bred his offspring: The Olguins. As bona fide bloodline relatives they were known as the Bosque Gang, and not a harder or meaner set lived or worked or robbed or murdered along the Río Bravo below El Paso. Patriarchal leader—the godfather—Clato Olguin at ninety-plus had opted for semi-retirement. Through natural succession the mantel of leadership was picked up by his sons, Pedro, Antonio, and Jesús María. In turn, the sons of Jesús María, Sebastian, Severio, and Pecilliano menacingly sat in their hand-tooled pancake-horned saddles serving as gangland lieutenants. As is clear, the family was of Mexican ancestry. They were, however, and long had been resident Texans. Well, not Antonio Olguin. He was a hard-boiled fugitive, an escapee from the Texas penitentiary, convicted of rape, and now put his head to rest on Mexico's side of the line. By the time Captain Frank Jones and Company D Rangers set up shop at Ysleta, Jesús María and Severio owned brand-new felony Indictments for Theft and Assault to Murder courtesy the El Paso County Grand Jury—warrants had issued.[45]

The Olguin clan—a tough subgroup in a tough landscape—were not intimidated by the new arrivals at Ysleta. They had ruled the roost for too many years. They took what they wanted. While somewhat short in stature, the meanest of the lot may have been Severio, squinting at likely victims and their accessible assets from behind his "piercing" brown eyes.[46] Just two days after the Texas Rangers ended their cross-country trip, and while Captain Jones and his Rangers were still orienting themselves about the neighborhood and ne'er-do-wells, the Olguins—at least several of them—whooped it up at the village of Guadalupe on the Mexican side of the river. There, if the hideous reports be true, they fatally gunned down one resident and during the drunken tequila spree shot three more inhabitants as they laughingly reeled in their saddles while galloping out of town.[47]

In their minds, the Olguins were simply untouchable. They were masters at conspiring when given sufficient time and mercilessly practiced at pulling off murders on the spur of the moment. On occasion, with superior numbers and itchy trigger-fingers, they had blatantly defied policing authorities sallying forth from both banks of the river. Not surprisingly then, the Olguins, ones with names on legally drawn after indictment warrants were at the top of Frank Jones' list. Bravado and badness didn't and wouldn't dissuade him.

Company D Rangers had arrived at Ysleta on the twenty-third day of June 1893. There may have been sufficient forage for the horses, but Captain Jones was not accustomed to, nor would he allow grass to grow under idle Rangers' feet. When dawn broke on the twenty-seventh, Company D's corporal and three privates rode south from historic Ysleta—the oldest town in Texas—to the quaint and pleasantly sited little village of San Elizario with specific instructions from Captain Frank Jones: Hunt hard for bandits Jesús María and Severio Olguin—or actionable intelligence about their whereabouts. That evening the Rangers returned empty-handed to Ysleta.[48] From the very best information at hand, Jones figured the fugitives and their unfailing and unscrupulous cronies would most likely be holed-up on Pirate Island.

By and large that was all Frank Jones needed to know. Not just a few folks throughout the Southwest referred to the captain "as a

Ranger's Ranger because he was always willing to set the example in leadership and energy."[49] This would not prove an exception. Less than a week after arriving at Ysleta, Captain Jones kissed Helen goodbye and pitched an *adios* the kiddos' way, then mounted his horse as headman of a scout with particular targets slated for arrest. Riding with Jones were Corporal Carl Kirchner, Private Eddie Aten, brother of ex-Rangers Ira and Cal, Private T. F. Tucker, Private Wood Saunders, who had reenlisted one more time, and Private Robert Edward "Ed" Bryant, a formidable fighter with impressive law-enforcing credentials due to prior Ranger service and as one of Sheriff Simmons' deputies, but as of three days earlier, now a Company D Ranger.[50] Although new to El Paso County, the Rangers wouldn't be totally clueless. Twenty-seven-year-old Ed Bryant had been born at Ysleta, had married Luisa Gonzalez, and from childhood spoke fluent Spanish.[51] Noteworthy, too, was Ed's familiarity with faces: the good guys and gals, as well as a few wicked guttersnipes and their girlfriends—like the Olguins. Private Bryant was also familiar with the county's geography; well, as knowledgeable as anyone could be taking into account the Rio Grande's twists and tangles, its dry beds and shifting sands.

At sometime and somewhere along the way the Texas Rangers met a local lad named Lujan. After friendly but inquisitive interrogation the Rangers concluded the teenager wasn't a spy, buying into his story that he was searching for horses stolen from the family's modest *rancho*. Lujan was permitted to accompany the scout. When the evening shadows began closing in on June 29, 1893, the Rangers made camp on the Texas side of the river, a handful of miles below San Elizario at La Quadrilla.[52]

Before sunup the Rangers were tightening cinches, stuffing cartridges into tubular magazines of Winchesters, and making sure there were "five beans in the wheel," a euphemism meaning their Colt's cylinders were fully loaded, except for one under the hammer, a safety precaution. Stepping into the stirrup and facing their horses' noses toward Pirate Island had been a precise maneuver, synchronized but virtually automatically and subconsciously executed. Conversely, thoughts spinning in each Texas Ranger's head were privately held. Fate would issue a real good day—or a damn bad day: Lawmen never knew?

They were, though, learning on-the-job about Pirate Island. Well before any of these Rangers celebrated their first birthday the ever erratic Rio Grande had jumped her banks, carving a new collateral channel and leaving a sandy island in her wake. Then she capriciously merged back with the mother river several miles downstream. She was tempestuous. The land mass between the ancient Rio Grande and the more recently cut channel was Pirate Island. Theoretically the island was mutually marked off, half in Mexico, half in the United States. Practically speaking the sandy strip several miles long and skirted with dense underbrush and untold secrets was a "No man's land!"[53]

A frontier-era Ranger—contemporary to the story—clarifies the confusion of place and time:

> In regards to the dividing line between the United States and Mexico, there is an old river bed where the water has not run since 1854 except when river is very high that is recognized by citizens of both nations as the line between the United States and Mexico. This old channel is very indistinct and there are two or three others very near like it on the island. . . . the Mexican side of this old channel that is recognized as the line but there are no marks of any international survey to show where the line is.[54]

Therefore what may have seemed to paper-pushers in plush-carpet embassy offices as real consequential, in truth was meaningless to Texas brigands and Mexican bandits, particularly those fiercely determined to stake claim on ground suggesting unofficial and unspoken asylum. Were one actually standing on Pirate Island's shifting sands, stepping in either direction might put one in Mexico or Texas or vice-versa. While Miss Vagueness was dealing the hand, crossing the river might yet leave the traveler in Texas, but breaching the ill-defined imaginary line would put the trekker inside Mexico's northern edge. A roadway—if that's what it could be called—ran the length of the island, frequently and confusingly crisscrossing between countries. Is there any wonder the Olguins called Pirate Island home?[55]

At first light the Rangers could be found outside Clato Olguin's place, on the Texas side of the line. They were there on business and they meant business. Unluckily for the lawmen their movements had been telegraphed by word of mouth to their persons of primary interest, allowing Severio and Jesús María to skip: Straight across the imaginary line into Mexico, seeking sanctuary that their blood relative Antonio—the escaped convict—could provide. Meanwhile, at Clato's abode, though he was old and nearly blind, Pirate Island's godfather of deviltry knew the Rangers' hunt at his house would be a bust. Hence, he bowed his neck and turned pissy, putting on a good show for the womenfolk, but the disappointed Texas Rangers paid him no never-mind. They were angry and hungry—having foregone breakfast trying to catch the Olguin owlhoots in bed. They mounted up and were gone.[56]

With a reasonably safe distance between themselves and prying eyes, Captain Jones ordered a halt. There was plenty of time that morning to boil a pot of Arbuckles, pull cold cathead biscuits and salt-dried pork from saddlebags—and mull over their next move. Captain Jones and his Rangers were under no silly illusion. They knew they'd been outfoxed, that more-than-likely the fugitives were lying low at Antonio's shanty, but they too were aware his place was in Mexico. He may have been a craven and brutish rapist, but Antonio was no dunce: Were he to live in Texas he'd be nabbed before the cows came home. Frank Jones was no dumbbell.

Probing deeply into the principled captain's way of rationalizing is admittedly speculative, but uncomplicated. As a thoroughly seasoned lawman and manhunter he knew not all chases ended rewardingly. Sometimes even good guys come up short. A helter-skelter dash into Mexico while not in hot pursuit might net prisoners, but would be counterbalanced by armchair howling from Austin and Mexico City. On Mexico's side of Pirate Island was the village of *Tres Jacales* but the plunder to be had by ravishing and raiding those poor peasants would be trifling and hollow. The cutthroats and crooks hanging out there were already mobbed-up. The Olguins were crime-bosses and thieves, not laborers and, sooner or later, treasure in Texas would tempt them into crossing the Rio Grande. Frank Jones could be patient, resting on drab driftwood like a Cottonmouth—until time to bare fangs and strike. He and his Rangers would head back to Ysleta this last day of June 1893.

Hardly were they screwed down in their saddles for a return trip to camp when the dejected Rangers espied two "Mexicans" riding hard, heading straight toward them hell-bent-for-leather. Upon seeing and nearly colliding with Rangers, the pair in unison not lightly jerked their horses' heads down, precipitating a sliding and hock-bumping stop, and at once "wheeled and ran back," clearly not fancying to fall into Texas lawmen's clutches. Although it's presumptive—but logical—it was likely Private Ed Bryant's recognition and shout that put Captain Jones on notice: One of those frantically spurring "Mexicans" was Jesús María. Mentioned elsewhere herein, at the time fleeing felons were fair game and could be shot while resisting or running from lawmen. Rather than holler orders for his Rangers to shoot men and/or horses, Captain Jones put iron to his gelding—the chase was on! The heat of hot pursuit was a game changer.

After running several hundred yards, Rangers Kirchner, Saunders, and Aten, riding faster horses, overtook and passed Captain Jones and Private Tucker, who until that time had been at the forefront. Purposefully jumping off or inadvertently falling off is immaterial but Jesús María was no longer horseback. He was afoot dodging back and forth across the road—sometimes in Texas, sometimes in Mexico—but at all times not too far from Antonio Olguin's adobe dwelling. At length Jesús María ducked through the open entrance of his brother's place, just as the three lead Rangers blew by, unable to check their horses' forward momentum. A bullet coming from the darkened doorway was faster than the Ranger's rides, and punched hard into the magazine of Corporal Kirchner's Winchester, the impact nearly tearing the rifle from the Ranger's hand. Though not rendered totally useless, from this point forward Kirchner's weapon had to be loaded one round in the chamber at a time—making it a slow single-shot and not a lever-action repeater. Private Saunders, hot on the heels of Kirchner, was next to receive attention from Antonio's address, but thankfully the salvo coming from windows, the doorway, and even a porthole went wild as he raced by. Next in line was Private Eddie Aten, who by this time had his Colt's .45 in hand. Leaning low in the saddle Eddie managed to luckily submarine himself underneath the next volley—which went high. He also earned distinction during this piece of non dime-novel warfare by firing a shot, the first discharge by any Ranger.

Fortuitously mounted on less speedy mounts than those three Rangers undergoing and surviving a hellacious barrage, Captain Jones and Private Tucker were yet physically placed on a tough piece of ground and, moreover, psychologically handed a hard choice. With what they had seen it was perfectly clear. They were not being challenged by one or two nitwits, outlaws not willing to be arrested, but by a whole gang—exact numbers unknown, but scorching gunfire was spitting forth from behind chest-high adobe walls jutting like outstretched buzzards' wings from Antonio's house, as well as from inside. Kirchner, Saunders, and Aten, having overshot the battleground, were dexterously slowing their horses so they could turn, reversing course—not necessarily an easy maneuver with bullets flying, booming noises, and veils of blue gun smoke coloring and clouding the morning air. Captain Jones, staying true to character, didn't retreat. He raced forward—to the sounds of roaring rifles and barking six-shooters, Private Tucker right on his coattails, and Private Bryant almost in his hip-pocket. When the charge—and that's what it was—ended, Captain Jones and Private Tucker were within thirty feet of the sniper's lair. Private Ed Bryant wasn't hunting safety but was flanking his buddies by only fifteen to twenty feet. It was mean, up close and personal, near knife fighting space.

Jumping from their horses and faced with scant cover, the Rangers were sitting ducks, like doves roosting on a telegraph line. Potshots were permissible for pirates. There was no time to pray, no damn time to aim! Frank Jones was furiously working the lever of his Winchester pouring hellfire into the house. Tucker and Bryant were feverishly backing his play. Amid the heat and eardrum-busting racket and stench and screamed expletives in two languages, at least a few of the Rangers' bullets were scoring blood and bone. Jesús María had caught a hot projectile with his right hand, one that punched clear through, and also had a couple of creases on his head thanks to bullets an inch or two off of the mark. Severio Olguin's wound was more critical, his upper arm shattered and broken "near the body." Just how the conclusion was reached might justifiably cry for scrutiny, but Captain Jones was, by a newspaper report, credited with firing the round that "hit Juan Agulerre in the forehead, killing him instantly. . . ."[57]

On the ground in real time, Captain Jones and the other Rangers may have seen the sickening drama unfolding before them as if it were in slow-motion, the bandits and bullets moving in grotesque and bizarre time-warp suspensions. Were their lives flashing before them as they dodged and shot and sorted flashbacks of better times? Did Frank see those goddamned bad Olguin gangsters lined up in the forefront, at the very same time picturing darling Helen and precious Grace Kathleen sitting on his shoulders whispering words of encouragement and pledging eternal devotion? Adrenalin is weird! Regardless, this lead-spitting episode was uncorking in real time, real fast, the clash consuming seconds: Certainly not one measured by more than a minute or two on Frank's cherished timepiece—the one gifted him by Rangers of Company D five years earlier.

One of those split-seconds carried a bullet to Frank. The impact knocked him to the ground. The hot lead boring through the sinew and muscle had not wasted all its energy. Unstoppably it had kept plowing its course through his thigh, smashing into bone and breaking it. Blood spurted. Excruciating pain swamped his nervous system. His Winchester took flight—now out of reach. Although suffering horribly, the capable Ranger captain gutted-up. Drawing from deep within he managed, somehow, to position his broken leg straight before him, remaining conscious and, miraculously, still focused. With nothing but pure grit and gumption Frank accessed his still holstered six-shooter. Exhibiting the heart of a lion and the tenacity of a wolverine Frank let the Colt's hammer drop, two or three times, inexplicably not letting the bucking six-shooter slip from his grip even as life's blood seeped into the sand beneath him. Privates Tucker and Bryant nearby were peppering Antonio's place, the scoring of their marksmanship unknown and untold. Further out Corporal Kirchner and Privates Saunders and Aten, hunting for a safe spot, were also letting rounds fly. Labeling this battle a gunfight would be silly; it was war.

During the chaos and confusion and crescendo of thunderous gunfire whether or not Frank noticed the sombrero and rifle's muzzle inching slightly higher than that jutting and sinister adobe wall is buried. Maybe two enemies made eye contact? For sure the gangster was quicker at touching the trigger. The zipping lead tore into Frank's torso. Private Tucker sharply turning his head screamed: "Captain, are you hurt?" Jones obviously sinking managed an answer: "Yes, shot all to pieces." The bushwhacker levered another round and was not about to abandon his work. The next bullet ripped into the captain's chest, ranging downward towards his heart. Feebly gasping for air, thirty-seven-year-old Frank Jones agonizingly mumbled, "Boys, I am killed." And he was!

★ ★ ★

There on the shifting sands of Pirate Island lay the lifeless and bloody body of Frank Jones: His biography a closed book. Penning words for successive chapters would not be furthering the fallen Texas Ranger's story. That, in effect, would be picking up on other folks' biographical profiles and/or showcasing after-the-fact episodes that Frank Jones' eyes had been eternally closed from witnessing. Nonetheless there is room in the storytelling arena to bring matters to a more complete close by hitting a few high-spots, even if ever so briefly.

For awhile, in reality a short time, the battle tapered off into the colloquial Mexican Standoff. Shootists pinned down at Antonio's abode and adobe breastworks were powerless to walk out. Had they, the Rangers would have gladly—free, gratis—gunned them down. The "Mexicans" did, however, hold a face-up Ace. Their field-of-fire covered ground where the dead Jones lay. The Company D boys could not dislodge the "Mexicans" nor could they recover their captain's remains. Private Ed Bryant brought his pals a morsel of cold and hard reality—they were in Mexico, barely traversing that imaginary line, but across they were. Even more upsetting news about the pickle they were in was delivered by Lujan; a courier from *Tres Jacales* was riding hard for the village of Guadalupe to fetch a platoon of Mexican troops. Corporal Kirchner was, by virtue of rank, now in command. Clearly exercising the best—at least most practical—option, he ordered the detachment back to sure-enough Texas soil, to San Elizario where via a telegraph authorities and the outside world could be told of the tragedy.[58]

Fashioning a heavily armed posse, Sheriff Frank Simmons rushed—almost to the crime-scene but smartly did not step across any imaginary line.[59] Accomplishing round one of negotiating through expressionless Mexican intermediaries, he sought the captain's body and property: Mexicans said no way!

Long a resident of the borderlands Frank Simmons knew how the game was played. He returned to El Paso for round two. Back channel work was on tap. Initiating contact with the right folks in Ciudad Juárez was on the politically savvy sheriff's program. It was delicate work. Wheeling and dealing would trump just saying "pretty please." An accord was reached. Although he wasn't actually present during any deal-making across the bridge at Ciudad Juárez and his official report to AG Mabry at Ranger headquarters makes use of an editorial "we," Corporal Kirchner dutifully confers proper credit but somewhat—intentionally it seems—skips around divulging too many specifics: "We then made a demand on the chief officer at Juarez, Mex. Who acted very nicely (I am told by Sheriff Simmons who made the demand) & ordered the body delivered to us at the State line."[60] Remembering that along the Rio Grande/Río Bravo *la mordida*—the bite—was then a well-oiled and common convention is, or may be, quite relevant. At ten o'clock on the morning following the fight, the sheriff took possession of Captain Jones' body. Readers may make their own well-reasoned judgments in regards to any under-the-table skullduggery or greasing palms with U.S. minter's ink, once posted about the existence of and exchange of two letters.

Only seven days after the captain's death Sheriff Simmons made inquiry to Governor Hogg: "I have been to quite an expense in getting the body of Capt. Frank Jones, Company D State Rangers from Mexico. Will the state help me pay these expenses. . . ." Bureaucracy bounced the ball downhill. AG Mabry having made the catch responded to the sheriff's claim for a payback: "I would say that your expenses for recovering the body of Capt. Frk. Jones, deceased, will be refunded to you, provided the amount is reasonable."[61] Not surprisingly the "quite an expense" is not itemized for posterity—perhaps purposefully so. At any rate, Captain Jones' body had been brought back to Texas wherein he was laid to rest at Ysleta under auspices of El Paso's Masonic Lodge No. 120 during the early evening of July 1, 1893.[62]

But even before Sheriff Simmons was making his pitch for reimbursement, Texas Ranger Sergeant John R. Hughes made his play—in writing—to fill Frank Jones' boots as captain of Company D. The company's rank and file—in writing—championed the sergeant's aspirations. Subsequent to, but quickly after noting other telegrams and letters supporting promotion of the top-sergeant, AG Mabry acted: Special Order No. 105 placed Captain John Reynolds Hughes in command of Company D.[63]

Although in certain history treatments it's dismissed as being but apocryphal, an armchair chronicler rushing to judgments out of hand might be doing so at his/her own peril—historically, of course—not physically. How much fabrication and folklore is built into the story is immeasurable. But, an assertion that Ernest St. Leon, south of the border and during moonlight, carried out a scheme of righting wrongs with a rope and dagger denied Rangers in the daytime—north of the Rio Grande, might not be only a legend. That would be—and is—another story.[64]

There was another story playing out regarding the murder near *Tres Jacales* and it wasn't on the state's backburner. At the time it was a diplomatic hot potato. After all, a government sponsored pre-planned armed invasion of Mexico had taken place, hadn't it? What virtuous Foreign Minister wouldn't protest that? Mexico's sovereignty had been breached. Secretaries of State were jumping, hurling spears built with words, sharpened on the grindstone of accusations, centered on drawing reparation not blood. It was a losing and bloodless battle, though, despite the customary comedy and silly sparring so well acquainted with honing the fine points of international diplomacy. Governor Hogg needed answers—and real quick. AG Mabry made his findings known to the state's chief executive, which in part countercharged a grand conspiracy on the part of *banditos*: "Under the circumstances the officers of the law naturally followed in pursuit and after chasing them about half of a mile the retreating Mexicans permitted themselves to be overtaken near an adjacent 'adobe' house. Hardly had the demand for surrender been uttered before a volley was fired into Capt. Frank Jones and his men from this 'adobe' house and from behind adjacent walls by parties there concealed. In the fight that ensued Capt. Jones was Killed. . . . There is no doubt but that Capt. Jones and detachment were decoyed into this trap just over line into Mexico by these criminals and the plan was to murder not only Jones but his entire detachment. . . ."[65]

There were, too, personal costs for family and friends. Helen Baylor Jones was heartbroken, the devastating loss near unbearable, so much so that she could not consciously bear to even sleep in the same room at her father's house that she and Frank had previously shared. George Wythe Baylor acquiesced and found his grieving—and perhaps somewhat spoiled—daughter suitable quarters outside his El Paso County home and rented same in her behalf.[66] Perhaps emotional strain prompted her premature delivery only ten days after her husband's untimely death, but Frank's one and only son came crying into Ysleta's world and soon carried part of his daddy's name, Frank Baylor Jones—for awhile.

Subsequent to her period of mourning, the widow Helen Baylor Gillett Jones married a manager of the posh and swanky Grand Hotel, Samuel M. Lee. Upon accepting new employment as superintendent for a railroad company Mr. Lee moved his new wife and stepsons—the two stepbrothers James Harper and Frank Baylor to Guadalajara, State of Jalisco, Mexico. Perhaps the grizzled old ex-Ranger and Indian-fighting grandfather wasn't really too surprised when he learned "with lingering hate for her first husband and a disavowal of her second, Helen [had] changed her two sons' names to Lee."[67] And from then until his untimely death due to natural causes at age fifteen, Captain Frank Jones' male heir was Francisco "Panchito" Baylor Lee.[68] Pitching a notable sidebar into the story is not out of place. Panchito's stepbrother Harper, while living in Mexico, became infatuated with bullfighting and obviously had quite a knack for it. Depending on one's outlook, his bullfighting practices were a skilled sport or a savage spectacle. In any case, the gutsy young man earned so much nationwide notice and notoriety, he piqued the interests of an author and a Boston publisher. Marshall Hail penned *Knight in the Sun: Harper B. Lee, First Yankee Matador*.

What of young Grace Kathleen? Lawmen sometimes have eerie and creepy thoughts ginning between their ears, often focused on "what if" scenarios. In this regard Frank Jones was normal. Whether or not at some point Jones' fortune and future had been predicted by a Gypsy mystic might wholly rest with passed-down oral history from family. That he had a premonition—like most brothers of the badge—that someday he might draw the short straw in a sudden gunplay is not anywhere near farfetched. With that in mind, Frank had asked for and extracted a pledge from Helen. Already with one child underfoot, and another on the way, and clearly thinking of Helen's well-being should the Grim Reaper knock, Frank wanted to lessen his wife's burden, having her short-time stepdaughter raised by his family at Boerne/San Antonio/Kendall County. The widow Jones had faithfully kept that promise.[69]

Across the border, as late as October 1893, according to a snippet in a *Dallas Morning News* article, Mexican authorities were moving slow on keeping their promise to release the personal effects of Captain Frank Jones. Whether any money changed hands is—in the big picture—moot. In due course—somebody else's timetable—Frank's cherished and engraved pocket-watch, hand crafted badge, and bloodstained Winchester were released to the family's representatives in Texas. The deceased captain's Colt's six-shooter and handcuffs remained unaccounted for, perhaps—for someone—macabre souvenirs of sorts.[70]

Also dawdling were any noticeable efforts underway at aptly awarding Captain Jones' service with the Texas Rangers and ultimate sacrifice due credit. As mentioned, life is for the living, and sometimes it's hectic. Often is the case dead men are overlooked in the short term. Though it would be anything but timely, eventually a heavy granite monument would be funded, appropriately inscribed, and erected on state-owned property near Ysleta as fitting tribute to Frank's career as a Texas Ranger and memorializing his line-of-duty death. Such public-spirited veneration and prestigious contribution by the Lone Star State—though posthumous—was distinction elusive to some of the Texas Ranger captains spontaneously festooned with "greatness" by early twentieth-century devotees.

The timing of Captain Frank Jones' demise had coincided almost perfectly with movements at the statehouse to defund the Frontier Battalion. Population numbers of Central Texas, East Texas, and the Gulf Coast, when measured against West Texas and the Rio Grande borderlands, were lopsided—moreover was the economic supremacy blossoming in the Lone Star State's emergent interior metropolitan centers. Proximity breeds predictability. In the main, the state's moneymaking movers and shakers were city folk heavily investing in the richness of promises Texas held. There were, now, sheriffs galore and policemen—in some towns not just a few policemen—certainly capable of catching crooks and scooping up drunks. Was there a frontier? Were Texas Rangers but a dollar draining anachronism? Captain Frank Jones was dead, but were the Rangers—institutionally? Some folks thought so; a few hoped so. Though the once fiery embers of his life had flickered, then extinguished, and Frank's figurative ashes had grown cold, memories of his life and legacy were very much alive. Killing a Ranger, well, regrettably that can happen: Killing the Rangers—as an outfit—preposterous! Adjutant General Mabry, comfortably aware that his responsibility was for all Texans—even those in faraway places and along remote river fronts—after lamenting Captain Frank Jones' death, had a message for the good governor of Texas and the good people of the Lone Star State:

> The members of the ranger force are young, quiet and determined fellows, animated with feelings of pride in the service they render. With the prairies their bed, and the saddle their home, and hands accustomed to the use of the rifle or revolver, they would have no time nor facility for the use of pen to tell of hardships they undergo upon the trail, or the desperate encounters in captures effected, upon the silent plain or in mountain fastness—the usual rendezvous for criminals who would evade the law's punishment for crimes committed.[71]

Finis!

Richard Clayton "Dick" Ware. A veteran Texas Ranger of the horrific shootout with Sam Bass and gang at Round Rock and later sheriff of Mitchell County, Ware would eventually beat Frank Jones out of the coveted job of United States Marshal for the Western District of Texas. FROM *TEXAS RANGER SKETCHES* COURTESY THE AUTHOR ROBERT W. STEPHENS.

Frank Louis Schmid shortly before his 1893 death as a result of the gunshot wound received during the 1889 Jaybird/Woodpecker street-fight at Richmond, Fort Bend County. FROM *TEXAS RANGER SKETCHES* COURTESY THE AUTHOR ROBERT W. STEPHENS.

Another veteran of the Pirate Island episode was Ranger Private Wood Saunders, pictured here armed and ready for war. *Courtesy Nita Stewart Haley Memorial Library & J. Evetts Haley History Center in Midland, Texas.*

Although this photograph was snapped subsequent to the Pirate Island tragedy, one of the participants in that fight is pictured: Edward Dunlap "Eddie" Aten is standing, Winchester in hand, fourth from left. Courtesy Armstrong Ranger Research Center, Texas Ranger Hall of Fame & Museum.

El Paso County Sheriff Frank Simmons. Although many others have been given or taken credit for recovering Frank Jones' body from Mexico, Sheriff Simmons was the Texas official delicately hammering out the details with Mexican officialdom—ultimately meeting with success. *Courtesy Mike Cox.*

Texas Ranger Corporal Carl Kirchner, Company D: A veteran of the horrific battle on Pirate Island that claimed Captain Frank Jones' life. *Courtesy Armstrong Ranger Research Center, Texas Ranger Hall of Fame & Museum.*

Peyton J. Edwards, El Paso County deputy sheriff at the time of the Pirate Island imbroglio and later the multi-term elected sheriff of El Paso County. *Courtesy the Armstrong Ranger Research Center, Texas Ranger Hall of Fame & Museum.*

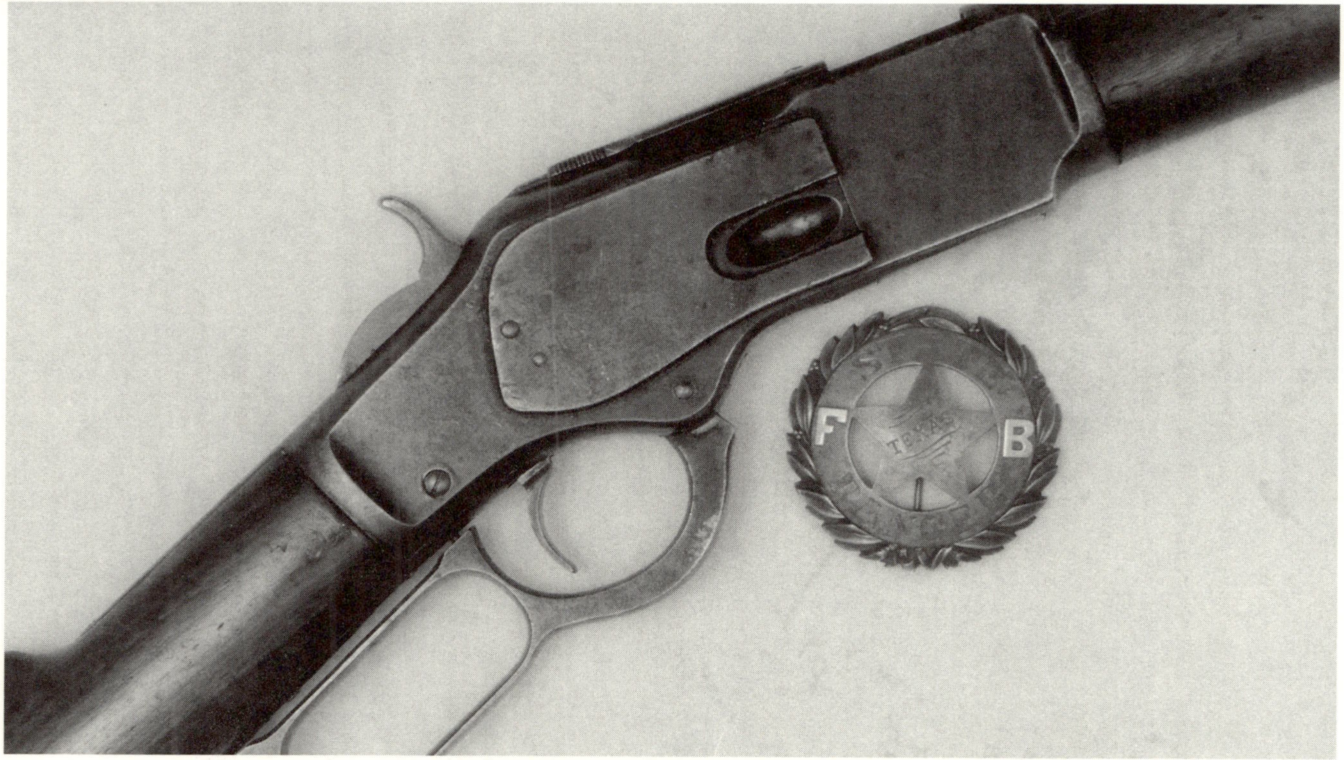

Blood-stained Winchester and jeweler's hand-crafted badge belonging to Captain Frank Jones at the time of his murder on Pirate Island. *Photo Courtesy Donald M. and Louise Yena. Badge and gun owned by well-known Old West collector Kurt House.*

Helen Baylor Jones, yet clothed in mourning attire, holding baby Frank Baylor Jones, the son Frank never saw. *Courtesy Lexie Van Tassel.*

Captain Frank Jones' old-time law enforcing comrades paying their respects at his memorial monument located near Ysleta, Texas. Standing from L to R: Eddie Aten, Ira Aten, and Ed Bryant. A kneeling John Reynolds Hughes is pointing to the carved inscription. Both Eddie Aten and Ed Bryant were six-shooting participants in the ruthless warfare on Pirate Island that claimed Captain Frank Jones' life. *Courtesy the Armstrong Ranger Research Center, Texas Ranger Hall of Fame & Museum.*

Notes

Chapter 1 "Dragged to the Ground Lanced and Scalped"

1. Gregory F. Michno and Susan J. Michno, *Forgotten Fights: Little Known Raids and Skirmishes on the Frontier, 1823–1890*, xxii–xxiii.
2. Luke Gournay, *Texas Boundaries: Evolution of the State's Counties*, 40–41. For exacting details of this historic incursion of Indians through the general area and as far south as the Texas Gulf Coast, see the seminal work of Donaly E. Brice, *The Great Comanche Raid: Boldest Indian Attack of the Texas Republic*. Also, Stephen L. Moore, *Savage Frontier: Rangers, Riflemen, and Indian Wars in Texas, 1840–1841*, Volume 3.
3. Gregory and Susan Michno, *A Fate Worse Than Death: Indian Captivities in the West, 1830–1885*, 79–82.
4. Candice DuCoin, *Lawmen on the Texas Frontier: Rangers and Sheriffs*, quoting William Kenner Jones, 80. Although there may be a slight appearance of negativity, none is intended. Candice DuCoin in her thoughtful and knowledgeable treatment of the Jones family, quite rightly includes a great deal of genealogical data, focusing her research on the lineage's contribution to Texas history, a more than worthwhile project. As a result, the tome's index enumerates 99 separate individuals under the Jones heading. This accounting is imperative for a family history, but not for a narrative like *Six-Shooters and Shifting Sands* with a much narrower focus. For investigative review of redrawing and creation and recreation of county lines the reader is again referred to the index in Gournay's *Texas Boundaries*.
5. A biography of William E. Jones and his service to Texas may be found in *The Encyclopedia of the New West*, William S. Speer, Managing Editor, John Henry Brown, Revising Editor, 579. Also, Frank Brown, *Annals of Travis County and of the City of Austin: From the Earliest Times to the Close of 1875*, 35.
6. John Stribling Moursund, Mabel Stribling, eds., *Blanco County Families*, 244; Hobart Huson, *District Judges of Refugio County*. Chapter 11 is devoted to sketching the life of William E. Jones. Interestingly, within this chapter is a lengthy first-person account by Jones regarding the circumstances of his

capture and subsequent incarceration at Mexico's notorious Perote Prison, 62–68.

7. Richard B. McCaslin, *Fighting Stock: John S. "Rip" Ford of Texas*, 50–51; also, W. J. Hughes, *Rebellious Ranger: Rip Ford and the Old Southwest*, 122–124.
8. Moursund, *Blanco County Families*, 245: "It should be noted that Judge William E. Jones lived on Currys Creek in that part of Blanco County which was taken in 1862 to form the new county of Kendall. He never did reside within the present territorial limits of Blanco County. . . ."; DuCoin, *Lawmen on the Texas Frontier*, 47.
9. Ibid.
10. Robert W. Stephens, *Texas Ranger Sketches*, 63–74. In many writings the nickname of Frank's brother Gerry is given as "Dude." However in this biography the nickname "Dood" will be utilized, as it was when Frank Jones referred to his brother in writings: "I enlisted by brother Dood on the 12th inst." See, Lieutenant Frank Jones to Captain L. P. Sieker, February 20, 1886, Texas State Library and Archives Commission, Austin, Texas, hereafter TSA. The handwriting of Frank Jones is distinct. The tabulation of acreage owned in 1860 is taken directly from Moursund, *Blanco County Families*, 245.
11. A. J. Sowell, *Early Settlers and Indian Fighters of Southwest Texas*, 246.
12. The letter written to the editor of the *Seguin Mercury* on July 21, 1855, by Judge Jones may be found in John Stribling Moursund, *Blanco County History*, 175.
13. Sowell, *Early Settlers and Indian Fighters of Southwest Texas*, 248; DuCoin, *Lawmen on the Texas Frontier*, for the given name of Jesse Lawhon's wife, 53.
14. J. W. Wilbarger, *Indian Depredations In Texas*, 660–661.
15. Robert M. Utley, *Lone Star Justice: The First Century of the Texas Rangers*, 95.
16. Sowell, *Early Settlers and Indian Fighters of Southwest Texas*, 429.
17. Frederick Wilkins, *Defending the Borders: The Texas Rangers, 1848–1861*, 50.
18. Ibid., 45: "There was a sharp increase in Indian attacks along the southwestern Texas frontier during the early summer of 1855, and petitions and calls for help were almost an everyday occurrence in the governor's office."
19. Moursund, *Blanco County History*, 176: "Captain James Callahon [*sic:* Callahan] who lived on the Martin's Fork of the Blanco River, together with the encouragement and support of Judge William E. Jones and other settlers of the entire area, became determined to pursue the Indians to the border. This idea spread rather quickly among the settlers along the frontier. By the latter part of September, a number of men had rallied to the support of Callahan and the Callahan Expedition began to organize with the avowed purpose of pursuing the Indians into Mexico, if need be, to destroy them."

20. Ernest C. Shearer, "The Callahan Expedition, 1855," *Southwestern Historical Quarterly*, April 1951. Specifically Governor Pease did not mention crossing the Rio Grande, but his orders were clear to a person of a military or fighting bent: "It is expected that you will be actively engaged in ranging in their vicinity unless it may become necessary to pursue any marauding parties of Indians that may be found in the neighborhood, in which case you are authorized to follow them up and chastise them *wherever they may be found* [emphasis added]," 432.
21. Ronnie C. Tyler, "The Callahan Expedition of 1855: Indians or Negroes?" *Southwestern Historical Quarterly*, April 1967, 574–585. Historian Tyler explores the intrigues and clandestine machinations within the context of an alleged conspiracy between Texas slaveholders and James Hughes Callahan's excursion into Mexico. While some of the evidence is provocative and well reasoned, to this writer, it seems the primary undertaking of James Callahan's Rangers was to severely punish Indians, and if they stumbled onto runaway slaves during the trip into Mexico, capturing them would not be neglected—but still a secondary goal within the overall operation of making Indians feel the pain of depredating in Texas and seeking refuge in Mexico. Readers may decide.
22. Michael L. Collins, *Texas Devils: Rangers and Regulars on the Lower Rio Grande, 1846–1861*, 79; Shearer, "The Callahan Expedition, 1855," 433.
23. DuCoin, *Lawmen on the Texas Frontier,* 233, for the given name of William Early Jones' first wife.
24. Muster Roll in TSA: "Muster Roll of Capt. William R. Henry's Company of Texas vols called into the Service of the State of Texas by order of his Excellency E.M. Pease and mustered into the service of state by J. H. Callahan for one month unless sooner discharged—at the Leona River, Sept. 15, 1855—and discharged at said place on the 15th of Oct. by said Capt. Callahan." At first blush it might seem that the valuation of Willis H. Jones' armament at $60 was overestimated. However, subsequent to an enlightening September 23, 2013, interview with an expert on arms of the Texas Rangers, Doug Dukes, Liberty Hill, Texas, such queries were more than adequately addressed. At the time in question, 1855, it would not have been uncommon for a Ranger to be armed with as many as three or four percussion cap revolvers, along with a rifle or shotgun—and possibly both. In the aggregate, a $60 valuation is certainly reasonable and not excessive.
25. Governor E. M. Pease to Gentlemen of the Senate and House of Representatives, 22 November 1855, TSA.
26. Shearer, "The Callahan Expedition, 1855," 436–437; Clarence C. Clendenen, *Bloody Border: The United States Army and the Mexican Irregulars*, 19; Darren L. Ivey, The *Texas Rangers: A Registry and History*, 79, 88.

27. Muster Roll, TSA: "Jones, Willis H.—Killed in the battle Escondido Oct. 3rd 1855—and lost horse and arms & equipment"; *Blanco County News*, publisher, John W. Speer, contributor, *Heritage of Blanco County, Texas,* 4: "he [Callahan] was attacked by a body of Indians and Mexicans, had a hard fight, and lost several of his men, among whom was the gallant Willis Jones, the eldest son of Honorable Wm. E. Jones"; the other Rangers killed alongside Willis H. Jones, as enumerated during an October 10, 2013, interview with Christina Stopka, Deputy Director and Head of the Armstrong Research Center, Texas Ranger Hall of Fame and Museum, Waco, Texas, were Augustus Smith, H. K. Holland, and William H. Clopton.
28. Tyler, "The Callahan Expedition of 1855: Indians or Negroes?" page 581: "There is a tradition among the Seminole Negroes even today that their ancestors chased the invaders from Piedras Negras by shooting fire arrows into the houses."
29. Governor Elijah M. Pease to Captain James H. Callahan, October 10, 1855, TSA.
30. Ibid.; Gary Clayton Anderson, *The Conquest of Texas: Ethnic Cleansing in the Promised Land, 1820–1875*, not surprisingly, in light of a preprogrammed schema to always bring an indictment against Texas Rangers, sidesteps any reproach of Callahan's actions at Piedras Negras by Governor Pease. Misleadingly, it would seem, on page 269 Anderson simply characterizes Texas' chief executive's reaction: "In Austin, Governor Pease jubilantly proclaimed the action as heroic and justified." True, he did congratulate Callahan's men for their bravery, but as cited in that same letter in the TSA Governor Pease severely scolded Callahan: "but you [Callahan] had not the right to take possession of or to occupy Piedras Negras or any other village or property of Mexican Citizens. After the termination of your engagement with the Indians you should have returned immediately to this side of the Rio Grande and I trust that you have already done so."
31. Governor Elijah M. Pease to General Persifor F. Smith, Commanding U.S. Army in Texas, October 13, 1855, TSA.
32. John Henry Brown, *Indian Wars and Pioneers of Texas*, 601; John Salmon Ford, Stephen B. Oates, ed., *Rip Ford's Texas*, 215–216; Mike Cox, *The Texas Rangers: Wearing the Cinco Peso, 1821–1900*, 136–139. Interestingly, Collins, *Texas Devils*, devotes a subsection of his coverage of the Callahan Expedition to the raid's aftermath, subtitled "The Fallout." Also worth noting is the author's down-to-earth and refreshingly practical assessment regarding whether or not Callahan was actively chasing after runaway slaves: "The truth shall probably remain buried with Callahan and Henry," 86–88. *¿Quién sabe?*

33. Huson, *District Judges of Refugio County,* 67, quoting the *San Antonio Sentinel* of October 16, 1855.
34. Gregory F. Michno, *Encyclopedia of Indian Wars: Western Battles and Skirmishes, 1850–1890*, 42.
35. Ibid., 43.
36. Telephone interview, Robert W. Stephens, November 24, 2013; DuCoin, *Lawmen on the Texas Frontier*, 50.
37. Michno, *Encyclopedia of Indian Wars*, 47.
38. DuCoin, *Lawmen on the Texas Frontier*. Quoting William Kenner Jones on page 81: "In 1856 our family moved to Austin on account of the dangers from Indians and lived there about eight months. While there my brother, Frank, was born and during that time my half brother, Willis H. Jones, was killed."
39. Stephens, *Texas Ranger Sketches*, 65.
40. Payroll of Captain William R. Henry's Company of State Volunteers, TSA.
41. Michno and Michno, *Forgotten Fights*, 142.
42. Ibid. The fight took place on 13 February 1857; Sowell, *Early Settlers and Indian Fighters of Southwest Texas*, 696–699.
43. Speer, *The Encyclopedia of the New West*, 579.
44. Bob Alexander, *Fearless Dave Allison: Border Lawman*, 19.
45. DuCoin, *Lawmen on the Texas Frontier.* Quoting the diary of a visitor to the Jones ranch on Curry Creek, Hermann Seele: "His twelve year old twins [William Kenner and James Russell] are armed with pistols and are out fetching the horses in this outpost of civilization," 49.
46. Sowell, *Early Settlers and Indian Fighters of Southwest Texas*, 703.
47. W. E. Jones to Governor E. J. Davis, 20 July 1870. Extracted from *Texas Indian Papers, 1860–1916*, by James M. Day and Dorman Winfrey, 324.
48. Alonzo Van Oden, *Texas Ranger's Diary and Scrapbook*, Ann Jensen, ed., 73; interestingly, the renowned exhibition shooter Adolph "Ad" Toepperwein (also Americanized as Topperwein) employed by Winchester Arms Company was from Boerne, Kendall County, Texas. See, Julie Gossell and Tina Little, eds., *Boerne: The History of Our Town*, 48. And, Roy R. Barkley and Mark F. Odintz, eds., *The Portable Handbook of Texas*, 884–885.
49. Huson, *District Judges of Refugio County*, 67; Speer, *The Encyclopedia of the New West*, 579: "He [Judge Jones] opposed annexation to the United States in 1845 and secession from them in 1861, but ever retained the public confidence from the acknowledged sincerity of his character"; during 1861 William E. Jones remarked to diarist Hermann Seele, who elaborated about

the conversation: "We talked about the troubled times. As a true patriot he [Jones] complains about the revolutionary situation which is causing our general feeling of insecurity. He considers the war to be a terrible calamity for the country and fears that the actions of mediocre politicians will seriously damage our freedom and our material wealth."

50. David Paul Smith, *Frontier Defense in the Civil War: Texas Rangers and Rebels*, Map 93, specifics of actions within the Third Frontier District, 156–167.
51. Ibid., 158–159.
52. Michno and Michno, *Forgotten Fights*, 186–187.
53. Ibid.; Sowell, *Early Settlers and Indian Fighters of Southwest Texas*, 564–565: "The forces were exactly even—eleven rangers and eleven Indians. . . . It was what they called in those days homemade powder, or Confederate powder, made in the south. "
54. Stephens, *Texas Ranger Sketches*, 63–64; DuCoin, *Lawmen on the Texas Frontier*, 41, reports Keziah Jones had lost two children, an unnamed baby at birth, and sometime during 1859, Albert Ernest Jones at the age of two and one half years.
55. Enlistment Records for W. E. Jones, May 1861 and February 1864, TSA; Moursund, *Blanco County Families*, 245; Ivey, *The Texas Rangers: A Registry and History*, 134.
56. Smith, *Frontier Defense in the Civil War*, 161, quoting report of General McAdoo.
57. Gregory Michno, *The Settler's War: The Struggle for the Texas Frontier in the 1860s*, xi.
58. Day and Winfrey, *Texas Indian Papers, 1860–1916*, 237–239, Extracted from a letter by W. E. Jones to Governor E. M. Pease, 7 August 1867.
59. Scott Zesch, *The Captured: A True Story of Abduction by Indians on the Texas Frontier*, 68–69.
60. O. C. Fisher, *It Occurred in Kimble*, 123. Dave Johnson, a well-recognized researcher and writer of historical happenings in the Mason County/Llano County region—and probably rightly so—takes issue with the assertion that a "Negro" participated in the brutal Legion Valley Massacre. Johnson to author, October 25, 2003: "No contemporary account mentions this [the presence of a black person], and neither of the two children who survived it made such a mention. . . . All of the contemporary facts indicate that there was no black man involved."
61. Michno and Michno, *A Fate Worse Than Death: Indian Captivities in the West, 1830–1885*, 386–395. Although not name specific, Lillian Bidal in *The Run of the Elk: A Biography of Angie Lydia Hendrix Cleve* writes of what seems to be

the same incident: "The early settlers of the Hill Country of Texas were under constant threat of Indian attack. During an attack on a neighboring family a young mother and her two children were killed. Another woman in the house was scalped. After scalping her, the Indians drove a sharp pointed arrow into her body. Although still alive she didn't flinch. She realized that if she did she would certainly be killed. The woman survived the ordeal, and afterwards always wore a lace cap to hide the ragged scar of her massive head wound," 9.

62. Ibid., 388–389; Wilbarger, *Indian Depredations in Texas,* 635: "we found a large rock, six or eight feet high, Mrs. Johnson's babe, with its brains knocked out."

63. Zesch, *The Captured*, 75.

64. Michno and Michno, *A Fate Worse Than Death*, 389. In a less than compelling treatment, Anderson in *The Conquest of Texas,* somewhat anemically proffers a twisted rationale for Comanches killing kidnapped children: "The murder of Mrs. Harris's three-month-old child, however, attests to a certain level of cruelty the Texans could never understand. Because of the long route home—from the Nueces River to New Mexico—the Indians knew the baby would never survive. He might also cry at an inopportune moment and give the party away," 137. Perhaps not satisfied that he has tendered a coherent explanation for Comanches killing infants, Anderson expounds, but once more seems to step on the neck of his own excuse making: "The savagery of such treatment was seldom lost on Texans. But the logic of it, from the Indian standpoint, is reasonable when considering the nature of Plains tribal societies. Indians too lost children; perhaps only one in two Indian babies lived to the age of three. With infant mortality extremely high, the loss of many of their own likely diminished the value of Anglo babies to the Indians. It likely even led to an acceptance of the notion that life began when a child could talk (rather than cry) and walk. Such children had economic value; they could pick berries or carry water. Infants took labor to keep alive," 137. Anderson does not cite sources for his infant mortality rates for Plains Indians in *The Conquest of Texas*. Though we cannot know for sure, it's a reasonably safe bet that three-year-old Nancy Johnson could walk and talk—but apparently her Comanche captors discounted her having any "economic value" and murdered her anyway. Testing the author's logic in this instance is not trying. If taking helpless babies was to be so problematic and had the potential to give war parties away, why take them in the first place? Though not wishing to be too pedestrian, isn't the definition of insanity consistently doing something time and again, but expecting different results? Nursing infants and dependent toddlers could hardly furnish meaningful intelligence to settlers striking out in pursuit of fleeing raiders. Second-rate excuse making is nearly always wobbly. Assuredly, on another front, the writer's generalized appraisal is

spot-on correct: Texans didn't "understand" the policy of murdering babies. The instances wherein Texans killed Indian children and, sadly, there were those cases, the unambiguous acts merit no conjectured defense. The hand that murders crying children is not clean, regardless of ethnicity—even apart from any engineered excuse making.

65. Ibid., 389. For a cogent reality check the reader is referred to the Michnos' final chapter, "Conclusions." Quite sagaciously the authors have pitched "political correctness" overboard, focusing—as historians and nonfiction writers should do—simply on "correctness." The authors' unvarnished study, sans any "sugarcoating, distortions, or denials," is a refreshing treatment. Their critique of more recent literature on the topic and its craftily designed misinformation is solidly grounded by strict application of two fundamentals: Solid evidence and sound interpretative logic. These basics seem elusive—not surprisingly though—to a cadre of raconteurs owning preprogrammed and partisan agendas. Zesch, *The Captured* is another chronicler not suffering from a compulsion to make artificial arguments at the expense of truth: "Minnie was present when her captors brutally terrorized, raped, and butchered her half sister, niece, and three cousins," 85. Likewise, S. C. Gwynne, *Empire of the Summer Moon: Quanah Parker and the Rise and Fall of the Comanches, the Most Powerful Indian Tribe in American History*, is not shy and retiring with the truth: "when Minnie's two aunts were raped and tortured as they wept and prayed aloud," 106.

66. Ibid., 390; James Wilson Nichols, *Now You Hear My Horn: The Journal of James Wilson Nichols, 1820–1887*, Catherine W. McDowell, ed., amplifies: "Crossing over the top of a cedar mountain they left the young lady dead and scalped, and she had been cruely [*sic*] outraged and her mangled body lay on the ground with her feete [*sic*] and hands tied to stakes," 165. Again, Anderson, *The Conquest of Texas*, less than persuasively avers: "While the women were quite safe then from sexual assault—and the captivity narratives demonstrate this—the raiding party would observe the time-honored ritual that Comanches had practiced for over a century," 135. Anderson further asserts, absent citation: "While the conduct of some raiders remained similar to that of earlier raids, other war parties in the 1860s and 1870s exhibited considerably more brutality. The increased violence may be explained by the fact that sometimes comancheros joined the raids, while at other times, the raiding parties were mixtures of warriors from various bands that included some renegades, some of whom were livestock dealers. In either case, the traditional Indian mechanisms that previously had limited violence mostly to men at times became inoperable," 348. Apparently because it's somewhat inconvenient for maintaining a weak thesis from the get-go, Anderson offers

this characterization: "The captivity narrative—often a short re-creation of some supposed Indian attack—became a staple of American reading," 37–38. Creditably, the Michnos, in *A Fate Worse Than Death*, explore the issue of sexual abuse by examining several of the modern-era politically correct treatments of the "captivity narratives." Their insight into certain authors' selectivity and purposeful omissions is illuminating. See pages 457–480. The writing team also identifies by name a more than significant number of Indian captives in a multi-page appendix: Not just a few of these folks, if they could, no doubt would be puzzled to refer to their sudden and violent abductions and involuntary confinements and murders of their infants as the culmination of a "supposed" Indian attack. Delicately sidestepping the hard truth is commonplace for certain nonfiction chroniclers, those trying to downplay the horrors and hardships inflicted on Indian captives. Kidnapping is not an act of compassion—anywhere, anytime! Likewise, it was not necessarily always hostile Indians that participated in gang rape. Noted Texas frontiersman and veteran Indian fighter Cicero Rufus Perry cites an example, one where he and his comrade looked the other way. With but minimal grammatical editing, Perry wrote: "the next day Stuc a trail and (followed) them to the Newaces[.] we kild too and tuc one Squa[.] got all of their outfit[.] the way the friendly Indians did to ceap hur was to Sleap with hur each one evry night as their time come[.] young Flaceo toald mee to tell Coln Lewis hee and mee could sleap with hur when thay all went around as hee was commander and I interpertor but wee did not but let them have hur to them selves[.]" See, C. R. Perry, *Memoir of Capt'n C. R. Perry of Johnson City, Texas: A Texas Veteran*, Kenneth Kesselus, ed., 13–14.

67. *San Antonio Daily Express*, March 34, 1868. Full text of Friend's letter to the newspaper may be accessed in Charles L. Kenner, *The Comanchero Frontier: A History of New Mexican-Plains Indian Relations*, 170.

68. Wilbarger, *Indian Depredations in Texas*, 633. Not surprisingly, Anderson, *The Conquest of Texas*, opts for whatever reason, not to even mention the Legion Valley raid and the subsequent abductions, sexual assaults, and murders carried out by Indians. The glaring omission is enough to make a nonpartisan writer and/or researcher "howl in pain" not just those "devoted to the [Texas] Ranger version of history" but, alas, at the expense of legit history. Clayton cleverly brushes across two years with dexterity, though unquestionably less than admirably or chronologically inclusive: "More violent attacks occurred in Texas in 1867 and in 1868, one of the worst years on record," 349. Assuredly, Matilda Friend, Lee Temple Friend, Fielty Johnson, Samantha Johnson, Nancy Johnson, Rebecca Johnson, Amanda Townsend, and Minne Caudle would concur—1868 was a bad year.

69. Sowell, *Early Settlers and Indian Fighters of Southwest Texas*, 700.
70. Ibid.
71. DuCoin, *Lawmen on the Texas Frontier*, 55–57. Emmett Jones, though but seven years old at the time of the incident, wrote this account for publication in the *San Antonio Express* on December 27, 1924, more than half a century after it took place.
72. Perry, *Memoir of Capt'n C. R. Perry Of Johnson City, Texas*, 28; Nichols, *Now You Hear My Horn*, supplements Perry's remarks: "This band of savages kilt [*sic*] and scalped ten persons and scalped Mrs. Friend alive. . . . Now nearly all of these raids was mad [*sic*] by Comanche Indians and nearly all mad in broad daylight. Other counties adjoining Blanco, especially the counties north and west, suffered about the same as Blanco, but as the saying is, 'let every dog shake his own tail,' I shall not shake it for them as I was not connected nor was I familer [*sic*] with but few of the outrages commited [sic] in other counties. I shall not attempt to cronical [*sic*] any of them except a few in Kerr and Gelispie [*sic*] counties which is too atrocious to leave out," 166.
73. Winfrey and Day, *Indian Papers of Texas and the Southwest, 1860–1916*, 326. Quite unfortunately old-time Texas Ranger Daniel Webster Roberts, writing his little classic, *Rangers and Sovereignty*, somehow—and no doubt innocently—confuses the killing of the Felpses with another which would spark action on his part and that of fellow settlers in 1872, a date he was also inadvertently mistaken about. Nonfiction writers—this one included—have in the past simply relied on Roberts' delightful little book at their own peril, or at least at historical accuracy's peril.
74. Ibid.
75. Capt. Dan W. Roberts, *Rangers and Sovereignty*, 20.
76. Wilbarger, *Indian Depredations in Texas*, 643. Alexander "Buck" Roberts, the father of Dan Roberts, a future Ranger Captain, penned a letter to the *Austin Republican*, August 4, 1869, highlighting the murder of Tom and Eliza Felps. Burnet County resident A. M. Cox, at least according to an editor for the *Austin Republican*, commented: "This party consisted of fifteen or twenty Indians. White men are supposed to be with them." See, Moursand, *Blanco County History*, 182–183.
77. Ann Patton Baenziger, "The Texas State Police During Reconstruction: A Reexamination," *Southwestern Historical Quarterly*, April 1969, 473.
78. W. E. Jones to Governor E. J. Davis, 20 July 1870. Extracted from Day and Winfrey, *Texas Indian Papers, 1860–1916*: "By a newspaper recd yesterday I see that you were kind enough to nominate me to the Senate for the position of District Judge. I thank you for this mark of confidence. I have no information as to the action of the Senate upon the nomination—Our mails here are badly

tangled & we are behind in the matter of news—Should the Senate have confirmed the nomination I hope to show by the administration of the laws that the confidence referred has not been misplaced," 325. DuCoin, *Lawmen on the Texas Frontier*, 38. As late as August, according to the Federal Census of 1870, the William E. Jones family were enumerated as residents of Kendall County, Precinct No. 3, Spring Branch Post Office. The letter cited above references "Hodges Mills, Kendall Co." The discrepancy is explainable: The Hodges Mill PO "on Guadalupe and Curry Creek, was in Blanco County when created in 1858." During the Civil War the Spring Branch PO suspended operations until U.S. Mail service was again established between New Braunfels and Fredericksburg in Gillespie County during July 1866. See Oscar Haas, *History of New Braunfels and Comal County, Texas, 1844–1946*, 132–133.

79. *Cleburne Chronicle*, April 12, 1873.
80. Carl H. Moneyhon, *Edmund J. Davis: Civil War General, Republican Leader, Reconstruction Governor*. 168–169; Carl H. Moneyhon, *Texas After the Civil War: The Struggle of Reconstruction*, 131–132; Otis A. Singletary, "The Texas Militia During Reconstruction," *Southwestern Historical Quarterly*, July 1956, 25–26: "In order to offset such defections, the Radicals assured passage of their two bills by having several conservative senators placed under arrest and excluded from the chamber while the vote was being taken."
81. Barry A. Crouch and Donaly E. Brice, *The Governor's Hounds: The Texas State Police, 1870–1873*, 27. The authors point out that the following year, 1871, the legislature revised and amended the enabling legislation: "The force would now comprise a chief, 6 captains, 12 lieutenants, 30 sergeants, and 210 privates. Base pay remained the same, but each officer received an additional $30 per month, noncommissioned officers $25, and privates $20 as compensation for use of their horses and arms and in lieu of all traveling expenses," 28.
82. Kenneth W. Howell, ed., *Still the Arena of the Civil War: Violence and Turmoil in Reconstruction Texas, 1865–1874*. Contributor and author of Chapter 6, Donaly Brice, "Finding a Solution to Reconstruction Violence: The Texas State Police," 192; Moneyhon, *Texas after the Civil War: The Struggle of Reconstruction*, 132.

Chapter 2 "Beneath the Heel of an Indignant Legislature"

1. Utley, *Lone Star Justice*, 136.
2. Ibid.
3. Zesch, *The Captured*, 17–19.
4. Ibid., 90–104; Hugh D. Corwin, *Comanche and Kiowa Captives in Oklahoma and Texas*, 187.

5. W. E. Jones to Governor E. J. Davis, 20 July 1870. Extracted from Day and Winfrey, *Texas Indian Papers, 1860–1916*, 325.
6. General Order No. 3, Headquarters State of Texas, Adjutant General's Office, An Act to Provide for the Protection of the Frontier, Austin, Texas, August 3, 1870. The terminology "Texas Rangers" is actually a part of Section 1, TSA.
7. Ibid., Section 11, TSA. "That the troops raised under and by virtue of this act shall be governed by the rules and regulations of the army of the United States, so far as the same may be applicable, but shall always be and remain subject to the authority of the State of Texas for frontier service."
8. Ibid., Section 1, TSA.
9. Ibid., Section 5. At the time, the handgun described would have been the Colt's Model 1860 Army, .44 caliber percussion (cap and ball) revolver.
10. Ibid., Section 4, TSA.
11. Stephens, *Texas Ranger Sketches*, 74; Sammy Tise, *Texas County Sheriffs*, 300; Frederick Wilkins, *The Law Comes to Texas: The Texas Rangers, 1870–1901*, 359.
12. Utley, *Lone Star Justice*, 138.
13. Alfred D. Evans, Paymaster, State of Texas, Frontier Forces: Certification of Pay and Deductions for James R. Jones, Sergeant, Company C, March 10, 1871, TSA. Final Statement of James R. Jones, Sergeant, of Capt. John W. Sansom's Company C, Frontier Forces, Camp Verde, Texas, 5th day of March, signed "John W. Sansom," TSA.
14. Muster Roll, Frontier Force, Company C, 1870, John W. Sansom, Commanding, TSA.
15. Cox, *The Texas Rangers: Wearing the Cinco Peso, 1821–1900*, 193.
16. *Daily State Journal*, August 19, 1870; Captain Franklin Jones to Adjutant General James Davidson, August 8, 1870. Interestingly, this letter indicates there was a fierce—and apparently bitter—competition between company commanders to enlist recruits, filling their ranks to the authorized staffing level, TSA.
17. *Daily State Journal*, August 24, 1870. "Captain [Franklin] Jones was for thirteen years a captive among the Comanches, and knows their ways and their manners."
18. *Daily State Journal*, October 15, 1870. This set of articles from the *Daily State Journal* courtesy Chuck Parsons.
19. Cox, *The Texas Rangers: Wearing the Cinco Peso, 1821–1900*, 195; Wilkins, *The Law Comes to Texas*, 10–12.

20. John W. Sansom, Company C, Frontier Forces, Camp Verde, Texas, to Adjutant General James Davidson, November 26, 1870, TSA; Franklin Jones, Company A, Frontier Forces, Mason, Texas: "Report of a Scout from Fort Mason to Fort Concho" during the month of October 1870. Courtesy the Texas Ranger Research Center, Texas Ranger Hall of Fame & Museum, Waco, Texas. Hereafter TRHF&M.
21. Utley, *Lone Star Justice*, 139.
22. DuCoin, *Lawmen on the Texas Frontier,* 38.
23. Wilkins, *The Law Comes to Texas*, 359–362.
24. Muster and Payrolls, Kendall County Minutemen, J. C. Nowlin, Commanding, TSA.
25. DuCoin, *Lawmen on the Texas Frontier.* 97–98; Muster and Payrolls, Company C, Kendall County Minutemen, TSA.
26. Crouch and Brice, *The Governor's Hounds*, 48–49.
27. Howell, *Still the Arena of Civil War*, 192.
28. Alwyn Barr, *Reconstruction to Reform: Texas Politics, 1876–1906,* 8: "The Davis administration, which lasted four years, continuously suffered from political bickering. Democrats charged extravagance and gross abuse of power, especially in appointments, control of the state police, and declarations of martial law. Davis found himself plagued with a variety of difficult problems such as frontier protection, lawlessness, widespread refusal to pay taxes, and bitter political opposition."
29. Sergeant J. M. Redmon, Texas State Police, to Texas Adjutant General F. L. Britton, February 17, 1873, TSA.
30. Crouch and Brice, *The Governor's Hounds*, 174–177.
31. Baenziger, "The Texas State Police During Reconstruction: A Reexamination," 477.
32. Bob Alexander, *Winchester Warriors: The Rangers of Company D, 1874–1901*, 6–7.
33. Clarence P. Denman, "The Office of Adjutant General in Texas, 1835–1881," *Southwestern Historical Quarterly*, July 1925, 317.
34. Crouch and Brice, *The Governor's Hounds*, 142–143.
35. Ibid. The facts belong to Crouch and Brice, the interpretation to this author.
36. David Johnson, *The Horrell Wars: Feuding in Texas and New Mexico.* Chapter 3 "The Lampasas Horror" is a proficient examination and analysis of the shooting wherein the Texas State Policemen were killed; Philip J. Rasch, "The Horrell War," *New Mexico Historical Review*, July 1956, 23. For quotation,

Frederick Nolan's *Bad Blood: The Life and Times of the Horrell Brothers*, 16–17. Alexander, *Winchester Warriors*, 2–3.

37. Clifford R. Caldwell and Ron DeLord, *Texas Lawmen: The Good and the Bad, 1835–1899*, 370–371; Program, *The Thirteenth Biennial Texas Peace Officers' Memorial Services*, Texas State Capitol, Austin, Texas. May 1–2, 2011, 67.
38. Insert for the *Dallas Daily Herald* of April 22, 1873.
39. *Austin Democratic Daily Statesman*, August 17, 1872.
40. Roberts, *Rangers and Sovereignty*, 20–21. Again, a note of caution: Dan Roberts implies this meeting at his daddy's home was a result of the murder of Tom and Eliza Felps. It was not, they being murdered on July 22, 1869. Roberts says after the Felps murders, "We did not have to wait long after the council of war was held. Within just a few days the report was received that the Indians were in the country to the north of us and were moving south." See page 21.
41. *Austin Daily Democratic Statesman*, August 17, 1872. Though Roberts would later write in *Rangers and Sovereignty* that the Deer Creek Fight took place in 1873, his memory was innocently mistaken or there was a simple typographical error. This 1872 edition of the Austin newspaper clearly references the participants and even mentions the wounds received by Roberts and Bird. Robert W. Stephens, *Texas Ranger Captain Dan Roberts: The Untold Story,* after dutifully competent investigation correctly determined the date of the Deer Creek Fight and so published, 5, 9 n. 15.
42. Roberts, *Rangers and Sovereignty*, 21–26; Ella Elgar Bird Dumont, Tommy J. Boley, ed., *Ella Elgar Bird Dumont: An Autobiography of a West Texas Pioneer*, 218–219. Though Dan Roberts offers a list of participants from his remembrances, that enumeration is supplemented by accessing Gammel, *The Laws of Texas*, Volume VII. "[No.8.] Joint Resolution Awarding Winchester Rifles to Certain Persons," 677.
43. *Austin Daily Democratic Statesman*, August 8, 1875. The date of the citation is correct, this edition, in part, recounts part of the drama surrounding the 1872 clash.
44. Roberts, *Rangers and Sovereignty*, 24. The *Austin Daily Democratic Statesman* of August 17, 1872, notes this fight and Dan Roberts' injury: "the Perdinales, where they ambushed ten men and a fight ensued, in which Mr. Dan Roberts was wounded in the thigh, young Buck Roberts shot through the nose, and Jo Bird, a son of Capt. bird of Birdville, slightly wounded."
45. Stephens, *Texas Ranger Captain Dan Roberts: The Untold Story*, 5–8; Alexander, *Winchester Warriors*, 10–11.
46. Roberts, *Rangers and Sovereignty*, 25–26.

47. H. P. N. Gammel, *The Laws of Texas, 1822–1897*, 10 vols., 7: 677–678; John Sayles and Henry Sayles, eds., *Early Laws of Texas: General Laws From 1836 to 1879*, Vol. III, 220: "JOINT RESOLUTION awarding Winchester rifles to certain persons," 220; Roberts, *Rangers and Sovereignty*, credits Texas State Senator H. C. King with introducing "a bill which provided for a gun to be given to each one of us who participated in the fight. . . ," 26. The primary source records as indicated in this citation, do not mention individual sponsors' names.
48. Wilbarger, *Indian Depredations in Texas*, 638–642; Alexander, *Winchester Warriors*, 11–12.
49. Michno, *Encyclopedia of Indian Wars*, 272–273; Alexander, *Winchester Warriors*, 40; William Sturtevant Nye, *Carbine and Lance: The Story of Old Fort Sill, 182–183*; Thomas T. Smith, *The Old Army in Texas: A Research Guide to the U.S. Army in Nineteenth-Century Texas*, 156–157.
50. Rick Miller, *Texas Ranger John B. Jones and the Frontier Battalion, 1874–1881*. Quoting a portion of Governor Coke's Inaugural Address on page 26.
51. General Laws of the State of Texas, Fourteenth Legislative Session, 1874: Chapter LXVIII; Gammel, *The Laws of Texas*, 8: 86.
52. Ibid.; Harold J. Weiss, Jr., "Organized Constabularies: The Texas Rangers and the Early State Police Movement in the American Southwest," *Journal of the West*, January 1995, 28–29.
53. Alexander, *Winchester Warriors*, 15–17.
54. Ibid., 21; George Durham, *Taming the Nueces Strip: The Story of McNelly's Rangers*, 20–21; Bob Alexander, *Riding Lucifer's Line: Ranger Deaths along the Texas-Mexico Border*, 44.
55. Ibid., 27.
56. Frontier Battalion, General Order No. 2, Adjutant General William H. Steele, May 6, 1874, TSA.
57. Ibid.
58. Alexander, *Winchester Warriors*, 29; Ben Proctor, *Just One Riot: Episodes of Texas Rangers in the 20th Century*, 23: "On September 1, 1988, forty-one-year-old Lee Roy Young, a fourteen-year veteran who was a DPS investigator in San Antonio, became the first black appointee in Ranger history, and on January 1, 1989 was joined by thirty-five-year-old Earl Ray Pearson, formerly a Highway Patrol sergeant, who proudly pinned on the Ranger badge"; Robert M. Utley, *Lone Star Lawmen: The Second Century of the Texas Rangers*, 315. Interestingly, the modern-era retired Texas Ranger Lee Young (with Nita Thurman) published his autobiography, *Lee Young: Memoirs of a Black Seminole Texas Ranger*.

59. *Waco Daily Examiner*, March 12, 1874.
60. Certainly and—thankfully—historians and Texas Ranger enthusiasts now have a definitive biography of the Frontier Battalion's first commander in the award-winning book by distinguished Old West researcher and writer Rick Miller, *Texas Ranger John B. Jones and the Frontier Battalion, 1874–1881*. Some of the light controversy concerning the appointment of Jones is spotlighted by Miller on pages 32–37.
61. Frontier Battalion, General Order No. 1, May 7 1874, TSA.
62. DuCoin, *Lawmen on the Texas Frontier,* 73.

Chapter 3"We Fought under the Black Flag"

1. Stephens, *Texas Ranger Sketches*, 73–5; DuCoin, *Lawmen on the Texas Frontier,* 73–76.
2. Michno, *Encyclopedia of Indian Wars*, 276–278; G. Derek West, "The Battle of Adobe Walls—1874," *English-Westerners' Brand Book*, January, 1962, 2–12.
3. Miller, *Texas Ranger John B. Jones*, 49–63.
4. Nye, *Carbine and Lance*, 200. Inexplicably it seems, Anderson, *The Conquest of Texas*, neglects to include mention of this, the Frontier Battalion's first clash with Indians and the Kiowa's beheading and disemboweling of Ranger Dave Bailey. Certainly with a predetermined agenda of pillorying Texas Rangers, the Kiowa mutilations of Private Bailey do—at least somewhat—become problematic and/or inconvenient.
5. Ed Carnal, "Reminiscences of a Texas Ranger," *Frontier Times*, December 1923, 24. Dutifully it must be reported that on occasion Texans, including Texas Rangers, were not simply satisfied with a scalp, not according to a snippet in the *Austin Daily Statesman*, November 28, 1874:

   > The boys brought some fresh scalps with them and they report that [Texas Ranger] Scott Cooley, who was fired at and run into camp, not only cut a wounded Indian's throat, but stripped a large piece of skin from his back, saying that he would make a quirt out of it.

   For other assertions that Rangers went further than just scalping fallen Indians, readers are referred to Glen Smith, "Some Early Runnels County History, 1858–1885," *West Texas Historical Association Yearbook*, 1966, 116.
6. Alexander, *Winchester Warriors*, 51–52.
7. Ibid., 53.
8. Major John B. Jones to Adjutant General William Steele, December 1, 1874, TSA.

9. Utley, *Lone Star Justice*, 150; Wilkins, *The Law Comes to Texas*, strikes the hammer of truth across the anvil: "Although the honors went to the Kiowa. . . ," 46.
10. Walter Prescott Webb, *The Story of the Texas Rangers*. Though Webb was largely responsible for building a twentieth-century mystique for the Rangers, in this later work, he had rethought and readjusted some of his earlier opinions. In relation to this imbroglio Webb concluded: "The fight at Lost Valley was a bad start for the Frontier Battalion," 68. Miller, in the updated and scrupulously honest appraisal of Jones, *Texas Ranger John B. Jones*, not hesitatingly deduced: "Jones' first conflict as commander of the Frontier Battalion can probably be rightfully criticized," 60. James Farber, *Texans With Guns*, credits closing darkness with saving Jones and his men: "Only the nightfall saved the Rangers," 107; Bern Keating, *An Illustrated History of the Texas Rangers* was not of two minds: ". . . Lone Wolf who dealt the Rangers one of their rare defeats . . . The battle at Lost Valley. . . ," 103.
11. Nye, *Carbine and Lance*, 236; Michno, *Encyclopedia of Indian Wars*, 291.
12. Major John B. Jones to Adjutant General William Steele, May 9, 1875, TSA.
13. Ibid. Andrew R. Graybill, *Policing the Great Plains: Rangers, Mounties, and the North American Frontier, 1875–1910*, 45. The reader interested in the comparative analysis of Mounties and Texas Rangers might also wish to access Eddie T. Woodard's "A Compare Contrast Study of the History of the R.C.M.P and the Texas Rangers and the Public Service Records of Personnel," presented to the Texas Ranger Hall of Fame & Museum, Waco, Texas, on April 11, 1992, and archived at the institution's Tobin and Anne Armstrong Texas Ranger Research Center.
14. Major Jones to AG Steele, May 9, 1875, TSA.
15. Miller, *Texas Ranger John B. Jones*, 99–100; Michno, *Encyclopedia of Indian Wars*, 291; Nye, *Carbine and Lance*, 236; Walter Prescott Webb, *The Texas Rangers: A Century of Frontier Defense*, 317.
16. Moursund, *Blanco County History*, 179–181.
17. Michno, *Encyclopedia of Indian Wars*, 291; Marion Humphreys Farrow, *Troublesome Times in Texas*. Quoting Major John B. Jones' description: "Another was a half-breed or quarter, & spoke broken English, was quite fair and had curly auburn hair," see page 65.
18. Ibid.; Miller, *Texas Ranger John B. Jones*, reports that it was the post surgeon at Fort Richardson that ordered the beheading of the Indians. See page 101. In his May 9, 1875, report to AG Steele, Major Jones does not mention cutting off the heads of any Indians, simply saying: ". . . . I must record it to their [Rangers] credit that they did not stop to scalp and plunder the Indians that was killed, as is too often done in such fights, but continued the rout

until the last Indians in sight was killed," TSA; Nye, *Carbine and Lance* is not confused: "the troops at Fort Richardson were asked to verify the fact that these were Indians. The soldiers therefore cut off the heads of the Indians, preserved them in jars of alcohol, and sent them to Washington," 236.

19. Ibid.; Graybill, *Policing the Great Plains*, 45: "Jones suspected that they had come from a reservation because they were well clothed and carried blankets bearing the initials of the U.S. Interior Department. . . ."
20. Michno and Michno, *Forgotten Fights*. "The posse considered the paper to be proof of what Texans already knew to be fact: reservation Indians were being protected in Indian Territory, but they continued to steal and kill in Texas," 298.
21. *Austin Daily Democratic Statesman*, August 25, 1875.
22. Dumont, *Ella Elgar Bird Dumont: An Autobiography of a West Texas Pioneer*. Tom Bird's presentation Winchester 1873, .44–40, SN 3518, with a silver inlaid shield in the stock, engraved with the wording, "Awarded to J. T. Bird by the XIII Legislature" is on display at the Panhandle-Plains Museum, Canyon, Texas. 157–158; Roberts, *Rangers and Sovereignty*, remarked about ownership of his specially awarded Winchester: "I have my gun yet, and I hardly need to add that it is among the most treasured of all my possessions," 26.
23. *Austin Daily Democratic Statesman*, August 25, 1875; *Austin Weekly Democratic Statesman*, August 26, 1875.
24. Payroll Records, Frank Jones, December 2, 1875, TSA; Frances T. Ingmire, *Texas Ranger Service Records, 1847–1900*, 3: 80; Major Jones to Adjutant General William Steel, May 9, 1875: "The courage and coolness of Lieutenant Ira Long was admirable during the whole day. When his horse was killed he fell very near to an Indian who had just been dismounted and instantly attacked him with his gun clubbed, and would have finished him on the spot, if the savage had not been 'an expert at dodging.' As soon as he could procure another horse, he joined in the pursuit again," TSA. A brief biographical sketch of Lieutenant Ira Long may be accessed in Robert W. Stephens' *Texas Ranger Indian War Pensions*, 64.
25. Stephens, *Texas Ranger Sketches*, 71.
26. Miller, *Texas Ranger John B. Jones*, 107, 110.
27. Payroll Records, Frank Jones, December 2, 1875, TSA.
28. James L. Haley, *The Buffalo War: The History of the Red River Uprising of 1874*.
29. Certainly the seminal study of the conflict is David Johnson's *The Mason County "Hoo Doo" War, 1874–1902*, an exhaustive multi-year research effort culminating in a first-rate factual accumulation and smart analysis of the feud and its aftermath.

30. Ibid., 91–95; Dave Johnson, "G. W. Gladden—Hard Luck Warrior," *National Association For Outlaw/Lawman History Quarterly* (NOLA), July-September 1991, 3.
31. Henry M. Holmes to Governor Richard Coke, September 8, 1875, TSA.
32. Major Jones to Lieutenant G. W. Stevens, Frontier Battalion, Company B, September 17, 1875, TSA.
33. Major Jones to Lieutenant B. S. Foster, Frontier Battalion, Company E, September 17, 1875, TSA.
34. Miller, *Texas Ranger John B. Jones*, 112.
35. Major Jones to AG Steele, September 28, 1875, TSA: "Sir, your courier with orders to send troops to Mason reached me at a late hour night before last . . ."; Henry M. Holmes to Governor Coke, September 8, 1875, TSA.
36. Major Jones to AG Steele, October 28, 1875, TSA; Johnson, *The Mason County "Hoo Doo" War*, 110; David Johnson, *John Ringo: King of the Cowboys—His Life and Times From the Hoo Doo War to Tombstone*, 87.
37. Major Jones to AG Steele, September 28, 1875, TSA.
38. Ibid.; Miller, *Texas Ranger John B. Jones*, 113.
39. Ibid.
40. Major Jones to AG Steele, September 30, 1875, TSA; Johnson, *John Ringo: King of the Cowboys*, 88.
41. Frontier Battalion Monthly Return, Company A, September 1875, TSA: Major Jones to AG Steele, September 30, 1875, TSA.
42. Ibid.
43. Walter Struve, *Germans in Texas: Commerce, Migration, and Culture in the Days of the Lone Star Republic*, 3–10.
44. Alexander, *Winchester Warriors*, 63–64.
45. Charles Kenner, "Guardians in Blue: The Untied States Cavalry and the Growth of the Texas Range Cattle Industry," *Journal of the West*, January 1995, 48.
46. *San Antonio Daily Herald*, June 16, 1876.
47. J. Frank Dobie, *Cow People*, 18.
48. Glenn James and Henri Rupe Capps, *The Life of Thomas W. Gamel*, 13.
49. C. L. Sonnichsen, *Ten Texas Feuds*, 91.
50. Ibid.
51. As would be anticipated, the inaction of a Texas Ranger during the mobbing and subsequent lynching of prisoners has drawn various but not necessarily conflicting opinions from numerous writers, such as *The Mason County*

"Hoo Doo" War by Johnson; *Texas Ranger John B. Jones* by Miller; *Winchester Warriors* by Alexander; *Texas Ranger Captain Dan Roberts* by Stephens; and Chuck Parsons and Donaly E. Brice, *Texas Ranger N.O. Reynolds: The Intrepid* who suggest: "Strangely Lieutenant Roberts made no report to Major Jones or Adjutant General Steele of his involvement in resisting the mob's action that night in Mason. Possibly he chose not to due to his obvious ineffectiveness," 52. Quite interestingly in Texas Ranger folklore there is the oft repeated parable that "A Texas Ranger would charge Hell with a bucket of water." Perhaps Harold J. Weiss, Jr. writing a piece for the April 1994 edition of *Southwestern Historical Quarterly*, "The Texas Rangers Revisited: Old Themes and New Viewpoints," knocks a homerun of reality concerning common sense and professionalism, writing that sometimes it's but smart to "call for more Rangers and more buckets," 640. This situation would have qualified.

52. Major Jones to AG Steele, September 30, 1875, TSA.
53. Petition from citizens of Loyal Valley, Mason County, to Major Jones, October 4, 1875, TSA.
54. Special Order No. 46. Frontier Battalion. October 6, 1875, TSA.
55. Lieutenant Dan Roberts, Company D, Frontier Battalion, to Major Jones, March 1, 1875, TSA.
56. Monthly Return, Company D, Frontier Battalion, October 1875, TSA; Special Order No. 47, October 7, 1875, TSA; Special Order No. 48, October 11, 1875, TSA.
57. Major Jones to AG Steele, October 28, 1875, TSA: "I have made twenty two arrests since I have been here."
58. Major Jones to AG Steele, October 20, 1875, TSA.
59. Monthly Returns, Company A, Frontier Battalion, September, October, and November 1875, TSA.
60. Major Jones to AG Steele, October 20, 1875, TSA.
61. Major Jones to AG Steele, October 28, 1875, TSA.
62. Ibid.
63. Stephens, *Texas Ranger Sketches*, 71.
64. Lieutenant Ira Long to Major Jones, December 31, 1875, TSA; Stephens, *Texas Ranger Indian War Pensions*, 5, 64; Tise, *Texas County Sheriffs*, 549; Monthly Return, Company A, Frontier Battalion, January 1875, TSA. The above letter to Major Jones, as cited, indicates that Corporal Nelson was in charge of the detail. The Monthly Return enumerates Sergeant (Kossuth) Aycock as the noncom in command. A hurried last-minute change in plans would rectify—and *probably* was—responsible for the discrepancy.

65. G. W. Todd to Major Jones, December 14, 1875, TSA.
66. Special Order No. 52, Frontier Battalion, December 14, 1875, TSA.
67. Lieutenant Long to Major Jones, December 20, 1875, TSA.
68. Lieutenant Long to Major Jones, December 26, 1875, TSA.
69. Petition to Adjutant General Steele, signed James M. Hunter, President, January 27, 1876, TSA.
70. Monthly Return, Company A, Frontier Battalion, August 1876, TSA.
71. Major Jones to AG Steele, April 13, 1876, TSA; Monthly Return, Company A, Frontier Battalion, April 1876, TSA.
72. Lieutenant Long to Major Jones, April 3, 1876, TSA; Major Jones to AG Steele, April 13, 1876, TSA.
73. Monthly Return, Company A, Frontier Battalion, May 1876, TSA.
74. Major Jones to Lieutenant Long, June 13, 1876, TSA.
75. Monthly Return, Company A, Frontier Battalion, July 1876, TSA.
76. Monthly Return, Company A, Frontier Battalion, August 1876. This MR was completed by Major Jones, Lieutenant Ira Long having discharged for this term of enlistment while Company A was in Wise County, TSA; Major Jones to AG Steele, August 12, 1876, TSA: "Will be at the former place [Menardville] about the 25th and the latter [Kerrville] about the last of this month."
77. General Order No. 10, Frontier Battalion, August 25, 1876, Sec. I, TSA: "Commanders of Companies will give discharges and final statements of their accounts to all the men of their respective Companies on the 31st of the present month." Stephens, *Texas Ranger Sketches*, 66.

Chapter 4 "Several Shots and Run Him into the River"

1. Major Jones to Lieutenant J. M. Denton, Company A, Frontier Battalion, September 26, 1876, TSA: "He [Lieutenant Dolan] is camped at or near old Camp Wood in N.W. Corner of Uvalde Co." Gournay, *Texas Boundaries*, reports that Real County was surveyed and organized in 1913 from portions of Bandera, Edwards, and Kerr Counties. There is no mention of Camp Wood being situated in Uvalde County. See Gournay, 121.
2. Special Order No. 67, Frontier Battalion, August 29, 1876, Sec. V, TSA: "On the first day of September next Pat Dolan of Co. 'F' will assume command of said Company with the rank of First Lieutenant, subject to the approval of the governor, and will be respected and obeyed accordingly. [signed John B. Jones, Maj. Comdg.]"; J. Marvin Hunter, ed. "Pioneer Dies In El Paso," *Frontier Times*, April 1930, 284; Tise, *Texas County Sheriffs*, 285, 503.

3. Stephens, *Texas Ranger Sketches*, 71; DuCoin, *Lawmen on the Texas Frontier*, 103.
4. Monthly Returns, Company F, Frontier Battalion, September and October 1876, TSA.
5. Certificate of Pay. Frank Jones, Private, Co. F, TSA.
6. Lieutenant Pat Dolan, Company F, Frontier Battalion to Major Jones. December 15, 1876, TSA.
7. Monthly Return, Company F, Frontier Battalion, December 1876, TSA.
8. Lieutenant Dolan to Major Jones, January 2, 1877; Major Jones to Lieutenant Dolan, January 10, 1877, TSA.
9. Lieutenant Dolan to Major Jones. February 17 (or 19), 1877, TSA.
10. Ibid.
11. Monthly Return, Company F, Frontier Battalion, February 1877, TSA: "Prvt. R.H. Kingsbury discharged Feby 20th by Special Order No. . . ."
12. Lieutenant Dolan to Major Jones, January 23, 1877, TSA.
13. Ibid.; Miller, *Texas Ranger John B. Jones*, 140–141.
14. Petition in support of Company F Sergeant Richard Jones, dated January 24, 1877, TSA.
15. Special Order No. 85, Frontier Battalion, February 8, 1877, TSA: "Private H. S. Joines of Co. F is hereby dishonorably discharged from the Service of the State for drunkenness and riotous conduct and disrespectful deportment towards his commanding officer. This discharge will have effect from January 15, 1877, and final statement of his account will be made to that date." Interestingly, due to a shortage of experienced supervisory noncoms, Lieutenant Dolan shortstopped the temporary reduction in rank for his 1st Sergeant: "Owing to the press of business I have been compelled to put Dick Jones on duty again." See, Lieutenant Dolan to Major Jones, February 15, 1877, TSA.
16. Monthly Return, Company F, Frontier Battalion, January 1877, TSA.
17. Lieutenant Dolan to Major Jones, January 23, 1877, TSA.
18. Monthly Return, Company F, Frontier Battalion, January 1877, TSA.
19. Kenner, "Guardians in Blue: The United States Cavalry and the Growth of the Texas Range Cattle Industry," 48.
20. Ibid.
21. Lieutenant Dolan to John C. Sullivan, District Attorney, 24th Judicial District of Texas, February 19, 1877, TSA.
22. Lieutenant Dolan to Major Jones, February 15, 1877, TSA.

23. Ibid. Certainly an arrest does not equate to a courthouse conviction. For an interesting and insightful biographical sketch of several of these players the reader is referred to *Nueces Headwater Country: A Regional History* by Allan A. Stovall, 13–41.
24. Ibid.; Tise, *Texas County Sheriffs*, 503.
25. Ibid.
26. Ibid.; Monthly Return, Company F, Frontier Battalion, February 1877, TSA.
27. Ibid.; DuCoin, *Lawmen on the Texas Frontier*, 114.
28. Miller, *Texas Ranger John B. Jones,* 142: "Dolan was understandably perturbed at the negligence of the two Rangers [Bowman and Chute] in allowing their prisoner to escape, but both kept their jobs."
29. Lieutenant Dolan to Major Jones, February 28, 1877, TSA.
30. Lieutenant Dolan to Major Jones, February 17, 1877, TSA.
31. Monthly Return, Company F, Frontier Battalion, March 1877, TSA.
32. Ibid.
33. Gournay, *Texas Boundaries,* 79.
34. Ranger H.B. Waddill to Major Jones, February 27, 1877, TSA.
35. Peter R. Rose, *The Reckoning: The Triumph of Order on the Texas Outlaw Frontier*, 46–72; Miller, *Texas Ranger John B. Jones*, 146–150.
36. Alexander, *Winchester Warriors*, 121–122; Parsons and Brice, *Texas Ranger N.O. Reynolds: The Intrepid*, 98; Rose, *The Reckoning*, 63.
37. Major Jones to Lieutenant Frank Moore, April 11, 1877, TSA.
38. Alexander, *Winchester Warriors*, 124:"Regardless of the finer points of legality the Texas Rangers had rounded up everyone in their path that didn't have a job or couldn't prove a good reason for being in Kimble County . . ."; Utley, *Lone Star Justice,* 179: "Every man who even looked suspicious wound up in Junction bound to a tree (Junction had no jail)." Cox, *The Texas Rangers: Wearing the Cinco Peso, 276*: "Constitutional guarantees of presumed innocence and due process meant nothing during the clean-up operation. Rangers surrounded houses and entered without warrants. Remote campfires drew rangers like moths. Anyone who could not convince the Rangers of his innocence went to Junction City for further interrogation."
39. Major Jones to AG Steele, April 16, 1877, TSA.
40. Ibid.
41. Major Jones to AG Steele, May 6, 1877, TSA.
42. Ibid.
43. Ed Blackburn, Jr., *Wanted: Historic County Jails of Texas*, 195–196.

44. Parsons and Brice, *Texas Ranger N.O. Reynolds*, 101.
45. Miller, *Texas Ranger John B. Jones*, 150; James B. Gillett, *Six Years With the Texas Rangers, 1875–1881*, 105.
46. Rose, *The Reckoning*, 71.
47. Gournay, *Texas Boundaries*, 80–81.
48. Tise, *Texas County Sheriffs*, 307: "Reynolds was appointed in October 1876 and served until May 3, 1877, when he resigned."
49. Rose, *The Reckoning*, 71. "J. M. Reynolds, sheriff since October 18, 1876, was delivered to jail in Mason County by Corporal Rhodes and two other Company D Rangers, who remained to guard the jail"; Alexander, *Winchester Warriors*, 124–125.
50. Testimony Taken by the Committee on Military Affairs in relation to the Texas Border Troubles, 45th Congress, 2nd Session, House of Representatives, Misc. Doc. No. 64. January 1878, 249. An excerpt from the *San Antonio Express* entered into evidence:

    > If there is any one thing more than another the people of Western Texas have to congratulate themselves upon in connection with the progress of the year 1877, it is the breaking up and almost entire eradication of the bands of cut-throat desperadoes that infested our section a year ago. Strong in numbers and the self-interest that banded them together, they had defied the officers of the law, and laughed at the idea of arrest and punishment for the serious crimes almost daily committed. But the rangers entered in among them, and their presence gave encouragement to the officers of the law and now the penitentiary and jails are almost crowded with the scoundrels; most of the ringleaders have been arrested, and the others have become demoralized; they are being hunted down and driven from the country. . . .

51. Major Jones to AG Steele, May 6, 1877, TSA.
52. *Galveston Daily News*, September 22, 1877.
53. Monthly Return, Company F, Frontier Battalion, April 1877, TSA; Lieutenant Dolan to Major Jones, April 30, 1877, TSA: "I have since found some hides out in a cedar brake supposed they were Killed by that party."
54. Lieutenant Dolan to Major Jones, February 28, 1877, TSA.
55. Major Jones to Lieutenant Dolan, March 1, 1877, TSA.
56. Lieutenant Dolan to Major Jones, March 15, 1877, TSA; Major Jones to AG Steele, April 16, 1877, TSA: "I have to request that you will ship to Lt. Dolan, Camp Wood, care Hugo & Schmeltzer, San Antonio, one case

of (10) improved Winchester Carbines, one case of Cartridges for them, and one case of Springfield Carbine Cartridges, and one case of pistol cartridges."

57. Citizens' Petition of Confidence, April 13, 1877, Camp Wood, Texas; Citizens' Petition of Confidence, May 8, 1877, Uvalde, Texas, TSA.
58. Public Written Statement of E. Hatch, Allan A. McDonnell, and S. B. Raney. April 18, 1877, TSA.
59. John C. Sullivan, District Attorney for the 24th Judicial District of Texas, to Major Jones, April 28, 1877, TSA.
60. Endorsement of Major Jones to AG Steele, on Petition of Confidence, Camp Wood, Texas, April 13, 1877, TSA.
61. Monthly Return, Company F, Frontier Battalion, June 1877 and August 1877, TSA.
62. Lieutenant Dolan to Major Jones, July 3, 1877, TSA.
63. Ibid.
64. Ibid.; *Galveston Daily News*, June 30, 1877.
65. Monthly Return, Company F, Frontier Battalion, July 1877, TSA. For the MR the murdered man is identified as Robert Kimble. Other Texas Ranger correspondence identifies the murder victim as Robert Trimble, as do the contemporary newspaper reports.
66. West Gilbreath, *Death from a Texas Gallows*, and interview with Gilbreath by author on November 7, 2013; The offense was later summarized in a recap appearing in the *Galveston Daily News,* July 8, 1879.
67. Lieutenant Dolan to Major Jones, July 18, 1877, TSA.
68. Ibid.; Miller, *Texas Ranger John B. Jones*, 154.
69. Ibid.
70. Lieutenant Dolan to Major Jones, July 31, 1877, TSA.
71. Ibid.
72. Miller, *Texas Ranger John B. Jones*, 155.
73. *New York Times*, July 8, 1879.
74. Gilbreath, *Death from a Texas Gallows.*
75. General Order No. 16, Frontier Battalion, August 9, 1877, TSA.
76. State of Texas, Settlement of Accounts, Company F, pay due from June 1, 1877 to August 18, 1877. Monthly Return, Company F, Frontier Battalion, August 1877, TSA; *San Antonio Daily Express*, August 24, 1877.

Chapter 5 "Sworn Enemy to Rangers and Sheriffs"

1. [Citizen] Frank Jones to Major Jones, December 17, 1877, TSA.
2. Ibid.; Jones asked Major Jones: "Was this the same John Gorman the same man that Sergt. Reynolds arrested on Gentry creek last spring?" Though the question is valid, there is no indication that the wanted John Gorman, and John B. Gorman the man replacing Kimble County's Sheriff J. J. Reynolds are the same—but there is more than sufficient room for understandable confusion. See, Parsons and Brice, *Texas Ranger N.O. Reynolds*, 169, 174; Tise, *Texas County Sheriffs*, 307. For additional mentions of the exciting life of Sheriff Gorman and photograph, an interested reader is referred to the index of Rose, *The Reckoning*.
3. Ibid.; in this same letter to Major Jones, Frank Jones characterizes another fellow quite well-known to students and scholars of Texas Outlaw/Lawman history, Isham J. Goode (or Good): "Goode is a notorious cow thief and if there is any chance [to arrest him] the authorities of this county [Kendall] would like to have him by the next term of the District Court, which will be next March."
4. Ibid.
5. U.S. Census, Curry's Creek, Kendall County, Texas, 1880, W. K. Jones, Enumerator, June 7, 1880.
6. DuCoin, *Lawmen on the Texas Frontier*, 91.
7. Ibid., 58; Stephens, *Texas Ranger Sketches*, 123–125.
8. Miller, *Texas Ranger John B. Jones*, 293–296.
9. *Galveston Daily News*, July 20, 1881.
10. Descriptive List, Frank Jones, July 28, 1881, TSA: "To fill vacancy of E. J. Pound, Discharged"; Monthly Return, Company D, Frontier Battalion, July 1881, TSA. Persons interested in following the activities of Company D during the Frontier Battalion epic, apart from the Frank Jones angle, might wish to peruse Alexander's *Winchester Warriors: Texas Rangers of Company D, 1874–1901*, an across-the-board study not focused on a single event or a particular personality.
11. Monthly Return, Company D, Frontier Battalion, August 1881, TSA. For comprehensive data about the notorious Bill Taylor, relatives and associates and enemies, an interested reader is referred to Chuck Parsons' *The Sutton-Taylor Feud: The Deadliest Blood Feud in Texas*. Citations throughout.
12. Ibid.; Tise, *Texas County Sheriffs*, 371.
13. Monthly Return, Company D, Frontier Battalion, September 1, 1881, TSA; Tise, *Texas County Sheriffs*, 204.

14. Occasionally it has been written that Emmett Jones enlisted in Company D on June 1, 1881. The Monthly Return for Company D, June 1881, is silent to that effect, while the Monthly Return for Company D, September 1881 in the TSA clearly enumerates Emmett Jones as having enlisted on the first day of the month. Also see DuCoin, *Lawmen on the Texas Frontier,* 139: "In good standing with the Jones boys' tradition, Emmett sallied forth and enlisted in Company D on September 1, 1881 for a year's service. . . ."
15. Captain Dan Roberts to Adjutant General W. H. King, September 13, 1881, TSA; Monthly Return, Company D, Frontier Battalion, October 1881, TSA; Stephens, *Texas Ranger Captain Dan Roberts: The Untold Story*, 211–213; Alexander, *Winchester Warriors*, 173–174.
16. Lieutenant Sieker to AG King, January 13, 1882, TSA: "It has been my experience that some men when Kept against their will or become dissatisfied, don't do their duty from a sense of duty as a true ranger should. . . ."
17. Lieutenant Sieker to AG King, April 24, 1882, TSA; Stephens, *Texas Ranger Sketches*, 144–146; Alexander, *Winchester Warriors*, 176.
18. Corporal Frank Jones to AG King, December 16, 1881, TSA; Monthly Return, Company D, Frontier Battalion, December 1881, TSA.
19. Lieutenant L. P. Sieker to Captain Neal Coldwell, Quartermaster, December 13, 1881, TSA.
20. Corporal Frank Jones to Lieutenant Sieker, February 18, 1882. "Pressing business demands my attention elsewhere and for this reason you are requested to recommend me a discharge from the service of the State to take effect March 1st 1882"; Monthly Return, Company D, Frontier Battalion, February 1882, TSA.
21. Lieutenant Sieker to AG King, February 20, 1882, TSA.
22. DuCoin, *Lawmen on the Texas Frontier*, 86.
23. Ibid. Interestingly, author and family historian DuCoin publishes in her book a photocopy of "An arcane letter from Frank Jones. . . ." That the content of the missive, written while Frank Jones was between Texas Ranger enlistments, is mysterious would be an accurate assessment. Written to someone named "Dan" the letter makes reference to the secreting of "money and five watches under the black rock 22 steps from where we eat dinner Sunday. . . ." And, puzzlingly, "I seen two Rangers yesterday on a scout so I took a skip at once. . . ." Also written, purportedly in Frank's hand (it certainly appears so), is the suggestion he and Dan should meet at El Paso and then "go to Frisco. . . ," 116. Absent any—even a hint—of context, the standing alone letter presents more questions than answers. Analyzing its content with rationalization or condemnation or idle speculation falls into the realm of first-class ambiguity.

24. Lieutenant Sieker to AG King, February 9, 1882, TSA.
25. Private S. D. Coalson to Lieutenant Sieker, March 6, 1882, TSA: "Sir, I most respectfully ask to be discharged from the service of the state on the 15th inst—reason to get married"; Lieutenant Sieker to AG King, March 6, 1882, TSA.
26. Lieutenant Sieker to AG King, March 17, 1882, TSA; Alexander, *Winchester Warriors*, 176; DuCoin, *Lawmen on the Texas Frontier*, 139–140. Regrettably, and in deference to Chuck Parsons in his *Captain John R. Hughes: Lone Star Ranger*, he misidentifies AG King as "Wilbur Hill King," rather than the correct "Wilburn Hill King," 36.
27. Monthly Return, Company D, Frontier Battalion, June 1882, TSA.
28. Report of Scouts, Pecos Detachment, Company D, Frontier Battalions, July 1882, TSA; Monthly Return, Company D, Frontier Battalion, July 1882; Tise, *Texas County Sheriffs*, 410.
29. Lieutenant Sieker to AG King, July 4, 1882, TSA.
30. Monthly Return, Company D, Frontier Battalion, August 1882, TSA; Report of Scouts, Pecos Detachment, Company D, Frontier Battalion, August 1882, TSA.
31. Monthly Return, Company D, Frontier Battalion, September 1882, TSA.
32. Lieutenant Sieker to AG King, August 31, 1882, TSA: "I will enlist and appoint 1st Sgt. Of this Co. Frank Jones, a former member and Corpl of Co. D."; State of Texas, Certificate of Pay, Sergeant Frank Jones, Frontier Battalion, September–November 1882, TSA; Monthly Return, Company D, Frontier Battalion, December 1882, TSA.
33. Monthly Return, Company D, Frontier Battalion, September 1882, TSA.
34. Stephens, *Texas Ranger Sketches*, 65; DuCoin, *Lawmen on the Texas Frontier*, 139.
35. Captain Sieker to AG King, September 30, 1882, TSA.
36. Monthly Return, Company D, Frontier Battalion, October 1882, TSA.
37. Telegram from Captain Sieker to AG King, November 1, 1882, TSA.
38. Captain Sieker to AG King, November 3, 1882, TSA.
39. Monthly Return, Company D, Frontier Battalion, November 1882, TSA.
40. Captain Sieker to AG King, November 27, 1882, regarding an article in the *San Antonio Daily Express*, TSA.
41. Ibid.; Report of Scouts, Pecos Detachment, Company D, Frontier Battalion, August 1882, TSA.
42. Ibid.; Captain Sieker was of the notion that the newspaper editor "embellished McCafferty's tale a little."

43. Captain Sieker to Captain Neal Coldwell, Quartermaster, Frontier Battalion, November 30, 1882, TSA. In a separate message about the Company D camp, Captain Sieker advised AG King on November 30, 1882, TSA: "I have fixed the camp up for winter and we are comfortably fixed. Health of men good. Stock in fine fix and plenty of grass, wood & water."
44. Monthly Return, Company D, Frontier Battalion, December 1882, TSA.
45. Captain Sieker to AG King, December 31, 1882, TSA.
46. Captain Sieker to Captain Coldwell, December 31, 1882, and Captain Sieker to AG King, December 31, 1882, TSA.
47. Monthly Return, Company D, Frontier Battalion, January 1883, TSA; Tise, *Texas County Sheriffs*, 503.
48. Ibid.; Captain Sieker to AG King, January 25, 1883, TSA.
49. Alexander, *Winchester Warriors*, 182. For more on the interesting and eventful life of C. B. McKinney, see Chuck Parsons and Gary P. Fitterer's, *Captain C. B. McKinney: The Law In South Texas*. In regard to the subject at hand refer to pages 54–55; Tise, *Texas County Sheriffs*, 321.
50. Sergeant Jones to AG King, March 13, 1883, TSA.
51. DuCoin, *Lawmen on the Texas Frontier*, 110.
52. Pinckney Jones to Governor John Ireland, March 13, 1883, TSA.
53. Captain Sieker to AG King, March 7, 1883, TSA. In addition to selling his horse without permission, it seems the Ranger also took an unapproved leave of absence. See Monthly Return, Company D, Frontier Battalion, March 1883, TSA: "E. P. Flagg dishonorably discharged March 1st by Capt. L. P. Sieker for desertion."
54. Alexander, *Winchester Warriors*, 183–184.
55. Robert W. Stephens, *Captain George H. Schmitt: Texas Ranger*, 21.
56. Cox, *The Texas Rangers: Wearing the Cinco Peso*, 329.
57. Stephens, *Captain George H. Schmitt: Texas Ranger*, 22: "In October of 1883 a petition was circulated by certain disgruntled members of Company D asking for Schmitt's resignation." During a November 17, 2003, telephone interview Bob Stephens commended the hardcore work ethics and bravery of George Schmitt, but did confirm that within Texas Ranger ranks he hardly had a friend and, due to his personality, was exceedingly disliked and unpopular; Alexander, *Winchester Warriors*, 184.
58. Captain Sieker to Captain J. O. Johnson, Quartermaster, Frontier Battalion, May 8, 1883, TSA.
59. Monthly Return, Company D, Frontier Battalion, April 1883, TSA.
60. Ibid. A well-documented biography of Austin Ira Aten is Bob Alexander's *Rawhide Ranger, Ira Aten: Enforcing on the Texas Frontier*.

61. Ibid.
62. Stephens, *Texas Ranger Sketches*, 123–124.
63. Sergeant Jones to AG King, May 25, 1883, TSA.
64. Captain Sieker to AG King, June 4, 1883, TSA.
65. Captain Sieker to AG King, June 21 and June 30, 1883; Captain Sieker to Captain Johnson, July 21, 1883, TSA: "I was compelled to move my camp from the Nueces on acct of water. I am now encamped on the Leona river about five miles S.E. of Uvalde." During a 24 July 1884 update (a year later) to AG King, Captain Sieker clarified the logic of his positioning the Ranger camp near Uvalde: "where I have mail, telegraph and Rail facilities and being a good place to get information from the surrounding country. Grass and water is good here and I can operate in a radius of 100 miles. Numerous reports of horse & cow stealing have reached me & I have just sent out a scout to investigate." See document in TSA.
66. For several scouts led by Sergeant Frank Jones not previously mentioned in text, refer to Monthly Returns, Company D, Frontier Battalion, June, September and October 1883, TSA.
67. Stephens, *Texas Ranger Sketches*, 73; DuCoin, *Lawmen on the Texas Frontier*, 110.
68. George Pfeuffer to AG King, September 13, 1883, TSA.
69. Monthly Return, Company D, Frontier Battalion, November 1883, TSA: "Lieutenant Schmitt transferred to Co. 'C' Front Batt Nov 10th by Gen King."

Chapter 6 "Sixty Thousand Dollars to Spend"

1. Captain Sieker to AG King. January 13, 1884, TSA: "and leave Sergt Jones in command of company during my absence."
2. General Order No. 15, May 13, 1884, TSA. Somewhat ironically it may seem, paralleling Frank Jones' elevation into the battalion's commissioned officers' corps, this same order also promoted Company C's lieutenant, George Schmitt, to captain of that distantly stationed company. Schmitt's accomplished biographer Robert W. Stephens pulls no punches regarding the political maneuvering landing Schmitt the new status. See his *Captain George H. Schmitt: Texas Ranger*, 23.
3. Representative housekeeping matters for Lieutenant Frank Jones is illustrated by just a partial sampling: Lieutenant Jones to Captain John O. Johnson, Quartermaster, June 9, 1884: "I have purchased 20 days rations for myself and 5 men to date from June 1st. I find it impossible to get corn

here and am buying sheaf oats. . . . I have given voucher for the supplies I have bought. I am only issuing six pounds per day but would like to obtain your consent to feed more as that is not enough in this Country." Lieutenant Jones to Captain Johnson, June 27, 1884; Lieutenant Jones to Harry Landa, July 24, 1884; Lieutenant Jones to Captain Johnson, August 15, 1884; and Lieutenant Jones to Captain Johnson, August 25, 1884: "Sir: I mailed you on the 16th inst. an account of money expended by me since taking charge of the detachment and have not heard a word from you in reply. I am in need of the money and hope that you will find it convenient to remit soon. I am also without blanks and am in need of them to settle for rations. Hoping that I will hear from you soon." All in TSA.

4. Monthly Return, Company D, Frontier Battalion, May 1884; Tise, *Texas County Sheriffs,* 357.
5. Captain Sieker to AG King, May 31, 1884, TSA: "I have promoted first corporal B. D. Lindsey to First Sergt. . . ."
6. Stephens, *Texas Ranger Sketches,* 83–86. Lindsey would later become a U.S. Mounted Customs Inspector, and yet later, the Sheriff of Bexar County at San Antonio; Tise, *Texas County Sheriffs,* 43.
7. Reports of Scouts, Llano Detachment, Company D, Frontier Battalion, May–August 1884, TSA.
8. Corporal B. D. Lindsey to AG King, May 19, 1884, TSA.
9. Corporal Lindsey to AG King, May 5, 1884, TSA.
10. Ibid.
11. Captain Sieker to AG King, May 31, 1884, TSA.
12. Lieutenant Jones to AG King, June 17, 1884, TSA.
13. Lieutenant Jones to AG King, June 30, 1884, TSA.
14. Lieutenant Jones to AG King, June 24, 1884, TSA
15. *San Saba News*, August 17, 1939. From an article, "60 Years Ago They Didn't Want Any Barb Wire Fences Here" regarding the Commissioners' Court meeting of February 11, 1879.
16. The reader interested in additional information about the major impact barbed-wire had in/on Texas both historically and sociologically might wish to review one or more of the following sources: R. D. Holt, "Introduction of Barbed Wire into Texas and the Fence Cutting War," *West Texas Historical Association Yearbook*, June 1930; Henry D. and Frances T. McCallum, *The Wire That Fenced the West*; Walter Prescott Webb, "The Fence Cutters' War," *True West*, May–June 1963; James L. Haley, *Passionate Nation: The Epic History of Texas*; Alexander, *Rawhide Ranger*, Chapter 7, "Curling Steel Tendrils"; Joanne S. Liu, *Barbed Wire: The Fence That Changed the West*; Wayne Gard, "The Fence

Cutters," *Southwestern Historical Quarterly*, July 1947. A video presentation on this subject was produced by WCCC-TV, Waco, Texas, and filmed at the Texas Ranger Hall of Fame & Museum, Waco, Texas , titled "Barbs, Bullets, and Blood: The Wire War That Revolutionized Texas" with oral presentations by Old West authors Clifford R. Caldwell, Harold D. Jobes, Bob Alexander, and Michael Barr.

17. Alexander, *Winchester Warriors*, 192; Harold D. Jobes, "Fence Cutting and a Ranger Shootout at Green Lake," *Wild West History Association Journal*, October 2009, 40.
18. Lieutenant Jones to AG King, June 24, 1874, TSA: "If it is your intention to keep this detachment in this County I would suggest that I remain here [Llano] for the grass is much better than at Bluffton." Lieutenant Jones to AG King, July 15, 1884, TSA.
19. Report of Scouts, Llano Detachment, Company D, Frontier Battalion, July 1884, TSA; Monthly Return, Company D, Frontier Battalion, July 1884, TSA.
20. Green B. Greer to Governor Ireland, July 19, 1884, TSA.
21. Monthly Return, Company D, Frontier Battalion, July 1884, TSA: "July 25th. . . . Corpl. Baird and 3 men made scout to Green lake Edwards Co. to protect the fence of Greer Bros. Not yet returned."
22. Captain Sieker to AG King, July 31, 1884, TSA: "I have just heard through Sheriff [Ira] Wheat of Edwards Co. that Greer Bros. fence was cut on the night of the 26th inst. Corpl. Baird & detachment should arrive there the 28th and I have strong hopes of his catching the cutters."
23. Jobes, "Fence Cutting and a Ranger Shootout at Green Lake," 45–46.
24. Corporal P. C. Baird's Report of Scout to Green Lake, August 8, 1884, TSA; Cox, *The Texas Rangers: Wearing the Cinco Peso*, 327: "But Baird wanted to catch them cutting the fence, a felony."
25. P. C. Baird, "The Fight at Green Lake Waterhole," *Frontier Times*, March 1926, 34.
26. G. B. Greer to Governor Ireland, July 30, 1884, TSA.
27. Corporal Baird's Report of Scout to Green Lake, August 8, 1884, TSA.
28. G. B. Greer to Governor Ireland, July 30, 1884, TSA; Monthly Return, Company D, Frontier Battalion, August 1884, TSA. In this report the estimate of rounds fired at Green Lake is 100 and it does note that Mason was "killed while resisting arrest."
29. Baird, "The Fight at Green Lake Waterhole," 34–35.
30. Telegram, Corporal Baird to Captain Sieker, August 5, 1884, TSA; Bob Alexander, "A Bloody Barbed-Wire Battle: Texas Rangers vs Fence Cutters," *True West*, May 2014, 42.

31. Captain Sieker to AG King, August 7, 1884, TSA.
32. Captain Sieker to AG King, August 8, 1884, TSA; Monthly Return, Company D. Frontier Battalion, August 1884, TSA: "in Barksdale arrested Brunston, delivered him to sheriff Edwards Co."
33. Private O. D. Baker to Captain Sieker, undated, but attached to Sieker's letter to AG King, August 21, 1884, TSA.
34. G. B. Greer to Captain Sieker, August 26, 1884, TSA.
35. G. B. Greer and W. J. Greer to AG King, August 26, 1884, TSA.
36. Captain Sieker to AG King, August 31, 1884, TSA: "I also enclose a letter from G. B. Greer and would advise Lt. Jones' detachment being sent to his aid at once."
37. Lieutenant Jones to AG King, September 6, 1884, TSA.
38. Lieutenant Jones to AG King, September 13, 1884, TSA.
39. Monthly Return, Company D, Frontier Battalion, October 1884, TSA.
40. Jobes, "Fence Cutting and a Ranger Shootout at Green Lake," 46.
41. Lieutenant Jones to AG King, September 23, 1884, TSA.
42. Lieutenant Jones to AG King, September 26, 1884, TSA.
43. Captain Sieker to AG King, September 29, 1884, TSA.
44. Captain Sieker to AG King, September 30, 1884, TSA.
45. Wilkins, *The Law Comes to Texas,* 247: "All the Rangers were cleared of any wrongdoing at an inquest. . . ." Alexander, *Winchester Warriors*, 200; Jobes, "Fence Cutting and a Ranger Shootout at Green Lake," 46: "Although we know that the three fence cutters who survived the shootout at Green Lake were apprehended, we find no record today of any one of the three men being charged, found guilty, or receiving a sentence for fence cutting and assault with intent to kill."
46. Monthly Return, Company D, Frontier Battalion, October 1884, TSA: "G.B. Greer/W.J. Greer—Enlisted by Genl. King and carried on the Rolls as specials without pay."
47. Captain Sieker to AG King, August 8, 1884, TSA.
48. Alexander, *Rawhide Ranger, Ira Aten*, 53–54.
49. Monthly Return, Company D, Frontier Battalion, September 1884, TSA.
50. Interview of Austin Ira Aten, El Cento, California, July 1941, by Earl Vandale, J. Evetts Haley, and Hervey Chesley. Hereafter Aten–1941. Typescript courtesy Nita Stewart Haley Memorial Library & History Center Midland, Texas, hereafter HML&HC; Monthly Return, Company D, Frontier Battalion, November 1884, TSA. Although the arrests are enumerated in the MR for

November, a descriptive narrative within places the actual date of the arrests as October 5, 1884.

51. Alexander, *Rawhide Ranger, Ira Aten*, 54; Blackburn, *Wanted: History of County Jails in Texas*, 37; Ira Aten, "Six and One-Half Years in the Texas Rangers," *Frontier Times* (Part 1) January 1945, 111: "We took them [the prisoners] to San Antonio, to a new jail, the best in the state—fool proof."
52. Monthly Return, Company D, Frontier Battalion, September 1884, TSA.
53. Monthly Return, Company D, Frontier Battalion, November 1884, TSA; Writ of Habeas Corpus regarding the incarceration of the prisoners: "said application for writ of habeas corpus against the Sheriff of Bexar County." Courtesy Gillespie County District Clerk, Fredericksburg, Texas.
54. Captain Sieker to AG King, January 22, 1885; Monthly Return, Company D, Frontier Battalion, January 1885; Captain Sieker to Captain Johnson, January 22, 1885; and Captain Sieker to AG King, January 31, 1885, TSA.
55. Interview of Austin Ira Aten, El Centro, California, by J. Evetts Haley, February 1928. Courtesy HML&HC. Hereafter Aten–1928.
56. Monthly Return, Company D, Frontier Battalion, February 1885, TSA. The proper spelling for the South Texas county is "Dimmit" while the county seat of Castro County in the Texas Panhandle is "Dimmitt."
57. Aten–1928, HML&HC.
58. Interview of Adolph Petree by J. Evetts Haley, July 1941, HML&HC. Hereafter Petree–1941.
59. Ibid.; Alexander, *Winchester Warriors*, 202; Tise, *Texas County Sheriffs*, 160.
60. Petree–1941, HML&HC.
61. Parsons and Fitterer, *Captain C. B. McKinney: The Law in South Texas*, 75.
62. Governor Ireland to AG King, February 7, 1885, TSA.
63. Monthly Return, Company D, Frontier Battalion, February 1885, TSA.
64. Captain Sieker to AG King, February 13, 1885, TSA.
65. Captain Sieker to AG Kind, February 20, 1885, TSA.
66. P. H. Wentworth, Jr. to Captain Sieker, February 20, 1885, TSA.
67. Captain Sieker to AG King, February 28, 1885, TSA.
68. Captain Sieker to Captain John O. Johnson, February 20, 1885, TSA.
69. Captain Sieker to AG King, February 28, 1885, TSA.
70. Monthly Return, Company D, Frontier Battalion, February 1885, TSA.

Chapter 7 "Most Bold, High-Handed Murder"

1. Captain Sieker to AG King, March 27, 1885, TSA; Captain Sieker to Captain Johnson, March 27, 1885, TSA.
2. Captain Joe Shely, Company F, Frontier Battalion to AG King, March 13, 1885, TSA; Alexander, *Rawhide Ranger, Ira Aten*, 64; Parsons and Fitterer, *Captain C. B. McKinney: The Law in South Texas*, 81–83.
3. Ibid.
4. Monthly Return, Company D, Frontier Battalion, March 1885, TSA.
5. Lieutenant Jones to AG King, April 1, 1885, TSA.
6. DuCoin, *Lawmen on the Texas Frontier*, 117.
7. Ibid. Precisely pinpointing where Frank Jones met Grace O'Grady is elusive.
8. Lieutenant Jones to AG King, April 10, 1885, TSA.
9. Monthly Return, Company D, Frontier Battalion, April 1885, TSA.
10. Captain Sieker to Captain Johnson, April 16, 1885, TSA.
11. John R. Baylor, Montell, Texas, to AG King, April 19, 1885, TSA. Even before John R. Baylor penned his letter to the adjutant general, Captain Sieker had learned of the burglary and burning of Mr. N. M. Gay's house in Edwards County and had dispatched Ranger Privates A. P. Barry and W. W. Collier to investigate. The two Rangers identified suspects and turned the information over to the county sheriff and then submitted a written report to AG King. See, Barry and Collier to King, April 16, 1885, TSA.
12. J. W. Jennings to Governor Ireland and AG King, May 3, 1885, TSA.
13. Monthly Return, Company D, Frontier Battalion, May 1885, TSA.
14. Report of Scouts, Edwards County Detachment, Company D, Frontier Battalion, May 1885, TSA. That Lieutenant Jones was temporarily headquartered in Edwards County is buttressed by his correspondence from there, as in, Lieutenant Jones, Barksdale, Texas, to AG King, May 13, 1885, TSA.
15. Captain Sieker to Captain Johnson, May 31, 1885, TSA.
16. Captain Sieker to AG King, May 31, 1885, TSA.
17. Captain Sieker to Captain Johnson, May 31, 1885, TSA. In the 31 May 1885 correspondence found in TSA to AG King, Captain Sieker reiterated: "after talking the matter over we are inclined to the opinion that they will try & cross the river about 18 miles above Eagle Pass. We have every point guarded and I think if they come this way they will be caught."
18. Alexander, *Rawhide Ranger, Ira Aten*, 71. Subsequent to publication the author learned that his reference to Griffin was incorrect. Thanks to informative and pleasant telephone interviews with Suzanne Giffin-Garcia the error has been

corrected for this, and future treatments. Also, though often Ben C. Riely's name is spelled "Riley" the former is correct. See, B. C. Riely to AG King, September 17, 1885, TSA.

19. Captain Sieker to AG King, April 30, 1885, TSA. That raging currents could also claim a Texas Ranger's life, as well as outlaws' bullets or Indians' arrows, is demonstrated by Caldwell and DeLord, *Texas Lawmen: The Good and the Bad, 1835–1899*, 330. During his part of a presentation in the program Barbs, Bullets, and Blood, at Nocona, Texas, on April 26, 2014, noted authority on the Texas Cattle Trails, Cliff Caldwell, highlighted the fact that drowning was the leading cause of death for cowboys pushing cattle north.
20. Aten–1928, HML&HC.
21. Sergeant B. D. Lindsey to Captain Sieker, July 10, 1885, TSA.
22. Alexander, *Rawhide Ranger, Ira Aten,* 75.
23. Sergeant Lindsey to Captain Sieker, July 10, 1885, TSA.
24. Telegram: Captain Sieker to AG King, June 1, 1885, TSA.
25. Captain Sieker to AG King, July 1, 1885, TSA: "The two Mexicans (Gonsales & Son) are in Mexico and are likely to remain there unless I can have them extradited."
26. Alexander, *Rawhide Ranger*, 80–88; Dudley G. Wooten, ed., *A Comprehensive History of Texas, 1685–1897*, Chapter 1, "The Texas Ranger Service and History of the Rangers, With Observations on Their Value as a Police Protection" by General W. H. King, page 363. Quite interestingly, though not surprising in light of Walter Prescott Webb's worshipful treatment of Rangers, his classic *The Texas Rangers : A Century of Frontier Defense* makes no reference to the killing of Private Sieker or incarceration of the Rangers at Laredo. Seemingly, he, like newspapermen and many border residents of the time, knew the episode was a "deplorable mistake" and historically embarrassing. Correspondingly and contemporaneously the Company D Monthly Return for June 1885 in the TSA makes mention of the shooting incident wherein Frank Sieker was killed, but wholly skips any mention of the Rangers being incarcerated at Laredo, simply saying the detachment in question was "out 30 day and marched 175 miles." Physical description of Webb County's Jail may be found in Blackburn's *Wanted: Historic County Jails of Texas*, 346–347.
27. Aten–1928, 58–59, HML&HC.
28. Captain Sieker to AG King, July 20, 1885, TSA.
29. *Galveston Daily News*, June 19, 1885, picking up a story from the *San Antonio Daily Express*.
30. Alexander, *Rawhide Ranger*, highlights the negative newspaper coverage, see pages 83–88.

31. Captain [subsequent to his promotion] Frank Jones to Adjutant General Woodford Haywood Mabry, March 1, 1892, TSA.
32. Captain Sieker to AG King, July 20, 1885, TSA: "I will leave Lt. Jones at Camp Ambrosia until I move everything from there." And, Captain Sieker to AG King, August 3, 1885, TSA: "Lt. Jones and three men are at Camp San Ambroia and will be here [Uvalde County] in about a week."
33. Captain Sieker to Captain Johnson, August 17, 1885, TSA.
34. Captain Sieker to AG King, August 17, 1885, TSA.
35. AG King to Lieutenant Jones, September 5, 1885, TSA; Certification of Dr. Fred Herff: ". . . I have examined and treated Mr. B. C. Riley [*sic*], Comp. D. Texas State Ranger ever since July 14th 1885 for a gunshot wound in his leg and that he is unfit for Duty and unable to trail on horseback. He will require an extension of his leave of absence for about two months longer." Lieutenant Frank Jones endorsed the request: "I recommend that the two months extension of time asked for by Private Riley [*sic*] be granted." Documents in TSA.
36. Certification of Private Riely's injuries and prognosis by Dr. Herff, September 15, 1885, TSA.
37. Lieutenant Jones to AG King, September 4, 1885, TSA.
38. Private B. C. Riely to AG King, September 17, 1885, TSA.
39. Monthly Return, Company D, Frontier Battalion, July 1885, TSA; Tise, *Texas County Sheriffs*, 160.
40. Monthly Return, Company D, Frontier Battalion, August 1885, TSA.
41. Frontier Battalion, Special Order No. 85, October 12, 1885, TSA.
42. Lieutenant Jones to Quartermaster Sieker, October 27, 1885 and December 4, 1885, TSA.
43. Monthly Return, Company D, Frontier Battalion, August 1885, TSA.
44. Monthly Return, Company D, Frontier Battalion, September 1885, TSA.
45. Supplement to the Monthly Return, Company D, November 1885, TSA.
46. Lieutenant Jones to Captain Sieker, QM, November 4, 1885, TSA.
47. Ibid.
48. AG King to Captain George Schmitt, November 5, 1885, TSA; AG King to Lieutenant Jones, November 5, 1885, TSA: "Capt. George N. Schmitt Co. C will probably call upon you for assistance in a contemplated descent on a gang of criminals in Karnes County. If he should do so, I desire that you go with all the men you can spare, leaving in camp only a sufficient number to guard the public property. . . ."
49. Stephens, *Captain George H. Schmitt, Texas Ranger*, 134.

50. Monthly Return, Company D, Frontier Battalion, November 1885, TSA.
51. Stephens, *Captain George H. Schmitt, Texas Ranger,* 135.
52. Robert W. Stephens, *Walter Durbin: Texas Ranger and Sheriff*, 26.
53. Supplemental Monthly Return, Company D, Frontier Battalion, November 1885, TSA.
54. Sergeant Lindsey to Captain Sieker, QM, November 28, 1885, TSA.
55. Lieutenant Jones to Captain Sieker, QM, December 4, 1885, TSA.
56. Lieutenant Jones to AG King, December 6, 1885, TSA.
57. Lieutenant Jones to Captain Sieker, QM, December 9, 1885, TSA.
58. Lieutenant Jones to AG King, December 7, 1885, TSA.
59. Ibid. Notation on above cited letter; AG King to Lieutenant Jones, December 10, 1885, TSA: "Leave of absence as requested in your letter of the 7th inst. is hereby granted him."
60. DuCoin, *Lawmen on the Texas Frontier,* 117.
61. Lieutenant Jones to AG King, December 17, 1885, TSA.
62. Lieutenant Jones to Captain Sieker, QM, December 17, 1885, TSA.
63. AG King to Lieutenant Jones, December 15, 1885, TSA.
64. Monthly Return, Company D, Frontier Battalion, December 1885, TSA.
65. Ranger C. W. Giffin to AG King, December 30, 1885, TSA.
66. Ruth Whitehead, "The Bloody Fence Cutting War," *The West*, December 1969, 20.
67. Monthly Return, Company D, Frontier Battalion, December 1885, TSA.

Chapter 8 "Damnable Act of Savagery"

1. Ranger Giffin to Captain Sieker, QM, January 19 and 29, 1886, TSA.
2. Lieutenant Jones to Captain Sieker, QM, January 1, 1885, TSA.
3. Monthly Return, Company D, Frontier Battalion, January 1886, TSA.
4. AG King to Lieutenant Jones, January 4, 1886, TSA.
5. Lieutenant Jones to Captain Sieker, QM, February 25, 1886, TSA.
6. AG King to J. A. and H. P. Maurice, February 3, 1886, TSA.
7. Monthly Returns, Company D, Frontier Battalion, January, February, and March 1886, TSA.
8. Alexander, *Rawhide Ranger, Ira Aten,* 92.
9. Monthly Return, Company D, Frontier Battalion, March 1886, TSA.

10. Alexander, *Rawhide Ranger, Ira Aten,* 108, 361, n. 26 and 27.
11. Monthly Return, Company D, Frontier Battalion, April 1886, TSA.
12. AG King to Lieutenant Jones, April 15, 1886, TSA.
13. AG King to Lieutenant Jones, April 26, 1886, TSA.
14. State of Texas Certification of Pay, Frank Jones, Captain, May 1, 1886, TSA.
15. AG King to Captain Frank Jones, May 3, 1886, TSA: "It is with pleasure I hand you herewith your Commission as Captain in Frontier Battalion. Hoping your Services in the future will be as well appreciated as they have been in the past."
16. Alexander, *Rawhide Ranger, Ira Aten,* 92–93.
17. Ibid., 94–95.
18. Ibid., 96–101; Aten–1928, HML&HC; Bob Alexander, "Square Deals and Real McCoys," *Wild West History Association Journal,* June 2011, 40–41. Parsons, *Captain John R. Hughes: Lone Star Ranger,* appears determined to fertilize John Hughes' participation in this arrest scenario by suggestion rather than substantiation: "Perhaps as Hughes had turned the knob to try the door, only to discover it was locked, did the slight sound alert Collier. With the fugitive thus distracted, Aten entered and uttered the words of 'Hold up, Wesley,' having the drop with his pistol in his hand." See page 28. Continuing with what smacks of hero worship, he writes on page 30: "Apparently he [Hughes] only observed what Aten had accomplished, but no doubt catching up with Collier was due to Hughes's tracking ability, which led the pair to the fatal doorstep of the Dayton house." Certainly, during this truly dangerous six-shooter state of affairs, Aten's real time contribution hardly earns any armchair degrading, nor does Hughes need a helping hand with any fanciful enrichment of his actual role. Both men were plucky.
19. Ibid., 99–100. The newspaper citation is taken from an undated copy of the *Liberty Hill Ledger* as contained in the Aten files at HML&HC. Also see, *Rawhide Ranger,* 357, n. 32, and 358, n. 33. A characterization by Parsons on page 29 in *Captain John R. Hughes: Lone Star Ranger* that Collier's .38 caliber Invincible model Iver-Johnson revolver was an "unreliable" weapon is nebulous and from a lawman's perspective meaningless: The revolver only has to be "reliable" once! Peace officers can ill-afford to let the hammer drop on a live round, and then decide if either the cartridge or the pistol is a dud.
20. AG King to A. L. Patterson, June 19, 1886, TSA.
21. Monthly Return, Company D, Frontier Battalion, June 1886, TSA.
22. Captain Frank Jones to Captain Sieker, May 31, 1886, TSA.
23. Captain Jones to AG King, June 6, 1886, TSA.
24. Monthly Return, Company D, Frontier Battalion, June 1886, TSA.

25. Captain Jones to Captain Sieker, July 9, 1886, TSA.
26. Captain Jones to Captain Sieker, August 1, 1886, TSA.
27. AG King to J.W. Saunders, August 17, 1886, TSA.
28. AG King to Captain Jones, August 17, 1886, TSA: "I would not under the circumstance reenlist him [Saunders] & assign him to any other Company & will not put him back in your Company unless by your endorsement you can show your willingness to try him once more." Monthly Return, Frontier Battalion, Company D, August 1886, TSA.
29. AG King to Captain Jones, August 2, 1886, TSA.
30. Monthly Return, Company D, Frontier Battalion, August 1886, TSA.
31. Monthly Return, Company D, Frontier Battalion, September 1886, TSA.
32. Ibid.
33. Captain Jones to Captain Sieker, September 18, 1886, TSA.
34. Captain Jones to Captain Sieker, August 31, 1886, TSA.
35. Monthly Return, Company D, Frontier Battalion, September 1886, TSA.
36. Monthly Return, Company D, Frontier Battalion, October 1886, TSA.
37. AG King to Captain Sieker, October 11, 1886, TSA.
38. Monthly Return, Company D, Frontier Battalion, October 1886, TSA.
39. Captain Frank Jones to Captain Sieker, November 8, 1886, TSA.
40. AG King to Captain Jones, October 19, 1886, TSA. As a matter of general interest it was Kinney County Sheriff Frank S. Fritter that arrested Carlotta Thompkins aka Lottie Deno for Keeping a Faro Bank, the good-timing gal's only known arrest for gambling infractions. Her other arrests throughout Texas were for Keeping a Disorderly House (Whorehouse). See, Devereaux, *Pistols, Petticoats and Poker: The Real Lottie Deno, No Lies or Alibis*.
41. Monthly Return, Company D, Frontier Battalion, November 1886.
42. Captain Jones to Captain Sieker, November 16, 1886, TSA.
43. Captain Jones to Captain Sieker, November 22, 1886, TSA.
44. Monthly Return, Company D, Frontier Battalion, December 1886, TSA.
45. Ranger Aten to AG King, November 26, 1886, TSA. The Brown County fence-cutting and subsequent nighttime shootout is covered in detail within Alexander's, *Rawhide Ranger, Ira Aten*.
46. AG King to Captain Jones, November 22, 1886, TSA.
47. Sheriff H. W. Baylor, Uvalde County, to AG King, December 12, 1886, TSA.
48. AG King to Captain Jones, December 15, 1886, TSA.
49. Captain Jones to Captain Sieker, December 1, 1886, TSA.

50. AG King to Captain Jones, December 18, 1886, TSA.
51. Monthly Return, Company D, December 1886, TSA.
52. Sergeant Lindsey to Captain Sieker, December 29, 1886, TSA.
53. Monthly Return, Company D, Frontier Battalion, January 1887, TSA.
54. Captain Jones to AG King, January 31, 1887, TSA.
55. Chief Deputy Sheriff, Mason County, P.C. Baird to AG King, January 4, 1887, TSA. For a chapter-length profile of the remarkable Old West lawman, banker, and rancher, P.C. Baird, see Bob Alexander's *Bad Company and Burnt Powder: Justice and Injustice in the Old Southwest* (University of North Texas Press, 2014), Chapter 7, "The Plum Was Ripening Fast." And see Bob Alexander, "A Bloody Barbed-Wire Battle: Texas Rangers vs Fence Cutters," *True West*. May 2014, 42–43.
56. AG King to P. C. Baird, January 7, 1887; AG King to Captain Jones, January 7, 1887, TSA.
57. Captain Jones to Captain Sieker, February 11, 1887, TSA.
58. Ibid.
59. Lampasas County Sheriff N. O. Reynolds to Captain Sieker, January 19, 1887, TSA.
60. Captain Jones to AG King, February 25, 1887, TSA.
61. Mrs. E. E. Johnson to Governor S.L. Ross, February 13, 1887, TSA.
62. Kerr County Clerk F. M. McFarland to AG King, February 26, 1887, TSA.
63. AG King to Captain Jones, February 21, 1887, TSA.
64. Monthly Return, Company D, Frontier Battalion, March 1887, TSA.
65. Captain Jones to AG King, March 31, 1887, TSA.
66. Ibid.
67. Ibid.
68. Monthly Return, Company D, Frontier Battalion, March 1887, TSA.

Chapter 9 "He Caught for a Pistol"

1. Sergeant Lindsey to Captain Sieker, March 30, 1887, TSA.
2. Val Verde County Judge William K. Jones to Captain Sieker, March 25, 1887, TSA.
3. Captain Jones to Captain Sieker, April 6, 1887, TSA. Undated letter from Mrs. Mattie Shutz to Governor Ross in the TSA: "Captain Jones, he said he did not know that his company is soon to be disbanded. . . ."

4. Aten–1941, HML&HC. Also, Alexander, *Rawhide Ranger, Ira Aten,* 130–131.
5. Monthly Return, Company D, Frontier Battalion, April 1887, TSA.
6. Captain Jones to AG King, May 4, 1887, TSA; Monthly Return, Company D, Frontier Battalion, April 1887, TSA. At this time the named of the Company D camp changes from Camp Sieker to Camp Ross, though both are located within the boundaries of Edwards County.
7. Alexander, *Rawhide Ranger, Ira Aten,* 131.
8. Captain Jones to Captain Sieker, May 2, 1887; Monthly Return, Company D, Frontier Battalion, April 1887, TSA.
9. Jeff Burton, "The Most Surprised Man In Texas," *Frontier Times*, 1973, 18–21, 50–53, 69; Alexander, *Rawhide Ranger*, 132; R. Michael Wilson, *Great Train Robberies of the Old West*, 64–65; Parsons and Brice, *Texas Ranger N.O. Reynolds*, 30; Jeff Burton, "A Great Man Hunt—Correspondence from W.B.S, Some Scenes of Outlawry and Gunplay in Texas," *English Westerners' Brand Book 18*, 11–34; Bill S. Price, *Bill Whitley, Outlaw*, 39–41.
10. Jeffrey Burton, *Western Story*, European Edition, 91, n. 17.
11. Richard Dillion, *Wells, Fargo Detective: A Biography of James B. Hume*, 236.
12. Sergeant Aten to AG King, August 11, 1887, TSA; AG King to Captain Jones, August 12, 1887, TSA; AG King to Captain Jones, August 21, 1887, TSA: "Hughes, however, is not intended to be a permanent member of your Company unless he desires so to be and favors himself a Suitable man; as the object of his present enlistment is to enable him to aid Aten in his efforts to catch some of the train robbers." Alexander, *Rawhide Ranger,* 136; Monthly Return, Company D, Frontier Battalion, August 1887; *Fort Worth Star-Telegram*, December 27, 1914.
13. Captain Jones to AG King, July 1, 1887, TSA.
14. Captain Jones to Captain Sieker, July 1, 1887, TSA.
15. Monthly Return, Company D, Frontier Battalion, July 1887, TSA. Interestingly this same Monthly Return enumerates an arrest for J. W. Basham, Theft of Cattle. Whether it was the Hide and Animal Inspector or a close or distant genealogical relative is as of this time indefinite.
16. AG King to Captain Sieker, July 19, 1887, TSA.
17. Captain Jones to AG King, August 23, 1887, TSA.
18. AG King to Captain Jones, August 26, 1887, TSA.
19. DuCoin, *Lawmen on the Texas Frontier,* 117.
20. Monthly Return, Company D, Frontier Battalion, September 1887, TSA; Captain Jones to AG King, September 27, 1887, TSA.

21. Monthly Returns, Company D, Frontier Battalion, September and October 1887, TSA.
22. Captain Jones to Captain Sieker, October 29, 1887, TSA.
23. Captain Jones to Captain Sieker , October 28, 1887, TSA.
24. Captain Jones to AG King, October 31, 1887, TSA.
25. Monthly Return, Company D, Frontier Battalion, October 1887, TSA: "[Oct.] 30. Co. D Front. Batt. Broke camp under orders from Genl. King and took up the line of march for Starr County." Interestingly for this document, in the blank provided for identifying the Company's Station is the notation "On the Road."
26. Captain Jones to AG King, November 1, 1887, TSA.
27. Captain Jones to AG King, November 25, 1887, TSA.
28. Captain Jones to Captain Sieker, November 25, 1887, TSA. "If you can have Durbin transferred to Co. D I would be glad to have him."
29. Captain Jones to AG King, November 17, 1887, TSA.
30. Monthly Return, Company D, Frontier Battalion, November 1887, TSA; Tise, *Texas County Sheriffs*, 559.
31. Monthly Return, Company D, Frontier Battalion, December 1887, TSA; Christina Stopka, Director, Texas Ranger Research Center, TRHF&M, *Partial List of Texas Ranger Company and Unit Commanders*: "Company F, Lt. Joseph Shely (March 1883–April 1884) Capt. Joseph Shely (May 1884–May 1885)."
32. Parsons, *Captain John R. Hughes: Lone Star Ranger* citing the *Galveston Daily News* of December 10, 1887 on page 38.
33. Elliott Young, *Catarino Garza's Revolution on the Texas-Mexico Border*, 66. For further explanation of *la ley de fuga*, see, Alexander's *Riding Lucifer's Line*, 42; Douglas V. Meed, *Bloody Border: Riots, Battles and Adventures Along the Turbulent U.S.–Mexican Borderlands*, 48; and Cornelus C. Smith, Jr., *Emilio Kosterlitzky: Eagle of Sonora and the Southwest Border*, 105–111.
34. Captain Jones to AG King, December 9, 1887, TSA.
35. Captain Jones to Captain Sieker, December 9, 1887, TSA.
36. Captain Jones to AG King, December 9, 1887, TSA; Alexander, *Winchester Warriors*, 214.
37. Monthly Return, Company D, Frontier Battalion, January 1888, TSA. Sometimes it's written that John R. Hughes acted as Barrera's bodyguard, but that seems belied by the Monthly Return, unless Hughes was assisting Rogers: "Private Rogers went to Roma with Juan Barrera to act as body guard. Out one day. Marched 30 miles."

38. Monthly Return, Company D, Frontier Battalion, December 1887, TSA; Stephens, *Walter Durbin: Texas Ranger And Sheriff*, 61.
39. Ibid.
40. Captain Jones to AG King, December 14, 1887, TSA.
41. Captain Jones to Captain Sieker, December 24, 1887, TSA.
42. Captain Jones to Captain Sieker, January 4, 1888, TSA.
43. Monthly Return, Company D, Frontier Battalion, January 1888, TSA.
44. Captain Jones to AG King, January 19, 1888, TSA.
45. Monthly Return, Company D, Frontier Battalion, January 1888, TSA.
46. AG King to S. H. Bass, Mexican National Railway—Texas Division, Laredo, Texas, January 27, 1888 and AG King to Captain Jones, Realitos, Texas, January 27, 1888, TSA.
47. Captain Jones to AG King, January 31, 1888, TSA.
48. Railway Passes, Mexican National Railway—Texas Division, for Captain Frank Jones, Company D, Frontier Battalion, February 6 and 8, 1888, Realitos to Corpus Christi and Corpus Christi to Realitos, TSA.
49. Monthly Return, Company D, Frontier Battalion, February 1888, TSA.
50. Stephens, *Walter Durbin: Texas Ranger and Sheriff*, 61: "Idolized by his men, the Captain [Frank Jones] was highly respected throughout the state. . . ."
51. Wooten, *A Comprehensive History of Texas*, 349.
52. Captain Jones to Captain Sieker, March 1, 1888, TSA.
53. AG King to Captain Jones, March 10, 1888, TSA; Tise, *Texas County Sheriffs*, 528.
54. Captain Jones to AG King, March 15, 1888, TSA.
55. Ibid.
56. Railway Pass, Mexican National Railway—Texas Division, for Durbin's detachment, March 15, 1888, TSA.
57. Monthly Return, Company D, Frontier Battalion, March 1888, TSA; Corporal J. Walter Durbin to Captain Sieker, March 23, 1888, TSA; Captain Jones to Captain Sieker, March 23, 1888, TSA: "I telegraphed B. F. Yokum of the San Antonio and Aransas Pass road and he gave me half rates on the road from Corpus Christi to Eagle Lake which Corporal Durbin paid. On this road my stock was billed to Corpus Christi at full rates. I strongly objected but the Agent said that he had no instructions to allow us reduced rates. I then saw the Agent in Corpus Christi and he knew nothing about the matter. When you get the bill $26.40 you must see that you are allowed your reductions for I couldn't do a thing with them."

58. Alexander, *Winchester Warriors*, 220–221
59. Stephens, *Walter Durbin: Texas Ranger and Sheriff*, 62.
60. Corporal Durbin to Captain Sieker, March 23, 1888, TSA.
61. Stephens, *Walter Durbin: Texas Ranger and Sheriff*, 62.
62. Ibid.
63. Corporal Durbin to Captain Sieker, April 18, 1888, TSA.
64. Corporal Durbin to AG King, May 14, 1888, TSA.
65. Monthly Return, Company D, Frontier Battalion, April 1888, TSA. For a chapter-length biographical profile of Calvin Grant Aten, see Alexander's *Bad Company and Burnt Powder: Justice and Injustice in the Old Southwest,* Chapter 1, "Battle at Bullhead Mountain."
66. Sergeant Aten to Captain Sieker, April 29, 1888, TSA: "The 25¢ is for my younger bother being sworn in."
67. Handwritten Memoir of Calvin Grant Aten, Courtesy Robert W. Stephens.
68. Ibid.; Monthly Return, Company D, Frontier Battalion, April 1888, TSA.
69. Memoir of Calvin Grant Aten.
70. Ibid.
71. Ibid. Apparently Dood Jones thought Cal taking potshots at the escaping prisoners was absurd, as Aten remembered that every time he would lob bullets at an escapee, Dood Jones "would grumble and tell me to quit."
72. Ibid. None of the escaping prisoners suffered any gunshot wounds, but one died during the escape attempt. Refer to the Monthly Return, Company D, Frontier Battalion, April 1888, TSA: "Capt. Jones & 2 men made scout to Carrizo, while there assisted in recapturing prisoners who broke jail, caught one and run another into the river who drowned while attempting to cross. . . ."
73. Ibid. Cal Aten also recalled Captain Jones' remarks about the incident on the horseback trip back to Realitos: "Cal, I have been with the rangers a good many years and seen many rangers come and go, but you are the first one I can remember of getting to shoot at a man on his first scout."
74. Memoir of J. Walter Durbin. Typescript courtesy Robert W. Stephens.
75. Captain Jones to AG King, April 9, 1888, TSA; Monthly Return, Company D, Frontier Battalion, May 1888, TSA.
76. Ibid.
77. Captain Jones to AG King, May 19, 1888, TSA.
78. Monthly Return, Company D, Frontier Battalion, May 1888, TSA.

79. Monthly Return, Company D, Frontier Battalion, May 1888, TSA. Although conclusiveness is difficult, it does seem logical that if Recéndez was a federal prisoner in the custody of U.S. Customs Inspector Sebree he would not be carried as a state prisoner on the Company D Monthly Return. That Sebree could have been present at the time of the shooting is not disputed, though apparently he did not stand trial due to the affair and Ranger Dillard (ex-Ranger) did.
80. Monthly Return, Company D, Frontier Battalion, June 1888, TSA; Stephens, *Walter Durbin: Texas Ranger and Sheriff*, page 69, by inference indicates that Dillard after separating from Company D became a Deputy United States Marshal.
81. Captain Jones to AG King, May 31, 1888, TSA.
82. Ibid.; Monthly Return, Company D, Frontier Battalion, June 1888, TSA.

Chapter 10 "A Strong Undercurrent of Excitement"

1. Captain Jones to AG King, July 31, 1888, TSA.
2. Young, *Catarino Garza's Revolution on the Texas-Mexico Border*, 31–41.
3. Ibid., 34: "In spite of his critique of Anglo supremacy, Garza seems to have internalized some of the dominant racial ideology that valued lighter over darker skin."
4. James N. Leiker, *Racial Borders: Black Soldiers Along The Rio Grande,* 122: "a popular following among working-class Mexicans. . . ."
5. Utley, *Lone Star Justice,* 255: "A Texas resident, he [Catarino Garza] had achieved notoriety as an eloquent newspaper editor and charismatic orator, but as a rebel general he proved altogether incompetent. Although he boasted an army of more than one thousand men, in three incursions he got less than a hundred across the border, and they accomplished no more than to prod Diaz into demanding that the United States enforce the neutrality laws." For a succinct overview of Spanish-language newspapers along the Texas/Mexico border, including Catarino Garza's enterprises, see Arnoldo De León, *The Tejano Community, 1836–1900*, 197–201. Mention of the fact Garza was subject material for *corridos* is cited by Américo Paredes, *With His Pistol in His Hand: A Border Ballad and Its Hero*, 146.
6. Paul N. Spellman, *Captain John H. Rogers, Texas Ranger,* 70; Jerry Thompson, *A Wild and Vivid Land: An Illustrated History Of The South Texas Border*, 131: "Within weeks, Garza and his men were decisively defeated. . . ."

7. Utley, *Lone Star Justice*, 255; Wilkins, *The Law Comes to Texas*, 302: "Very likely, many of the people who joined him were motivated by revolutionary zeal, but a goodly number were border ruffians out for whatever plunder might be available."
8. Spellman, *Captain John H. Rogers, Texas Ranger*, 68; Andrew R. Graybill, *Policing the Great Plains: Rangers, Mounties, and the North American Frontier, 1875–1910* confirms the stridence: "given Garza's harsh editorial treatment several years earlier. . . ." See page 105.
9. Professor Emeritus Louis R. Sadler to author, April 21, 2012: "the Federal Records Center in Fort Worth has 600 case files/indictments of Catarino Garza supporters."
10. Young, *Catarino Garza's Revolution on the Texas-Mexico Border*, 66.
11. Parsons, *Captain John R. Hughes: Lone Star Ranger*, 43; Arnoldo DeLeón, *They Called Them Greasers: Anglo Attitudes Toward Mexicans in Texas, 1821–1900*, 93.
12. De León, *They Called Them Greasers*, 93.
13. Cox, *Wearing the Cinco Peso*, 343.
14. Young, *Catarino Garza's Revolution on the Texas-Mexico Border*, 67.
15. Monthly Return, Company D, Frontier Battalion, August 1888. The primary source document is clear as to where the charges had actually been filed, and where Catarino Garza was taken into custody: "Pvt. Hughes and one man arrested C. E. Garza in Realitos, wanted in Starr County for Criminal libill [*sic*]." Document in TSA. Interestingly, but somewhat deceptively, occasionally a writer will reference Jack Martin's *Border Boss: Captain John R. Hughes—Texas Ranger* as source material for recounting Catarino Garza's arrest for Libel at Realitos, Duval County, not infrequently disparaging the melodramatic account penned during 1942. For quite some time now—years—the overblown rendition of the story with contrived dialogue has been recognized for what it was, exaggeration akin to Harold Preece's *Lone Star Man, Ira Aten: Last of the Old Texas Rangers*, a part fictional and part factual account of Company D's top-sergeant and later sheriff of two Texas counties. Even John R. Hughes' most recent biographer, Chuck Parsons, in *Captain John R. Hughes: Lone Star Ranger* is put off—it seems—by the creative dialogue: "This appears to be yet another example of Martin's addition of 'color' to his narrative with little basis in fact." See page 313, n 60.
16. Ibid. "Brought him [Catarino Garza] to camp. . . ," TSA; Tise, *Texas County Sheriffs*, 163; Chuck Parsons and Marianne E. Hall Little, *Captain L. H. McNelly, Texas Ranger: The Life and Times of a Fighting Man*, 196–200.

17. Ibid. "Pvt. Roberson [Robinson] and 3 men conveyed Garza to Rio Grande City and delivered him to proper authorities, out 7 days, marched 230 miles." The assertion that Captain Jones personally fashioned the prisoner escort detail is conjecture, but based on the fact that his correspondence suggests he was in Camp Collins at the time, and as such, was the man in charge of Rangers stationed there.
18. Stephens, *Captain George H. Schmitt, Texas Ranger*. The author cites arrests made by Ranger Jim Robinson throughout, check index; Young, *Catarino Garza's Revolution on the Texas-Mexico Border*. 67; Cox, *Wearing the Cinco Peso*, 343: ". . . Garza quickly posted bond."
19. Young, *Catarino Garza's Revolution on the Texas-Mexico Border*, 67.
20. Parsons, *Captain John R. Hughes: Lone Star Ranger*, 43–44; Stephens, *Walter Durbin: Texas Ranger and Sheriff* includes Dillard as one of the persons the run-amok crowd wanted. Quoting from page 69: "Sebree and U.S. Marshal Tooney Dillard, who was backing him against the mob, barricade themselves in a thick walled adobe house ready to fight but were persuaded by the County Judge to go to Fort Ringgold, a mile from town, in an effort to avoid bloodshed among innocent citizens."
21. Alexander, *Riding Lucifer's Line*, 120–121.
22. Telegram: AG King to Captain Jones, September 22, 1888, TSA.
23. Telegram: Captain Jones to AG King, September 23, 1888, TSA.
24. Captain Jones to AG King, September 24, 1888, TSA.
25. Captain Jones to AG King, September 26, 1888, TSA.
26. Monthly Return Company D, Frontier Battalion, September 1888, TSA; Corporal Durbin to Captain Sieker, October 2, 1888, TSA: "We arrived here [Rio Grande City] Sunday morn. the 30th after 3 hard days travel. Capt Jones arrived the Day before."
27. Monthly Return, Company D, Frontier Battalion, TSA.
28. Captain Jones to AG King, September 30, 1888, TSA. Interestingly the aggregate number of possemen rushing to the scene of purported rioting at Rio Grande City under the command of area sheriffs was 145. In turn, the financial cost billed to the State of Texas was $5,477.00 which was later somewhat discounted, as reported in the *Dallas Morning News* edition of January 21, 1895.
29. AG King's answer to the foregoing letter from Jones, attached to the September 30, 1888, communication, TSA.
30. Corporal Durbin to Captain Sieker, October 9, 1888, TSA.

31. Parsons, *Captain John R. Hughes: Lone Star Ranger*, 44. Quoting the *Galveston Daily News*, picking up a story from Austin, September 27, 1888; Leiker, *Racial Borders: Black Soldiers Along the Rio Grande*, p. 121, seems to award the Rio Grande City Mexicanos the status of rioters, which even the commander of Fort Ringgold was reluctant to do: "At Laredo in 1886 and Rio Grande City in 1888, American troops (all white) suppressed Mexican riots caused by resentment of local political machines."
32. Ibid.; Cox, *Wearing the Cinco Peso*, 343: "Sebree, charged in connection with the shooting went free on $2,500 bond." Young, *Catarino Garza's Revolution on the Texas-Mexico Border* does not deny Sebree was required to post bail, but his wording on page 70 seems designed to leave such an impression: "After noting the irony that the victim of the shooting, Garza, was arrested while the perpetrator, Sebree, was free, . . ." As noted in the text, who in fact fired the first shot is unsettled and, likely, will remain so.
33. Captain Jones to AG King, October 17, 1888, TSA; Monthly Return, Company D, Frontier Battalion, October 1888, TSA.
34. Alexander, *Winchester Warriors*, 221.
35. Recapitulation of Arrests Made by Co D, F.B. [Frontier Battalion] Oct. 1888, TSA; Monthly Return, Company D, Frontier Battalion, October 1888, TSA.
36. Stephens, *Walter Durbin: Texas Ranger and Sheriff*, 69.
37. Ibid.; Alexander, *Riding Lucifer's Line*, 120–121.
38. Monthly Return, Company D, Frontier Battalion, November 1888, TSA.
39. AG King to Captain Jones, October 18, 1888, TSA.
40. For full-length biographical profiles of these two prominent Rangers the reader is referred to the previously mentioned and first-rate treatments by Paul Spellman, *Captain J. A. Brooks, Texas Ranger* and *Captain John H. Rogers, Texas Ranger*. For a look at John R. Hughes, the watchful and circumspect student or aficionado might access the biography, *Captain John R. Hughes: Lone Star Ranger* by Parsons as previously cited. And, as alluded in the Preface to this volume, there is a widely reported assertion suggesting that there were "four great Ranger captains," the fourth being William Jesse "Bill" McDonald, the subject of an outstanding biography, *Yours To Command: The Life And Legend of Texas Ranger Captain Bill McDonald*, by Professor Emeritus Harold J. Weiss, Jr. Of particular note is the fact that all four of these volumes were published by the University of North Texas Press, the premier publisher for preserving and promoting well-documented Texas Ranger history, and by extrapolation, Texas history. Additionally, as cited in the text, during the 1888 assignment to Rio Grande City, Captain Frank Jones supervised three

of these four captains-to-be, and the fourth, McDonald, was not even a Texas Ranger at the time and would not be for several years.

41. Spellman, *Captain J. A. Brooks, Texas Ranger*, 69.
42. Monthly Return, Company D, Frontier Battalion, October 1888, TSA.
43. Private John R. Hughes to Captain Sieker, June 13, 1888, TSA.
44. Monthly Return, Company D, Frontier Battalion, November 1888, TSA.
45. Monthly Return, Company D, Frontier Battalion, December 1888, TSA.
46. Captain Jones to Captain Sieker, November 5, 1888, TSA.
47. Captain Jones to AG King, November 14, 1888, TSA.
48. Tise, *Texas County Sheriffs*, 473.
49. Young, *Catarino Garza's Revolution on the Texas-Mexico Border*, 66: "Later, after pleading guilty to libel, Garza was released."
50. AG King's endorsement on Captain Jones letter of November 14, 1888, TSA; AG King to Captain Jones, November 23, 1888, TSA: "you will proceed to move your Company by easy Marches back to the section formerly held by you in Uvalde & Edwards Counties unless your presence is still needed at your present point. Lieut. Brooks & Company will remain at Rio Grande City until further orders."
51. Captain Jones to AG King, November 29, 1888, TSA.
52. F. A. Piper to Captain Sieker, December 10, 1888, TSA.
53. For a reasonably thorough look at the lengthy undercover operation conducted by Ranger Sergeant Ira Aten in the Navarro County fence-cutting case and his most ingenious and historic exit strategy for removing himself from same, the interested reader is referred to Alexander's *Rawhide Ranger, Ira Aten: Enforcing Law on the Texas Frontier*, Chapter 9, "Wild boy among the villains."
54. Sergeant Aten to Captain Sieker, December 14, 1888, TSA.
55. Monthly Return, Company D, Frontier Battalion, December 1888, TSA. In his 29 November letter to AG King, Captain Jones says, "I will leave here today for Uvalde Co. . . ." Apparently there was a delay, as this Monthly Return, under the date December 1, 1888 reveals, "Company 'D' Frontier Battalion under orders from Genl. King broke camp in Starr County and came to Uvalde County. . . ." The discrepancy is insignificant.
56. Sergeant Aten to Captain Sieker, December 14, 1888, TSA.
57. AG King to Captain Jones, December 13, 1888, TSA.
58. Captain Jones to AG King, December 21, 1888, TSA. Eventually Neeley would be issued a governor's pardon.
59. Captain Jones to AG King, December 31, 1888.TSA.

60. Sheriff W.H. Baylor to AG King, April 6, 1888, TSA.

Chapter 11 "By God, They Will Never Come Back"

1. Monthly Return, Company D, Frontier Battalion, January 1889, TSA.
2. Monthly Return, Company D, Frontier Battalion, February 1889, TSA. Although written on page 47 in Parsons' *Captain John R. Hughes*, that Captain Frank Jones and Private John R. Hughes arrested John Chapman, charging him with cattle theft, such is not the case. The arrest was made, according to the Monthly Return, by "Privates" Hughes and Jones, which would have in fact been W. W. Jones, no relation to Captain Frank Jones. The unintentional error is understandable.
3. Letterhead Stationery, *The Tariff Saloons*, Lindsey & Collier: B.D. Lindsey, Eagle Pass, W.W. Collier, Uvalde, TSA.
4. B. D. Lindsey to Captain Jones, March 5, 1889, TSA.
5. Captain Jones to AG King, March 6, 1889, TSA; Tise, *Texas County Sheriffs,* 363.
6. AG King to Captain Jones, March 9, 1889, TSA: "as the question of the retention of the battalion has not & will not be settled for some time."
7. AG King to Captain Jones, March 18, 1889, TSA.
8. Alexander, *Rawhide Ranger, Ira Aten,* 173; *Forth Worth Gazette*, September 19, 1891.
9. Eugene Cunningham, "Frontier Justice: How Old-Time Rangers Solved a Baffling Texas Murder Mystery," *Startling Detective Adventures,* September 1935, 34–35; J. Marvin Hunter, "The Famous Dick Duncan Murder Case," *Frontier Times*, February 1939. Quite obviously both of these pieces were written in the twentieth-century after Captain John R. Hughes had garnered a degree of celebrity as a Texas Ranger, but preceding publication of Jack Martin's rather rich *Border Boss: Captain John R. Hughes—Texas Ranger*. Contemporary primary source records are less charitable regarding Hughes' actual involvement in this particular criminal investigation.
10. Chris Weatherby, "From No Account to Plain Mean," *Old West*, Summer 1974, 27; Aten–1941, HML&HC; Aten–1928, HML&HC. "Hughes helped me in this case a great deal. . . . It was a very noted case."
11. *Dallas Morning News*, September 19, 1891; Tise, *Texas County Sheriffs*, 363 and 312.
12. Paul Havens, "Border Boss: The Saga of Captain John R. Hughes, Texas Ranger," *True Detective*, July 1940, 35.

13. Cunningham, "Frontier Justice," 37; Aten–1941, HML&HC. During the 1941 interview Ira Aten confirms the general outline of this conversation, but does identify the wagon as being manufactured by the Bain Wagon Company. The discrepancy is meaningless for the story at hand.
14. Monthly Return, Company D, Frontier Battalion, March 1889, TSA.
15. Alexander, *Rawhide Ranger, Ira Aten,* 174.
16. Ibid.; Tise, *Texas County Sheriffs,* 454.
17. Ibid., 175.
18. *Eagle Pass Guide*, December 7, 1889.
19. *The San Saba News*, March 29, 1889. "Dick and Tap Duncan, who are charged with murder of the Williamson family on the Rio Grande came in Saturday about noon and surrendered to Sheriff Howard."
20. Sergeant Aten to Captain Sieker, March 29, 1889, TSA.
21. *San Saba Weekly News*, September 25, 1889; Gournay, *Texas Boundaries*, 102.
22. Ibid., March 29, 1889; *San Antonio Daily Express*, September 19, 1889.
23. Alexander, Ra*whide Ranger, Ira Aten,* 176.
24. Aten–1941, HML&HC; Cunningham, "Frontier Justice," 39.
25. Refer to Alexander's *Rawhide Ranger, Ira Aten* for a more in-depth, day by day investigation conducted by Sergeant Aten concerning the movements of Dick Duncan to Eagle Pass and his return to San Saba. See especially pages 177–179.
26. Ibid.; Gilbreath, *Death from a Texas Gallows.*
27. Mike Whittington, "Hughes and Aten Solve the Williamson Family Murders," *Texas Ranger Dispatch*, 2003; Cunningham, "Frontier Justice," 58.
28. Aten–1941, HML&HC; Weatherby, "From No Account to Plain Mean," 27: "Some people suspected that he [Landers] had been killed by Duncan to eliminate the only witness to the slayings."
29. Gilbreath, *Death from a Texas Gallows*; *Fort Worth Gazette*, September 19, 1991; *Dallas Morning News*, September 19, 1891; *San Antonio Daily Express*, September 19, 1891.
30. Monthly Return, Company D, Frontier Battalion, April 1889, TSA.
31. AG King to Captain Jones, April 15, 1889, TSA.
32. Two letters, Captain Jones to AG King, April 16, 1889, TSA.
33. AG King to Captain Jones, April 18, 1889, TSA.
34. Monthly Return, Company D, Frontier Battalion, April 1889, TSA; Captain Jones to AG King, April 30, 1889, TSA.

35. Corporal Durbin to Captain Sieker, May 8, 1889, TSA. For additional information regarding this arrest the reader is referred to Stephens, *Walter Durbin: Ranger and Sheriff*, 73. Though the suspect is not actually named in this account, the facts seem to parallel the ones mentioned in this text.
36. DuCoin, *Lawmen on the Texas Frontier*, 122.
37. Captain Jones to Captain Sieker, May 21, 1889, TSA; Sergeant Aten to Captain Sieker, May 23, 1889, TSA: "Three of our best men quit a few days since and went to Old Mexico to work at the mines." Monthly Return, Company D, Frontier Battalion, May 1889, TSA; Stephens, *Bullets and Buckshot in Texas*. The author, a quite prominent researcher of Texas Ranger history, clarifies the muddle sometimes surrounding the issue of Outlaw's first name, fully explaining on pages 33–34 that at various times by various persons he was know as "Baz" or "Bass." Alexander, *Winchester Warriors*, 224.
38. Ibid.; Alexander, *Riding Lucifer's Line*, 102; Stephens, *Walter Durbin: Texas Ranger and Sheriff*, 77.
39. Captain Jones to AG King, June 5, 1889, TSA.
40. Corporal C. H. Fusselman to AG King, June 5, 1889, TSA; Monthly Return, Company D, Frontier Battalion, June 1889, TSA: "Corpl Fusselman went to Maxom Springs after Donaciano Beslanga charged with Murder. Found him on the 3rd and exchanged shots, Beslanga making his Escape. Found him again on the 4th where Beslanga was killed after firing 8 shots at Fusselman."
41. AG King to Captain Jones, June 25, 1889, a follow-up letter subsequent to telegram of same date.
42. Captain Jones to AG King, June 25, 1889, TSA.
43. Telegram, Captain Jones to AG King, June 28, 1889, TSA.
44. C. L. Sonnichsen, *I'll Die Before I Run: The Story of Great Feuds of Texas*. Quoting the *Houston Post*, 267–268. Aside from "Doc" Sonnichsen as cited, a reasonably comprehensive look at Texas Ranger involvement in the Jaybird/Woodpecker Feud may be gleaned from Alexander's *Rawhide Ranger, Ira Aten*, 189–233. Although written from a somewhat partisan perspective, the interested reader may wish to access Pauline Yelderman, *The Jay Birds of Fort Bend County*. Also, for a chapter-length biographical sketch of one of the foremost players in the feud on the Woodpecker side, Deputy Sheriff Thomas Calton "Tom" Smith, see Bob Alexander's *Lawmen, Outlaws, and S.O.Bs*, Volume II, 178–199.
45. Monthly Return, Company D, Frontier Battalion, June 1889, TSA.
46. Captain Jones to AG King, July 12, 1889, TSA.
47. Captain Jones to Captain Sieker, August 8, 1889, TSA; Captain Jones to AG King, August 8, 1889, TSA.
48. Monthly Return, Company D, Frontier Battalion, August 1889, TSA.

49. Henry Orsay, Chief Clerk, Adjutant General's Office [also sometimes referred to as Captain] to Captain Jones, August 12, 1889, TSA.
50. Ira Aten, "The Woodpecker and Jaybird Feud," *Frontier Times*, June–July 1978, 21, a facsimile reprint of "The Jaybird and Woodpecker War" with a slightly altered title as it appeared in the April 1939 edition of *Frontier Times*.
51. Aten–1941, HML&HC.
52. Alexander, *Rawhide Ranger, Ira Aten*, 204–207.
53. Stephens, *Bullets and Buckshot in Texas*, 172.
54. AG King to Captain Jones, August 24, 1889, TSA.
55. Captain Sieker to AG King, August 25, 1889, TSA; Corporal J. R. Robinson to AG King, August 28, 1889, TSA.
56. Sheriff Austin Ira Aten, Fort Bend County, to Captain Sieker, September 3, 1889, TSA; Monthly Return, Company D, Frontier Battalion, August 1889, TSA: "Co 'D' Rangers assisted Sheriff Aten arresting 23 of the parties engaged in the fight of the 16th charged with murder."
57. Monthly Return, Company D, Frontier Battalion, August 1889, TSA; AG King to Captain Jones, August 26, 1889, TSA; Captain Jones to AG King, August 29, 1889, TSA. "I will send the Co. 'B' men back as soon as transportation can be obtained."
58. Captain Jones to AG King, September 1, 1889, TSA.
59. Sheriff Aten to Captain Sieker, September 3, 1889, TSA.
60. AG King to Captain Jones, September 3, 1889, TSA.
61. Captain Jones to AG King, September 4, 1889, TSA.
62. Captain Jones to AG King, September 9, 1889, TSA.
63. DuCoin, *Lawmen on the Texas Frontier*, 122.
64. Ibid., 123.
65. Captain Jones to AG King, September 21, 1889, TSA: "I arrived here [Richmond] last night. . . ."
66. AG King to Captain Jones, October 10, 1889, TSA; Captain Jones to AG King, October 10 and 11, 1889, TSA; Monthly Return, Company D, Frontier Battalion, October 1889, TSA: "Oct. 14 . . . . Capt. Jones under orders from Genl. King, broke Camp in Fort Bend County and returned to Uvalde. . . ."

Chapter 12 "Just Plain Legal Assassination"

1. Monthly Return, Company D, Frontier Battalion, November 1889, TSA. Assuredly, lifting but four sentences from Captain Jones' letter of October 25,

1889, to AG King is suggestive that he was on the psychological mend after losing his wife the preceding month: "Can't you come and make the trip with me? It will only take about two weeks and we will have splendid hunting. I can furnish you a good saddle horse and outfit. Capt. Coldwell killed 186 deer out there last year." In TSA.

2. Captain Jones to AG King, January 3, 1890, TSA.
3. A series of letters on the letterhead stationery of W. K. Jones, Del Rio, Texas: Captain Jones to AG King, November 29, 1889, and December 4 and 7, 1889, TSA. Although in some accounts it has been written that Frank Jones' sickness sojourn with his brother at Del Rio was of several months' duration, such was not the case. Within the December 16 letter from Jones to AG King, the Company D captain is quite particular and clear: "I stayed with my brother in Del Rio from the 27th [November], until last night when I returned to Uvalde." Document in TSA.
4. Captain Jones to AG King, December 7, 1889, TSA.
5. Captain Jones to AG King, December 16, 1889, TSA.
6. AG King to Captain Jones, December 12, 1889, TSA.
7. Captain Jones to AG King, December 16, 1889, TSA.
8. United States Marshal for the Western District of Texas, Paul Fricke, San Antonio, Texas to AG King, December 12, 1889, TSA.
9. AG King to Captain Jones, December 14, 1889, TSA.
10. The reader interested in further exploring the practice of cross-deputation should access two excellent volumes by the eminent Larry D. Ball, *The United States Marshals of New Mexico and Arizona Territories, 1846–1912* and *Desert Lawmen: The High Sheriffs of New Mexico and Arizona, 1846–1912*. As encapsulated in Alexander's *Riding Lucifer's Line*, although Ball's treatment is specific to the territorial years of New Mexico and Arizona, the practice of United States Marshals appointing local lawmen as provisional Deputy U.S. Marshals is, likewise, applicable to Texas. This particular topic will, in a subsequent six-shooter scenario involving Sergeant Charley Fusselman, resurface.
11. Baz Outlaw reenlisted with Company D on September 1, 1889, and John Hughes was on the Muster & Payroll as of December 1, 1889. See Monthly Returns, Company D, Frontier Battalion, September and December 1889, TSA. Although it's been written J. Walter Durbin also signed on with Company D Rangers again, such is in error.
12. Tise, *Texas County Sheriffs*, 199. Durbin served as the sheriff of Frio County from November 8, 1892, until November 3, 1896. Stephens, *Walter Durbin: Texas Ranger and Sheriff*, 78.
13. Stephens, *Bullets and Buckshot in Texas*, 52.

14. Alexander, *Bad Company and Burnt Powder*.
15. Calvin Grant Aten to Austin Ira Aten, December 12, 1936.
16. Stephens, *Bullets and Buckshot in Texas*, 54.
17. Memoir of Calvin Grant Aten. The engraved Colt .45 taken from Alvin Odle is currently on extended loan through the exceptional courtesy of Aten descendant Joseph Trobaugh II and is part of an extraordinary exhibit at the Texas Ranger Hall of Fame & Museum, Waco, Texas, honoring the three Aten brothers' (Austin Ira, Calvin Grant, and Edward Dunlap) contributions to Texas Ranger history.
18. Private John R. Hughes to AG King, December 25, 1889. For an undisclosed reason, despite what the primary source document indicates, Parsons, *Captain John R. Hughes: Lone Star Ranger,* opts to place the shoot-out during the wee morning hours of Christmas rather the decidedly more correct evening hours after sundown, 55.
19. Captain Jones to Captain Sieker, December 29, 1889, TSA.
20. Captain Jones to Captain Sieker, December 31, 1889, TSA.
21. Monthly Return, Company D, Frontier Battalion, December 1889, TSA.
22. Supplement to the Monthly Return, Company D, Frontier Battalion, December 1889, TSA.
23. Captain Jones to Captain Sieker, December 19, 1889, TSA. "I will have 3 men in Edwards County. It is hard to do much work there as the Sheriff will not work with Rangers."
24. Sheriff Ira Aten to Cal Aten, April 10, 1890.
25. Corporal James R. Robinson, to Captain Sieker, January 2, 1890, TSA.
26. Supplement to Monthly Return, Company D, Frontier Battalion, December 1889, TSA.
27. Corporal Robinson to Captain Sieker, January 10, 1890, TSA.
28. Captain Jones to Captain Sieker, December 19, 1889, TSA.
29. R. W. Callahan, Pat McHugh, and C. F. Adams, Proprietors, The Sonora Supply Company, to AG King, January 3, 1890, TSA.
30. Petition submitted to AG King, January 4, 1890, signed by G. F. Smith, et al., requesting removal of Company D Rangers from their neighborhood on "the Rio Leona about Six miles South of the town of Uvalde. . . ." Document in TSA.
31. AG King to Captain Jones, January 8, 1890, TSA.
32. Captain Jones to Captain Sieker, January 14, 1890, TSA; Gournay, *Texas Boundaries*, 113; Tise, *Texas County Sheriffs,* 106; Monthly Return, Company D, Frontier Battalion, January 1890, TSA.

33. Captain Jones to AG King, January 31, 1890, TSA.
34. Captain Jones to AG King, February 10 and 19, 1890, TSA; AG King to Captain Jones, February 15, 1890, TSA: "Replying to your letter of the 10th inst. you are hereby authorized to return to your Hdqts camp & leave Pvt. Hughes & his detch of 2 men in Coke County to keep the peace & quiet any excitement which may arise."
35. Captain Jones to AG King, February 22, 1890, TSA.
36. DuCoin, *Lawmen on the Texas Frontier,* 123.
37. Captain Jones to AG King, February 22, 1890, TSA. And see, Robert W. Stephens, "A Ranger's Grave: The Murder of Jim King," *National Outlaw/Lawman History Association Quarterly*, October–December 2005.
38. Captain Jones to Captain Sieker, March 4,1890, TSA.
39. AG King to Captain Jones, March 25, 1890, TSA.
40. Alexander, *Winchester Warriors*, 235–236; Stephens, *Bullets and Buckshot in Texas*, 117–121; Captain Jones to AG King, March 21, 1890, TSA: "Sheriff Akers of Zavalla County will need help shortly in making some important arrests in the King murder case and I will not break camp here until I assist him unless specially instructed to do so."
41. Caldwell and DeLord, *Texas Lawmen: The Good and the Bad, 1835–1890*, 346–347.
42. Captain Jones to AG King, March 21, 1890, TSA.
43. Monthly Return, Company D, Frontier Battalion, March 1890, TSA.
44. Blackburn, *Wanted: Historic County Jails of Texas*, 206.
45. Petition to AG King, from J.M. Williams, et al., January 3, 1890; AG King to Captain Jones, March 17, 1890, TSA.
46. Monthly Return, Company D, Frontier Battalion, March 1890, TSA: "Corpl. J.R. Robinson discharged March 31st 1890 by Capt. Jones"; Captain Jones to AG King, April 20, 1890, TSA; Stephens, *Bullets and Buckshot in Texas*, 37.
47. Captain Jones to Captain Sieker, April 5, 1890, TSA; Captain Jones to AG King April 7, 1890, TSA.
48. Private Frank L. Schmid to Captain Sieker, April 7 and 30, 1890, TSA. As of May 4, 1890, Ranger Schmid was still hospitalized in San Antonio and yet worried not only about his medical condition, but expenses as well: See, Private Schmid to Captain Sieker in TSA: "he [the doctor] said that it was very necessary that I had remained at the Hospital as long as I have, and that I will have to remain a week longer as he says there is one suspicious looking place which requires close watching and attention twice daily that I can only get here. . . . Capt. if I can find a better and cheaper boarding place than at Uvalde and nearer to San Antonio I thought I would try it. . . ."

49. Captain Jones to AG King, April 21, 1890, TSA.
50. Monthly Return, Company D, Frontier Battalion, April 1890, TSA.
51. Private Hughes to Captain Sieker, April 18, 1890, TSA.
52. Telegram, From Captain Jones, Cotulla, Texas, to Private Hughes, Marfa, Texas, April 19, 1890, TSA.
53. Captain Jones to AG King, April 19, 1890, TSA; *El Paso Times*, April 20, 1890; *Dallas Morning News*, April 18, 1890; *Arizona Daily Star*, April 19, 1890; Robert Ernst, *Deadly Affrays: Violent Deaths of the U.S. Marshals*, 97–98.
54. Alexander, *Fearless Dave Allison: Border Lawman*, 44; Stephens, *Bullets and Buckshot in Texas*, 172–175. Also see, an article titled "A Brave Soldier" in the May 1890 edition of *The National Police Gazette*.
55. *El Paso Times*, April 19, 1890; and see, C. L. Sonnichsen, *Pass of the North: Four Centuries on the Rio Grande*, 312. Also, Antonio Croce, "In the Line of Duty," *The Texas Gun Collector*, Fall 1996.
56. Alexander, *Riding Lucifer's Line*, 106–110. For an encyclopedic format highlighting Ranger Fusselman's death the reader is referred to Caldwell and DeLord, *Texas Lawmen: The Good and the Bad, 1835–1999*, 347–348.
57. AG King to Captain Jones, April 18, 1890, TSA; Stephens, *Bullets and Buckshot in Texas*, 37: "late in April was made first sergeant of Company D. . . ." Alexander, *Winchester Warriors*, 253; Captain Jones to Adjutant General Woodford Haywood Mabry, June 21, 1892, TSA. Inexplicably Parsons in *Captain John R. Hughes: Lone Star Ranger* appears loathe to acknowledge that Outlaw was selected over Hughes to fill the 1st Sergeant's vacancy created by Fusselman's death. See page xv: "When his sergeant was killed in action in 1890, Hughes was promoted to take his place; when his captain was killed fighting bandits in Mexico in 1893, he was promoted to take his place." The first half of the sentence is fictitious. And on page 61 Parsons opts to leave Baz Outlaw's promotion to 1st Sergeant in the abyss of incompleteness: "With the death of [Sergeant] Fusselman on April 17, Adjutant General King had to determine who would take his place. On the following day, John Reynolds Hughes became 1st Corporal of Company D, Frontier Battalion of the Texas Rangers." Certainly the latter statement—though not incorrect—is misleading, an implication by omission. Notwithstanding any hero worship, Baz Outlaw was promoted to fill Fusselman's supervisory shoes and would remain Company D's 1st Sergeant for more than two years. See Stephens, *Bullets and Buckshot in Texas*, 37–42 as well as a wealth of primary source documents.
58. S. J. Henley to AG King, May 17, 1890, TSA.
59. Petition of citizens of Presidio County to Governor L. S. Ross, May 3, 1890, TSA.

60. AG King to Captain Jones, May 3, 1890, TSA; Captain Jones to AG King, May 25,1890, TSA; Monthly Return, Company D, Frontier Battalion, May 1890, TSA.

Chapter 13 "The Shooting Was Promiscuous and Lively"

1. AG King to Captain Jones May 3 and 7, 1890, TSA; Spellman, *Captain J. A. Brooks, Texas Ranger*, 66; Captain J. A Brooks, Company F, Frontier Battalion to AG King, May 15, 1890, TSA: "Having arrived here [Cotulla] and consulted Capt. Jones have decided to establish Camp at the same place that he is now located. My men and outfit will arrive Saturday." Monthly Return, Company D, Frontier Battalion, June 1890, TSA; Parsons' remark on page 63 of *Captain John R. Hughes:* "Later that same month Captain Jones also moved the main camp from La Salle County to Presidio. The work of the Rangers in the counties of La Salle and Brewster had been so effective that their efforts would now be better spent elsewhere," seems to be a weird application of logic taking into account Company D was forthwith replaced by Company F at Cotulla.
2. W. H. Denman to AG King, June 22, 1890, TSA. Here the letter writer, though understandable, is confused: The Mexican border town of Palomas is in the state of Chihuahua, not the state of Sonora. Captain Jones to AG King, May 2, 1890, TSA; Alexander, *Riding Lucifer's Line,* 109: "The murdering thieves had sneakily made off with Sheriff White's saddle horse and Deputy U.S. Marshal Ross' gun—a Winchester. Sergeant Fusselman wasn't on any federal business in the Franklin Mountains when he was killed: it was an easy call. Lawmen White and Ross sought reimbursement from the State of Texas: $40 for a horse, $15 for a gun. Doctor Sowers also submitted his bill for $10 to the state, not the federal government, 'for going out to where Fusselman was Killed.'"
3. *El Paso Times*, April 19, 1890; Captain Jones to AG King, June 30, 1890, TSA.
4. Private C. G. Aten to Captain Sieker, April 22, 1890, TSA; Corporal Hughes to M. A. Dolan, May 17, 1890, TSA; Corporal Hughes to Captain Sieker, May 6, 1890, TSA: "I moved camp from Marfa to Presidio. . . . arrived at Presidio May 5th . . ."; Ignaly Klienman to Captain Sieker, June 2, 1890, TSA. Shortly after Fusselman was buried at El Paso's Concordia Cemetery, his brother arrived at El Paso. Subsequent to attending to the necessary legalities, John Fusselman had his brother's body disinterred and accompanied Sergeant Fusselman's remains to Live Oak County, were he was finally laid to rest in the cemetery at the community of Lagarto on April 29, 1890. See Alexander, *Riding Lucifer's Line,* 109.

5. Corporal Hughes to Captain Sieker, May 6, 1890, TSA.
6. Captain Jones to AG King, July 31, 1890, TSA; Captain Jones to Captain Sieker, July 31, 1890, TSA.
7. Alexander, *Riding Lucifer's Line*, 111–112; Corporal Hughes to Captain Sieker, April 18, 1890, TSA.
8. Robert J. Casey, *The Texas Border and Some Borderliners*, 298.
9. *Brooklyn Daily Eagle*, August 5, 1890. The story of Ranger Private Gravis' death was also headlined in the *Galveston Daily News* of August 5, 1890, and the *El Paso Times* on August 6, 1890.
10. *The Luling Signal*, August 7, 1890.
11. Captain Jones to Captain Sieker, August 9, 1890, TSA.
12. Monthly Return, Company D, Frontier Battalion, August 1890, TSA. Also see, Virginia Madison, *The Big Bend Country of Texas*, 171–172.
13. Caldwell and DeLord, *Texas Lawmen: The Good and the Bad, 1835–1899*, 348: "While one newspaper account in September 1890 reported that a man was to be tried at Marfa for the murder of Private Gravis, it is unknown if anyone was ever convicted."
14. Report of Adjutant General: State of Texas 1889–1890, TSA.
15. AG King to Captain Jones, August 22, 1890, TSA.
16. Captain Jones to AG King, September 25, 1890, TSA.
17. Monthly Return, Company D, Frontier Battalion, October 1890, TSA; Captain Jones to Captain Sieker, October 14, 1890, TSA; Captain Jones to Captain Sieker, October 28, 1890, TSA.
18. Captain Jones to AG King, October 24, 1890, TSA.
19. AG King to Captain Jones, October 20, 1890, TSA.
20. Wooten, *A Comprehensive History of Texas, 1685–1897,* 349; Utley, *Lone Star Justice*, 253.
21. Circular to all Frontier Battalion Company Commanders, from Adjutant General Woodford Haywood Mabry, January 27, 1891, TSA; Captain Jones to AG Mabry, January 29, 1891, TSA; Captain Jones to Captain Sieker, January 31, 1891, TSA.
22. Captain Jones to AG Mabry, January 31, 1891, TSA; Lucy Miller Jacobson and Mildred Bloys Nored, *Jeff Davis County, Texas*, 131–132; Monthly Returns, Company D, Frontier Battalion, January and February 1891, TSA.
23. Captain Jones' and Private Putman's sworn certifications regarding the destruction of Putman's horse: February 13, 1891, TSA. And, Statement of Walter Gillis and Frank Patterson, Neutral Appraisers for establishing a dollar

value for the mercifully destroyed horse, February 13, 1891, before Brewster County Judge Van Sickle, TSA.

24. Captain Jones to AG Mabry, February 1, 1891, TSA; Captain Jones to Captain Sieker, February 12, 1891, TSA; Appraisal and Description of Horses, Company D, Frontier Battalion, April 17, 1891, TSA; Ron C. Tyler, *The Big Bend: A History of the Last Texas Frontier,* 134. Three additional secondary accounts of the gunfight between the lawmen and Fine Gilliland may be accessed in Stephens' *Texas Ranger Sketches*, 44–46, Alexander's *Winchester Warriors*, 241–242, and Parsons' *Captain John R. Hughes*, though the latter author's assertion that Ranger John R. Hughes, who was not present, "no doubt would have preferred to have been a participant" is but speculation. See pages 66–67.
25. Captain Jones to AG King, January 22, 1891 (just prior to King's resignation), TSA; Monthly Return, Company D, Frontier Battalion, January 1891, TSA.
26. Captain Jones to AG Mabry, March 17, 1891, TSA; AG Mabry to Captain Jones, March 19, 1891, TSA.
27. Monthly Return, Company D, Frontier Battalion, March 1891, TSA; Captain Jones to AG Mabry, March 27 and 31, 1891, TSA.
28. J. Morgan Broaddus, *The Legal Heritage of El Paso*, 131–132, other citations throughout; AG Mabry to Captain Jones, April 23, 1891, TSA.
29. AG Mabry to Captain Jones, April 29, 1891, TSA.
30. AG Mabry to Captain Jones, April 23, 1891, TSA; District Judge Winchester Kelso to Governor J. S. Hogg, February 2, 1891, TSA.
31. Captain Jones to AG Mabry, April 26, 1891, TSA.
32. Captain Jones to AG Mabry, April 30, 1891 and May 8, 1891, TSA.
33. Captain Jones to AG Mabry, May 26, 27, and 31, 1891, TSA; AG Mabry to Captain Jones, May 29, 1891, TSA.
34. Captain Jones to Colonel John F. Camp, June 28, 1891, TSA; Captain Jones to AG Mabry, July 31, 1891, TSA.
35. Don Graham, *Kings of Texas: The 150-Year Saga of an American Ranching Empire*, 63–64. For this rich historic account the esteemed author is not beguiled by an underlying compulsion to bend to political correctness and shatters long-standing myths. The treatment cuts to the bone with factuality, logical thinking, and evenhandedness: Refreshing!
36. Rick Miller, *Rube Burrow, Desperado*. The author, a quite prominent nonfiction chronicler of the Old West, brings the heretofore less glamorized outlaw to life. Although often ignored in Wild West writings, Ruben Houston Burrow actually participated in more train robberies than the James-Younger gang,

the Daltons, Butch Cassidy and the Sundance Kid, or Sam Bass. See pages ix–viii.

37. Bob Alexander, *Lynch Ropes and Long Shots: The Story of an Old West Train Robbery*. From the Introduction by one of the renowned experts on this particular criminal offense as it was perpetrated in the American Southwest, the late John D. Tanner, Jr., page 2.
38. *El Paso Daily Times*, September 3, 1891; *San Antonio Daily Express*, September 7, 1891. The painstakingly researched and meticulously written works of another renowned authority on this class of Southwestern gangsters of the era must not be overlooked. See Jeff Burton's *Dynamite and Six-Shooter*, 31 and *The Deadliest Outlaws: The Ketchum Gang and the Wild Bunch*, 71.
39. Captain Jones to AG Mabry, September 11, 1891 and May 1, 1892, TSA. Written with particular emphasis on the Rangers' participation and pursuit of the train robbers, a reasonably inclusive account may found in Chapter 1 of Alexander's, *Lawmen, Outlaws, and S.O.Bs.*, "Cigar Stumps and Peach Peels." Another oft-cited account, with much valuable data about the Big Bend Country's geography on the front end and fascinating details of courtroom happenings on the backend, may be found in the excellent piece by Franklin W. Daugherty, "Las Vegas de los Ladrones and the Flynt Gang," *The Journal of Big Bend Studies*, 1991, 1–28. Two additional good primary source documents are also obtainable, one frequently cited and one seldom mentioned. One is Frank Jones' letter about the episode to Pauline Baker, as contained in the January 1929 edition of *Frontier Times* under the title of "The Killing of Captain Frank Jones." The less frequently cited but extraordinarily worthwhile and enlightening paper is the handwritten statement, "Joe Sitter's Account of the Trailing and Capture of the Train Robbers," as recorded by Harry Warren during a first-person interview. This fascinating document may be found at the Bryan Wildenthal Memorial Library, Archives of the Big Bend, Sul Ross University, Alpine, Texas. For factually recounting the train robbing tale in this narrative, rather than specifically breaking down the story sentence by sentence with a specifically corresponding citation, these sources were amalgamated into the text for overall completeness and easier readability.
40. Ibid.; Monthly Return, Company D, Frontier Battalion, September and October 1891, TSA.
41. AG Mabry to Captain Jones, September 28, 1891, TSA.
42. Captain Jones to Pauline Baker as quoted in the *Frontier Times*' article previously cited.
43. AG Mabry to Captain Jones, October 22, 1891, TSA; Governor J. S. Hogg to Captain Jones, October 29, 1891, TSA. Rather curiously it's been written from

a secondary perspective that had Corporal John R. Hughes not been busy elsewhere he would have naturally headed up the Texas Ranger scout hunting for the elusive train robbers. See Parsons, *Captain John R. Hughes: Lone Star Ranger,* 70: "Corporal Hughes was with a detachment down at Shafter, or else he would have been in charge of the scout after the train robbers." In real time, had AG Mabry wanted to put any Texas Ranger—from anywhere in the state—on that manhunt he was the man holding power to do so. Apparently, at that time, the adjutant general was not as overawed with the policing reputation of Hughes as some modern-era chroniclers would be. Even with that misguided fantasy aside, the Frontier Battalion was built on a military model and in the chain-of-command structure corporals do not have command authority over sergeants—in this case Baz Outlaw—or captains—in this case Frank Jones.

Chapter 14 "We Have Been Compelled to Do Some Killing"

1. C. E. Van Horn, Zamloch's Congress of Wonders, San Francisco, California, to Texas Governor James S. Hogg, November 4, 1891, TSA.
2. Captain Jones to AG Mabry, November 6, 7, and 12, 1891, TSA; AG Mabry to Captain Jones, November 30, 1891. Clearly, AG Mabry guarded against overreaction: "If Sergt. Outlaw has made a faithful Ranger and conscientious officer in the performance of his duties heretofore, same should be taken into consideration. If he was provoked by certain extenuating circumstances he should have the benefit of such and you will reprimand him and assure him that any more of such Conduct will cause his dismissal from the service." Document in TSA.
3. Captain Jones to AG Mabry, December 1, 1891, TSA.
4. Captain Jones to AG Mabry, November 27, 1891, TSA: "Sergt. Outlaw and 4 men left last night in pursuit of a Mexican who brutally murdered Bill McCutcheon, a prominent rancher of Jeff Davis County yesterday morning." Jacobson and Nored, *Jeff Davis County, Texas*, 161–162; Monthly Return, Company D, Frontier Battalion, December 1891, TSA.
5. Captain Jones to AG Mabry, December 5, 1891, TSA.
6. Captain Jones to AG Mabry, December 22, 1891, TSA.
7. Captain Jones to AG Mabry, December 31, 1891, TSA. This was Captain Jones' second request to be redeployed, at least temporarily, to the South Texas borderlands: See, Jones to Mabry November 11, 1891, TSA: "If you move any Company down about Rio Grande City or Brownsville would like very much to go. I know the Country and people well and think I could do good work."

8. Alexander, *Riding Lucifer's Line,* 146–147.
9. Leon Claire Metz, *The Encyclopedia of Lawmen, Outlaws, and Gunfighters,* 233–234; *Los Angeles Times*, August 31, 1898; *El Paso Daily Times*, September 1, 1898.
10. Captain Jones to AG Mabry, January 15, 1892, TSA.
11. Monthly Return, Company D, Frontier Battalion, January 1892, TSA.
12. *Chicago Daily Tribune*, July 3, 1892.
13. Captain Jones to AG Mabry, March 9, 1892, TSA; Corporal Hughes to AG Mabry, January 15, 1892, TSA.
14. Monthly Return, Company D, Frontier Battalion, January 1892, TSA.
15. Captain Jones to AG Mabry, January 31, 1892, TSA.
16. Captain Jones to Governor Hogg, March 8, 1892, TSA; AG Mabry to Captain Jones, March 14, 1892, TSA; Captain Jones to AG Mabry, March 17, 1892, TSA.
17. Captain Jones to AG Mabry, March 1, 1892, TSA. History would bear witness, on this subject Frank Jones was forward thinking and right. Today, even though many plainclothes law enforcement personnel—city, county, state, and federal—do not wear uniforms, during raid and arrests scenarios they are mandated by internal policy to don clearly marked insignias, such as armbands, raid caps, raid jackets, etc .
18. Sheriff H. W. Baylor to Captain Jones, May 9, 1892, TSA.
19. Captain Jones to AG Mabry, March 27, 1892, TSA.
20. Captain Jones to AG Mabry, March 13 and 19, 1892, TSA; AG Mabry to Captain Jones, March 22, 1892, TSA.
21. M. R. Daniels to AG Mabry, May [?], 1892, TSA; Typed itemization of complaints submitted to AG Mabry, May [?], 1892. A notation on this document after it reached the adjutant general's office is dated June 9, 1892, TSA.
22. Daugherty, "Las Vegas de los Ladrones and the Flynt Gang," 15–16; Broaddus, *The Legal Heritage of El Paso*, 111–136; Alexander, *Lawmen, Outlaws, and S.O.Bs*, 22; Captain Jones to AG Mabry, April 16, 1892, TSA.
23. Captain Jones to AG Mabry, May 24 and 31, 1892, TSA. From the latter, "about the 10th of June a letter or telegram will reach me at Boerne. After that will inform you where I am." AG Mabry to Captain Jones, May 26, 1892, TSA.
24. Captain Jones to AG Mabry, June 1, 1892, TSA; AG Mabry to Captain Jones, June 3, 1892, TSA. For more on the life and death of Tom Carson, see Cliff Caldwell, "Davey Thomas 'Tom' Carson, Texas Ranger," *Wild West History Association Journal*, June 2009.

25. Captain Jones to AG Mabry, June 15, 1892, TSA; AG Mabry to Captain Jones, June 16, 1892, TSA.
26. Captain Jones to AG Mabry, June 21, 1892, TSA.
27. Alexander, *Winchester Warriors*, 253; Oden, *Texas Ranger's Diary and Scrapbook*, 59.
28. Monthly Return, Company D, Frontier Battalion, June 1892; Captain Jones to AG Mabry, July 1, 1892; Mike Cox, *Texas Ranger Tales: Stories That Need Telling*, 97–98; Parsons, *Captain John R. Hughes*, 73.
29. Monthly Returns, Company D, Frontier Battalion, July and August, 1892, TSA.
30. Captain Jones to AG Mabry, April 2, 1892, TSA.
31. Captain Jones to AG Mabry, August 3, 1892, TSA; AG Mabry to Captain Jones, August 5, 1892, TSA.
32. Captain Jones to AG Mabry, August 5, 1892, TSA.
33. Oden, *Texas Ranger's Diary and Scrapbook*, 40.
34. Ibid., 20.
35. Captain Jones to AG Mabry, September 18, 1892, TSA; AG Mabry to Captain Jones, September 27, 1892, TSA; Monthly Return, Company D, Frontier Battalion, September 1892, TSA.
36. Captain Jones to AG Mabry, September 30, 1892, TSA; April 18, 2014, interview by author with Robert W. Stephens: More than forty years ago Mr. Stephens, during his research, conversed with Lelia Jones Neibert, a daughter of one of Frank's brothers, and was furnished the exact quotation as cited.
37. For a close look at George Wythe Baylor, the reader must access *Into the Far Wild Country: True Tales of the Old Southwest*, edited by the esteemed Jerry D. Thompson.
38. Monthly Return, Company D, Frontier Battalion, August 1891, TSA.
39. DuCoin, *Lawmen on the Texas Frontier*, 124.
40. Baylor, *Into the Far Wild Country*. On page 25 in the Introduction editor Thompson introduces Helen Baylor: "It was there, [Ysleta] that Baylor's oldest pampered daughter, Helen, married Ranger sergeant James Buchanan Gillett on 10 February 1881."
41. DuCoin, *Lawmen on the Texas Frontier*, 124.
42. Ibid.
43. Ibid.
44. AG Mabry to Captain Jones, October 3, 1892, TSA.
45. Captain Jones to AG Mabry, October 23, 1892, TSA. The sheriff Frank Jones mentioned was Presidio County Sheriff S. R. Miller, although he is

not referenced in Sammy Tise's *Texas County Sheriffs*. See, Sheriff Miller to Governor Hogg, November 5, 1892, TSA, written on Presidio County preprinted letterhead stationery: "S.R. Miller, Shff & Tax Collector." Also, S. R. Miller to AG Mabry, July 7, 1893, TSA: "S.R. Miller, ex-Sheriff Presidio Co. Texas."

46. AG Mabry to Captain Jones, October 26, 1892, TSA. For specifics of political chicanery associated with this election contest the reader is referred to *Little Known History of the Big Bend* by Glenn Justice, pages 40–41.
47. Tise, *Texas County Sheriffs*, 65, 424; Parsons, *Captain John R. Hughes*, 276.

Chapter 15 "Boys, I Am Killed"

1. El Paso County Judge F. E. Hunter to Governor Hogg, December 16, 1892, TSA.
2. AG Mabry to Captain Jones, December 20, 1892, TSA.
3. Captain Jones to AG Mabry, December 22, 1892, TSA: "I will leave for El Paso tonight. . . ."
4. Monthly Return, Company D, Frontier Battalion, December 1892, TSA: "22—Captain Jones went to El Paso as per instructions from Genl. Mabry to investigate reported lawlessness, returned on the 24th and made report by letter. Out 3 days, marched 520 miles."
5. Captain Jones to AG Mabry, December 25, 1892, TSA; Parsons, *Captain John R. Hughes: Lone Star Ranger,* page 93, fires a shot at Sheriff Frank B. Simmons: "Simmons also asked for a full company of Rangers 'if only for a few months.' He concluded, 'I am going to try and catch all these Mexicans that had been doing the Stealing and Robbing [*sic*] in this county for years.' One wonders why he had not already attempted to do just that." One may posit that Sheriff Simmons, living in the real world in real time reality, could not avail himself of recruiting Hoppy or Matt Dillon, but was desperately trying to fulfill his law-enforcing mission with the meager resources and insufficient manpower at his disposal.
6. Captain Jones to AG Mabry, December 30, 1892, TSA. "If you have no objection I would like to visit Austin about the 6th of January on some business connected with my candidacy for the Marshal's office. I am very anxious to meet some parties who will be in Austin when the Legislature convenes."
7. AG Mabry to Captain Jones, January 2, 1893, TSA.
8. Rick Miller, *Sam Bass and Gang*, 241–262; Tise, *Texas County Sheriffs,* 378; Stephens, *Texas Ranger Sketches*. 152; Alexander, *Winchester Warriors*, 259.

9. Stephens, *Texas Ranger Sketches*, 130; Private Frank Schmid to AG Mabry, January 19, 1893, TSA.
10. Captain Jones to AG Mabry, January 17, 1893, TSA.
11. AG Mabry to Captain Jones, January 23m 1893, TSA.
12. Petition to Governor Hogg from El Paso County Grand Jury. January 31, 1893, TSA.
13. El Paso County Sheriff Frank B. Simmons to Adjutant General's Office, February 1, 1893, TSA.
14. Captain Jones to Captain G.A. Wheatley, Quartermaster, February 5, 1893, TSA; Stephens, *Texas Ranger Sketches,* 145: "[Sieker] was made Assistant Adjutant General."
15. George Wythe Baylor to AG Mabry (who had just been replaced as adjutant general), February 15, 1893, TSA.
16. Ibid.
17. Captain Jones to AG Mabry, February, 17, 1893, TSA.
18. Captain Jones to AG Mabry, March 9, 1893, TSA.
19. Monthly Return, Company D, Frontier Battalion, March 1893, TSA. "Capt. Frank Jones went to Val Verde Co. on official business." Note the "official business" was not further particularized, an appropriate move for maintaining the integrity of an ongoing but secretive criminal investigation.
20. Captain Jones to AG Mabry, March 31, 1893, TSA.
21. Alexander, *Lawmen, Outlaws, and S.O.Bs.* The life and times of Charles Small are biographically sketched in Chapter 6, "He Was Killed By Me: Charley Small, Southwest Badman."
22. Telegram, Ranger Sergeant D. L. Musgrave, Company F, Frontier Battalion to AG Mabry, July 22, 1893, TSA.
23. Captain Jones to AG Mabry, April 16, 1893, TSA.
24. Monthly Return, Company D, Frontier Battalion, April 1893, TSA: "Capt. Jones and 2 men went to Langtry under instructions of Genl. Mabry."
25. Telegram, Captain Jones to AG Mabry, April 21, 1893, TSA.
26. Alexander, *Winchester Warriors*, 260.
27. Captain Jones to AG Mabry, April 22, 1893, TSA.
28. Hughes McCormick to AG Mabry, May 30, 1893, TSA.
29. Captain Jones to AG Mabry, April 22, 1893, TSA.
30. Monthly Return, Company D, Frontier Battalion, April 1893, TSA; Captain Jones to AG Mabry, April 22, 1893, TSA. A biographical profile of Ranger Kirchner may be found in Stephens' *Texas Ranger Sketches,* 77–80,

31. Company D, Scout Report, Langtry Detachment, Frontier Battalion, May 1893, TSA.
32. Captain Jones to AG Mabry, May 14, 1893, TSA.
33. Captain Jones to AG Mabry, May 7, 1893, TSA.
34. Sheriff Frank Simmons, El Paso County to AG Mabry, June 7, 1893, TSA.
35. Captain Jones to AG Mabry, June 2, 1893, TSA.
36. AG Mabry to Captain Jones, June 9, 1893, TSA. Unfortunately, Parsons in *Captain John R. Hughes*, once again stirs in a bit of confusion regarding the adjutant general. In this instance he proffers that AG Wilburn H. King was responsible for transferring Captain Jones to El Paso County. See page 82. Long before the transfer took place King had been replaced by AG Mabry, and it was he who signaled the okay for the redeployment to El Paso County.
37. Petition, W. M. Noyes, et al, to AG Mabry, June [?] 1893, TSA.
38. J. M. Dean to AG Mabry, June 19, 1893, TSA.
39. Captain Jones to AG Mabry, June 11 and 13, 1893, TSA. From the latter, "I broke Camp this morning. . . . It will take us about ten days to make the trip." Monthly Return Company D, Frontier Battalion, June 1893, TSA.
40. Parsons, *Captain John R. Hughes*, page 82, citing the *San Antonio Daily Express*, suggests one of the first things Captain Jones did upon Company D's arrival at Ysleta was "to set up tents."
41. Monthly Return, Company D, Frontier Battalion, June 1893, TSA.
42. Stephens, *Texas Ranger Sketches*, 129.
43. Ibid.
44. Alexander, *Riding Lucifer's Line*, xv.
45. Ibid., 130.
46. DuCoin, *Lawmen on the Texas Frontier*, 127; Carlysle Graham Raht, *The Romance of Davis Mountains and Big Bend Country*, 321.
47. Parsons, *Captain John R. Hughes: Lone Star Ranger*, 82.
48. Monthly Return, Company D, Frontier Battalion, June 1893, TSA.
49. Bruce A. Glasrud and Harold J. Weiss, Jr., eds., *Tracking the Texas Rangers: The Nineteenth Century*, "Rangers on the Last Frontier of Texas" by James M. Day, 269.
50. Alexander, *Riding Lucifer's Line*, 131.
51. Stephens, *Texas Ranger Sketches*, 33.
52. Alexander, *Bad Company and Burnt Powde: Justice and Injustice in the Old Southwest*, 323; George W. Baylor to AG Mabry, July 2, 1893, TSA; Alexander, *Riding Lucifer's Line*, 131.

53. AG Mabry to Governor Hogg, September 9, 1893, TSA; Leon C. Metz, *Border: The U.S.–Mexico Line*, 295: "A portion of disputed territory involved *La Isla de San Elizario* (the Island of San Elizario), usually just referred to as 'the island' or sometimes 'Pirate Island,' twenty miles downstream from El Paso. The island extended nine miles and comprised thirteen thousand acres, two hundred in cultivation, the rest in tangled *bosque* (thickets)."
54. Captain John R. Hughes to AG Mabry, September 6, 1893, (Subsequent to promotion to captain), TSA.
55. Utley, *Lone Star Justice*, 264–265. For particular attention to the Rio Grande changing course, 341, n.24.
56. The following story relating to the infamous shoot-out on Pirate Island, aside being drawn from myriad secondary sources, is basically a synthesis of three outstanding—and oft cited—primary sources: George W. Baylor to AG Mabry, July 2, 1893, TSA; Corporal Carl Kirchner to AG Mabry, July 2, 1893, TSA; and AG Mabry to Governor Hogg, September 9, 1893, TSA.
57. Baylor to AG Mabry, July 9, 1893, TSA; *Dallas Morning News*, July 2, 1893.
58. Telegraph, Corporal Kirchner to AG Mabry, June 30, 1893, TSA: "Have just had fight with Mexican outlaws near the line of Mexico. Capt. Jones killed. We were overpowered and have just come in for reinforcements. Only had six men." The cited telegram was repeated verbatim by newspapers throughout Texas, including the *Dallas Morning News* of July 1, 1893.
59. *Dallas Morning News*, July 1, 1893: "A special train carrying a well-armed posse of twenty-five men led by Sheriff Simmons and Col. W. Baylor, an ex-ranger captain, reached San Elizario at 3 p.m. and left at once for the trouble determined to rescue the rangers and secure the body of Capt. Jones. . . ." Also, see, Robert K. DeArment, *George Scarborough: The Life and Death of a Lawman on the Closing Frontier*, 47–48.
60. Corporal Kirchner to AG Mabry, July 2, 1893, TSA; *Dallas Morning News*, December 18, 1893: "Sheriff F. B. Simmons of El Paso county was in the city yesterday. It was he who on the 30th of last June recovered the body of Capt. Frank Jones, who was killed at Tres Jacales, in the state of Chihuahua, Mexico."
61. Sheriff Simmons to Governor Hogg, July 7, 1893, TSA; AG Mabry to Sheriff Simmons, July 19, 1893, TSA.
62. *Dallas Morning News*, July 2, 1893; Parsons, *Captain John R. Hughes: Lone Star Ranger*, 87–88.
63. Sergeant Hughes to AG Mabry, July 5, 1893, TSA; Corporal Kirchner to AG Mabry, July 5, 1893, TSA; Petition of Company D Rangers to AG Mabry, July 5, 1893, TSA; Captain John R. Hughes to AG Mabry, July 8, 1893, TSA.

64. Alexander, *Riding Lucifer's Line*, 136–138, 150.
65. AG Mabry to Governor Hogg, September 13, 1893, TSA.
66. Baylor to AG Mabry, July 9, 1893, TSA.
67. Baylor, *Into the Far, Wild Country*. Quotation from the Introduction by Jerry D. Thompson, 30.
68. DuCoin, *Lawmen on the Texas Frontier*, 130.
69. Stephens, *Texas Ranger Sketches*, 68. During the author's 18 April 2014 interview with writer Robert W. Stephens, he advised and believes, based on his interviews with Jones' relatives some forty-odd years ago, that Grace Kathleen Jones did in fact live with her stepmother, Helen Baylor Jones, and Frank Jones, until her father's untimely death on Pirate Island.
70. Alexander, *Riding Lucifer's Line*, 134–135; Frank Jones' pocket-watch, rifle, and badge until quite recently were on extended loan and display at the Texas Ranger Hall of Fame & Museum, Waco, Texas, courtesy the then owners, Old West memorabilia collector and renowned Western artist Donald M. Yena, and his gracious wife Louise. These historic treasures, however, changed hands at auction on March 1, 2014, at Burley Auction Gallery, New Braunfels, Texas, purchased by Kurt House. Interestingly, for the Fall 2013 edition of *The Texas Gun Collector,* noted collector Kurt House, in "Cold Steel and Warm Gold: Arms and Badges of Three Texas Ranger Captains," 26–30, makes mention of shields credited as being "Pirate Island" badges later presented to legit veterans of the battle inside Mexico's borderline, including Captain John R. Hughes. It is, however, but fair to acknowledge in deference to the Texas Rangers who were actually there and survived the horrific warfare, that John Reynolds Hughes, at the time Company D's 1st Sergeant, was not within 100 miles of Pirate Island at the time Captain Frank Jones was killed. Additional data regarding the collecting of Old West-era badges may be found in the exceptional piece by Donald M. Yena, "Texas Authority In Metal: Badges, History and Related Artifacts," *The Texas Gun Collector*, Spring 2003.
71. *Dallas Morning News*, January 21, 1895, quoting adjutant general's biannual report to the governor.

Bibliography

The non-published sources—manuscripts, typescripts, theses, dissertations, tape recordings, official documents, courthouse records, tax rolls, petitions, correspondence, prison records, census records, licensing records, interviews, etc.—are cited with specificity in chapter endnotes.

Books

Alexander, Bob. *Bad Company and Burnt Powder: Justice and Injustice in the Old Southwest*. Denton: University of North Texas Press, 2014.

________ . *Riding Lucifer's Line: Ranger Deaths along the Texas Mexico Border*. Denton: University of North Texas Press, 2013.

________ . *Rawhide Ranger, Ira Aten: Enforcing Law on the Texas Frontier*. Denton: University of North Texas Press, 2011.

________ . *Winchester Warriors: Texas Rangers of Company D, 1874–1901*. Denton: University of North Texas Press, 2009.

________. *Lawmen, Outlaws, and S.O.Bs.: Gunfighters of the Old Southwest*. Silver City, NM: High-Lonesome Books, 2004.

________ . *Lawmen, Outlaws, and S.O.Bs.: Gunfighters of the Old Southwest*. Vol. II. Silver City, NM: High-Lonesome Books, 2007.

________ . *Lynch Ropes and Long Shots: The Story of an Old West Train Robbery*. Silver City, NM: High-Lonesome Books, 2007.

________ . *Fearless Dave Allison, Border Lawman*. Silver City, NM: High-Lonesome Books, 2003.

Anderson, Gary Clayton. *The Conquest of Texas: Ethnic Cleansing in the Promised Land, 1820–1875*. Norman: University of Oklahoma Press, 2005.

Ball, Larry D. *Desert Lawmen: The High Sheriffs of New Mexico and Arizona Territories, 1846–1912*. Albuquerque: University of New Mexico Press, 1992.

________. *The United States Marshals of New Mexico and Arizona Territories, 1846–1912*. Albuquerque: University of New Mexico Press, 1978.

Barkley, Roy R., and Mark F. Odintz, eds., *The Portable Handbook of Texas*. Austin: The Texas State Historical Association, 2000.

Barr, Alwyn. *Reconstruction to Reform: Texas Politics 1876–1906*. Austin: University of Texas Press, 1971.

Baylor, George Wythe. *Into the Far, Wild Country: True Tales of the Old Southwest*. Edited by Jerry Thompson. El Paso: Texas Western Press, 1996.

Bidal, Lillian, *The Run of the Elk: A Biography of Angie Lydia Hendrix Cleve*. El Paso: The Robert E. and Evelyn McKee Foundation, 1996.

Blackburn, Ed. *Wanted: Historic County Jails of Texas*. College Station: Texas A&M University, 2006.

Blanco County News. *Heritage of Blanco County, Texas*. Blanco, TX: Blanco County News, 1987.

Brice, Donaly E. *The Great Comanche Raid: Boldest Indian Attack of the Texas Republic*. Austin: Eakin Press, 1987.

_______. and Barry A. Crouch. *The Governor's Hounds: The Texas State Police, 1870–1873*. Austin: University of Texas Press, 2011.

Broaddus, J. Morgan. *The Legal Heritage of El Paso*. El Paso: Texas Western College Press, 1963.

Brown, Frank. *Annals of Travis County and of the City of Austin: From the Earliest Times to the Close of 1875*. n.p. n.d. Copy in Texas State Library & Archives, Austin, Texas.

Brown, John Henry. *Indian Wars and Pioneers of Texas*. Austin: State House Press, 1988.

Burton, Jeffrey. *The Deadliest Outlaws: The Ketchum Gang and the Wild Bunch*. Denton: University of North Texas Press, 2009.

_______. *Western Story*. European Edition. England: Palomino Books, 2008.

_______. *Dynamite and Six-Shooter*. Santa Fe, NM: Press of the Territorian, 1970.

Caldwell, Clifford R., and Ron DeLord. *Texas Lawmen: The Good and the Bad, 1835–1899*. Charleston, SC: The History Press, 2011.

Casey, Robert. *The Texas Border and Some Borderliners*. New York: Bobbs-Merrill Co., 1950.

Clendenen, Clarence C. *Blood on the Border: The United States Army and the Mexican Irregulars*. Canada: The Macmillan Company, 1969.

Collins, Michael L. *Texas Devils: Rangers and Regulars on the Lower Rio Grande, 1846–1861*. Norman: University of Oklahoma Press, 2008.

Corwin, Hugh D. *Comanche and Kiowa Captives in Oklahoma and Texas*. Guthrie, OK: Cooperative Publishing Co., 1959.

Cox, Mike. *The Texas Rangers: Wearing the Cinco Peso, 1821–1900*. New York: Forge Books, 2009.

_______. *Texas Ranger Tales: Stories That Need Telling*. Plano, TX: Republic of Texas Press, 1997.

Day, James M., and Dorman Winfrey. *Texas Indian Papers, 1860–1916*. Austin: Texas State Library, 1961.

DeArment, Robert K. *George Scarborough: Life and Death of a Lawman on the Closing Frontier*. Norman: University of Oklahoma Press, 1992.

DeLeón, Arnoldo. *They Called Them Greasers: Anglo Attitudes Towards Mexicans in Texas, 1821–1900*. Austin: University of Texas Press, 1983.

_______. *The Tejano Community, 1836–1900*. Albuquerque: University of New Mexico Press, 1982.

DeLord, Ronald G. *The Ultimate Sacrifice: Trials and Triumphs of the Texas Peace Officer, 1823–2000*. Austin: Police Officers Memorial Fund, 2000.

Devereaux, Jan. *Pistols, Petticoats and Poker: The Real Lottie Deno, Nor Lies or Alibis*. Silver City, NM: High-Lonesome Books, 2008.

Dillion, Richard. *Wells, Fargo Detective: A Biography of James B. Hume*. Reno: University of Nevada Press, 1986.

Dobie, J. Frank. *Cow People*. Boston: Little Brown and Company, 1964.

DuCoin, Candice. *Lawmen on the Texas Frontier: Ranger and Sheriffs*. Round Rock, TX: Riata Books, 2007.

Dumont, Ella Elgar Bird. *Ella Elgar Bird DuMont: An Autobiography of a West Texas Pioneer*. Edited by Tommy J. Boley. Austin: University of Texas Press, 1988.

Durham, George. *Taming the Nueces Strip: The Story of McNelly's Rangers*. Austin: University of Texas Press, 1962.

Ernst, Robert. *Deadly Affrays: The Violent Deaths of the U.S. Marshals*. Lafayette, IN: Scarlet Mask, 2006.

Farber, James. *Texans With Guns*. San Antonio: The Naylor Company, 1950.

Farrow, Marion H. *Troublesome Times in Texas*. San Antonio: The Naylor Company, 1960.

Fisher, O. C. *It Occurred in Kimble*. San Angelo, TX: Talley Press, 1954.

Ford, John Salmon. *Rip Ford's Texas*. Edited by Stephen B. Oates. Austin: University of Texas Press, 1963.

Gammel, Hans Peter. *The Laws of Texas, 1822–1897*. Ten Vols. Austin: Gammel Books, 1898.

Gilbreath, West. *Death From a Texas Gallows*. Fort Worth: Eakin Press, 2014.

Gillett, James B. *Six Years With the Texas Rangers*. New Haven, CT: Yale University Press, 1921.

Glasrud, Bruce A., and Harold J. Weiss, Jr., eds. *Tracking the Texas Rangers: The Nineteenth Century*. Denton: The University of North Texas Press, 2012.

Gossell, Julie, and Tina Little, eds. *Boerne: The History of Our Town*. Boerne, TX: Boerne Education Foundation, 2011.

Gournay, Luke. *Texas Boundaries: Evolution of the State's Counties*. College Station: Texas A&M University Press, 1995.

Graham, Don. *Kings of Texas: The 150-Year Saga of an American Ranching Empire*. Hoboken, NJ: John Wiley & Sons, 2003.

Graybill, Andrew W. *Policing the Great Plains: Rangers, Mounties, and the North American Frontier, 1857–1910*. Lincoln: University of Nebraska Press, 2007.

Gwynne, S. C. *Empire of the Summer Moon: Quanah Parker and the Rise and Fall of the Comanches, the Most Powerful Indian Tribe in American History*. New York: Scribner, 2010.

Haas, Oscar. *History of New Braunfels and Comal County, Texas 1844–1946*. Austin: The Steck Co., 1968.

Hail, Marshall. *Knight in the Sun: Harper B. Lee, First Yankee Matador*. Boston: Little Brown and Co., 1962.

Haley, James L. *Passionate Nation: The Epic History of Texas*. New York: Free Press, 2006.

_______. *The Buffalo War: A History of the Red River Uprising of 1874*. Norman: University of Oklahoma Press, 1985.

Harris, Charles H. III, and Louis R. Sadler and Frances E. Harris. *Texas Ranger Biographies: Those Who Served, 1910–1921*. Albuquerque: University of New Mexico Press, 2009.

Horgan, Paul. *Great River: The Rio Grande in North American History*. Two vols. New York: Rinehart & Company, Inc., 1954.

Howell, Kenneth W., ed. *Still the Arena of Civil War: Violence and Turmoil in Reconstruction Texas*. Denton: University of North Texas Press, 2012.

Hughes, W. J. *Rebellious Ranger: Rip Ford and the Old Southwest*. Norman: University of Oklahoma Press, 1964.

Huson, Hobart. *District Judges of Refugio County*. Refugio, TX: Refugio Timely Remarks, 1941.

Ingmire, Frances T. *Texas Ranger Service Records, 1847–1900*. Six vols. St. Louis, MO: Ingmire Publications, 1982.

Ivey, Darren L. *The Texas Rangers: A Registry and History*. Jefferson, NC: McFarland & Co., 2010.

Jacobson, Lucy Miller, and Nored, Mildred. *Jeff Davis County, Texas*. Fort Davis, TX: Fort Davis County Historical Society, 1993.

James, Glenn, and Henri Rupe Capps. *The Life of Thomas W. Gamel*. Mason, TX: Mason County Historical Commission, 2003.

Justice, Glenn. *Little Known History of the Big Bend: Documented Chronicles from Cabeza De Vaca to the Era of Pancho Villa*. Odessa, TX: Rimrock Press, 2001.

Johnson, David. *The Mason County "Hoo Doo" War, 1874–1902*. Denton: University of North Texas Press, 2006.

______. *John Ringo, King of the Cowboys: His Life and Times From the Hoo Doo War to Tombstone*. Denton: University of North Texas Press, 2008.

______. *The Horrell Wars: Feuding in Texas and New Mexico*. Denton: University of North Texas Press, 2014.

Keating, Bern. *An Illustrated History of the Texas Rangers*. New York: Rand McNally & Co., 1975.

Kenner, Charles L. *The Comanchero Frontier: A History of New Mexican-Plains Indian Relations*. Norman: University of Oklahoma Press, 1969.

Leiker, James N. *Racial Borders: Black Soldiers Along the Rio Grande*. College Station: Texas A&M University Press, 2002.

Liu, Joanne S. *Barbed Wire: The Fence That Changed the West*. Missoula, MT: Mountain Press Publishing Company, 2009.

McCaslin, Richard B. *Fighting Stock: John S. "Rip" Ford of Texas*. Forth Worth: Texas Christian University Press, 2011.

McCullum, Henry D., and Frances T. McCullum. *The Wire That Fenced the West and Southwest*. Norman: University of Oklahoma Press, 1965.

Martin, Jack. *Border Boss: Captain John R. Hughes—Texas Ranger*. Austin: State House Press, 1990.

Madison, Virginia. *The Big Bend Country of Texas*. New York: October House, Inc., 1968.

Meed, Douglas V. *Bloody Border: Riots, Battles and Adventures Along the Turbulent U.S. Borderlands*. Tucson, AZ: Westernlore Press, 1992.

Metz, Leon Claire. *Encyclopedia of Lawmen, Outlaws, and Gunfighters*. New York: Checkmark Books, 2003.

______. *Border: The U.S.-Mexico Line*. El Paso, TX: Mangan Books, 1989.

Michno, Gregory F. *Encyclopedia of Indian Wars: Western Battles and Skirmishes, 1850–1890*. Missoula, MT: Mountain Press Publishing Company, 2003

______, *The Settlers' War: The Struggle for the Texas Frontier in the 1860s*. Caldwell, ID: Caxton Press, 2011.

______, and Susan J. Michno. *A Fate Worse Than Death: Indian Captivities in the West, 1830–1885*. Caldwell, ID: Caxton Press, 2007.

______, and Susan J. Michno. *Forgotten Fights: Little Known Raids and Skirmishes on the Frontier, 1823–1890*. Missoula, MT: Mountain Press Publishing Company, 2008.

Miller, Rick. *Texas Ranger John B. Jones and the Frontier Battalion, 1874–1881*. Denton: University of North Texas Press, 2012.

_______. *Sam Bass and Gang*. Austin: State House Press, 1999.

_______. *Rube Burrow, Desperado*. Bloomington, IN: iUniverse LLC, 2014.

Moneyhon, Carl H. *Edmund J. Davis: Civil War General, Republican Leader, Reconstruction Governor.* Fort Worth: Texas Christian University Press, 2010.

_______. *Texas After the Civil War: The Struggle of Reconstruction*. College Station: Texas A&M University Press.

Moore, Stephen L. *Savage Frontier: Rangers, Rifelmen, and Indian Wars in Texas*. Four vols. Denton: University of North Texas Press, 2002–2010.

Moursund, John Stribling. *Blanco County History*. Burnet, TX: Nortex Press, 1979.

_______. *Blanco County Families for One Hundred Years*. Edited by Mabel Stribling. Burnet, TX: Nortex Press, 1981.

Nichols, James Wilson. *Now You Hear My Horn: The Journal of James Wilson Nichols, 1820–1887*. Edited by Catherine W. McDowell. Austin: University of Texas Press, 1967.

Nolan, Frederick. *Bad Blood: The Life and Times of the Horrell Brothers*. Stillwater, OK: Barbed Wire Press, 1994.

Nye, W. S. *Carbine and Lance: The Story of Old Fort Sill*. Norman: University of Oklahoma Press, 1937.

Oden, Alonzo V. *Texas Ranger Diary and Scrapbook*. Edited by Ann Jensen. Dallas: Kaleidograph Press, 1936.

Paredes, Américo. *With His Pistol in His Hand: A Border Ballad and Its Hero*. Austin: University of Texas Press, 1958.

Parsons, Chuck. *Captain John R. Hughes: Lone Star Ranger*. Denton: University of North Texas Press, 2011.

_______. *The Sutton-Taylor Feud: The Deadliest Blood Feud in Texas*. Denton: University of North Texas Press, 2009.

_______, and Donaly E. Brice. *Texas Ranger N.O. Reynolds: The Intrepid*. Honolulu: Talei Publishing, 2005.

_______, and Marianne E. Hall. *Captain L. H. McNelly, Texas Ranger: The Life and Times of a Fighting Man*. Austin: State House Press, 2001.

_______, and Gary P. Fritterer. *Captain C. B. McKinney: The Law in South Texas.* Wolfe City, TX: Hennington Publishing Co., 1993.

Perkins, Clifford Alan. *Border Patrol: With the U.S. Immigration Service on the Mexican Boundary, 1910–1954.* El Paso: Texas Western Press, 1978.

Perry, C. R. *Memoir of Capt'n C. R. Perry of Johnson City, Texas; A Texas Veteran.* Edited by Kenneth Kesselus. Austin: Jenkins Publishing Company, 1990.

Preece, Harold. *Lone Star Man: Ira Aten, Last of the Old Texas Rangers.* New York: Hastings House, 1960.

Price, Bill S. *Bill Whitley: Outlaw.* Austin: Nortex Press, 1995.

Proctor, Ben. *Just One Riot: Episodes of Texas Rangers in the 20th Century.* Austin: Eakin Press, 1991.

Raht, Carlysle Graham. *The Romance of Davis Mountains and the Big Bend Country.* Odessa, TX: The Rahtbooks Company, 1963.

Roberts, Dan W. *Rangers and Sovereignty.* Austin: State House Press, 1987.

Rose, Peter. *The Reckoning: The Triumph of Order on the Texas Outlaw Frontier.* Lubbock: Texas Tech University Press, 2012.

Sayles, Henry, and John Sayles, eds., *Early Laws of Texas: General Laws From 1836–1879.* St. Louis, MO: Gilbert Book Company, 1891.

Smith, Cornelius C., Jr. *Emilio Kosterlitzky: Eagle of Sonora and the Southwest Border.* Glendale, CA: The Arthur E. Clark Company, 1970.

Smith, David Paul. *Frontier Defense in the Civil War: Texas's Rangers and Rebels.* College Station: Texas A&M University Press, 1992.

Smith, Thomas T. *The Old Army in Texas: A Research Guide to the U.S. Army in Nineteenth-Century Texas.* Austin: Texas State Historical Association, 2000.

Sonnichsen, C. L. *Ten Texas Feuds.* Albuquerque: University of New Mexico Press, 1971.

_______. *I'll Die Before I'll Run: The Story of the Great Feuds of Texas.* Lincoln: University of Nebraska Press, 1964.

_______. *Pass of the North: Four Centuries on the Rio Grande.* Two vols. El Paso, TX: Texas Western Press, 1968.

Sowell, A. J. *Early Settlers and Indian Fighters of Southwest Texas.* Austin: State House Press, 1986.

Speer, William S., ed. *The Encyclopedia of the New West.* Marshall, TX: The Untied States Biographical Publishing Company, 1881.

Spellman, Paul N. *Captain J. A. Brooks, Texas Ranger.* Denton: University of North Texas Press, 2007.

_______. *Captain John H. Rogers, Texas Ranger.* Denton: University of North Texas Press, 2003.

Stephens, Robert W. *Texas Ranger Sketches*. Dallas: Self-published, 1972.

_______. *Bullets and Buckshot in Texas*. Dallas: Self-published, 2002.

_______. *Walter Durbin: Texas Ranger and Sheriff*. Clarendon, TX: Clarendon Press, 1970.

_______. *Texas Ranger Captain Dan Roberts: The Untold Story*. Dallas: Self-published, 2009.

_______. *Captain George H. Schmitt, Texas Ranger*. Dallas: Self-published, 2006.

_______. *Texas Ranger Indian War Pensions*. Quanah, TX: Nortex Press, 1975.

Stovall, Alan A. *Nueces Headwater Country: A Regional History*. San Antonio: The Naylor Co., 1959.

Struve, Walter. *Germans in Texas: Commerce, Migration, and Culture in the Days of the Lone Star Republic*. Austin: University of Texas Press, 1996.

Thompson, Jerry D. *Cortina: Defending the Mexican Name in Texas*. College Station: Texas A&M University Press, 2007.

_______. *A Wild and Vivid Land: An Illustrated History of the South Texas Border*. Austin: Texas State Historical Association, 1997.

Tise, Sammy. *Texas County Sheriffs*. Hallettsville, TX: Tise Genealogical Research, 1989.

Tyler, Ron C. *The Big Bend: A History of the Last Texas Frontier*. College Station: Texas A&M University Press, 1996.

Utley, Robert M. *Lone Star Justice: The First Century of the Texas Rangers*. New York: Oxford University Press, 2002.

_______. *Lone Star Lawmen: The Second Century of the Texas Rangers*. New York: Oxford University Press, 2007.

Webb, Walter Prescott. *The Texas Rangers: A Century of Frontier Defense*. Austin: University of Texas Press, 1965.

_______. *The Story of the Texas Rangers*. Austin: Encino Press, 1957.

Weiss, Harold J., Jr. *Yours to Command: The Life and Legend of Texas Ranger Captain Bill McDonald*. Denton: University of North Texas Press, 2009.

Wilbarger, J. W. *Indian Depredations in Texas*. Austin: Eakin Press. 1985.

Wilkins, Frederick. *The Law Comes to Texas: The Texas Rangers, 1870–1901*. Austin: State House Press, 1999.

_______. *Defending the Borders: The Texas Rangers, 1848–1861*. Austin: State House Press, 2001.

Wilson, R. Michael. *Great Train Robberies of the Old West*. Guilford, CT: TwoDot, 2007.

Wooten, Dudley G., ed. *A Comprehensive History of Texas, 1685–1897*. Two vols. Dallas: William Scharff, 1898.

Yelderman, Pauline. *The Jay Birds of Fort Bend County*. Waco, TX: Texian Press, 1979.

Young, Elliott. *Catarino Garza's Revolution on the Texas-Mexico Border*. Durham, NC: Duke University Press, 2004.

Young, Lee, and Nita Thurman. *Lee Young: Memoirs of Black Seminole Texas Ranger*. McKinney, TX: Old Alton Press, 2013.

Zesch, Scott. *The Captured: A True Story of Abduction by Indians on the Texas Frontier*. New York: St. Martin's Press, 2004.

Periodicals

Alexander, Bob. "A Bloody Barbed-Wire Battle: Texas Rangers vs Fence Cutters." *True West*. May 2014.

________. "Square Deals and Real McCoys." *Wild West History Association Journal*. June 2011.

Aten, Ira . "Six and One-Half Years in the Ranger Service." Part I. *Frontier Times*. January 1945.

________. "The Jaybird and Woodpecker War." *Frontier Times*. April 1939.

________. "The Woodpecker and Jaybird Feud." *Frontier Times*. July 1978.

Baenziger, Ann Patton. "The Texas State Police During Reconstruction: A Reexamination." *Southwestern Historical Quarterly*. April 1969.

Bailey, Tom, and Ralph J. Weaver. "The Nine Lives of Captain Frank Jones." *Frontier Times*. Spring 1960.

Baird, P. C. "The Fight at Green Lake Waterhole." *Frontier Times*. March 1926.

Barton, Henry W. "The United States Cavalry and the Texas Rangers." *Southwestern Historical Quarterly*. April 1960.

Burton, Jeff. "A Great Manhunt—Correspondence From W.B.S.: Some Scenes of Outlawry and Gunplay in Texas." *English-Westerners' Brandbook*. 1975–76.

________. "The Most Surprised Man in Texas." *Frontier Times*. March 1973.

Caldwell, Cliff. "Davey Thomas 'Tom' Carson, Texas Ranger. *Wild West History Association Journal*. June 2009.

Carnal, Ed. "Reminiscences of a Texas Ranger." *Frontier Times*. December 1923.

Croce, Antonio. "In The Line of Duty." *The Texas Gun Collector*. Fall 1996.

Cunningham, Eugene. "Frontier Justice: How Old-Time Rangers Solved a Baffling Murder Mystery." *Startling Detective Adventures*. September 1935.

Daughtery, Franklin W. "Las Vegas de los Ladrones and the Flynt Gang." *Journal of Big Bend Studies*. 1991.

Day, James M. "El Paso's Texas Rangers." *Password*. Winter 1979.

Denman, Clarence P. "The Office of Adjutant General in Texas, 1835–1881." *Southwestern Historical Quarterly*. July 1925.

Gard, Wayne. "The Fence Cutters." *Southwestern Historical Quarterly*. July 1947.

Havens, Paul. "The Saga of Captain John R. Hughes, Texas Ranger." *True Detective*. June–September 1940.

Holt, R. D. "The Introduction of Barbed Wire Into Texas and the Fence Cutting War." *West Texas Historical Association Yearbook*. 1930.

House, Kurt. "Cold Steel and Warm Gold: Arms and Badges of Three Texas Ranger Captains." *The Texas Gun Collector*. Fall. 2013.

Hunter, J. Marvin . "The Killing of Captain Frank Jones." *Frontier Times*. January 1941.

________. "The Famous Dick Duncan Murder Case." *Frontier Times*. February 1939.

________. "Pioneer Dies in El Paso." *Frontier Times*. April 1930.

Jameson, W. C. "Incident at Pirate Island." *True West*. November 1988.

Jobes, Harold D. "Fence Cutting and a Ranger Shoot-out at Green Lake." *Wild West History Association Journal*. October 2009.

Johnson, David. "G.W. Gladden—Hard Luck Warrior." *National Association For Outlaw/Lawman History Quarterly*. July–September. 1991.

Kenner, Charles. "Guardians in Blue: The United States Cavalry and the Growth of the Texas Range Cattle Industry." *Journal of the West*. January 1995.

Meed, Douglas V. "Daggers on the Gallows: The Revenge of Texas Ranger Captain 'Boss' Hughes." *True West*. May 1999.

Parrish, Joe. "Ranger Killed in Gunbattle Gave Fusselman Canyon Name." *Sundial Magazine*. September 26, 1965.

Rasch, Phillip. "The Horrell War." *New Mexico Historical Review*. July 1956.

Shearer, Ernest C. "The Callahan Expedition, 1855." *Southwestern Historical Quarterly*. April 1951.

Sherman, Jean Dale. "A Century With the Texas Rangers." *The Cattleman*. March 1937.

Singleterry, Otis A. "The Texas Militia During Reconstruction." *Southwestern Historical Quarterly*. July 1956.

Smith, Glen. "Some Early Runnels County History." *West Texas Historical Association Yearbook*. 1996.

Spellman, Paul. "Dark Days of the Texas Rangers, 1915–1918." *Journal of South Texas Studies*. Spring 2001.

Stephens, Robert W. "A Ranger's Grave: The Murder of Jim King." *National Outlaw/Lawman History Association Quarterly*. October–December 2005.

Tyler, Ronnie C. "The Callahan Expedition of 1855: Indians or Negroes?" *Southwestern Historical Quarterly*. April 1967.

Webb, Walter P. "The Fence Cutters." *True West*. May–June 1963.

Weiss, Harold J., Jr. "The Texas Ranger Revisited: Old Themes and New Viewpoints." *Southwestern Historical Quarterly*. April 1994.

________. "Western Lawmen: Image and Reality." *Journal of the West*. January 1985.

________. "Organized Constabularies: The Texas Rangers and the Early State Police Movement in the American Southwest." *Journal of the West*. January 1995.

Weatherby, Chris. "From No Account to Plain Mean." *Old West*. Summer 1974.

West, G. Derek. "The Battle of Adobe Walls—1874." *English-Westerners' Brand Book*. January, 1962.

Whitehead, Ruth. "The Bloody Fence Cutting War." *The West*. December 1969.

Whittington, Mike. "Hughes and Aten Solve the Williamson Family Murders." *Texas Ranger Dispatch*. 2003.

Yena, Donald M. "Texas Authority in Metal: Badges, History, and Related Artifacts." *The Texas Gun Collector*. Spring 2003.

Newspapers

Arizona Daily Star
Austin Democratic Daily Statesman
Austin Weekly Democratic Statesman
Brooklyn Daily Eagle
Chicago Daily Tribune
Chicago Times
Cleburne Chronicle
Corpus Christi Caller
Corpus Christi Gazette
Daily State Journal
Dallas Daily Herald
Dallas Morning News
Eagle Pass Guide
El Paso Times
Fort Worth Gazette
Fort Worth Star-Telegram

Galveston Daily News
Houston Post
Liberty Hill Ledger
Los Angeles Times
Luling Signal
New York Times
San Antonio Sentinel
San Antonio Daily Express
San Saba News
Seguin Mercury
Union Land Register
Waco Daily Examiner

Index

C

D

S

Y

Z